African Gifts of the Spirit

Pentecostalism
& the Rise of a Zimbabwean
Transnational Religious Movement

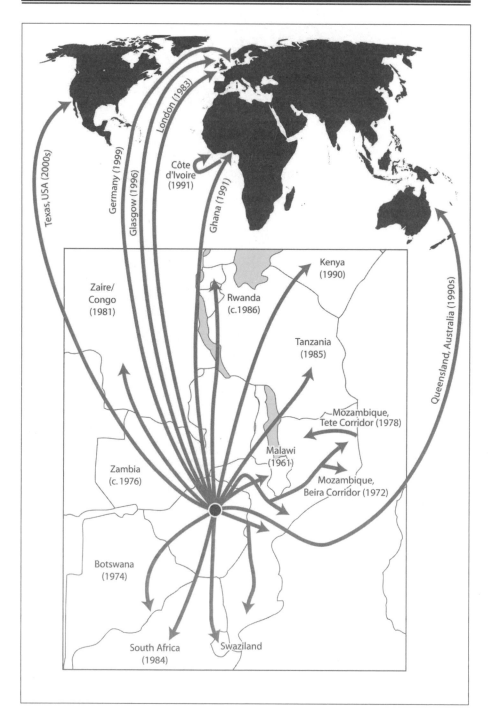

Zimbabwe Assemblies of God Africa (ZAOGA) Transnational Expansion 1961–c.2000s

African Gifts
of the Spirit

Pentecostalism
& the Rise of a Zimbabwean
Transnational Religious Movement

DAVID MAXWELL

Senior Lecturer in History
Keele University

James Currey
OXFORD

Weaver Press
HARARE

Ohio University Press
ATHENS, OH

James Currey Ltd
73 Botley Road
Oxford OX2 0BS

Ohio University Press
19 Circle Drive, The Ridges
Athens, Ohio

Weaver Press
Box A1922
Avondale, Harare

1 2 3 4 5 10 09 08 07 06

British Library Cataloguing in Publication Data

Maxwell, David, 1963–
African gifts of the spirit: Pentecostalism & the rise of a
Zimbabwean transnational religious movement
1. Assemblies of God – Africa 2. Zimbabwe Assemblies of God
Africa 3. Pentecostal churches – Zimbabwe – Harare
I. Title
289.9'4

ISBN 10: 0-85255-965-8 (James Currey cloth)
ISBN 13: 978-0-85255-965-9 (James Currey cloth)

ISBN 10: 0-85255-966-6 (James Currey paper)
ISBN 13: 978-0-85255-966-6 (James Currey paper)

Library of Congress Cataloging-in-Publication Data
available upon request

ISBN 10: 0-8214-1737-1 (Ohio University Press cloth)
ISBN 13: 978-0-8214-1737-9 (Ohio University Press cloth)

ISBN 10: 0-8124-1738-X (Ohio University Press paper)
ISBN 13: 978-0-8124-1738-6 (Ohio University Press paper)

ISBN 10: 1-77922-052-9 (Weaver Press paper)
ISBN 13: 978-1-77922-052-3 (Weaver Press paper)

Typeset in 10.5/11.5 Monotype Ehrhardt
by Frances Marks, Harare
Printed in Great Britain
by Woolnough, Irthlingborough

For Mandy
&
In memory of
John Moran

Contents

Contents

List of Maps, Photographs
& Tables

Maps

Photographs

All photographs © David Maxwell unless otherwise stated

Tables

List of Abbreviations

ADAZA	Assemblée de Dieu au Zaïre, Afrique
ADDA	Assemblee De Deus Africana
AFM	Apostolic Faith Mission (Lyndhurst, South Africa)
AIC	African Independent Church/African Initiated Church
AMFCC	Africa Multination for Christ College
AOGA	Assemblies of God African (post-1977 Assemblies of God, Africa)
AOGSA	Assemblies of God South Africa
AOGSCA	Assemblies of God of Southern and Central Africa
AOGUSA	Assemblies of God United States of America (Springfield)
AOGZ	Assemblies of God Zimbabwe (Borrowdale) (formerly Springfield USA)
BSAC	British South Africa Company
BSAP	British South Africa Police
CFAN	Christ for All Nations
CFNI	Christ for the Nations Institute
CNC	Chief Native Commissioner
DCG	Donald Gee Centre for Charismatic Research (Doncaster, England)
DRC	Dutch Reformed Church
EGEA	Ezekiel Guti Evangelistic Association
ESAP	Economic Structural Adjustment Programme
FIFMI	Forward in Faith Mission International
FGBMFI	Full Gospel Business Men's Fellowship International
IAOG	Independent Assemblies of God
ITWLA	International Third World Leaders Association
JK	(Papers in the Possession of) Jeremiah Kainga
LMS	London Missionary Society
MDC	Movement of Democratic Change
NAZ	National Archives of Zimbabwe
NCA	National Constitutional Assembly
NC	Native Commissioner
NDP	National Democratic Party
NGO	Non Government Organisation
PAOC	Pentecostal Assemblies of Canada
PAOZ	Pentecostal Assemblies of Zimbabwe (formerly Canada)
RF	Rhodesian Front
RICU	Reformed Industrial Commercial Union
SADOP	Sons and Daughters of the Prophets
SDA	Seventh Day Adventist
SRANC	Southern Rhodesia African National Congress
TPZ	Think Progressive ZAOGA
WMA	Wesleyan Methodist Archives
ZAOGA	Zimbabwe Assemblies of God Africa
ZANLA	Zimbabwe African National Liberation Army
ZANU	Zimbabwe African National Union
ZANU/PF	Zimbabwe African National Union Patriotic Front
ZAPU	Zimbabwe African People's Union
ZAW	ZAOGA Archives, Waterfalls (Zimbabwe)
ZCTU	Zimbabwe Congress of Trade Unions
ZIPA	Zimbabwe People's Army
ZIPRA	Zimbabwe Peoples' Revolutionary Army

Place Names

Numerous place names in Southern Africa have been corrected or changed in the post-colonial era. Many Zimbabwean names have been returned to their pre-colonial name (real or imagined) or are now spelt using African orthographies. Generally, I have tried to follow the convention of using the name appropriate to the period in question, thus before 1890 Mutoko, after 1890, Mtoko, after ca.1980, Mutoko. Below is a fairly comprehensive list of name changes referred to in this text.

Colonial	Pre-Colonial Post-Colonial
Fort Victoria	Masvingo
Gatooma	Kadoma
Gwelo	Gweru
Harare Township	Mbare
Hartley	Chegutu
Hunyani	Manyame
Inyanga	Nyanga
Manica	Manyika
Marandellas	Marondera
Mangula	Mhangura
Mazoe	Mazowe
Mtoko	Mutoko
Northern Rhodesia	Zambia
Nyasaland	Malawi
(Southern) Rhodesia	Zimbabwe
Portuguese East Africa	Mozambique
Que Que	Kwekwe
Sabi	Save
Salisbury	Harare
Selukwe	Shurugwi
Sinoia	Chinhoyi
Umtali	Mutare

Acknowledgements

A small army of friends and colleagues helped make this book possible. Peter Griffiths originally gave me the idea for a study of ZAOGA in 1991. When his description of the movement's massive transnational expansion and growing public significance captured my imagination he kindly set up a meeting with ZAOGA's leader, Ezekiel Guti. The idea developed as I finished my doctorate and then Richard Werbner saw its potential and facilitated a Fellowship at Manchester University to pilot the research. Dick's insightful comments on research reports and draft chapters have had the effect of pushing my work to new levels of sophistication. In the process of working with Dick I have also learned a good deal from Pnina Werbner who has been a valuable interlocutor throughout my time at Keele University. Terence Ranger has remained a constant inspiration. During country walks and pub-lunches he has kept me abreast of new literatures and developments within Zimbabwe. I have learnt much from David and Bernice Martin. David in particular encouraged me to have confidence in my own ideas. John Peel, Paul Gifford and Harri Englund have all read, refereed and commented upon various papers and articles and this study is much enriched because of their different perspectives. Norman Etherington has been a great supporter. Both he and Adrian Hastings encouraged me to integrate the story of African Pentecostalism into the broader history of African Christianity. It was an honour, if not sometimes rather daunting, to work as Adrian's understudy on *The Journal of Religion in Africa (JRA)*. His knowledge was encyclopaedic and his insights often profound. If there is any clarity in my prose much of it springs from Adrian's irritation with fashionable and unnecessary jargon. I have also learned much about writing from Ingrid Lawrie. Ingrid, Kevin Ward and Brad Weiss have been my editorial colleagues on the *JRA*, and it has been a pleasure to work with such dedicated and fair-minded people.

In the History Department at Keele University I have been fortunate to find a community of scholars who have engaged with my research in a critical but supportive fashion. I am grateful to Ian Atherton, Malcolm Crook, Ann Hughes, Philip Morgan and particularly my fellow Africanist, Murray Steele. Such collegiality is a rare commodity in our highly competitive academic world. As always, Andrew Lawrence did sterling work on my maps while Kath McKeown and Amanda Roberts helped prepare the photographs. The University of Zimbabwe has also provided me with a convivial working environment whenever I have conducted research in that country. I remain indebted to Ngwabe Bhebe, John Makumbe, Gilbert Pwiti and Brian Raftopolous for their help.

Mai Chesve, David Choto, Jean Henderson, John James, Jeremiah Kainga and Wilson Mabasa all kindly lent me their own correspondence and diaries. And the leaders of the Assemblies of God Zimbabwe and the Pentecostal Assemblies of Zimbabwe graciously allowed me access to important files. Archivists and librarians in the Apostolic Faith Mission, South Africa, Christ for the Nations, Dallas, USA, the Donald Gee Centre for Charismatic Research, Mattersey, England, Fuller Theological College, Pasadena, USA, and the National Archives of Zimbabwe were all immensely helpful. But Des Cartwright, the most 'knowledgeable Pentecostal in Britain' stands out for his friendship and support. Other Pentecostal historians and scholars offered advice and encouragement at important moments. Harold Hunter and Mel Robeck deserve special thanks.

Most importantly, the arguments in *African Gifts* have been sharpened in discussions at seminars and conferences convened on four continents. Numerous friends and colleagues, too many to name, have provided me with the opportunity to give papers in Basel, Bayreuth, Bellagio, Cambridge, Canberra, Copenhagen, Edinburgh, Exeter, Harare, Houston, Leeds, Leiden, London, Manchester, New Orleans, Oslo, Oxford, Pasadena, Perth, Pretoria, Uppsala and Washington. I am grateful to them all for their invitations and interest.

During fieldwork in Zimbabwe, ZAOGA Congregations in City Assembly and Highfields Revival Centre offered great hospitality. Special thanks must go to Pastors Enoch Gwasira and Steve Simango for their help. In Pretoria, South Africa and Pemba, Mozambique I received a hearty welcome from Pastors Wilson Mabasa and Jorge Joaquim Matus. Many ZAOGA members offered me help and advice secretly but none were as fearless as Jason and Elizabeth Marowa in their desire that I should get to the bottom of things. They opened many doors for me and drew my attention to issues that I had hitherto overlooked. Elisha Manzou was a kind and generous helper with regard to ZAOGA's archives. In England, Joshua and Mabel Samasuwo initiated me into London's assemblies. While tracing ZAOGA's connections with the United States, Ronnie Meek and his family opened up their home to me, and Bruce Coble, Gayle Erwin and Howard Reents offered me their time and insights. Much of the research would not have been possible without the initial welcome from Ezekiel Guti, who gave me complete access to his movement's papers and encouraged his leaders and members to talk to me. Although I have reservations about his methods and the direction of his leadership I retain a great admiration for his gifts, creativity, vision and immense energy. He has indeed 'brought his people a long way'.

Family members and friends have provided support of another kind. In Zimbabwe I received hospitality from Geoff and Erica Saunders, Steve, Anna and Brenda Griffiths, John and Amy McRobert. Simba Chikodo, Samson Mudzudza, Titus Murefu, Emmanuel Nyarumba, Tom Riyo, Erica Saunders helped as research assistants. Phineas Dube, Pious Munembe, Bobbie Rapson and Ephraim Satuku offered help and advice. I would like to thank Dudly and Janice Pate for their hospitality in Mozambique. In Britain, the friendship of Nigel Biggar, Gerrard Hughes, Hedwig Lammers, John Moran and Harry Sherwood has been very important, along, of course, with the support of my family. My wife, Mandy, has been a great helper and companion. She willingly proofed the first draft of each chapter and more importantly dragged me away from my books. I dedicate this book to her and to the memory of my great friend, John Moran.

Two grants from the Economic and Social Research Council and the Harry Frank Guggenheim Foundation funded the research and writing of much of this book. A Keele University Research Award also freed up extra time for writing. The Introduction and Conclusion were written during my stay at Villa Serbelloni at Bellagio on Lake Como. I am grateful to the Rockefeller Foundation for awarding me the Fellowship that made writing in such glorious surroundings possible, and to Giana Celli and her team for their hospitality in Bellagio. Amongst a stream of interesting people who passed through and asked helpful and probing questions about my work thanks must go to Allen Franzen, Barbara Gillman, Saidiya Hartman, Dick and Jing Lyman, Graham and Jill Nuthall and David and Sheila Rothman.

Parts of the book have appeared in *The Journal of African History* 39, 2, (1999), *Africa* 70, 2, (2000), *The Journal of Religion in Africa* 28, 3, (1998) and 35, 1, (2005) *Comparative Studies in Society and History* 43, 3, (2001), and D. Maxwell & I. Lawrie (eds.) *Christianity and the African Imagination: Essays in Honour of Adrian Hastings,* chapter 10. In each case the presentation has been revised, supplemented and re-situated within an overarching narrative. *African Gifts* has been a long time in production. The story of the religious movement that became ZAOGA is a complex one, as inspiring as it is depressing. I hope that I have arrived at a fair and balanced account of all I encountered, but I take responsibility for all the imperfections that remain.

Introduction

Prelude

On Sunday 7 January 1996 I attended a service of Zimbabwe Assemblies of God Africa (ZAOGA) at Highfields Revival Centre in Harare, the 'Mother' of the Movement's churches. The meeting encapsulated much of ZAOGA's history and contemporary character. The service was the climax of the annual prayer convention and so it began with a lengthy and noisy period of intercession. Many of those present had devoted much of the previous three nights to prayer and, although fatigued, they prayed with a greater than usual sense of urgency. The theme of the convention had been unity (an issue of much concern within a movement as schismatic as ZAOGA) and so the service began with prayer for unity. But this was no ordinary prayer meeting. The congregation split into pairs, men with men, women with women, tightly embracing, eyes firmly closed, as they prayed for unity and for each other. A man I barely knew from headquarters grasped me in a bear hug. He prayed for my soul with much zeal as I fought to overcome my English reserve. I then prayed for him but ran out of words too quickly, leaving us facing each other awkwardly as others continued their intercessions. After a while the master of ceremonies directed the pairs to split up and pray for the cleansing of the church. All present moved into familiar Pentecostal mode: perambulating, punching the air, jumping up and down as they interceded loudly for pure hearts and a church kept free from the works of the Devil. Two young men praying in tongues into microphones added to the intensity.

At this moment, 'the Prophet and Servant of God' Archbishop Ezekiel Guti arrived, accompanied by his wife Eunor. They entered amidst great fluster as deacons and elders fussed to place special armchairs on the stage and cover them with crocheted blankets. The lay leadership appeared shocked, even worried. The Gutis' arrival was unplanned though not unexpected. In a recent reshuffle, the Archbishop had appointed his young son-in-law Steve Simango and daughter Laverne as pastors of Highfields Revival Centre. Given that the Revival Centre was so central to the movement's history, such an appointment is seen as a great honour, usually reserved for senior high-flying pastors, soon to become Overseers. Although the new appointees were able and charming, many within the local church and beyond had grumbled that they were too young and had gained the position through nepotism. The Archbishop and his wife had arrived to endorse, even enthrone, their daughter and son-in-law.

Proceedings rapidly came to a standstill as the episcopal entourage took their seats. Adding to a growing sense of drama, a female deacon stood up to tell the congregation that the Gutis' visit had been foretold in a vision the night before: 'When I was praying the spirit of God spoke to me. I saw the roof of this church opening up and angels coming into it. The spirit of the Lord was falling and angels were moving amongst us. And the lord said "I am amongst you".' As Eunor Guti got up to speak, the regional Overseer Elson Makanda arrived, claiming that God had told him to come to Highfields. (Though more cynical informants told me that, on hearing that the Gutis were in town, he had desperately phoned round to discover their whereabouts).

Mrs Guti then shared with the gathering. Throughout the Prayer Convention she had been at Bindura, the mythical birthplace of ZAOGA. She had gone up the mountain where Ezekiel had prayed and there she had found herself praying the same things that God had given to the Servant of God for 1996, the coming year. The Holy Spirit had directed the Archbishop to come to Highfields that morning. Like Makanda, Eunor Guti was keen to associate herself as strongly as possible with her husband. But more than that, she seemed to claim a special access to his revelations, which at times she sought to amplify.

Finally Ezekiel Guti got up to speak. His subject was 'upgrading', his chosen theme for the forthcoming Deeper Life Conference. His text was Hebrews 6: 9 'Even though we speak like this, dear friends, we are confident of better things in your case, things that accompany salvation'. He began by observing that modern companies, television and radio stations are continually upgrading. They are exchanging new computers for old; they are straightening roads. He continued, 'If companies are using new equipment how can the church use old equipment? The theme of Deeper Life will be "Better things: better organisation, better preaching, better equipment, better, better, better, better, better ... better performance"'. He then proceeded to rebuke the congregation for not putting a nice ceiling under the church roof:

> You are not working hard enough. By this time you are supposed to have new stands in Lusaka [an adjacent area] and Old Highfields and there is no office yet. In our church we don't just worship, we want good things. That is why we watch pastors, leaders and Overseers ... This church I built myself. You young people build a church in Lusaka and Old Highfields ... If you stay in the Church too long and don't do anything you will become critical. ... This is the Mother church. What pleases me is that from this church we have spread all over the world ...

> Steve and Laverne are the new Pastors of Highfields. Wherever Steve has been they always cry for him: England, South Africa, even where he has just come from. I began to see Laverne, that when she quit UCT [University of Cape Town] and when she quit UZ [University of Zimbabwe] she just wanted to serve God.

> We have to move on to better preaching, better organisation, everything better. Better praise and worship, better singing ... if the world is upgrading, how can we remain behind? Better preaching, better Christians. In the beginning of this church we used to have the accordion. People would buy accordions and then sell them. They would think that if the Holy Spirit came upon them they would be able to play it. The Holy Ghost does not work like that. Fasting does not work on its own. Only when you pray and read and read the word of God. You can be speaking in tongues but lying against the word of God. Preach the word, explain the word, verse by verse. Then you will become strong Christians. It is not by the Holy Ghost. I was watching a video of the laughing spirits at the conference. There was a woman not laughing. She was pretending ...

The meeting spoke of many things. There was vintage Ezekiel Guti, with his impromptu but nevertheless inspired preaching, a mixture of shrewd observation and engagement with the contemporary world. His message extolled the virtue of the instruments and institutions of modernity, yet at the same time exhibited a real concern that his people cultivated sincere and pious devotion. In a fascinating combination of the two, the electronic media was used as a means of internal reflexive commentary, where the faith of a female adherent was seen on video and judged. There was also family politics: an ambitious wife and an aspiring son-in-law. There was the growing leadership cult, in which the Archbishop's arrival was heralded by the voice of God and visions of angels, and which merged his person with the person of Christ. It was a cult sustained by a heavily edited sacred history in which Guti stood out as the sole agent in the movement's past, where he alone was responsible for the construction of the mother church. It was a cult that thrived on sycophancy and created fear. But there were hints of another history, of a more humble, less sophisticated past out of which the movement had emerged. There were also hints of the movement's contemporary transnational reach. And finally there was an intense spirituality among the laity, which persisted regardless of the visits of church leaders.

*

This book is an account of the origins, evolution and dynamics of one of Africa's most vital religious movements, Zimbabwe Assemblies of God Africa (ZAOGA) known in its transnational incarnation as Forward in Faith Mission International (FIFMI). ZAOGA is one of many African Pentecostal movements recasting the shape and character of world Christianity. Since the 1980s Pentecostalism has grown in prominence across sub-Saharan Africa, mirroring developments in Latin America a decade earlier. Huge air-conditioned tabernacles and chapels mark its growing visibility in towns and cities. Pentecostal music, film and radio fill the airwaves, transforming popular culture in the process. Pentecostal leaders wield their enormous followings to influence governments to re-moralise politics. Some Pentecostals have formally entered the political arena, standing in presidential and parliamentary elections. African Pentecostalism has ambitions that transcend the nation-state. It is vigorously transnational, planting assemblies in neighbouring countries and European cities through its Diaspora and missionaries. African Pentecostalism occupies much of the space held by Christian Independency in colonial and early post-colonial times. And like Christian Independency it focuses its activities on prayer, healing and family stability as a value for the poor.

Despite the appearance of newness, African Pentecostalism has deep roots in the colonial past, arising either directly or indirectly from waves of American and European Pentecostal missionary activity. It therefore presents an intriguing mix of religious, political and economic themes concerning African nationalism, American commodification of religion, and interracial ambivalence. It is a religious movement animated by a dialectic between primitive egalitarian ideals on the one hand and hierarchy and authoritarianism on the other. This inherent tension influences civic culture and practice. Township youth and student elites who are Pentecostals draw upon egalitarian and pluralist sentiments to connect with radical politics, while their authoritarian religious leaders find common cause with politicians and party bosses.

Through detailed study of ZAOGA and its antecedents, *African Gifts* explores and differentiates the full chronological sequence of religious change within African Pentecostalism, considering the local seeds and transnational moves that preceded recent globalisation. I analyse how the African Pentecostal movement evolved throughout the colonial and immediate post-colonial eras, illuminating the antecedents and conditions surrounding its 'take-off' and subsequent transformations in the neo-liberal era.

ZAOGA has grown mightily in size, influence and resources since the 1960s. It has evolved from a small urban-based sectarian organisation strongly linked to Christian Independency into a vast transnational movement supported by a complex bureaucracy. In its contemporary concern for respectability and recognition ZAOGA has come to resemble the type of mission Christianity it initially disparaged. Where the movement remains distinctive is in the cult of leadership that surrounds its head, Archbishop Ezekiel Guti, who has risen to eminence over the past forty years. In his tempered criticism of African culture and commentary on modernity the Archbishop embodies a powerful and appealing fusion of roles – apostle, prophet, culture broker and community leader – representing both continuity and change in an era of immense social flux.

The changing nature of African Christianity calls for new modes of research, analysis and historical explanation. This study provides a richly documented and 'insiderly' account of ZAOGA. Research derived from two periods: First, a period close to the leadership, providing a rich harvest of behind-the-scenes observation and access to the movement's innermost papers; secondly, a time with the movement's critics and opponents offering new data and alternative views of the past. This unusual two-sided view of the movement is incorporated throughout the study. *African Gifts* also innovates in the attention paid to ZAOGA's own published literature, sources which until recently have been almost completely ignored by historians of Africa (Ellis and ter Haar, 1998: 2; Maxwell, 2001). The movement has produced a host of tracts, pamphlets and, most importantly, spiritual autobiographies that function as canonical history. This literature has been used to shape its contemporary identity, control its historical reputation, and influence its direction. The study of these sources contributes to a recovery of the role of Africans as agents as they make history and themselves, exploring their idioms and notions of significance.

A noticeable feature of the sacred texts produced by Christian Independency and recent Born-again movements is their tendency to construct hagiographies of their leaders, casting them as great resistance figures and pioneering Christians. Although these prophetic founders were often courageous and creative individuals, it is the acolytes, intent on maintaining religious establishments, who have told their stories, producing texts that overlook the abuse of power inside churches. One-dimensional characterisations of African Christian prophets have found their way into scholarship on African Christianity, as historians, theologians and missiologists have sought to counter a missionary-dominated narrative of the continent's Christian history (Sundkler, 1948; Daneel, 1971; A. Anderson, 1992). But it follows that, if these prophetic leaders are missionaries to their own people, then their practices should be interrogated with the same rigour as those of their white forebears and contemporaries (Murray, 1999). Furthermore post-colonial, more particularly post-apartheid, southern Africa now deserves a more rigorous consideration of religious leadership. Thus this study pays heed to the use of ritual and sacred text in the construction of religious authority and in shaping power struggles. It also considers the popular concerns of ordinary adherents about excess and hypocrisy, often expressed obliquely in rumour or theological critique within religious movements. The intention here is not just 'church history' or journalistic exposé, but an insight into power relations within civil society in colonial and post-colonial Africa, which stresses the centrality of religious ideas and images.

ZAOGA, Africa and World Christianity[1]

On the turn of the twenty-first century Zimbabwe Assemblies of God Africa (ZAOGA) numbers 300–400,000 adherents in Zimbabwe. It also has branches in at least a dozen other African countries, as well as Britain, Germany, Australia and the USA. In terms of numbers of adherents and transnational reach, ZAOGA/FIFMI is one of Africa's most important Pentecostal movements. Moreover, Born-again luminaries such as the Ghanaian, Mensa Otabil, and the Jamaican, Kingsley Fletcher, have paid tribute at international conventions to the movement's leader, Ezekiel Guti, hailing him as the 'Father' and pioneer of an entire generation of churches.[2] ZAOGA/FIFMI is a powerful exemplar of the recent shifts and contemporary character of African, even world, Christianity.

As Elizabeth Isichei observes in the 'Prelude' of her *A History of Christianity in Africa*, the expansion of Christianity in twentieth-century Africa has been so dramatic that it has been called 'the fourth great age of Christian expansion'. According to much-quoted, if somewhat unreliable, statistics, there were 10 million African Christians in 1900, 143 million in 1970, and approximately 393 million in the year 2000, which would mean that one in five of all Christians would be an African (Isichei, 1995: 1). Andrew Walls paints an even broader picture. He writes: 'perhaps one of the two or three most important events in the whole of Church history has occurred ... a complete change in the centre of gravity of Christianity, so that the heart lands of the church are no longer in Europe, decreasingly in North America, but in Latin America ... and in Africa' (Walls, 1976: 180).

A few examples illustrate the seismic nature of the global shifts that have taken place. The first series refer to the Anglican Communion. At the 1998 Lambeth Conference, the highest consultative body of the Church, 224 of the 735 Bishops were from Africa, compared with only 139 from the United Kingdom. At the time of the Conference there were 17 million baptised Anglicans in Nigeria compared with 2.8 million in the United States (Robert, 2000: 53). More recently *The Sunday Times* (of London) reported that 'The average Anglican [in the world] is a 24 year old African woman'.[3] In the Roman Catholic Church a similar picture emerges. In 1999, there were 18 million official baptisms, of which 8 million took place in Central and South America and 3 million in Africa, and an impressive 37 per cent of the African baptisms were adult. In the same year, India eclipsed the United States as the nation with the largest chapter of the Jesuits (Jenkins, 2002: 96, 194). The widespread notion that secularisation follows modernisation is simply not true. The rest of the world has not kept to European parameters in matters of faith and Europe increasingly appears to be the exception (Davie, 2002). Two articles published on consecutive days by *The New York Times* in October 2003 made the point powerfully. The first, entitled 'Faith Fades Where Once It Burned Strong', discussed the widespread process of secularisation within Europe. The second, 'Where Faith Grows, Fired by Pentecostalism', surveyed the vibrancy of the Christian faith within Africa, Latin America and the USA.[4]

World Christianity has not only shifted its centre. As the second *New York Times* piece suggested, Christianity has also radically altered its denominational and theological appearance. At the turn of the twenty-first century, vast numbers of African Christians describe themselves as 'Born-again'. They comprise a diverse and at times uneasy coalition of Evangelicals, Charismatics and Pentecostals who co-operate on national and international Church Councils and Fellowships. These groups share a belief in the infallibility of scripture and, more importantly, stress the centrality of a 'Born-again' experience of conversion. However, given that the Charismatic and Pentecostal strands in the African Born-again movement are very much in the ascendant, a third defining characteristic grows increasingly important, namely that of possessing the 'gifts of the Spirit': divine healing, glossolalia, exorcism and prophecy. Indeed, within Pentecostalism, the most dynamic part of the Born-again movement, growth has led to an enormous diversity of movements, far removed from classic Pentecostalism. In Ghana for instance, some Pentecostal churches place more emphasis on prosperity and success than personal moral reformation. In such cases the token Born-again label has little or no significance (Gifford, 2004).

Africa's contemporary Christian landscape looks very different from a century ago when the historic mission churches — Catholic, Anglican, Methodist, Baptist and Lutheran — dominated the scene. And it barely resembles the ecclesiastical scene of just three decades ago, when African Independent churches *appeared* to be in the ascendancy (Hastings, 1994, 1979). Accurate figures are hard to obtain, especially because Born-agains are obsessed with size and prone to exaggeration. But the examples available indicate that considerable changes have taken place. In South Africa, the Apostolic Faith Mission is numerically as strong as the Dutch Reformed Church. The Church of Pentecost is probably Ghana's largest Protestant Christian body. And a ca.1991 survey of Kenya's capital, Nairobi, revealed that the Assemblies of God was the fastest growing church, with an annual growth rate of 38 per cent (Kimau, 1991:1). Indeed in Ghana, Kenya, South Africa, Uganda, Zambia and Zimbabwe, Born-agains are so numerous and their leaders so influential that they are just as 'mainstream', 'mainline' or 'established' as Anglicans. Besides rendering former organisational categories meaningless, the Born-again movement has also created new fault-lines in African Christianity, transcending previous denominational boundaries. Charismatic renewal in the older historic mission churches has caused traditional Anglicans, Catholics and Methodists to seek the 'gifts of the Spirit', dividing them from their 'unrenewed' brethren within their congregations who ignore the prompting of the Holy Spirit and retain links with ancestral religion. And this type of Christianity is unashamedly proselytising, creating its own missionary movements. South Africa had over 500 missionaries in over 50 countries by 1998, while Nigeria had 250 by 1992 all working under the auspices of Nigeria-based agencies. If it were not for financial constraints, African Born-agains have a proselytising zeal that could doubtless match the 5,800 missionaries from South Korea and the 2,000 sent by Brazil (Freston, forthcoming).

Across the African continent Born-again Christianity grows ever more strident and publicly visible. In many African cities urban dwellers are continually provoked to reflect upon the state of their souls, by scriptural banners heralding the latest convention led by the most recent Born-again celebrity. At weekends, cinemas, schools, hotels and warehouses become theatres of the Holy Spirit for new churches and assemblies, or are permanently bought up and transformed into air-conditioned venues for new mega-churches (Ukah, 2003). Places where people congregate — parks and market places, bus stations and buses, even taxis — are targets for brash young preachers, or the low-key purveyors of tracts. Moreover, Born-again Christianity has seized hold of popular culture. 'Worship stores' have sprung up in many African cities selling a range of commentaries, devotional texts, spiritual biographies, magazines, Bibles and song-books. Like the tracts that helped shape the early Pentecostal movement at the turn of the twentieth century, many of these religious tomes would outsell normal academic texts twenty or thirty times over. Added to these, and no less prolific, are the latest lines in a burgeoning electronic media. The religious consumer can buy gospel songs on audio-cassettes and CDs, video-taped recordings of sermons and conventions, or the latest religious film such as the recent Nigerian productions *Living in Bondage*, *Out of Bounds* and *Endtime*. These electronic media are also accessible to rural dwellers in an age in which the mobile video parlour has replaced the flannel graph and magic lantern, and radio or cassette players are widely available. Cash-strapped African broadcasting companies buy subsidised American tele-evangelism, such as the popular '700 Club', and beam it into front rooms in townships and suburbs where the television is rarely switched off. In Zimbabwe, the local television chart show, *Mutinhimira WeMimhanzi/Ezomgido*, regularly features 'Gospel' alongside more secular music, and bands such as The Family Singers or The Holy Spirits are as mainstream as the famous Bundu Boys. The accompanying gospel videos of singing and dancing, vivid scenes or deliverance, or believers symbolically 'stepping on Satan', are as compelling as the secular alternatives.

In countries such as Zimbabwe or Nigeria, Born-again graffiti, stickers and hand-bills pervade institutions of higher education, re-designating lecture halls, offices and hostels as sites of fellowship and worship. In Ghana '[A]bout 50% of vehicles have Christian slogans painted across the front: "God is King"; "Abide with Me"... Even firms are frequently given Christian names: "Jesus Way Upholstery"; "King of Kings electrical"' (Gifford, 1998: 61). The body has become a temple to religious advertising. It is not uncommon to see Born-agains sporting T-shirts, baseball caps, scarves and neckties emblazoned with Christian symbols, Church logos or phrases such as 'Jesus is Life' or 'God loves you'.

The changing nature of African Christianity is replicated globally. Pentecostalism has also made great headway in the Pacific Rim and China, and more recently in Eastern Europe, particularly Romania. And none of these regions yet rival Latin America, which experienced its 'take off' a decade or so earlier, in the 1960s. David Martin offers an estimate of the number of people involved in the Charismatic/Pentecostal movement at around a quarter of a billion (Martin, 1996: 26). Vinson Synan, the Pentecostal historian, recently argued that these groups now represent 25 per cent of the world's two billion Christians,[5] while the statistician David Barrett casts his net further and assigns 750 million to the Evangelical category (see also A. Anderson, 2004: chapter 1).[6]

Pentecostalism, on which this study will focus, has similarities with its close relative, Evangelicalism.[7] It is not new, though its *forceful* presence in African and beyond has comparatively recent roots.[8] Its theological and cultural origins will be discussed at length in Chapter 1, but in brief Pentecostalism is a form of Christianity which fuses four theological antecedents, or sets of beliefs. The first element in this Foursquare Gospel was personal salvation, the belief that forgiveness follows an act of repentance in the light of God's grace. The second element was a stress on sanctification, a second work of grace received by baptism in the Holy Spirit. Thirdly, the movement placed

7

great emphasis on divine healing. The final tenet was adventism, the belief in the imminent return of Christ. These individual beliefs, witnessed in different parts of the Christian Church through the ages, came together in an ambience of interrelated waves of 'revivalist' activity which occurred between 1900 and 1910 in places as diverse as Azusa Street in Los Angeles, Oslo, the Welsh valleys, Calcutta and Johannesburg. In practice the doctrines combined to form a powerful religion of the body, promising healing and personal security to those who believed. It was religion of enormous practical value to the numerous marginal communities which initially embraced it. News of revival soon reverberated around the international circuits of holiness and evangelical missions and their churches by means of tracts and itinerating missionaries and clergy. Others moved to centres of revival in search of 'gifts of the spirit', subsequently returning to share them with their own communities. Missionaries describing themselves as Pentecostal were driven by an adventist zeal and embarked on a third wave of missionisation, following the established and non-conformist mission endeavours of the previous two centuries. As early as 1908, American missionaries bearing news of the 'Apostolic Faith' arrived in South Africa. By 1920, missionaries from the earliest Pentecostal denominations in America, Canada, Sweden, Norway and Britain were at work in Africa. This missionary Pentecostalism often combined with revivalistic tendencies in the historic mission churches to stimulate the rise of a host of 'Zionist' or 'Aladura' type Independent churches in Southern and West Africa. Generally the missionary-derived Pentecostal denominations remained relatively small. Other missionary organisations such as the US Pentecostal Holiness Church, the Apostolic Church of Pentecost of Canada, and the British Elim Movement arrived on the scene during or after the Second World War. This second wave of missionisation grew out of the Restorationist Movement within Pentecostalism -- a desire by second-generation Pentecostals to revive the enthusiasm of the original outpourings of the Holy Spirit dampened by bureaucratisation and a growing clericalism. But it was not until the 1980s that Pentecostalism 'took off' with the growth of movements such as ZAOGA.

In part, the growth of the Pentecostal movement in Africa can be situated within the steadily increasing missionary input from the older Pentecostal denominations such as the American and British Assemblies of God and the Pentecostal Assemblies of Canada. Some African pastors and evangelists, including Guti and his acolytes, broke away from these missionary movements to found their own churches, retaining part of the original name in their new organisations. The take-off can also be traced to broader interdenominational evangelical ministries such as Scripture Union, Campus Crusade, and the Navigators, which targeted Africans in secondary and higher education: a sector that expanded rapidly in the 1960s to meet the needs of newly independent states. These African elites, joined by others with a similar Christian experience in higher education in the West, began ministries in cities amongst the educated middle classes forming movements like the Redeemed Christian Church in Nigeria. The growing momentum of Pentecostalism caused others to leave mainline churches to found new movements as was the case with Mensa Otabil, who left the Anglican Church to found the Ghana-based International Central Gospel Church in 1984.

The growth of these new movements coincided with important shifts in American Christianity. Between 1965 and the 1990s, attendance in older churches such as the Catholic, Methodist and Episcopalian declined 20 per cent, while Evangelical attendance increased by 50 per cent. This in turn affected the world missionary movement. By 1989, 65 per cent of all Protestant missionaries in the world were North American, and most of these were evangelicals (Gifford, 1994). Thus, the African Born-again movement was funded and catalysed by a host of Evangelical, Charismatic and Pentecostal organisations, many of which originated in the USA. Although different in theology and practice, these bodies agreed on the centrality of the Born-again conversion experience and sought to foster it. Parachurch bodies such as Women Aglow, the Full Gospel Business Men's Fellowship International and the Haggai Institute promoted an interdenominationalism. American Bible colleges, for example Gordon Lindsay's Christ for the Nations Institute, Dallas, and the Oral Roberts University, Tulsa, provided the new Pentecostal leaders like the Nigerian, Benson Idahosa, and the Zambian, Nevers Mumba, with training, and more importantly a vast pool of resources and international contacts. Lastly, the crusading activities of western Charismatics and Pentecostals, initially Billy Graham and Oral Roberts and more recently Reinhard Bonnke, Benny Hinn and John Avanzini, boosted local African initiatives.

In many respects the Born-again take-off of the late 1970s and early 1980s coincided with a new era in Pentecostalism, sometimes termed 'neo-Pentecostalism'. Recent high-profile African movements such as ZAOGA can be distinguished from their forerunners. The older Pentecostal denominations like the Apostolic Faith Mission of South Africa and Nicholas Bhengu's South African Assemblies of God preached a doctrine of holiness that made them highly sectarian, rejecting the many pleasures and luxuries of everyday life. The newer movements are often mass-based and embrace many more aspects of the contemporary world. As we have already seen, contemporary Pentecostalism is characterised by an association with media technologies. Although other churches, particularly the Roman Catholic Church, have made good use of print media and religious broadcasting, Pentecostals have come to appropriate the electronic media with such a zeal that it is almost a defining characteristic. Audio- and video-tapes produced locally and internationally now augment gospel tracts, Bible study guides and Christian monthlies as tools of teaching and proselytism.

The strong reliance by African Born-agains on literature and electronic media derived from America contributes to two other markers of new Pentecostalism: its supposedly global, homogenous character and its interdenominationalism. The appearance of African Pentecostal leaders at Born-again conventions and conferences in Europe, Asia and America and the activities of Western Born-again leaders in Africa enhance these tendencies. African Pentecostals are proud to be part of a global Born-again community. Their convention centres are decked out in the flags of other nations, and many ministries include the word 'International' in their name.

The fourth characteristic of contemporary Pentecostalism is its embrace of the faith gospel. The holiness strand in older missionary-derived Pentecostal denominations emphasised the socially humble character and was suspicious of material success. More recent strains of African Pentecostalism have drawn from the teachings of American preachers including Oral Roberts, T.L. Osborn, Kenneth Hagin and Kenneth Copeland to argue that material success is a sign both of faith and of God's blessing. The stereotype of the African Pentecostal who drives to church in a Mercedes, wearing the finest clothes and jewellery, is not far from the truth in the new urban mega-churches found in large African cities. Contemporary Pentecostalism's final marker is its tendency to produce oligarchic governments whose leaders often retain power for decades before passing it on to their immediate kin. Some of these leaders have formed cosy alliances with equally authoritarian secular politicians.

To summarise, at the dawn of the twenty-first century the global Born-again movement stands beside renewed Catholicism as the most vital strand of contemporary Christianity (Robert, 2000: 54). And after Catholicism the Born-again movement now constitutes 'the largest segment of world Christianity' (Freston, 2001: 3). Its recent rapid expansion makes it 'comparable to the recent growth of conservative Islam' (better described as Islamicism), forming some of the most dynamic social movements in the world today (Martin, 1996: 3). There have been studies of global Catholicism, and its African variations have been well represented in recent surveys (Hastings, 1989, 1994; Isichei, 1995; Baur, 1994). Likewise, since the Iranian Revolution in 1979 Islamicism has received a good deal of scholarly attention (Marty and Appleby, 1991, 1993a, 1993b, 1994, 1995; Sivan and Friedman, 1991).

The Study of African Pentecostalism[9]

Until recently, however, historians have somewhat ignored African Pentecostalism. There are a number of reasons for this. In the first survey of relations between global Evangelicalism and politics, Paul Freston observes how globalisation theory, often strongly associated with Americanisation or Westernisation, has actually failed to describe and account for what has happened to global Christianity. For instance, Christianity is entirely absent from Arjun Appadurai's influential list of global cultural scapes (Appadurai, 1990). And, when religion is considered within the framework of globalisation, it is often studied in an overly abstract manner or with empirical examples restricted to the West. Such an approach ignores Christianity's spread in the Southern Hemisphere and Pacific Rim, which has occurred mostly independently of Western initiatives. Even when other regions are covered, the focus is often too limited. Liberation theology and Islamic 'fundamentalism' remain the usual candidates (Freston, 2001: 4, and forthcoming). Thus, a scholarly enterprise as allegedly comprehensive as the Chicago-based Fundamentalism Project (Marty and Appleby, 1991, 1993a, 1993b, 1994, 1995) marginalised Christian developments in sub-Saharan Africa. Driven by the exigencies of American foreign policy, its concern with movements that potentially threaten US security or global hegemony meant that Africa was given hardly any consideration in any of its five enormous volumes. The important question of America's religious and spiritual imperialism in Africa never reached the research agenda.

The initial paucity of research on Born-again religion also reflected the biases and prejudices of the academic community. As this study will show repeatedly, Pentecostals exhibit an aggressive intolerance toward aspects of their own local culture, which they label 'tradition'. This assault on their own heritage is not well received by those who interpret 'cultural conservation' as an aspect of human rights (Martin, 1996: 9). Neither does it square with the preference of some social scientists to ignore the religious choices made by their subjects and seek instead to elevate certain versions of a pristine culture over society. The problem with contemporary non-Western Pentecostalism, observes David Martin, is that it 'is not quite foreign enough. Were it composed of ancestor worshippers in Vietnam or shamans in Siberia, we would suspend judgement and not impose our own categories' (1996: 13-14; see also Robbins, 2004b: 27-34). Moreover, Western intellectuals are often quick to dismiss Pentecostals as disappointing subalterns. Poor, and distant from the corridors of power, Pentecostals have often eschewed formal politics, or backed the wrong, usually Conservative, horse. In a world where moral judgements are so enmeshed with political attitudes, Pentecostals score low marks in our moral scripts, in spite of our supposed relativism. Despite the fact that female Pentecostals claim liberation through their faith, their religion is still dismissed simplistically as patriarchal. Likewise the prosperity gospel may appear unsavoury to many Western intellectuals, but those who analyse it in ironic tones often fail to grasp the context of poverty and hopelessness that drives African Christians to embrace it. Interrogations of political rectitude often miss the significance of the transformation of manners and mores that Pentecostalism engenders.

The cult of authenticity has also affected African theologians and religious studies departments within Africa. These have mistakenly continued to advance so-called African Independent Churches, or African Initiated Churches (AICs), as models of authentic Christianity, ignoring the very real disjunctures such movements themselves have with local culture (Etherington, 1996, Hastings, 1979: 9 & chapter 3). Driven by funding from secular agencies in search of the authentic, and by the pervasive force of cultural nationalism, African religious studies departments initially gave little attention to the religious activities of their own students within university campuses and across African cities. The major exception was a committed group of Nigerian scholars led by Ogbu Kalu (1998a, b) and Matthews Ojo (1988a, b).

To be fair, the initial growth of the African Born-again movement throughout the 1970s and early1980s did remain invisible to many observers. Often starting in houses and progressing to classrooms, theatres and community centres, it did not have the resources to inscribe itself on the landscape of African cities. Large, plush church complexes did not arrive until the 1990s. Moreover, given the ecstatic nature of Born-again worship and the totalising and intrusive demands preachers make on their audiences, fieldwork could be a 'shocking experience' deterring all but the most determined of researchers (Lehmann, 1996: 9).

However, by the end of the 1980s African Pentecostalism was increasingly hard to ignore. The first scholars to observe and analyse it within the southern African context were often not sure what they had encountered, categorising it as Independency, or Puritanism, rather than grasping its global connections.[10] Paul Gifford did much of the ground-breaking work by exploring the political implications of the Born-again explosion. Noting the high incidence of American Born-again missionary activity in Southern Africa and the reliance of many African Born-agains on the US Bible Belt for literature and audio–video media, Gifford argued that Africa's latest Christianisation was really a process of Americanisation. Initially, writing in the late 1980s in the closing stages of the Cold War, he attributed the Born-again upsurge to American missionary activities that furthered the agenda of the American Religious Right. He argued that organisations like Youth With A Mission, Campus Crusade, the Full Gospel Business Men's Fellowship, Africa Enterprise, the Rhema Bible Church, Jimmy Swaggart Ministries and Christ For the Nations were bound up with a message of anti-communism, anti-Islam, and a far right stand against women's rights, the welfare state and abortion. Moreover, he argued that this American missionary movement's theological message was totally inappropriate for Africa's socio-economic malaise, mystifying a condition which needed sound analysis of the structural causes of injustice and oppression, and radical political and theological solutions (Gifford, 1987, 1989, 1991).

The end of the Cold War, the brief demise of autocratic or one-party regimes along with the short-lived emergence of a democratisation movement in Africa, and the seemingly relentless advance of global capitalism under neo–liberal auspices and American patronage, prompted a series of new questions. Gifford's study, *African Christianity*, was again influential. By means of a series of rich case studies, he emphasised the sheer weight of US resources entering the continent. However, this time he did not emphasise their potential political influence so much as their 'paradigm enforcing power', which serves 'to hold sub–Saharan Africa in the Western embrace' (1998: 317).

Other scholars have debated with Gifford in the discourse of civil society. Civil society is defined as the domain of organised social life between the family and the state, concerned with public or collective goals and needs. The concept, which has a genealogy stretching back as far as Adam Ferguson (1767) and the Scottish Enlightenment, came back into vogue with the demise of communism in the Soviet Union and the Eastern Bloc. It was argued that civil society was central to the democratisation of the former communist regimes. Democracy is characterised by both conflict and consensus, allowing for conflict and consensus between parties but containing that conflict within bounds. The management of conflict depends on 'developing a political culture of moderation, co–operation, tolerance, pragmatism, accommodation, trust, civil political discourse and respect for other views' (Gifford, 1995: 6). The emergence of a rich associational life comprising, amongst other things, lawyers' groups, student bodies, trade unions and an independent press, was believed to have been key to the transition to multi–partyism in Eastern Europe, and African scholars and activists came to see it as crucial to the democratisation of their own continent (Sachikonye, 1995). The historic mission churches played a high–profile role in constitutional reform in many Francophone countries as well as Kenya, Malawi and Zambia in the late 1980s and early 1990s. Scholars also began to ponder the political significance of the continent's burgeoning Born–again movement.

Drawing from the Latin American literature, Ruth Marshall highlighted civil and egalitarian tendencies of Charismatic and Pentecostal Christianity in Lagos, Nigeria. She showed how these movements created an autonomous space against the corruption and abuses of power by military, political and business elites, in which social relations can be recast in favour of youth, women and the poor (1993). These findings built on earlier work on Pentecostalism in Malawi, highlighting how young men and women could undermine patriarchy by demonising ancestor cults, which legitimate male heirship (Schoffeleers, 1985; see also Maxwell, 1999). A similar argument about Born–again religion's capacity to act as a force of delegitimation was made by Stephen Ellis in the case of war–torn Liberia. Liberian Pentecostal churches became like cults of 'counter violence'. They rejected the ritualised cults of murder that underpinned the authority of military leaders such as Charles Taylor and Prince Johnson, and instead claimed a higher purer authority and spiritual power, deriving from the Holy Spirit (Ellis, 1995). A subsequent article by Marshall on Nigerian Born–agains was less optimistic about its democratic and egalitarian potential. Like Gifford, she observed the increasing politicisation of Pentecostalism whereby its leaders have joined the dominant elite in a culture of neo–patrimonialism (1995). A more recent research project on evangelicals and democracy in six African states, co–ordinated by Terence Ranger, has shown just how complex that encounter has become (forthcoming).

Contemporary Pentecostals' fixation with commodities and media technologies, their emphasis on rupture with the past through conversion and rhetoric about individualisation have been debated by anthropologists in terms of their relation to modernity. Birgit Meyer argued that Pentecostalism provides adherents with 'a space and a discourse for reflecting upon the pitfalls, if not the impossibility, of the project of modernity' (2000: 242; 1999); Harri Englund and James Leach pointed to the danger of allowing the meta-narrative of modernity to become the organising feature of analysis. Drawing on his own research concerning township-based Pentecostals in Lilongwe, Englund argued that the abstractions associated with modernity obscure believers' 'specific existential passions', for example the desire for healing, fertility and a successful family life (Englund and Leach, 2000: 234). Scholars have also begun to think more specifically about the media and its relation to the construction of transnational identities, which extend beyond, and even reject, the notion of the nation-state, (Marshall, 1998) while more recent work by Asonzeh Ukah and Gifford has explored the growing fixation of West African Pentecostals with success and material prosperity (Ukah, 2003; Gifford, 2004).

These are important issues and this study will engage with them. However, much of the recent research on African Pentecostalism gives the impression that it is new to Africa. It is true that Pentecostalism did not take off in the continent until the 1980s and has evolved since then in significant ways, as Paul Gifford's ongoing research powerfully illustrates. But what is missing is an in-depth historical account of a single African Pentecostal movement that situates Pentecostalism within the broader sweep of Africa's Christian history.

Situating African Pentecostalism: Nationalism, Transnationalism and Modernity

ZAOGA's trajectory is not easily captured by the meta-narratives of class and nationalism, although both of these forces shaped its development. Emerging from Zimbabwean townships in the 1950s and '60s it had no formal relation with the nationalist movement. It followed a different path, which focused its adherents' energies on transforming themselves, and their families, rather than the nation. At times the movement espoused Pan-Africanist sentiments, but it also made connection with the evolving global Born-again movement.

Analysis of ZAOGA's development has to move beyond the Zimbabwean context and challenge 'the national order of things', in which colonial and post-colonial African history is often set (Cooper, 1994: 1542).[11] This study reconstructs a movement that has extended beyond the boundaries of the nation-state into the region and beyond. But I resist the current sociological fashion that would categorise ZAOGA/ FIFMI as 'global'. The more modest label 'transnational' is preferred for a number of reasons. First, while ZAOGA/FIFMI does transcend state frontiers, it is not 'global' in the sense of having an effect which is 'worldwide'. It does not intensify 'worldwide social relations' in a manner that links 'distant localities in such a way that local happenings are shaped by events occurring many miles away and vice-versa'(Giddens, 1990: 64). Neither can ZAOGA/FIFMI claim to be *international* 'in the strict sense of involving nations as corporate actors' (Hannerz, 1996: 6). Its key agents are economic migrants, refugees, African missionaries, roving bishops and pastors. Secondly, while globalisation theory grows ever more nuanced, there is still a widespread belief that globalisation involves cultural homogenisation and the obliteration of the locality

(Featherstone, Lash and Robertson, 1995). ZAOGA has, at times, claimed to be part of the global Born-again movement, and it has derived both ideological and material resources from this 'international community of the saved', exhibiting 'astonishingly similar techniques of oratory and proselytization, and similar forms of organisation and leadership'(Lehmann, 1996: 8). Nevertheless it has put these resources to use to create its own collection of adherents and placed very firm boundaries around them. Its success lies partly in its own distinctive character. Finally, ZAOGA's transnational connections are not new, in fact they pre-dated the supposed 'global age' and lie in an established trajectory of regional and transcontinental activity.

ZAOGA/FIFMI is a movement that originates from one base, and operates at supra-national and sometimes intercontinental level, but with uneven and varied effects. This study locates the movement within a long history of African transnational religious mobilisation, tracing its shifting boundaries as they occur. Attention is given to the multi-directional flows of ideas, images and practices out of which the movement was formed, but also to the small-scale, face-to-face interactions within regional networks of labour migrancy and religious association which carried and appropriated these religious phenomena. This historical approach to transnationalism pays heed both to the mechanisms that make the connections work and also to their limitations. It analyses *who* is being transnational and in *what context* they are operating and it identifies the specific networks and circuits in which Zimbabwean Pentecostals operate. Furthermore it investigates processes of localisation, tracing the means by which ideas and objects move from imitations to appropriations. It asks how and why they were taken up at a specific juncture and what their new meaning is (Cooper, 2001).

As with globalisation, I also avoid the totalising explanations of fundamentalism and modernity. Rather than using modernity's transformations as shorthand to explain all religious phenomena, this study nuances Pentecostalism's position within it. Throughout the twentieth century Pentecostals have been animated by two impulses: the primitive and the pragmatic. The primitive represents a powerfully destructive urge to smash all human traditions in order to return to a first-century world where the Holy Spirit reigned supreme. In that realm, miraculous signs and wonders are the stuff of daily life, dreams and visions constitute normative authority, and the Bible is immune to higher criticism. The pragmatic impulse, in contrast, reflects a desire 'to do whatever is necessary in order to accomplish the movement's purposes'. Though pragmatism does not 'logically require the acceptance of the technological gains and governing social arrangements of modernity – structural differentiation, procedural rationalism and centralised management' – as a practical matter Pentecostals have slowly come to live with them. However, although some observers assume that cultural modernism and social modernisation come together in the same package, Pentecostals like other ardent Christians have approached them selectively. They have generally preferred to borrow from modernity's tools, such as the print and electronic media or rational bureaucracies, rather than its relativistic approach to truth (Wacker, 1995: 142, 154-5). This study explores how these tools have come to profoundly shape their churches.

Moving to fundamentalism, the popular sociological definition often situates it in opposition to modernity. The influential *Fundamentalism Project* defines it as 'movements of religiously inspired reaction to aspects of global processes of modernisation and secularisation ... the struggle to assert or reassert the norms of traditional religion in the public order'(Marty and Appleby, 1993b: 2-5). Pentecostalism is located within this model along with Islamicism, Hindu Nationalism and radical Judaism as

14

the Project struggles to map and explain the huge shifts in religious adherence in the contemporary world. It is important to study constructions of religio-political authority in comparative terms. Indeed there are some instructive commonalities shared by Pentecostalism and other supposed examples of fundamentalism, for example the tendency to make totalising demands on the believer's body, time and resources, and the tendency to create firm boundaries between the believer and the world (Marty and Appleby, 1991: chapter 15). However, the notion of fundamentalism has proved to be so inclusive that it obscures more than it enlightens. For instance, whereas Islamicism seeks to make an organic relation between law, society and faith, Pentecostalism represents a fissiparous extension of voluntarism and competitive pluralism. It seeks to create 'autonomous spiritual space *over against* comprehensive systems' (Martin, 1996: 10-11). While Pentecostalism's rejection of philosophical and moral pluralism and its belief in a sacred text stand in opposition to some of modernity's key values, its desire to break with traditional hierarchies and legitimations places it firmly in modernity.

Contemporary Pentecostalism has multiple discourses. Its business culture, its fascination with the electronic media, and its fixation with the accumulation and retention of commodities, shape lives as fundamentally as scripture itself. But what particularly animates the movement is 'the free and democratic availability of gifts of the Spirit' (Martin, 1996: 10-11). It is these pneumatic *practices* of speaking in tongues, prophecy, divine healing and exorcism that are central to Pentecostals' self-definition, and those seeking to understand Pentecostalism must remain mindful of them. Questions about Pentecostals' relations to the workplace, and broader structures of society and governance are crucial. They, of course, operate in these domains. However, given the choice, Born-agains spend their free time in the assembly hall, the convention centre, the township cottage, the suburban home, the rural homestead, or under shady trees, studying the Bible, praying and worshipping God. There is a great danger that questions about Pentecostalism's relation to economics and politics are too reductive, viewing religion only from an instrumental perspective. By focusing on 'what is central to religion: belief, ritual, the religious community' this study will show that Pentecostals are motivated by a genuine pious devotion, a sincere desire to act decisively on their faith (Isichei, 1995: 8). While other scholars working on Pentecostalism have offered insight into specific aspects of adherents' spirituality, the latter chapters of *African Gifts of the Spirit* bring the religious life of the believer to the fore.

My intention is to situate Pentecostal Christianity in the social history of Southern Africa. A significant portion of the book is devoted to the last two decades of the twentieth century, when ZAOGA and other African Pentecostal churches 'took off', and as such it addresses the fundamental question of why Pentecostalism as a religious movement should emerge with such force in the neo-liberal era. In the 1950s and '60s, movements such as ZAOGA were small sectarian communities of little significance to the larger story of African Christianity. Writing on one of ZAOGA's antecedents, Nicholas Bhengu's Assemblies of God, South Africa, Philip Mayer observed that it had 'of all forms of *ukurumusha* [the adopting of town ways] the greatest explosive force, blasting away not only old values but old networks'. Nevertheless, at the time of his research and writing in the 1960s, Mayer concluded that the rigours of Bhenguism were 'too drastic to appeal to any but a small minority' (Mayer, 1961: 205). The metaphor of 'blasting' is particularly appropriate for Pentecostalism and in essence this study is a reconstruction of that process; it is an analysis of Pentecostals' struggle against traditions, mentalities and interests, material and metaphysical, as they fashioned their own religious movement. It begins as a 'decentred narrative' of 'protean and transgressive' religious forms in both Africa and the West (Bayly, 2004: 329) and ends as an account of a new orthodox global religion.

Notes

[1] For a broader survey of recent shifts in African Christianity see Maxwell, 2006.
[2] Pers. comm. Paul Gifford.
[3] *The Sunday Times* (London), 15 March 2001.
[4] *The New York Times*, 13 & 14 October 2003. I am grateful to Matthew Engelke for drawing my attention to these articles.
[5] Synan, 'Current News Summary', religiontoday.com October 5 1998 cited in Robert, 2000: 59.
[6] David Barrett and T. Johnson, 1998, 'Annual Statistical Table on Global Mission 1998', *International Bulletin of Missionary Research*, January, 26-27, cited in Freston, 2001: 3. While Pentecostals happily accept the Evangelical tenets of conversionism, activism, biblicism, and crucicentism, their additional emphasis on gifts of the spirit brings them into conflict with some Evangelicals. Hence they are often placed in a separate or sub-category of Christianity.
[7] Evangelicalism has far deeper roots than Pentecostalism, stretching back to the German Pietistic and British Evangelical Revivals of the eighteenth century, movements which soon developed missionary impulses (Hastings, 1994: 242-47; Isichei, 1995: 74-84).
[8] For a synthesis of the history of Pentecostal interactions with Africa since the early twentieth century, see Maxwell 2002, 2006.
[9] For two excellent reviews of the recent literature on Pentecostalism, see Robbins, 2004a; Meyer, 2004.
[10] In the early 1980s, Adrian Hastings sensed the movement's significance through essays and projects submitted by students while teaching at the University of Zimbabwe. Some of these are now in my possession. He describes movements which were self-consciously 'Born-again' as 'a new independency' (Hastings, 1989: 33). Rijk van Dijk (1992) initially cast the brash Born-again youth he encountered on the streets of Malawi as 'young Puritan preachers'.
[11] A major exception has been social and economic historians concerned with Southern Africa's regional economy and flows of labour. The pre-eminent example is Van Onselen, 1976.

1

Print, Post & Proselytism in the Making of Global Pentecostalism

Travellers from afar wind their way to the head quarters at Azusa Street...
The demonstrations are not the shouting, clapping or jumping so often seen in camp meetings. There is a shaking such as the early Quakers had which old Methodists called the 'jerks'. It is while under the power of the Holy Spirit you see hands raised and hear speaking in Tongues....
No instrument that God can use is rejected on account of colour or dress or lack of education....
The singing is characterised by freedom. 'The Comforter has come' is sung everyday, also 'Heavenly Sunlight' and 'Under the Blood'....
The Lord is saving drunkards and taking the appetite for liquor and tobacco completely away.
[*The Apostolic Faith* (Los Angeles), November 1906]

Brother and Sister G.W. Batman to go to Monrovia, Liberia
After that I received baptism in the Holy Ghost and fire and now I feel the presence of the Holy Ghost, not only in my heart but in my lungs, my hands, my arms and all through my body and at times I am shaken like a locomotive steamed up and prepared for a long journey.
[*The Apostolic Faith* (Los Angeles), December 1906]

The burning message of another Pentecost is now flying to the ends of the earth. 'The Apostolic Faith' edited in Los Angeles has only published three numbers, the last of which was a 30,000 edition!
[*The Apostolic Light* (Salem, Oregon), November 1906]

Rising at the dawn of the twentieth century, the Pentecostal movement crossed the globe within the first decade of its existence. At that stage it was known variously as the Fourfold or Foursquare Gospel, the Apostolic Faith, the Latter Rain of the Holy Spirit or the Holy Ghost Revival, and its adherents spent little time reflecting on its origins. Instead they were preoccupied with the task of proclaiming their new message, which bore a resemblance to the Acts of the Apostles. Struck by the seeming spontaneity of the Revival and its rapid dissemination, most were content to assume that its origins were supernatural, an act of God beyond the bounds of ordinary human history (Cerillo and Wacker, 2001: 390-405). This sense of spontaneity and divine intervention infused the first written histories of the movement a decade or two after its foundation (see Bartleman, 1980 [1925]). A 'providential' interpretation of Pentecostal origins also found its way into later, more scholarly, accounts of the movement written by Pentecostal ministers, church officials and more detached scholars. Thus one historian from the Assemblies of God, USA, asserted that Pentecostals had 'no earthly father', the movement being a 'child of the Holy Ghost'.[1] Nevertheless, a formal academic historiography of Pentecostalism has emerged. Its most influential strand, termed the genetic approach, stems from the recognition that early Pentecostalism shared many of 'its doctrinal beliefs, leadership and organisational polities, behavioural practices and social thought' with prior nineteenth-century Protestant movements (Cerillo and Wacker, 2001: 400). Hence scholars have written intellectual histories debating the strength and significance of the various theological strands and traditions in Pentecostalism's genealogy. Vinson Synan and Donald Dayton stressed the Wesleyan Holiness roots of the movement, while Edith Blumhofer emphasised its Reformed and Keswick influences (Synan, 1971; Dayton, 1987; Blumhofer, 1993).

The second category of Pentecostal historiography known as the 'multicultural approach' has focused on the African American and Latino histories of Pentecostalism. It has explored the black origins of the Azusa Revival, and sought to redefine Pentecostalism as a multicultural rather than white religion. Lastly, historians have taken a functional approach to Pentecostalism, connecting it 'to its cultural setting and Pentecostal adherents to their place in ... social and economic structure'. The functional approach is exemplified by the important work of Robert Anderson who demonstrated the appeal of Pentecostal thought and practice to marginalised poor farmers, working and lower class city dwellers, new immigrants and black Americans in rapidly industrialising and urbanising America (Cerillo and Wacker, 2001: 401-405; R. Anderson, 1979).

The genetic, multicultural and functional interpretations offer important insights into the origins of Pentecostalism. But it is worth returning to notions of spontaneity and rapidity that animated the accounts of participants in the first histories of the movement. The propensity of witnesses to resort to naturalistic imagery of the wind, rain and fire to describe the appearance of the early movement highlights an important gap in Pentecostal historiography, concerning modes of transmission. This chapter charts the neglected material history of the movement. It analyses how existing networks of radical evangelical Protestantism, often sustained by the British Empire, facilitated Pentecostalism's rapid uptake. In particular it shows how Pentecostal ideas and practices were transmitted by print media and by the movement of people. The chapter demonstrates how Pentecostalism was transnational from the outset.

The Cultural and Theological Origins of Pentecostalism

Before considering Pentecostalism's material history it is useful to place the movement in its cultural context. Grant Wacker's remarkable study, *Heaven Below: Early Pentecostals and American Culture*, provides an admirable synthesis of scholarship on the movement's theological and intellectual origins. Wacker identifies 'four distinct though frequently confluent streams' of ideas comprising the movement. The first stream 'theologically and historically, emphasised heartfelt salvation through faith in Jesus Christ'. This idea was rooted in the Great Awakening of the mid-eighteenth century, when it was usually referred to as 'new birth'. Late-nineteenth-century evangelicals perpetuated 'the ideology and experience of new birth', making it a 'nonnegotiable marker' of the Christian faith. This emphasis on salvation grew stronger in the twentieth century, with those who experienced personal transformation calling themselves 'Born-again Christians'.

The second ideological stream contributing to the fourfold gospel – Holy Ghost baptism – 'flowed from three closely related though historically distinct tributaries'. One tributary began in eighteenth-century England with John Wesley's notion of entire sanctification. Wesley believed that 'though new birth marked the beginning of the Christian life, corrupt desires persisted'. This '"in-bred" sin needed to be eradicated in a lifelong process of moral cleansing'. However, in the mid-nineteenth century, American Holiness Wesleyans 'came to view entire sanctification less as a process than as a state one entered at a definable moment in time'. At this moment, termed 'the second blessing', Christians were empowered to rise above the power of sin. The second tributary derived from the teachings of Oberlin president, Charles G. Finney, and other Reformed or broadly Calvinist writers in the 1870s. Like Holiness Wesleyans these Oberlin Perfectionists, as they came to be known, 'emphasised a definable, life-transforming experience after conversion' but understood it as 'an ongoing process', focusing the believer's life completely on service to Christ. The final tributary came from the annual 'higher life' conferences held at Keswick, England. Teachers at these camps argued that 'the second experience in the order of salvation was properly understood as a series of experiences that equipped believers for extraordinary feats of witness and service'. 'Baptism with the Spirit' was not intended to make Christians holy or happy but rather endue them with a power to serve. Wacker writes that 'by the end of the century Christians in each of these three tributaries had come to label the post-conversion experience (or experiences) "baptism with the Holy Ghost"'. Some advocates emphasised purity, others spoke of power, but 'grass-roots believers typically blurred those lines and talked about purity and power in the same breath'. A century later, Pentecostals tend to describe the experience as 'baptism in the Holy Spirit'.

Wacker identifies divine healing and anticipation of the Lord's imminent return as constituting the third and fourth streams of the fourfold gospel. On the former he writes:

> Divine healing was as old as Christianity itself, but the distinctive form it took in American radical evangelical circles emerged from mid-nineteenth century developments in Switzerland, Germany, and Britain. This pattern departed from historic Christian doctrine (which had enjoined elders to anoint and pray for the sick) by insisting that Christ's atonement on the cross provided healing for the body just as it provided healing for the soul.

The most notable advocate of the 'atonement-healing' idea was A.B. Simpson, founder of the Christian and Missionary Alliance. At the same time, anticipation of Christ's imminent return 'expressed itself in the language of dispensational premillennialism, which called for an imminent secret rapture of the saints, immediately followed by seven years of terrible tribulation, and the second coming of the Lord, the millennium and the final judgement'. This idea was initially articulated by the British Plymouth Brethren and then spread to the United States via the journal, *Missionary Review of the World*.

These four broad theological streams – personal salvation, Holy Ghost baptism, divine healing and dispensational premillennialism – interacted and took force in a 'vast institutional network'. It was a network that 'included conferences, summer camps, books, magazines, colleges, Bible institutes, and a web of national, regional, and local associations'. The establishment of 'faith homes' in the American mid-west and north-east boosted the theology and practice of divine healing. Some of the most notable pioneers of these healing centres were Charles Cullis in Boston and A.B. Simpson in New York City. But for this study, John Alexander Dowie, founder of Zion City, Illinois, was the most important. The influence of his healing mission extended far beyond the healing revivals of North America into the receptive soil of Southern Africa.

Wacker also identifies traditions within late-nineteenth-century Christianity, which, though not directly contributing to Pentecostalism, flowed alongside its theological tributaries adding to the cultural milieu from which it emerged. Groups like the Churches of Christ and the Latter-day Saints 'brimmed with restorationist impulses', looking to a final miraculous outpouring, 'a latter rain' of the Holy Spirit and the imminent return of the Lord. Other groups such as the Adventists, Mormons, Spiritualists and Christian Scientists, all shared one or more radical evangelical interests in 'the immediacy of the supernatural, the healing of the physical body, and the imminent apocalyptic ending of history' – all portended in 'a special reading of a sacred text'. Even more broadly, liberal modernist Protestants, while having considerable differences with radical evangelicals, shared with them a belief in the 'nearness and salvific power of God's Spirit in history'. Similarly, Roman Catholics also displayed a growing interest in the work of the Spirit in everyday life.

Finally, Wacker considers how forces in popular culture also shaped the radical evangelical world-view. Probably the most important influence was the growing interest in physical health. 'The presumption that a long-lived, pain-free body should be normative for all people spurred the growth of recreational sports, fitness regimes, and institutional expressions of a muscular Christianity such as the YMCA and YWCA.' There was a widespread fascination with millennial schemes found in popular texts such as Edward Bellamy's *Looking Backward* (1888) and Charles Sheldon's *In His Steps* (1896). Millions were looking to the dawn of a new era, and all the more so as the twentieth century drew closer (Wacker, 2001: 1-4).

While Pentecostalism took force through its continuities with Holiness and Revivalist traditions, and its connections with aspects of popular culture, it also broke with certain religious traditions. Broadly, it emerged in opposition to what Pentecostals perceived to be the corrupting influences of priestly supremacy and liberal theology in Established churches. Certainly within Britain it emerged at a time of declining interest in religion, exemplified by falling church attendance, increasing secularism and the growth of anti-supernaturalism (Hollenweger, 1972: chapter 2; Taylor, 1994: 123).

It is difficult to discern precisely when this fusion of theological ideas and practices 'began to crystallise into institutional shapes' in the USA (Wacker, 1996: 509). Some commentators argue that the movement began in the mountains of North Carolina in the late 1890s. Many more point to the significance of the revival in Topeka, Kansas, in January 1901. Its leader, Charles Fox Parham, an itinerant Methodist healer, believed speaking in tongues to be essential evidence of Baptism in the Holy Spirit, and encouraged it among a tiny prayer band meeting in Bethel Bible School. But this remarkable revival, although covered by several regional newspapers, went largely unnoticed by the majority of the American public. And so it is the Azusa Street Revival in the summer 1906 that is generally understood to be the defining moment of the Pentecostal movement. Its links with the earlier Topeka Revival are clear. Buoyed up by their new message of the 'Apostolic Faith', Parham and his followers took it to other American cities. By 1905 it had found acceptance in Houston, Texas. A black Holiness preacher, William J. Seymour, embraced the message and carried it to Los Angeles where he sparked revival in the former African Methodist Episcopal Church on Azusa Street. The revival continued non-stop for three years. Blacks and whites worshipped together; men, women and children received Spirit Baptism and spoke in tongues. The services were characterised by singing, shouting, glossolalia, divine healing, deliverance from evil spirits and the expectation of Christ's imminent return. Conversion often led to dramatic personal transformations, with new believers turning from lives of crime and alcoholism.

By November 1906, revival had spread among the Native Americans and Mexicans of downtown Los Angeles.[2] Others, hearing news of the outpouring of the Holy Spirit, came in search of it, taking revival back home to their communities. One such couple was G.B. Cashwell and his wife, who read of the Pentecost revival in *The Way of Faith* and travelled 3,000 miles from North Carolina to receive it.[3] In the meantime Parham's followers spread the Apostolic Faith to Chicago and then to urban centres of the north-east, especially New York. By the early 1910s the revival had reached most parts of the United States, Canada and northern Mexico, with as many as 50-100,000 converts (Wacker, 2001: 6; McGee, 1988: 58). The movement took root so rapidly because of the fertile religious environment of late-nineteenth-century America. As Wacker observes, the radical evangelical agenda had already prompted 'tens of thousands of Baptists and Methodists, along with a smaller number of Quakers, Mennonites, and Presbyterians to leave their natal fellowships' and form numerous transitional sects 'with defiantly "come-outer" labels as Shiloh, Pillar of Fire, Fire Baptised Holiness Association, Christian and Missionary Alliance, and Missionary Bands of the Worlds' (2001: 1). These transitional organisations seeking an 'apostolic faith' of personal salvation, Holy Ghost baptism, divine healing and the Lord's imminent return rapidly became Pentecostal once these strands combined in Azusa Street.

Pentecost across the World

The Pentecostal movement spread rapidly across the globe. As early as March 1907, *The Apostolic Faith*, the periodical of the Azusa Street Revival, reported that Pentecost had spread to Hawaii in the West and England, Norway, Sweden and India in the East.[4] As remarkable as the initial numerical growth of the Pentecostal revival was its impact on the lives of ordinary people. Within a decade, hundreds of previously 'humble folk' were scattered across the globe as missionaries. Some left Los Angeles almost immediately. At the turn of 1907, Alfred and Lillian Garr were in Calcutta on their way to China. In August 1907, Brother A. Post left for Ceylon, and by May 1908, only 'one and a half years after his Pentecost', G.S. Brelesford left Colorado Springs for Egypt. Many of the first missionaries were single women, for example Sister Nelson and Sister Johnson who left for Calcutta in 1910 (McGee, nd: 1).[5]

The very first Pentecostal missionaries were of the independent or 'faith' variety and travelled overseas without pledged support or the backing of traditional mission societies, believing that God would supply their needs. They therefore stood in a tradition of faith missions that had emerged in the 1880s in response to the teachings of radical evangelical A.T. Pierson, who had popularised the watchword 'the evangelisation of the world in this generation'. Their renouncing of salaries and pastoral appointments represented a rejection of Western materialism, an affirmation of super-naturalism in theology and history, a dependence on God's daily providence, and a belief that they were fulfilling biblical prophecies (Robert, 2003: 181). As we shall see in the following chapter, some of these were rugged individualists or mavericks and positively shunned ties with mission organisations. However, formal Pentecostal missionary societies were founded to co-ordinate the activities of faith-based mission-aries. In the United States the Pentecostal Missionary Union (PMU) emerged from the Pentecostal Camp Meetings in Alliance, Ohio in 1909. This initiative floundered within a year. Nevertheless, it helped spur over 185 Pentecostals overseas in that short space of time. Its sister organisation, the PMU of Great Britain, took things a little more slowly, founding missionary homes and Bible schools (Kay, 1996). Two women, Misses K. Miller and L. James, immediately sailed for India under its aegis, having previously worked there with other societies. The first missionaries trained completely by the PMU were dispatched to China in September 1910. By 1925 the PMU had sent out sixty missionaries, 36 women and 24 men, and at least half a dozen other Pentecostal mission societies had formed in Europe and the USA.

All these missionaries, and those who supported them financially and in prayer, had been captured by the key ideas of the Foursquare Gospel, the most significant being Adventism. Many believed that they literally lived in the 'Last Days' and had a duty, or 'burden', to spread the Christian message before Christ's return. Importantly though, Christ's return did not depend on the wholesale conversion of the world. Many Pente-costals followed Pierson in believing that the Great Commission commanded believers simply to proclaim the gospel to the world, not to convert everyone. '[T]he purpose of missions was to gather out Christians from all nations, not to Christianise the nations themselves' (Robert, 2003: 136). Nevertheless, the millennial urgency to spread the gospel in end times drove many Pentecostal missionaries forward. In 1907, a writer in the Washington-based periodical, *The Apostolic Light,* noted that missionaries from Minnesota were leaving for Japan, China, the Philippines and Korea. He went on to observe that '[t]he pleading cry to hasten the gospel message to the ends of the earth is being answered, and the Holy Ghost has in wrought the Pentecostal "60" [Revival] into humble followers'.[6] After recounting the events at a Pentecostal conference in Fyzabad, India, the indefatigable missionary Alfred Garr wrote: 'The rapture will be wonderful. It will take all the oil we can hold to be able to partake in its wonders. Pray for us, and let us keep humble, for his coming draweth nigh'.[7] Others were spurred on by the signs of the time, of which they were continually reminded in Pentecostal broadsheets:

We know that he is near
Signs of the Last Days: Signs on the Heavens – The Jews Return –
Earthquakes and Judgements – Preparation for a World War – Increase of
Riches and of Crime – The Great Falling Away – The Anti-Christ Spirit –
The Latter Rain.[8]

Other aspects of the Pentecostal faith also fired the missionary impetus. A number of the early missionaries believed in the existence of missionary tongues, or *xenola-lia*, 'the ability to speak an actual though unstudied foreign language at will'. Early accounts of the revival list instances of missionaries writing in Syriac and Armenian, singing in Chinese and speaking in Basotho.[9] Such accounts were short on detail and Wacker's analysis of them cast doubt on their veracity. Missionaries ultimately had to submit themselves to the discipline of foreign language study if they were to succeed. Nevertheless, between 1906 and 1909 'more than a dozen zealots journeyed' to the mission fields 'armed with the conviction that they would be empowered to speak the native language when they arrived' (2001: 44-51). Moreover, accounts of miraculous missionary tongues doubtless stimulated interest in 'regions beyond', as described in *The Upper Room,* and countered the prevailing impression created by social Darwinism that non-Western cultures were unintelligible.

More generally, missionaries such as Brother G.W. Batman (cited at the beginning of this chapter) were 'steamed up' by the Holy Spirit, empowered for Christian witness. In addition, those who attended the revival services believed the 'apostolic signs and wonders that had characterised the advance of early Christians in the book of Acts had been restored in the last days'(McGee, 1988: 58). The gifts of the spirit – prophecies, divine healing and exorcism, as well as tongues – had been given for the advance of the gospel. Such gifts were more than an adequate substitute for the formulaic mission strategies adopted by the Established missionary societies. The power of the mantra 'the evangelisation of the world in this generation' lay in the simplicity of the notion of evangelism. Rather than mission being a complex operation requiring theological formation, the construction of schools and hospitals, the creation of indigenous leadership, and the eradication of regressive social customs, evangelism simply meant the preaching of the gospel to all. Success was not to be measured in terms of the number of converts. 'At stake was not the conversion of the world, but the faithfulness of the church to Christ's mandate' (Robert, 2003: 154). In his *Practical Points Concerning Missionary Work* (1916), Cecil Polhill, founder of PMU, warned missionaries 'to consider yourself an evangelist throughout your term of service. Let others educate, doctor, do philanthropy … avoid also the incubus to the evangelist of day schools, orphanages, and the 101 things which may be accumulated in station life'.[10] As we shall see in the following chapter, this outlook did not sit well with the British colonial project.

Networks and Niches

Although missionary enthusiasm contributed to the global spread of the Pentecostal message, the speed of its movement across frontiers and its rapid assimilation cannot be attributed to that alone. Given that the American revival flowed from converging streams of Wesleyan and Keswick teachings with faith healing and dispensational premillennialism, it was hardly surprising that radical evangelical Christians all over the world were swept along by similar currents. Protestant Europe, its mission fields and their indigenous progeny experienced a similar convergence of pietistic ideas and shared a climate of expectancy. All were seeking a more profound and immediate religious experience not present in their particular denominations. Many of the doctrinal and experiential streams that flowed into the Azusa Street Revival originated from Europe: Wesleyan Holiness, Keswick, the Plymouth Brethren and the Welsh Revival of 1904. Indeed, the Azusa Pentecost might well not have happened in 1906 without the events in Wales two years earlier. Joseph Smale, Minister of the 1st Baptist

Church, Los Angeles, returned hotfoot from the Welsh Revival, adding to the sense of expectation in the city. That story was repeated across the world. Missionaries working as far away as Madagascar read of the Welsh Revival and prayed for it with the same sense of expectancy.[11] There was a clear link between Wales and Azusa Street in the minds of many Pentecostal pioneers.[12]

By 1906 the world was a deeply interconnected place. People, ideas and texts moved rapidly across frontiers, aided by the structures of empire, crucially the British Empire, in what has been called the first globalisation. Such movement was made possible by the nineteenth-century communications revolution of the steamship and the telegraph that accompanied the industrialisation of steel and electricity, oil and chemicals (Atterbury, 2001; Barraclough, 1967; Bayly, 2005: 19-21). The 1858-9 revivals in America and Britain touched the rest of the globe within a year (Austin-Broos, 1997: 55). Many radical evangelicals had attended the globe-trotting Torrey/Alexander revival campaigns at the turn of the twentieth century. The Protestant world was well primed for revival in 1906.

Moreover, given the truth of David Martin's observation that Pentecostalism emerges in certain socio-economic contexts, or 'niches', there were many locations across the world ready for Pentecostal take-off. As capitalism disrupted agrarian economies, relocating people in industrial agglomerations and their homes in large conurbations, so citizens were ready for a new religion that created new communities patterned on new sets of social relations (2002: chapter 1). As we shall see in the following chapter, Pentecostalism would transplant itself easily from the industrial heartland of the USA to a similar context in South Africa.

Although Pentecostalism was often quickly appropriated by local Christians because of its emphasis on lay empowerment, missionaries were usually the first points of connection in its global spread. They had greater freedom of movement, returning home on furlough or attending missionary conferences funded by mission boards and faith offerings. Missionaries also had greater access to new ideas and developments. It was they who often received the first letters from Pentecostal friends and the first literature from Pentecostal organisations. And mission stations were often the first port of call for new Pentecostal missionaries with their radical fourfold message. Indeed converts to Pentecostalism often began by encouraging the Revival among their home mission societies. Former China Inland Missionary (CIM) Cecil Polhill sought to do so indirectly through the formation of a council of missionary societies working in China, while the Anglican minister Alexander Boddy, often described as the Father of British Pentecostalism, actively proselytised the Church Missionary Society (CMS). At one meeting in Sunderland in 1910 he chided a gathering of CMS clergy for their lack of faith in the miraculous, reminding them that:

> The Lord's healings were not through medicines. Paul used no medicine in healing dysentery. Peter and John did not use a galvanic battery to make the lame man leap at the Beautiful Gate of the Temple. They simply used the mighty name of the Lord Jesus himself.[13]

Because of the prior circulation of revival literature, Pentecostal missionaries sometimes encountered wide-open church doors when they arrived in the mission field. Thus H.M. Turney and his wife travelled to Honolulu within a year of the Azusa Street outpouring and were given free range of an unnamed mission. Pentecost soon followed.[14] At other times missionaries began to preach the Pentecostal message within the historic missionary societies, sometimes with painful consequences. One local missionary, D.E. Dias Wanigasekera, working in Colombo, Ceylon, wrote to *The Upper Room* to tell of his dismissal from the CMS after he had begun to teach the fourfold gospel. Undeterred, he had stayed on as a missionary, surviving on faith. He had prayed for three and a half years to receive baptism in the Holy Spirit. His prayers were finally answered after travelling 2,500 miles to a missionary conference in Fyzabad.[15]

India was a prime example of how a rich combination of existing networks, traditions and Pentecostal missionaries could come together to make a revival. As Gary McGee notes, there were earlier Pentecostal-like revivals in Tinnevelly (1860-65) and Travacore (1873-81), but the first stirrings of the 1905 revival occurred in March of that year among peoples of the Khassia Hills. At stations staffed by Welsh Calvinist missionaries, Christians began to confess their sins in noisy 'prayer-storms' that continued for hours. Revival also occurred in the Mkuti Mission at Kegon, a Christian community founded by the remarkable Pandita Ramabai, a former high-caste Hindu who had converted to Christianity. At one of its high points, revival erupted in the girls' dormitories. Witnesses reported powerful manifestations of the Holy Spirit as flames of fire. A keen participant in the Mkuti Revival was Minnie Abrams, a former Methodist missionary and staunch supporter of Ramabai. Moved by what she witnessed, she wrote *The Baptism of the Holy Ghost and Fire* (1905), which was serialised by two major Christian newspapers, *The Bombay Guardian* and *Christian Patriot* (Madras), as well as the Methodist journal *The Indian Witness* (McGee, nd: 5-6). News of the revival thus spread rapidly, so that when Pentecostal missionaries Kate Knight and a Miss Gardener arrived in Gujarat in February 1907, they found the missionaries in situ 'a prepared people and earnestly expecting the Holy Spirit'. By November 1908, *The Apostolic Messenger* could report that more than twenty mission stations had been 'flooded with Pentecostal power and light', and that fifty missionaries had received 'Pentecost'. Many of these missionaries accepted the message of a restored Apostolic Faith and received Baptism in the Holy Ghost in a series of conferences held in Calcutta and Fyzabad in 1909-10. Examples of converts to Pentecostalism were: Mrs Agnes Hill, general secretary of the YWCA India, a Miss Luce of the CMS, a Miss Mudge of the Women's Union Missionary Society of New York, and many 'local lady school teachers'.[16]

Mission publications soon carried accounts of Pentecostal revival throughout India, particularly in the south. The revival spread dramatically across denominations embracing Anglicans (usually associated with the CMS), the Christian Missionary Alliance (CMA), the London Missionary Society (LMS), the Church of Scotland, the Open Brethren, Danish Lutherans, the YMCA, American Methodists, Presbyterians, and Reformed and Wesleyan Methodists among others. 'Along with confessions of sin and prayer storms (the most striking features)' other salient characteristics of the Indian outpouring were 'dancing, visions, dreams, reception of the "burning" (purifying work of the Spirit), repayment of debts, and even miraculous provisions of food' (McGee, nd: 5).

The Calcutta Revival of January 1907, which began at a conference of missionaries addressed by Alfred and Lillian Garr from Los Angeles, was often credited in Pentecostal histories as the first general outpouring of the Spirit in India.[17] But it is now perfectly clear that regions of India had been 'awakened by the Spirit' well before the Garrs arrived on the scene.[18] Even the phenomenon of tongues had occurred prior to their arrival, first recorded at a CMS-sponsored conference in Aurangabad in April 1906. This occurrence of glossolalia had involved the ministry of Minnie Abrams and a 'prayer band' from Mkuti Mission where revival occurred the following December. Nevertheless, the arrival of the Garrs, fresh from Azusa Street, had the effect of differentiating the Indian Pentecostal revival from the classical Western model, a model that came to set the benchmarks for the global movement. Although Abrams and Ramabai endorsed the experience of speaking in tongues, neither saw it 'as indispensable evidence of Spirit baptism'. There were other differences too. While ecstatic phenomena such as visions and prophecies were central to the Indian movement, 'divine healing and premillennialism never found the levels of acceptance that they did in the West'. McGee explains the low incidence of divine healing in terms of the 'intimidation of praying for the sick' in India where the suffering was of enormous proportions. He puts the weakness of a premillennial outlook down to the local strength of postmillennial thinking, particularly in Methodist missionary traditions (nd: 5–8).

After an intensive period in India preaching the Pentecostal message of the Los Angeles vintage, the Garrs moved to China, the other major target of Pentecostal missionary endeavour. They arrived in Hong Kong in October 1907 where they joined a group of single Pentecostal women who had arrived from Seattle a few months earlier. Alfred Garr was to have 'a considerable impact' in Hong Kong, preaching from a base in a Congregational Church of the American Board. Hong Kong was one of the three places where Pentecostal missionaries put down roots in China. The second was Hebei Province in the north of the mainland, where a Mr Berntsen had been working as a missionary since about 1904. In late 1906 he came across one of the first issues of the Azusa Street publication, *The Apostolic Faith*, and was so gripped by its description of the revival that he immediately sailed for the United States and headed for Los Angeles. Having received baptism in the Holy Spirit, he gathered around him a dozen Pentecostal missionaries and returned to found a new independent mission in Zhengding, Hebei. In addition to Hong Kong and Hebei, a third early Pentecostal group was established in Shanghai. Again, there were oblique connections with Azusa Street. In the summer of 1906, Pastor M.L. Ryan heard of the events in Los Angeles and was profoundly moved by them. He relocated to Spokane (Washington) where he founded a Pentecostal congregation. Within a year, a band of Pentecostal missionaries led by Ryan left the Spokane gathering for Asia. By 1910 a number of them, along with missionaries who had left other congregations, had founded a Pentecostal work in Shanghai.

Daniel Bays has shown how a dynamic indigenous Pentecostal church soon emerged from this missionary initiative. Once again, Protestant networks were crucial. Like their missionary leaders who rapidly changed allegiance, 'the earliest Chinese participants in the Pentecostal movement ... were nearly all already Christians, but searching for a deeper and more immediate religious experience that they did not find in particular denominations'. Thus, early adherents came from a variety of backgrounds: Methodist, China Inland Mission, Congregational, Seventh Day Adventist. From this predominantly radical evangelical context, indigenous leaders emerged to found Chinese Pentecostal movements, often blending key aspects of their prior denominational formation with classic Pentecostalism. Thus the strongly Sabbatarian character of the True Jesus Church owed much to the Seventh Day Adventist background of some of its founders. But there were also continuities with non-Christian religion. Bays argues that the dynamism of the Chinese Pentecostalism also owed a good deal to its congruence with 'traditional Chinese popular sectarian "heterodox" religion', which centred upon millenarianism, self-interpreting direct divine revelation and divine healing. These continuities help explain the intense millennial character of the True Jesus Church and the startling visions and prayers of one of its founders, Paul Wei (Bays, 1995: 127-38). They also help explain the preponderance of remarkable healing miracles described by Berntsen in *The Upper Room*.[19]

Given the foundational role of Protestant, especially radical evangelical, networks in the global Pentecostal movement, it is not surprising that India and China received the greatest attention from Pentecostal missionaries and their churches back home. India and China had been the classic mission sites for the historic mission churches and remained so for Pentecostals well into the 1930s, as illustrated by their profiles at the World Missionary Conferences held in Edinburgh in 1910 and Tambaram, Madras, in 1938. Nevertheless, Pentecostalism did spread elsewhere. Close behind the two big Asian mission fields came South Africa, considered in following chapter. Within Africa, Pentecostal missionaries also quickly gained footholds in Sierra Leone and Liberia, and were well established in Belgian Congo by the 1910s.[20] Beyond Asia and Africa, Jamaica was as well primed for Pentecostal revival as mainland America. In March 1907 a local periodical described how Browns Town Baptist Chapel 'caught fire' along with 'half a dozen other chapels' and one or two Episcopalian churches.[21] Latin America was also rapidly initiated. The story surrounding the Chilean Pentecost is particularly noteworthy. In late 1906, Minnie Abrams, a leading figure in the Indian Revival, revised her book, *The Baptism of the Holy Ghost and Fire*, to include the restoration of tongues and sent it to a former classmate from Bible school in Chicago, May Hoover. Mrs Hoover and her husband, Dr Willis, were Methodist missionaries in Valparaiso, Chile. Dr Hoover was the leading missionary in the church, superintendent of the central district and pastor of the largest parish. Moved by Abrams's account, he encouraged Chilean Christians to seek a similar experience. When forced out by missionary opposition he helped found the National Methodist Church, a Pentecostal brand of Methodism, in 1910 (McGee, nd: 11; Cleary and Sepulveda, 1997: 99-100).[22]

Print and Pentecost

Both the Chilean story and the remarkable account of Berntsen, a missionary in northern China, receiving the periodical *The Apostolic Faith*, highlight another important factor influencing Pentecostalism's rapid worldwide expansion: the print media. By the turn of the twentieth century the theological strands that comprised the movement were in place across much of the Protestant world. New Pentecostal missionaries and itinerant preachers, conferences and conventions, correspondence from home churches and old college friends, all contributed to the spread of revival once it occurred, but they did not account for the sheer rapidity of its dissemination. A rich Pentecostal literary tradition, supported by a host of small publishing houses, was essential in the global distribution of Pentecostalism's main tenets.

The nineteenth-century communications revolution spurred global Pentecost. New mechanised typesetting in the form of Linotype and Monotype systems developed in the 1880s meant that publications could be produced more quickly and cheaply. Once tracts and journals were produced, the Universal Postal Union of 1875, which linked the inhabitants of participating countries by a system of flat-rate postage, massively increased the volume and speed of dissemination. Mail subsidies from the US Congress to steamship companies were crucial in linking North America to Europe and the rest of the world (Taylor, 1994: 48; Ryan, 2001).

By far the most important type of Pentecostal publication was the broadsheet periodical, brought out on a monthly or bi-monthly basis, or whenever funds permitted. Privately produced by Pentecostal pioneers and their zealous bands, these were the height of simplicity:early issues were usually no more than one folded sheet printed on both sides. They were experiential rather than doctrinal, containing vivid accounts of Pentecostal revival around the globe. Their intention was simply to inform. The news was often unedited letters from participants in the revival with their names and addresses supplied. Where editors did intervene, it was to report what they had read in other like-minded journals. There was a good deal of cutting and pasting.

The prototypical broadsheet was Seymour's *The Apostolic Faith*, published between 1906 and 1908. Based in Azusa Street, it was the first publication to carry news of the revival around the world with first-hand reports of Pentecostal phenomena. Aiming simply to reflect 'a revival in Bible Salvation and Pentecost as recorded in the book of Acts', it proved a great success. The first issue of 5,000 copies was distributed throughout the USA and across the globe. The second issue ran to 10,000 copies and the third doubled again to 20,000. The sixth issue of February/March 1907 amounted to 40,000 copies. As early as December 1906 Seymour could report 'we are receiving letters from all over the world ... People from thousands of miles have been coming to Los Angeles to get into the rivers of salvation.'

The success of Seymour's broadsheet led to a flurry of similar publications. The March 1907 issue of *The Apostolic Faith* noted that '[t]here are a number of papers on the Apostolic line which are springing up', listing the following as 'out and out for Pentecost': *The Apostolic Light* (Salem, Oregon); *The New Acts* (Alliance, Ohio); *The Apostolic Evangel*, (Royston, Georgia). The following year *The Apostolic Messenger* published what it described as a 'partial list' of approximately 30 Pentecostal publications. The bulk, 25, were of American origin, but there were a number of others: *Pentecostal Truths* (Hong Kong); *Liberty and Gladness* (Edinburgh); *Spade Regen* (*The Latter Rain*) (Amsterdam); *Cloud of Witness*, (Bombay); *The Reign of Christ on Earth* (Cairo); *The Promise of the Father* (Jerusalem). Although most of these never came anywhere near rivalling the circulation figures of *The Apostolic Faith*, some did do extremely well. *Pentecostal Wonders* (Alliance, Ohio), one of the first broadsheets, printed 5,000 for its initial issue in 1906 and expected to double that in its second issue of January 1907. W.H. Durham began to publish *Pentecostal Testimony* (Chicago, Illinois) slightly later, in 1909. Its first issue had a print run of 25,000 and its first three amounted to 100,000 copies.[23]

Pentecostal broadsheets were successful for a number of reasons.They stood in a well-established culture of religious print. In Victorian Britain, for instance, the missionary periodical was the most widely circulated form of literature (Gray, 1990: 88). Alongside the missionary journal came a host of denominational and doctrinal publications, many of which were of Holiness or Revivalist orientation. Such publications helped Pentecostal literature to get off to a 'flying start'. In his doctoral dissertation, Malcolm Taylor (1994: 70-71) shows how editors received the Pentecostal experience and simply incorporated the new ideas into the existing publications, moving them into the Pentecostal genre. Prime examples were Charles Parham's *Apostolic Faith* (Kansas, 1897), J. M. Pike's *Way of Faith* (1890) and S. Otis's *Word and Work* (1879). Other journals, such as *Revival News*, actively encouraged Pentecost; subtitled *The Organ of the Revival League of Jamaica* and operating under the motto 'work and wait', it published accounts of revival worldwide.

The processes involved in the production and dissemination of Pentecostal broadsheets were also crucial. Advances in print technology and universal postage made them both cheap and easy to print and dispatch around the world. It was relatively easy for Pentecostal pioneers to found a publishing house or press and gather around them a group of dedicated assistants. Seymour's prototype journal was printed by a former Baptist who had worked for a Los Angeles daily newspaper. It was compiled and dispatched by a small, predominantly female, band of co-workers at the Azusa Street mission. To rival Seymour's *Apostolic Faith*, Charles Parham re-launched his own version by the same name. Likewise, the two patriarchs of British Pentecostalism each had publications of their own: Alexander Boddy published *Confidence* and Cecil Polhill, *Flames of Fire*. Such publications were a vital part of their ministries. The well known 'firebrand preacher' W.H. Durham observed in the editorial of the second issue of his *Pentecostal Testimony* that he did not have time to attend all the camp meetings and conventions to which he was invited across the United States. Instead he would send copies of his paper.[24]

Large numbers of Pentecostal papers could be sent out at very low costs because they were heavily subsidised by both faith offerings and cheap postage. Forty thousand copies of *The Apostolic Faith* were printed for as little as $200 an issue. Durham's *Pentecostal Testimony* was produced at just 2 cents per copy, while the first four editions of *Confidence* cost just £72.12s.2d to print and post. The latter regularly recorded costs and tables of donors to remind readers that its existence depended on their generous faith offerings. If not always regular, funds were nevertheless forthcoming, allowing broadsheets such as *The Apostolic Light* to be sent free to any address for six months on receipt of a postcard requesting it. And, despite the huge numbers sent out, *The Apostolic Faith* was also free of charge.[25] Compilation costs were minimal because writers sent reports, articles and sermons for the sake of mission rather than mammon. They happily accepted carte blanche syndication of their productions. In the Pentecostal case, capitalism and print technology parted ways (B. Anderson, 1991: 33-6). Pentecostal publications were not commodities hawked around the market place by publishers in search of profit. Although some of the great pioneers exhibited holy pride and jealousy, even at the beginnings of the revival, for the most part the architects of this trans-denominational movement co-operated to 'quicken' the moment of Christ's return. The texts themselves were important instruments of proselytism. *Revival News* instructed readers to 'Help spread revival by sending extra copies of this paper to your friends and foes, after praying for them'. *The Children's Paper*, published by the AFM Oregon 'at no set time, but as often as the Lord permits', warned subscribers that '[the broadsheets] are the Lord's and none must be wasted'. Given their sacred quality, it was not surprising that reading them could have a miraculous effect. *The Upper Room* triumphantly reported that a 'Sister in Dundee' had been healed while reading it.[26] It was not only in Africa (Hofmeyr, 2002) and pre-modern Europe that sacred texts were put to non-literary uses.

Although the early Pentecostal movement did not always endorse the values of capitalism, with typical pragmatism Pentecostal pioneers used some of its best strategies. As well as 'aggressively' targeting enemies of the movement, publishing houses compiled lists of 'opinion formers' whose souls they wished to win. Thus 20,000 of the first 100,000 copies of *Pentecostal Testimony* were sent to church ministers world-wide.[27] As will be highlighted below, well-kept subscription lists were crucial to those seeking to lead the movement.

Tracts and short booklets supplemented Pentecostal broadsheets. These required even less of a printing operation and were often produced by local churches in small runs and handed out at meetings free of charge. Some had a very short shelf life, and gave details of forthcoming meetings on the back cover. Also on the back cover were advertisements for other tracts, including details of where to get them and how to make a donation towards costs. Messages such as 'Kindly pass on' or 'We trust that friends will *do their best* to spread this free Pentecostal literature' were typical. The evangelistic tracts were mostly simple testimonies: conversion stories or plain accounts of the gifts of the Spirit at work in believers' lives. Thus on the back of a 1908 edition of *Confidence* was an advertisement for *Pentecost at Sunderland: Testimony of a Lancashire Builder*. This was no more than a six-page account of the conversion of a Mr H. Mogridge from Northlands, Lytham. For the most part it remained in its original form, a letter to his pastor, Alexander Boddy. The latter simply prefaced the account with a few verses of scripture and added a footnote attesting to the veracity of what followed. Where the broadsheets aimed at a wide readership, tracts could be targeted at specific social categories. Along with the advertisement for Mogridge's testimony, readers could also acquire copies of *Pentecost for Tram-Car Men* and *A Trained Nurse's Testimony*.[28] Tracts could also be devoted to promoting specific Pentecostal issues such as divine healing. One such tract, entitled *Healed through Praise* (c.1915), told the story of Rosa Smith, a nurse who contracted smallpox while working as a missionary in Kwai Ping, South China. Undaunted, she was healed by jumping up and down and praising the Lord.[29] Pocket-sized and amounting to a few pages, such literature was quickly consumed and passed on. Again, a sense of shared mission overcame the forces of copyright and commerce. On the back cover of T.B. Barratt's *The Twentieth Century Revival. Some Facts and General Information* was the notice: 'Anybody is at liberty to reprint, in part or in whole, any of these publications. *Translations* into other languages for *free* distribution are also desirable.'[30]

Pentecostal literature, particularly the broadsheets, was more successful than that of other denominations because it was a compelling read. Using the genre of the Acts of the Apostles, the writers and publishers did not so much believe that they were living in the dawn of a great new Christian age but rather in the *last age,* and that it was their duty to hasten end times. Their accounts engendered excitement, expectation and faith. And their emphasis on experience made their prose far more accessible and entertaining than the classic religious journals such as *The Expository Times* or *Life of Faith* which were highbrow, impersonal and turgid. News of the Azusa Street Revival did much to stir spiritual passions around the globe. In March 1907 *The Apostolic Faith* reported letters 'from hungry souls that want their Pentecost' in China, Germany, Switzerland, Norway, Sweden, Ireland and Australia. As we have seen, Pentecostal pilgrims were drawn to Los Angeles, the 'American Jerusalem', not just from within the USA but beyond. One important pilgrim was the Norwegian-based minister of Cornish descent, T.B. Barratt. Barratt did not make it to Azusa Street but encountered Pentecost in A.B Simpson's healing home in New York during the autumn of 1906. His letters home to Christiania (Oslo) did much to create expectancy, and revival commenced on his return on New Year's Day, 1907. Soon he was holding Pentecostal meetings in a large gymnasium where as many as 1,500-2,000 attended from 'all denominations'.[31] Christiania itself became a sacred centre for Europeans, attracting the attentions of the British Anglican, Alexander Boddy. Boddy made his way there in 1907 and subsequently began to encourage the revival in Britain, receiving tongues himself in December 1907. Soon his own Pentecostal broadsheet *Confidence* was dispatched to Sweden and Norway and British readers received Pentecostal papers from Norway and the Netherlands.[32]

Pentecostal literature, however, did far more than simply disseminate the message of revival. Together the multitudes of the texts created a discursive arena in which the global movement took shape. Pentecostal pioneers were prolific publishers. They were well aware that the burgeoning revival needed voice and direction. A great Pentecostal sacred text never emerged. There was no equivalent of Bunyan's *Pilgrim's Progress* or Augustine's *Confessions* that captured the essence of the movement, but the sheer volume of Pentecostal literature did much to fill the gap. The early broadsheets and tracts aimed to inform readers of the existence of the movement. Examples of key texts were: Minnie Abrams's *The Baptism of the Holy Ghost and Fire* (1905/1906), Alexander Boddy's *Pentecost at Sunderland: A Vicar's Testimony* (1909) and T.B. Barratt's *The Twentieth Century Revival. Some Facts and General Information* (nd). Vast numbers of 'technical' tracts instructing members on Pentecostal practice supplemented these testimonies. Thus the March 1912 edition of *The Latter Rain* advertised *Forty-Eight Hours in Hell*, *Signs and Spiritual Gifts*, *Conserve the Power*, *Hints on Divine Healing*, while *Showers of Blessing*, 1914, advertised *Pathway to Pentecost* by Rev. C. Musgrave Brown, for the price of 1s.2d, postage free, and informed readers that *Faith in the Blood of Jesus Christ* by Pastor W.O. Hutchenson currently in Malayam [sic], would shortly be issued in English.

Pentecostals also published for defensive or apologetic purposes, though true to their convictions their writing could quickly shift onto the offensive. Boddy had founded *Confidence* because the two major evangelical journals *The Christian* and *Life of Faith* had closed their doors to Pentecostalism. Some evangelicals objected to glossolalia and other ecstatic practices, finding them indecorous or difficult to control. Another related gripe was the high profile of female Pentecostals both in services and within the movement in general. Other evangelicals, often from a Brethren background, objected to divine healing. It was with such criticisms in mind that W.H Durham founded *Pentecostal Testimony*. Its purpose was to help convince people of the 'scripturalness' of Pentecostalism. His intention was 'not so much to publish reports of what is being done, here or in other lands, as it is to set forth the teachings and what the Lord used to bring this great work into existence'. Hence he addressed issues such as '[t]he genuineness of the outpouring', and 'the evidence of what constitutes baptism in the Holy Ghost'.[33] Well into the 1920s Pentecostalism was often conflated with Spiritualism and Christian Science, two of its mortal enemies.[34] Tracts were therefore of prime importance in defending religious boundaries. Prime examples were Barratt's *The Gift of Tongues: What Is It? Being a Reply to Dr A.C. Dixon* and *Pentecost not Hypnotism*, and H. Musgrave Reade's *Christ or Socialism*, also translated into French and German.[35]

Finally, within the confines of the Pentecostal press, debates took place over doctrine, ethics and lifestyle. There was a heated controversy about when spirit baptism was received and its relation to sanctification between Durham on the one hand and Parham and Seymour on the other. Another polemical exchange took place over the correct formula to apply during water baptism. And debate raged over a number of issues that were to continue to haunt the more fundamentalist wings of American evangelicalism: snake handling, pork eating, feet washing, pacifism and female preaching. Over the three years of its existence, Seymour's *Apostolic Faith* developed a didactic side to complement its evangelistic thrust, engaging with many of these concerns as well as issues such as marriage and divorce, and attitudes towards medicine, jewellery and other denominations (Taylor, 1994: 776-7, 96-7).

Although individual Pentecostal broadsheets were never as frequent as daily newspapers, they nevertheless did help create a religious community. The sheer number of broadsheets promoting the same message circulated among fellow Christians was enough to foster a sense of global Pentecostal 'communion' (B. Anderson, 1991: 6, 34-5). Through syndication and mutual advertising the broadsheets authenticated each other and authenticated the movement as a global phenomenon. Editorials drew together diverse revivals into one great outpouring of the Spirit. In 1913 Polhill advised readers of *Showers of Blessing* of 'the Holy Spirit revealing the same truths in South Africa in regard to the Apostolate, that He is doing in England, Scotland, and Wales'.[36] Another means of legitimating the movement was projecting it backwards into the past, making genealogical connection not just with the Welsh Revival but also with the American Revivals of 1825, 1858 and 1859. The reprinting and promotion of the works of the great Holiness and Revivalist preachers such as Charles Finney, D.L Moody and Andrew Murray facilitated such tradition building.[37] Thus the movement's architects located it in the radical evangelical tradition and added to the impression that its happenings were the culmination of Christian history.

Beyond the realms of the printed word, the evolving Pentecostal community took flesh through the movement of its leading practitioners. Many of the Pentecostal pioneers were 'inveterate travellers' (Wacker, 1995: 149). Boddy crossed the Atlantic at least fourteen times and made trips to Africa, Europe and Siberia. As well as visiting the United States, T.B. Barratt journeyed to Britain in 1907 and India in 1908. A great advocate of missionary endeavour in China, Cecil Polhill travelled there a number of times, stopping off in Los Angeles on the way home.[38] In June 1910 *The Upper Room* reported that the tireless Brother Berntsen of northern China planned to visit Norway via the Trans-Siberian railway, but would also journey to 'Sweden, Denmark, and England and other countries as the Lord leads'.

Visiting pioneers brought the latest teachings and news of the most recent doctrinal developments, which gave impetus to fledgling movements. The movement in Sunderland, Britain, received much encouragement from a visit of seven weeks by Barratt in 1907 and also from a Mr and Mrs Mead from Akron, Ohio.[39] Conferences were a more important source of homogenisation. The annual Sunderland International Pentecostal Congress, held from 1908 to 1914, was vital in establishing a distinctive corpus of doctrines and practices for the movement, particularly those regulating the gifts of the Spirit. The congress drew an impressive array of Pentecostal luminaries from around the globe, in 1909 attracting 300 delegates from Germany, Italy, France, Russia, Norway, Sweden, the USA, Canada, Ceylon and India.[40] Likewise, annual conferences in Calcutta and Fyzabad were important in shaping Pentecostalism in Asia. These *new* networks, drawing together leaders from diverse denominational backgrounds, did much to energise the emergent Pentecostal movement. But, beyond texts, the key mechanism in homogenising the movements was denominationalism.

Denominationalism: The Urge to Pragmatism

Within a decade of its beginnings the Pentecostal movement was beginning to form identifiable denominations. In the United States the most significant was formation of the Assemblies of God in 1914 from a cluster of Wesleyan sects in the south-east and radical evangelicals of Reformed (particularly Baptist and Presbyterian) background in the central and south-central states. In Britain the first Pentecostal denomination emerged even more rapidly, riding on the back of the Welsh Revival. The Apostolic Church was founded by a former Welsh miner, D.P. Williams, in 1913. In 1915 the Elim Evangelistic Alliance (re-named in 1919 the Elim Pentecostal Alliance) combined assemblies which had emerged from the revival campaigns of George and Stephen Jeffreys. What was to be the largest British denomination, the Assemblies of God, came into being in 1924 out of a coalition of 37 English assemblies, one from Ireland and 38 from Wales. As denominationalism took force, so the Pentecostal movement changed in nature. There was a shift from the charismatic individualism of the pioneers to more institutional forms of government. With the change came younger men, better equipped at managing large organisations, and founding figures became increasingly marginal (B. Wilson, 1961: 39-50). The effects of denominationalism were immediately apparent within Pentecostal print culture. The co-operative interdenominational ethos rapidly diminished. Although some of the rugged individualists that characterised the early movement continued to publish their own broadsheets within new denominations, many of the early publications withered away. Some broadsheets were subsumed by the publications of new denominations. In the USA, *The Christian Evangel* (1913) and *Word and Witness* (1911) were given to the Assemblies of God. Other broadsheets, for example Boddy's *Confidence*, ceased publication, unable to compete with the official print media of the denominations such as *Redemption Tidings* (Assemblies of God) and the *Elim Evangel* (Elim Pentecostal Alliance). These more recent denominational publications had a greater concern for allegiance and conformity to doctrine, employing editing and censorship to that end. Other interdenominational initiatives also went by the wayside. In 1925 the PMU folded into the Assemblies of God, and with it vanished Polhill's broadsheet *Flames of Fire*. After the First World War, Boddy's annual congress was relocated to London, evolving into a series of denominational events.

The drive to denominationalism had both internal and external motors. The internal or developmental motor was the growing pressure of institutionalisation. Although many of the pioneers earnestly believed they were the 'last generation', the practicalities of making the best of an alien world ultimately impinged. Leaders found it worthwhile to register their adherents for tax advantages, and for cheap travel and postal rates. There was a need to found Bible schools, to train pastors and missionaries and to construct worship and meeting places. And thorny issues of succession had to be faced. More generally there was the need to build an increasingly complex bureaucracy to regulate and manage a large and expanding movement. The external impetus toward denominationalism came from the wider Christian milieu. Although the apostolic faith attracted many from Holiness and Nonconformist networks, it aroused great opposition from some who remained, and criticism from the Established Church. The vision of most leaders of the nascent movement was that 'Pentecost should represent

33

a unifying spiritual experience among Christians of all denominations' (Taylor, 1994: 54). But accusations of hypnotism, emotionalism, spiritualism and counterfeit religious experiences left many ordinary Pentecostals desirous to create a new spiritual home. Boddy and Polhill remained committed Anglicans to the end, but at the cost of being written out of the first Pentecostal histories.

Other early casualties of the movement were Parham and Seymour. Their biographies shed light on two key themes of this chapter. First, they show how the primitive impulse to holiness can rapidly dissipate. Secondly, they illustrate the importance of material and organisational phenomena in the making of Pentecostalism. Parham never reconciled himself to the fact that the direction of the Pentecostal movement escaped his control and for a while passed into the hands of one of his own students, Seymour. His resentment was fuelled by the racism that permeated the Southern USA at the time. In the beginning his prejudice was trammelled by missionary paternalism but it soon got the better of him. When founding his Bible school in Houston in 1905 he observed Jim Crow Protocols yet allowed Seymour to attend school by listening in an adjacent classroom. The two men preached together on the same platform in a mission to Houston's black community and were allies in their struggle with Durham on issues of doctrine. The turning-point came when Parham visited Azusa Street in late October 1906. He was shocked by the multi-racial nature of the meetings and by their emotionalism. He described them in his own revived broadsheet, *The Apostolic Faith* (Kansas), as no more than 'spiritual power prostrated to the awful fits and spasms of the holy rollers and hypnotists'. In Parham's eyes the revival bore a 'disgusting similarity to Southern darkey camp meetings' (Wacker, 2001: 231-2). Inevitably Parham and Seymour parted company, the former founding a rival mission near to Azusa Street. In a final attempt to regain influence Parham sought to seize control of John Alexander Dowie's Zion City, Chicago. Dowie had founded a large and successful publishing empire based on his influential magazine *Leaves of Healing*, of which we shall hear more in the following chapter. By 1905 he seemed to have lost his senses, claiming to be Elijah the Prophet. But Parham's hopes of gaining control of the publishing operation were dashed by Dowie's successor, Wilbur Voliva. Increasingly shunned by other Pentecostals, Parham became a 'prophet without honour' within the movement (Taylor, 1994: 83).

For a while Seymour's work in Azusa Street flourished. But by the end of 1908 the revival there had come to an end. Perhaps the overarching explanation was religious fatigue. The demands of those seeking cleansing, healing, exorcism or simply a deeper experience of the Holy Spirit at intense nightlong meetings, combined with the rigorous demands of purity and probity that Pentecostalism placed upon its leaders, took their toll after three years. It was impossible for Seymour and his team to sustain the high note that long without pausing for breath. Tensions between Seymour and Florence Crawford began to manifest themselves. These took a number of forms. Crawford accused Seymour of unorthodox views on holiness. The accusation may have been false but it seemed to stick. More importantly, Crawford disapproved of Seymour's courtship and eventual marriage to Jenny Evans Moore, a co-worker at the mission. Although her disapproval may have sprung from her own unrequited love for Seymour, the public explanation was that it showed lack of faith in the imminent return of Christ. And closely related to the above reason, Seymour was highly critical of Crawford's separation from her husband in 1907 on the grounds that he could not share her faith. In Seymour's eyes Crawford was flouting the teachings of scripture.

Rubbing salt in the wound, he made apparent his strongly held views on Christian marriage in the columns of *The Apostolic Faith* in 1907 and 1908. With tensions rising, Crawford, in alliance with Clara Lum, made secret plans to transfer the publishing operation of *The Apostolic Faith* to Portland, Oregon. By May 1908 their plans were complete and that monthly issue of the broadsheet carried an announcement in the masthead that read: 'For the next issues of this paper address The Apostolic Faith Camp-meeting, Portland, Ore'[sic]. Taylor leaves us in no doubt as to why this act of Pentecostal espionage was so easy. Crawford had in her possession Seymour's mailing list containing the names of 40,000 subscribers around the world. Seymour's downfall was rapid and complete.'Stripped of access to a publishing medium, he was literally a voice in the wilderness' (Taylor, 1994: 84; Wacker, 2001: 230).

Seymour's loss of influence ended his vision of an inter-racial Pentecostal movement. By 1914 the Azusa Street mission was a local black church with the occasional white visitor. In the same year Pentecostals also witnessed the outbreak of the Great War. Despite the apocalyptic nature of the hostilities, the war did not herald the return of Christ as Pentecostals had hoped, but rather a good deal of this-worldly physical hardship and mental anguish. The conflict and ensuing economic chaos also curtailed the globalisation of communications that had contributed to the Pentecostal Revival.

Conclusion

The Azusa Street Revival was crucial in shaping the worldwide Pentecostal movement although there were other epicentres of revival such as Oslo, Sunderland, Calcutta and Hong Kong. Los Angeles may well not have been the place where Pentecostalism was first born but the Azusa Street Revival was certainly the dynamo, and most subsequent revivals emerged directly or indirectly from its tutelage. Questions concerning exactly where, when and who were involved in the first manifestation of the apostolic faith are of secondary importance. Such a quest is driven by the Pentecostal fascination with issues of birth and rebirth rather than by a desire to understand the movement's causation. The key to the movement's rapid spread across the globe lay in the religious networks already in place. Energised by Holiness and Revivalist ideas, radical evangelicals were actively seeking what was to be the Pentecostal experience. Once the revival took place it was spread by the movement of missionaries and pious adventurers, but more importantly by a well-established tradition of religious print underpinned by the communications revolution in the latter half of the nineteenth century. The centre of this worldwide revival was the United States. There were, of course, European missionaries and Pentecostal print operations scattered even further afield, aided in Africa and Asia by the structures of empire, particularly the predominantly Protestant British Empire. But the bulk of the resources came from North America. In this third wave of Pentecostal and evangelical missionary activity (following the earlier Established and Nonconformist movements) we begin to see a shift from Europe to America as the major source of missionary enterprise. The shift became far more apparent in the last three decades of the twentieth century where the focus of this study lies. But from the outset it is important to consider North America, the metropole and the colony in the same analytic field, exploring how developments in one shaped the other.

In this first manifestation of global Pentecostalism, we begin to see tensions that would animate the movement for the rest of the century and beyond. First there was the tension between forces of homogenisation and localisation. The print media, conferences and conventions, Bible schools, colleges, and denominations provided the movement with a fairly uniform set of doctrines and practices. At the same time many of them helped give the movement a specific local character across the globe. Belief in Christ's imminent return along with emphasis on the gifts and empowerment of the Spirit meant that missionaries were rapidly dispatched with little formal missiological training. Moreover, given that such gifts had great authority in themselves, the Pentecostal movement was open to local leadership and innovation. There were other forces of localisation, too. Pentecostalism often took root in existing Christian networks and these influenced the colour of local movements. Existing networks contributed Sabbatarianism to some Chinese Pentecostalism and a postmillennial flavour to India Pentecostalism. Local Pentecostal churches also encountered very different traditional religious systems. Pentecostalism could gain added force through continuity with existing beliefs and practices, or be slowed by discontinuity. These local variations were often formalised in printed publications produced by a widely available print technology.

A second set of tensions emerged from the dialectic between the primitive egalitarian ideals of the early movements and the forces of hierarchy and authoritarianism as they institutionalised. Often beginning in small face-to-face prayer bands, the early movements ignored divisions of race, class and gender. Black and white, manager and worker, male and female ministered to each other. But as the movements aged and formed bureaucracies, so they adopted the conventions and prejudices of wider society. By the 1910s, American Pentecostalism was travelling parallel but separate black and white routes. After similar beginnings, South African Pentecostalism would go the same way. Within denominations patriarchal and gerontocratic patterns usually reasserted themselves. As denominations grew, so they were vulnerable to power struggles and could be shaped by the very worldly designs of their leaders.

In May 1908 *The Apostolic Faith* (Los Angeles) informed readers that 'Eleven Apostolic Faith Missionaries from Indianapolis have lately sailed for South Africa'. It is to Pentecostal developments in southern Africa and to the first encounters of these eleven missionaries that we now turn.

Notes

[1] C. Brumback, 1961, *Suddenly ... from Heaven: A History of the Assemblies of God*, cited in Cerillo and Wacker, 2001: 397. Donald Gee, a prominent figure in the British Assemblies of God contended that Pentecostalism was 'a spontaneous revival appearing almost simultaneously in various parts of the world' (Gee, 1967: 3).

[2] *The Apostolic Faith* (Los Angeles), November 1906.

[3] *The Apostolic Faith* (Los Angeles), November and December 1906.

[4] *The Apostolic Faith* (Los Angeles), March 1907.

[5] *The Apostolic Faith* (Los Angeles), May 1908. *The Upper Room*, November 1910.

[6] *The Apostolic Light*, August 1907.

[7] *The Upper Room*, July 1910.

[8] *The Apostolic Faith* (Portland), no. 20 ca. 1912.

[9] *The Apostolic Faith* (Los Angeles), March 1907. *The Upper Room*, November 1910.

[10] C. Polhill, 1916, *Practical Points Concerning Missionary Work* cited in Kay, 1996: 9.

[11] *Revival News*, March 1907.

[12] C. Polhill, c.1908, *A China Missionary's Witness*; A. Boddy, ca. 1907, *Pentecost at Sunderland*, file, Tracts, Donald Gee Centre for Charismatic Research, Mattersey (henceforth DGC).

13 *Confidence*, March 1910.
14 *The Apostolic Faith* (Los Angeles), March 1907.
15 *The Upper Room*, February 1910; *The Latter Rain Evangel*, October 1911.
16 *The Apostolic Faith* (Los Angeles), May 1908; *The Apostolic Messenger*, November and December 1908; *The Upper Room*, March & May 1910.
17 *The Apostolic Herald*, February 1909.
18 See *Apostolic Light*, November 1906 with a story entitled, 'Pentecost in India'.
19 *The Upper Room*, March 1910.
20 T*he Apostolic Faith* (Los Angeles), June 1906; *The Apostolic Messenger*, November/December 1908; *Confidence*, June 1911, October & December 1916.
21 *Revival News: Being the Organ of the Revival League of Jamaica*, March 1907.
22 *The Upper Room*, May 1910.
23 *Pentecostal Wonders*, January 1907; *Pentecostal Testimony*, vol.1, nos. 2, & 4, 1909.
24 *Pentecostal Testimony*, vol.1, no. 2, 1909. See also Wacker, 1995: 149. On Durham, see Wacker, 2001: 22.
25 *Pentecostal Testimony*, 1, 4, December 1909; *Confidence*, July 1908; *Apostolic Light*, November 1906.
26 *Revival News*, March, 1907; *The Children's Paper* (nd); *The Upper Room*, July 1910. See also *The Apostolic Faith* (Portland) no.19, ca. 1912: 'God is blessing this paper. We print four tons and send them all over the world ... remember these papers have been prayed over'.
27 *Pentecostal Testimony*, December 1909.
28 *Confidence*, April 1908; *Pentecost at Sunderland: Testimony of Lancashire Builder*, c.1907, file, Tracts, DGC.
29 *Healed Through Praise*, ca.1915, file, Tracts, DGC.
30 T.B.Barratt (nd), *The Twentieth Century Revival. Some Facts and General Information*, file, Tracts, DGC.
31 *The Apostolic Faith* (Los Angeles), March 1907.
32 A. Boddy, 1909, *Pentecost at Sunderland: A Vicar's Testimony*, Sunderland, England, published by author. *Confidence*, May 1908.
33 *Pentecostal Testimony*, vol.1, no. 2, 1909.
34 See for example *Intercessory Missionary*, vol. 1, no. 4, January 1908.
35 File, Tracts, DGC. Those who were seen to have erred from Pentecostal pathways were often formally identified and castigated in broadsheets. See for instance the attack on J.G. Lake in *Pentecostal Testimony*, vol. 4, 1909. Lake is discussed in the following chapter. Likewise the movement dissociated itself from Charles Parham. *Pentecostal Wonders* vol. 1, no. 2, January 1907. On Parham, see below.
36 *Showers of Blessing*, no. 12, ca.1913.
37 *The Latter Rain Evangel*, vol. 4, no.1, October 1911; vol. 6, no. 24, March 1912.
38 *Confidence*, May 1908. C. Polhill, *A China Missionary's Witness* ca.1908, file Tracts, DGC.
39 Boddy, *Pentecost at Sunderland*.
40 *Confidence*, June 1909.

2

Missions & Independency
The Southern African
Pentecostal Movement
ca. 1908–1950

The party of Pentecostal missionaries whose imminent arrival in South Africa had been announced in *The Apostolic Faith* stepped ashore in Cape Town on 14 May 1908, having set sail in early April. The group comprised Mr and Mrs John G. Lake, their children and John's sister, Mr and Mrs Tom Hezmalhalch, Mr Jacob O. Lehman and Miss Ida Sackett. Sackett, who was paralysed from the waist downwards, had to be carried onto the platform prior to embarking on the journey. She set sail in faith that God would heal her. While at sea Lake and Hezmalhalch took full advantage of their large captive audience, conducting services for passengers and crew in the dining room and on deck. During a brief sojourn in Liverpool, Lake attended services at a Methodist Church and preached at a rescue mission. Lake had little time for 'formal' services held in the Methodist church and found the members of the rescue mission more to his liking, describing them as a 'real New York bum congregation'. With these hardened dock-workers he shared a message of deliverance from illness and drink by the power of the Holy Spirit. None of this Pentecostal band had an organisation behind them. They had only been able to purchase one-way tickets courtesy of the last-minute generosity of a friend (Burton, 1934:1; Lindsay, 1994: 24; Burpeau, 2002: 106-109).

The arrival of these Apostolic Faith missionaries catalysed a rapid and far-reaching Pentecostal revival in South Africa and beyond. These Pentecostal workers, like others across the Protestant world, encountered Christian networks already primed for revival by the activities of radical evangelicals and news from Azusa Street carried by a proliferation of tracts and broadsheets. As in India and China, the southern African Pentecostalism took a variety of forms, reflecting the rich constellation of Christian traditions and non-Christian religions with which it collided. This chapter considers issues of the local reception and appropriation of Pentecostalism. It illuminates the different trajectories taken by Pentecostalism, paying particular attention to the origins and evolution of Christian independency. Some missiologists and theologians have asserted that African Independent Churches (AICs)[1] are a separate 'authentically African' category of African Christianity (Daneel, 1971, 1974, 1988), but this chapter draws the early history of the movement together, illuminating its common origin and global character. In the following sections I explore the dialectic between Pentecostalism's localising and globalising strands. While it had a remarkable capacity to localise itself and take on different forms in different contexts, Pentecostalism resonated with

38

communities across the globe sharing common experiences of marginalisation from established religion and from the values of twentieth-century industrial capitalism.

The recovery of the southern African Pentecost will be accomplished by focusing on the Apostolic Faith Mission (AFM) founded in 1908 and associated with the work of the Lakes and Hezmalhalchs.[2] The AFM was not the only Pentecostal movement in southern Africa. It existed alongside the American and South African Assemblies of God, and the Pentecostal Assemblies of Canada and other smaller movements, such as the British Apostolic Faith Church (Watt, 1992: chapter 1).[3] However, the AFM was the region's largest Pentecostal church and it was a catalyst for Pentecostal advance (Burger, 1995; Langerman, 1983). Its evolution from religious movement to institutional church, and its relations with 'spirit type' independency will be analysed in both South African and Southern Rhodesian contexts. At the heart of this chapter lies a comparative analysis of the radically different responses the movement engendered from the South African and Southern Rhodesian states.

The Origins of the South African Pentecost

News of the Azusa Street revival soon reverberated around the international Evangelical and Holiness missions and churches by means of tracts and itinerant missionaries. By 1908, South Africa had its own Pentecostal awakenings, characterised by a strong interaction with the American movement. The first factor creating the climate for South African Pentecostalism was the 1860 revival in the Dutch Reformed Church (DRC), itself part of a worldwide movement. It was followed by two more local revivals in 1874 and 1884. All three awakenings were characterised by a deep conviction of sin followed by conversion, fervent prayer and ecstatic phenomena. When Pentecost began in South Africa in 1908, its character was familiar to older DRC members, many of whom came in search of it. Another crucial influence was the Dutch Reformed minister, Andrew Murray. Murray was a key exponent of holiness teachings and helped create the climate for the local and global revivals (Burger, 1995: 2-3). Radical evangelical workers distributed his writings on prayer and the Holy Spirit amongst Afrikaner prisoners interned during the South African War. Manifestations of spirit endowment, visions and tongues followed. Bengt Sundkler has also suggested that refugee camps for Africans fleeing the war may also have functioned as stimuli for apocalyptic visions (Sundkler, 1976: 44; Burpeau, 2002: 93-4, 101-2).

The third factor shaping the South African Pentecost was the Zionist movement originating from John Alexander Dowie's Zion City, Chicago, USA. Dowie had formed the American Zion in 1896, drawing a following from the impoverished urban communities of the industrial mid-west. This new community was characterised by a set of teachings that resisted the values of modernity, though not necessarily its tools (Comaroff, 1985: 177-84). Johannes Buchler, P.L. Le Roux and Edgar Mahon solicited and cultivated links with Zion City, Chicago, briefly forming a triangle of Zion activity in Wakkerstroom, Krasfontein and the Rand from 1904 to 1908. All were moved by what they had read of Dowie's movement in his church paper, *Leaves of Healing* (Sundkler, 1976: 19, 29, 35).[4] Dowie's Zionism contributed two key practices in the Pentecostal movement: triune immersion (baptism in the names of the Trinity), and divine healing.

The final influence – the ecstatic phenomena associated with baptism in the Holy Spirit – came with Pentecostal missionaries, particularly those from Indianapolis. Lake's personal religious trajectory was an embodiment of some of the major doctrinal streams comprising Pentecostalism. He had been raised as a Methodist and had engaged with the Holiness movement. In later years he and his wife worked in Zion City, Chicago alongside the Hezmalhalchs. Most importantly all four had experienced the Azusa Street outpourings in Los Angeles. As in the Indian case, there may well have been pre-Azusa Street manifestations of Pentecost in South Africa, particularly amongst Afrikaners incarcerated during the South African War, 1899-1900. But Lake and his colleagues were instrumental in homogenising and catalysing the movement. In the rainy season, when it was impossible to preach outside, Lake would spend days in correspondence with brethren and broadsheet editors providing news of revival in South Africa and soliciting funds and seeking information on Pentecostal outpourings elsewhere (Burger, 1995: 6-10; Burpeau, 2002, chapter 1; Lindsay, 1994: 48-55).

South Africa's Pentecost was inaugurated in Doornfontein's Zion chapel in the suburbs of Johannesburg shortly after the Lakes arrived on 23 May. The movement bore remarkable resemblance to the Azusa Street revival, particularly in its *initial* multi-racial character. While recent Pentecostal historiography has diminished the significance of the black roots of the Revival, in the South African case Lake's Azusa Street experience directly influenced his practice in Johannesburg and beyond (Cerillo & Wacker, 2001: 390-405). A paternalist to the last, his experience of working with Seymour nevertheless left him with a great openness toward black ministry and spirituality that shaped the early development of the South African movement. As with Azusa Street there were also similar ecstatic phenomena such as glossolalia, 'holy laughter', shaking and prostration under the power of the spirit, and a pronounced public confession of sin.[5] There were revisions of personality that came with conversion, the most dramatic of which were changes in the aggressive male psyche. The syndicated salvation narratives found in the first Pentecostal journals tell of the transformation of hardened male criminals, drunkards and female prostitutes.[6]

Most remarkable were the instances of divine healing: A man pronounced medically incurable, whose wrist tendons were useless after a machine accident, and whose foot and leg were damaged by the fall of a heavy pulley, and Swanepoel, whose eye was burst in a mining accident on the Rand, were both miraculously healed; a dead girl called Maggie Truter was raised to life (Burton, 1934: 43-8). Lake himself saw parallels between the South African and the American and Welsh revivals, but remarked that never before had he witnessed such manifestations of Pentecostal power.[7] In South Africa, Pentecostalism was a visual and instrumental religion, a religion of the body. Indeed, as in the Chinese Pentecostal movement explored in the previous chapter, divine healing was a distinctive feature of the South African movement (Lindsay, 1995: 123-38).[8] Lake claimed a 75 per cent success rate during his South African ministry (Burger, 1995:10).

The Americans' influence soon moved beyond the chapel in Doornfontein to the Central Tabernacle, Bree Street, Johannesburg, formerly owned by the Christian Catholic Church in Zion. News of miraculous healings and conversions was propagated by word of mouth and by the press, which was often hostile. Members of other denominations came to witness the events, often receiving spirit baptism in the process. Soon the movement had expanded into the western suburbs of Vrededorp and Newlands. Sometimes a new group of zealous believers would take over a tabernacle or church, but often they would start neighbourhood cottage meetings – praying, singing and confessing into the late hours of the night. By October 1909 the movement was established in the Orange River Colony.[9]

The Expansion of the South African Pentecost

In these early accounts of South Africa's Pentecostal movement, its defining features were already apparent. The first was a trans-denominational character whereby its emissaries had intense interactions with other churches. These solicited and unsolicited contacts with other Christians explain the second characteristic. Although the movement had the appearance of a spontaneous and rapid growth, which initially defied central control, it expanded along existing Church networks. South African Pentecostalism moved along channels of Methodism and other types of radical evangelicalism as it had done in the USA, Europe and other 'mission fields', but also took force along circuits of Ethiopianism, and most importantly, within the Dutch Reformed Church.

The Pentecostal movement appealed to Boers and blacks alike. Many Africans and Afrikaners suffered the social hardships that accompanied the country's mineral discoveries and the subsequent rapid industrialisation of the Rand. Population in the urban areas around Johannesburg swelled through the influx of refugees from the South African War. Afrikaners and Africans were plunged into drunkenness, gambling, promiscuity and poverty in what some described as a 'New Babylon'. The movement arrived in the closing stages of the 1906-08 depression, a period of high unemployment amongst Afrikaners. The first Afrikaner suburbs it took root in, Vrededorp and Newlands, were locations receiving poor relief (Van Onselen, 1982, vol.1, chapter 1, vol.2, chapter 3). Pentecostalism's rationale was obvious. Having no need for church buildings or for the presence of professional clergy, it established itself in local neighbourhoods, pulling people away from alcoholism, petty crime and corruption. A counter-society was born in which the newly empowered believers, black or white, reordered their social lives around church meetings and the nuclear family, learnt to discipline their speech and sexuality, and adopted a puritan work ethic.

Pentecostalism also expanded rapidly amongst African farm workers in the Orange River Colony and Wakkerstroom (Kiernan, 1994: 70-75),[10] where the movement's strong taboo on tobacco may well have worked as an ideology of resistance against rural capitalist exploitation. Farm workers received scant reward for their labour: often it took the form of payment in kind, usually in tobacco. The Zionist and Pentecostal workers, emboldened by the Spirit, had a legitimate reason for rejecting this type of exchange (Sundkler, 1976: 43-4). Certainly the condition of African tenants and labourers was particularly bleak in the decade of drought, war, and pestilence beginning in the late 1890s. The depletion of African economic reserves would inevitably have tightened the grip of their landlord-employers. In this context of rural poverty, divine healing practised by prayer alone, without recourse to traditional or bio-medicine, would also have had great appeal (Kiernan, 1994: 72), as would Pentecostals' rain-making skills.[11]

Once converted, the Afrikaners made extremely effective missionaries. They took up a peripatetic life, living in ox-wagons, tents and African villages as they moved throughout the Transvaal and Orange River area propagating the Pentecostal message. In the first half of 1910 over 30 'Dutch' evangelists volunteered for missionary service. The significance of Afrikaner evangelists was not lost on Lake. In a letter, written in 1909, to the American Pentecostal journal *The Upper Room* he observed that missionaries were not needed: 'We have men here far superior to any that can come from America ... Among baptised people here are men who can speak English, Dutch, Zulu and Basuto.'[12] In their effectiveness, the Afrikaners were only surpassed by African missionaries (usually unnamed in the sources), who had an even greater linguistic ability as well as affinity with their people. Lake commented: 'Some of the most used men in Africa are these young converts ... God is using the timber right on the field to make missionaries of'.[13] And African preachers were far more numerous than Afrikaners, who barely had time to 'oversee' this rapidly expanding work. In 1909, Le Roux alone was responsible for 35 native 'under-preachers'.

As we have seen in the previous chapter, the ideology of the movement propelled it forward in its early stages. Adventist theology added urgency to the work. And in South Africa the doctrine of the priesthood of all believers was carried to the nth degree. Missionaries and evangelists followed on the heels of ordinary church members who took evangelistic initiatives, and subsequently sent back word for a full-time worker, or membership cards. It was by this process that Pentecost first entered Natal and Tsolo, Transkei. A key missionary strategy was to target concentrated populations in towns and mining compounds. A national census of 1928 revealed that 60 per cent of AFM members lived in urban areas.[14] From its urban base, the movement expanded into the rural areas, often through the agency of returning labour migrants or native preachers. In November 1909, Afrikaner missionary Kretschmar wrote a remarkable report of the expansion of the movement into Orange River Colony: 'whole native churches have been converted, and whole native churches have given their hearts to God'. By May of the following year he wrote, with a fair degree of exaggeration, that there were now tens of thousands of believers but that he had only managed to visit a quarter of them. By that date an Apostolic Faith missionary had still not visited Pentecostal villages in the environs of Ladybrand, Ficksburg, Hoopstadt, Bothaville, Woolvehoek, Villiers Dorp and numerous other towns. A similar pattern was beginning to occur in Basutoland – a region for which the fatigued Kretschmar was also responsible.[15]

The early practices of the South African Pentecostal movement were institutionalised in the formation of the Apostolic Faith Mission. The AFM grew out of a committee based at the Central Tabernacle in Bree Street. The first minuted meeting occurred in September 1908, and the first constituted executive meeting in May 1909. Rather than co-ordinating work, this 'Mother' church initially acted as a catalyst, only slowly taking control of the movement. The AFM was not registered until November 1913, because its leaders were in no hurry to set up as another religious body. No church or mission organisation sent either Lake or Hezmalhalch to South Africa. They came as 'apostolic faith' missionaries seeking to testify to, and demonstrate, the power of the Holy Spirit. The American Pentecostal missionaries had intended their work to be inter-denominational and began with their contacts in the Zionist movement. It was only when they encountered hostility from mainline clergy, who were threatened by ecstatic phenomena, that they began to form their own organisation. Indeed, it was very much an 'organisation' rather than a denomination. The founder members of the AFM became so disillusioned by the established churches' resistance to Pentecostalism that in November 1913 they registered it as an unlimited company rather than a denomination. Professional church leaders were viewed with scepticism and only Lake, Hezmalhalch and a few others were in full-time ministry. Others who kept to church standards were simply given a 'worker's certificate'. 'As early as 1909 the Pentecostal missionaries accepted the consequences of Pentecostal doctrine that the most important qualification for the office of pastor was baptism in the Holy Spirit – a qualification acquired with extraordinary speed by black converts' (Langerman, 1983: chapter 3; Hollenweger, 1972: 150). Ecclesiastical hierarchy was shunned. Everyone, including Lake and Hezmalhalch, was given the title 'brother' or 'sister'. None of the full-time workers could expect an income and all lived by faith that God would provide for their material needs. The Central Assembly owned nothing and only convened a financial committee in 1911.

Given the inter-denominational aims of the early Pentecostal movement, its pioneers attempted both to relate to other denominations and to retain links with their former churches. This was crucial in the shaping of Zionist-type independency. It is often argued that the Apostolic Faith Mission sprang from the earlier Zionist movement (Hastings, 1994: 501; Sundkler, 1996: chapter 1). It is true that Lake and Hezmalhalch began their work in the Zion chapel in Doornfontein and quickly took over white Zionist congregations in the Bree Street Central Tabernacle and in the town of Krugersdorp. But the relationship between Zionism and the AFM was one of symbiosis rather than simple succession. The career of Le Roux is a case in point. Though he left the Zionist movement in 1908 to join the AFM, he stayed with his Zion congregation in Wakkerstroom until 1913, when he moved to Johannesburg. Before he left he had baptised many in the Spirit. His wife, meanwhile, cared for the family and the church until 1926, supported by Le Roux's periodic visits. Whilst some of the Wakkerstroom congregation eventually followed Le Roux into the AFM, others like Daniel Nkonyane, Elias Mahlangu and Michael Ngomezulu used their relative autonomy and the informal links they had with AFM to develop their own Zionist followings. Once free from missionary supervision, these leaders developed Africanised versions of Pentecostalism very different in form and intent from the original American packages.

A similar pattern is discernible in the case of Edward Lion. Prior to the South African Pentecost, Lion had cultivated links with white Zionist Edgar Mahon, but from 1910 to 1919 maintained relations with the AFM. Lion was considered AFM Overseer for Basutoland and his delegates attended the 1918 Native Conference. As we have seen, his churches received little formal missionary supervision and in 1921 he decided to become independent again, printing identification cards which bore remarkable resemblance to the ones previously issued to him by the AFM. He subsequently developed a very distinctive and controversial set of Zionist practices (Haliburton, 1976; Murray, 1999). In 1932, 112 out of 400 Zionist groups could be shown to be offshoots of the AFM (Hollenweger, 1972: 172).

As in other parts of the Protestant world, intense Pentecostal interaction with radical evangelicals such as the Plymouth Brethren or the International Holiness movement often ended with individuals or whole congregations joining the AFM. But the 1928 census cited above revealed that most AFM converts came from 'Dutch churches', especially the Dutch Reformed churches (Burger, 1995: 35). What has often escaped scholarly attention is the interaction of the AFM with Ethiopian-type churches. For example, in 1909 Lake attended a conference of the African Methodist Episcopal Church in Bloemfontein and accepted 45 preachers with their respective churches into the AFM.[16] Some of these affiliations turned out to be no more than clever scams by Ethiopian churches to ameliorate their perennial problem of funding, the new bodies leaving as soon as they received an injection of cash (Burton, 1934: 84-5). Nevertheless, many were introduced to ecstatic phenomena in the process. Shortly after accepting the group of African Methodists into the AFM, Lake made a tour of their circuit, 'seeing baptism [in the spirit] fall in every church'.[17] Pentecost exploded across South Africa in the same manner as African Methodism had done a decade earlier. The South African Pentecostal movement shared much of African Methodism's organisational and doctrinal character. It forged many of the trails already blazed by itinerant Methodists. Once again, Methodism had prepared a fertile soil for the growth of Pentecostalism.

It is from this early interdenominational symbiosis that many of the distinctive rituals and taboos of Zionist churches derive. Admittedly, some practices were congruent with traditional religion: melodies, hand-clapping, ecstatic dancing, the appeal to visions and dreams, purity laws, leadership styles and polygamy. Nevertheless, those features which one leading scholar of independency asserts as 'typically African' are in fact the most Christian aspect of these churches (Daneel, 1971: 321, 1987). Dowie in Chicago first preached the message of divine healing and the Levitical-style taboos on alcohol and pork. And smokers, or 'dirty stinkpots' as Dowie called them, could expect a fine of as much as $20 if caught in the act in his Zion City. Despite their theological rejection of Old Testament legalism, Lake and Hezmalhalch taught some of these taboos during their South Africa ministry.[18] Other Zionist-type practices such as triune immersion during baptism (Hollenweger, 1972: 121), pacifism (Burger, 1995: 39), the style of preacher's certificate, derive from Zion City, Chicago and the AFM. And the tendency for fission in Zionist-type churches need not be explained by anything as exotic as 'kraal-splitting' (Sundkler, 1961: 116). Such schism was 'endemic to Anglo-Saxon Protestantism once it ceased to be a State Church' (Hastings, 1994: 498). Some Zionists appealed to Luther for legitimation (Hollenweger, 1972: 151). Even the Zionists' distinctive white robes with coloured sashes and accompanying staffs seem to have derived from a cocktail of other church sources: Protestant Sunday school illustrations distributed at the turn of the century (Comaroff, 1985: 204); flirtations with Ethiopian churches (Burton, 1934: 84) and borrowings from Catholicism (Hastings, 1994: 583-4). And of course, from Dowie and his followers who wore a variety of robes (Sundkler, 1976: 48). This is not to contend that Zionist doctrines and practices have not taken on new meanings in the different socio-political context of southern Africa. Rather, Zionism's appeal highlights the 'structural equivalence between the two populations of the newly proletarianised dispossessed in South Africa and the United States', and their shared struggle 'to protest the inappropriate image of themselves presented in the established church and in the dominant culture at large' (Comaroff, 1985: 177).

The AFM would doubtless have looked more like Zionism if Lake and Hezmalhalch had not returned to America. Le Roux was elected President of the AFM in 1913 and remained in office until 1943. He was also elected Superintendent of mission work. From about 1915, relations between the emerging black Zionist movement and fledgling AFM began to sour. The very first minutes of the AFM's Native Committee record that the African membership had emerged out of a separation from Mahlangu's Zion Apostolic Church. Le Roux's strong Dutch Reformed inclinations had grown increasingly uneasy with the distinctive taboos and dress of Zionism in Wakkerstroom, thus many black Zionists went their own way (Sundkler, 1976: 51; Kiernan, 1994: 73;

Hollenweger, 1972:151). The AFM took a different path. Although retaining a large black membership, the leadership of the movement remained in white hands. The laity kept a prominent role until 1935 when David du Plessis was elected General Secretary. Under his leadership the movement was rapidly institutionalised. A professional leadership with a higher standard of theological training began to emerge, backed by a strong bureaucracy. The anti-denominational sentiment of the first generation of Pentecostals was replaced by a desire for respectability. By the 1940s AFM assemblies no longer met in simple halls but in buildings with pulpits and layout inspired by DRC architecture (Langerman, 1983: chapter 4). The strong DRC antecedents of the AFM also reasserted themselves in the introduction of elders and deacons in 1945. By the 1960s the frosty relations between the two churches had subsided.[19]

The black AFM evolved in a different way from the white church. Mirroring the trajectory of Azusa Street Revival, the early practice of multi-racial worship changed to one of segregation. Within a few months of the genesis of the AFM, Lehman was conducting special meetings for 'natives' in Zulu, later opening a special black chapel in Doornfontein. In July 1909 it was decreed that the baptism of blacks, whites and coloureds would be separate. The black work was co-ordinated by a separate committee controlled by whites. This combination of paternalism and racialism contributed to the numerous secessions from the AFM (Burton, 1934: 38; Sundkler, 1976: 54). Nevertheless, those blacks who chose to stay in the AFM still retained a large amount of autonomy in their local assemblies. Hence the symbiosis between AFM and Zionism never completely ceased. The meetings of the Native Workers' Council in the late 1940s and early 1950s were dominated by discussion of 'The Laws of Moses', feet-washing, the purification of women, the wearing of robes and carrying of staffs. The AFM and Zionism exchanged memberships and, inevitably, ideas. Uniforms that started out as simple blue blouses, lengthened into robes, and developed long sleeves upon which wings sometimes sprouted.[20]

It is from the perspective of this grassroots competition for black membership that the discourse of syncretism must be contextualised. 'Although some historians and phenomenologists of religion observed long ago that syncretism is a feature of all religions', in the South African context the clerical definition has come to dominate. Here, much of the early scholarship on religion came from a committed Christian viewpoint and syncretism has become an 'othering' term to denote an ambiguous or deviant religion. As a form of religious politics, anti-syncretism was not evident in the contemporary descriptions of initial relations between the Apostolic Faith Mission and Zionism, nor in the early historical accounts, but developed as the AFM leaders sought respectability, and lost membership to Zionism (Shaw and Stuart, 1994: 5; Burton, 1934).[21]

In 1916 the AFM entered Southern Rhodesia, with all the tensions and tendencies outlined above. Its reception was to be markedly different but its impact no less significant.

The AFM in Southern Rhodesia

The first recorded entrance of the AFM into Southern Rhodesia came in 1916. In that year an AFM evangelist, Zacharias Manamela, entered Gwanda reserve, Southern

Rhodesia as part of the movement's expansion from the northern Transvaal. Manamela was certainly not the first Pentecostal missionary or worker to enter the colony and perhaps not even the first AFM representative. As early as 1910, Lake reported in the journal *The Upper Room* that several missionary families were working amongst blacks in the Zambezi region. Three years later the British Apostolic Faith Church had elders working in churches 'as far north as Bulawayo'. There had been an abortive attempt by the AFM to send missionaries to work among the 'Mashonas' in 1909, terminating with their death from malaria and blackwater fever.[22] Prior to the 1910s Rhodesian and Nyasa labour migrants had doubtless already returned home with a new Pentecostal faith.

However, when Manamela arrived in Gwanda he was not welcome. The Rhodesian state was busy assessing the impact of the Chilembwe rising in Nyasaland and viewed the AFM with suspicion.[23] By February 1917 there were about 400 AFM adherents in Gwanda but the movement still had no official recognition. Consequently a 'deputation of 12 Rhodesian natives' attended a co-ordinated meeting of the Native AFM in South Africa requesting white missionaries. The following year AFM sent two missionary families. The Goldies went to Gwanda and the Luttigs to the mining town of Gatooma.[24] The work soon flourished, again under the dynamism of African preachers.[25] Of these, Isaac Chiumbu, a Nyasa labour migrant from Malawi, made the most significant contribution. Initially a Zionist Pentecostal, Chiumbu had founded and led the work at Gatooma for two years before Luttig's arrival. After their fairly rapid departure he became *de facto* leader once again, eventually becoming head black minister of the Rhodesian movement. Around 1927/28 he also played a key role in the conversion of the Gwanzura brothers: Enoch, Samson, Petros and John, the next generation of black leaders. Of the brothers, the former Methodist preacher Enoch was the most significant. His conversion was accompanied by a dramatic healing of his recurrent stomach ulcers, and henceforth he became a zealous Pentecostal practitioner.[26] In the oral tradition of the Zimbabwean AFM, Enoch has mythical status. He is remembered for his undoubted healing powers, but also for his St Francis-like trait of preaching to animals. And those possessed by demons would cry out at the sight of him approaching a village wearing a white pith helmet.[27] Gwanzura was also renowned for his outspoken criticism of the government. He was extremely vocal at a Gwanda meeting of black and white AFM leaders in 1935, shortly after the government had restricted the movement. A plain-clothes policeman reported: 'ENOCH in his speeches became very heated and repeated continually that the Government is rubbish, they cannot prevent us expanding our faith ... ENOCH's manner was very disrespectful toward authority when he made these statements...'.[28]

In the east, an Afrikaner railway ganger, Lucas Holtzhousen, started meetings in his garage in Umtali. Holtzhousen seems to have left Umtali soon after that, and Joel Juma, one of the converts, was left in charge from 1929 onwards. Juma was also to become a prominent evangelist. Such was his zeal that he was popularly known as 'alleyulah' [sic].[29] There were many other evangelists. By 1930 there were 16 operating in Charter, Gwanda, Marandellas, Wedza and Hartley districts alone.[30] Their methods appeared to those from the older missionary traditions as somewhat unorthodox: night meetings, exorcism, witch-finding, divine healing and ecstatic possession by the spirit, but they certainly had results. By 1931 there were between 3,000 and 6,000 adherents in Southern Rhodesia.[31]

Pentecostalism and the State

Despite its numerical success, the AFM came into immediate conflict with the Rhodesian state. The movement was denied formal recognition. Its missionaries found their work in reserves restricted, and in 1934 they were banned from entry. The reasons for the conflict are not at first obvious. The movement's promotional literature professed obedience to the state, and asserted that spiritual regeneration fostered peace and civic virtue. 'Industrial unrest', it argued, was 'a manifestation of the anti-Christ'. Indeed there did seem to be something in the AFM's claims of 'civilising' influence.[32] Farmers and mining compound managers were impressed with the sobriety and good behaviour of AFM members and allowed church gatherings on their property.[33] Only Enoch Gwanzura appeared to present a political threat, and even his supposed disloyalty sprang from a desire to evangelise.

The AFM was viewed with suspicion by the state and mission churches for two related reasons. First, its practices undermined the state's own narrowly defined civilising mission. Secondly, the AFM threatened the colonial order, particularly through its links with Zimbabwean Christian independency. The predominantly rough and ready Afrikaner Pentecostal missionaries suffered from the racial and class bias of urbane British Native Commissioners (NCs). The Pentecostal missionaries' emphasis on the gospel of personal transformation put them out of sorts with colonialism's new-found notion of development. Their focus on 'God in the person' led to a deterritorialising strategy that engendered conflict between the state-cum-established missionary thrust to territorialise. And AFM encouragement of ecstatic subjectivity clashed with the state's desire for a disciplined subject.

The AFM arrived in Southern Rhodesia in the post-Versailles age – a period epitomised by Lugard's *Dual Mandate* (1922) and the Phelps-Stokes Commissions on African Education, when colonial powers were increasingly called upon to justify their presence in Africa. They made much of their civilising mission. The advancement of African agriculture, health care and education were key elements in this new colonial enterprise and missionaries were to play a leading role. Missionaries' relationship with the Rhodesian state was not always harmonious. A few liberal troublemakers like Arthur Shearly Cripps and John White spoke up for African rights. Nevertheless, most missionaries knuckled down and built schools and hospitals, sharing colonialism's key ideological concerns and willing to act as informal representatives of civilisation (Hastings, 1994: chapter 12; Fields, 1985: chapter 2).

The Apostolic Faith Mission really let the side down. Its white representatives did not look like missionaries, act like missionaries, or even sound like missionaries. Like many of the first Pentecostal pioneers they were arch-mavericks, only loosely affiliated to the AFM of South Africa. Luttig, or *Lulu* as he was popularly known, was really a freelance Pentecostal. He received little financial support from South Africa and took up secular work to save the Mission expenditure. When *Lulu* finally resigned from the AFM, he cultivated links successively with the Pentecostal Mission, the Assemblies of God and the Full Gospel Church, in order to regain control over his flock. An American Pentecostal couple, the Goldies, ended up working for the AFM in Gwanda. They affiliated to the mission only when they arrived in Southern Rhodesia.[34]

47

Like the workers of the Pentecostal Missionary Union discussed in the previous chapter, AFM pioneers rejected conventional missionary ideology. They had no desire to build schools or hospitals, and purchased Gobateme farm in Gwanda only because 'It was clear there was no other way of getting into the territory to preach the true gospel'. Their sole goal was to win converts for Christ.[35] Worse still, they blatantly undermined the colonial mission by preaching divine healing. Their arrival in the colony could not have been worse timed, coinciding with the 1918 influenza pandemic. One of their angry critics wrote to the Superintendent of Natives, Bulawayo: 'These people here persuade the natives not to take medicines from doctors but trust only in prayer, and this is when the town is stricken with a plague ...'. And, much to the chagrin of the Native Administration, the AFM did not invest in local infrastructure. Instead, the missionaries preached tithing and remitted the African offerings back to South Africa.[36]

Neither did the majority of AFM missionaries form an easy rapport with the Native Administration. Most missionaries entering Africa in the inter-war period were professionally trained teachers, doctors and nurses. In this context AFM whites were sadly lacking. Their poor educational qualifications were a matter of continuous concern to the state, which prevented them from opening schools even when the missionaries finally appreciated the utility of mission education. Neither Swanepoel nor Harris, two of the movement's key missionaries in the 1920s, had anything better than a standard 6 qualification.[37] Worse still, all the AFM missionaries shared their African colleagues' liking for ecstatic phenomena, even witchcraft eradication, and some saw nothing amiss in such activity taking place at night and in African villages.[38] These were not the sort of Europeans Native Commissioners would have felt comfortable inviting for afternoon tea. As members of the British middle class with predominantly established church backgrounds, NCs were appalled by the uninhibited exclamations of AFM whites. The NC Sinoia wrote of one white AFM worker, 'I have picked up some queer stories of the manner this Mr Oberholzer conducts baptismal services; the manner he has in writing letters is fervent with expressions like "the lovely work of the Lord"'. The Chief Native Commissioner described another Pentecostal as 'full of faith and ignorance'.[39] Neither did it help that the majority of the early AFM missionaries to Southern Rhodesia were Afrikaners. Rhodesian whites in the 1920s were deeply suspicious of Afrikaner penetration north of the Limpopo and had voted against closer links with South Africa in 1923.

The white AFM pioneers and their African workers also rejected widely shared missionary conventions. The colony had been split into discrete packages of missionary territory rather like tribal areas. But AFM evangelists roved across them in a carefree fashion. 'They recognise no boundaries', the Reverend Holman Brown of the Methodist Epworth Mission fumed in 1931. 'If only they would leave my people alone.'[40] Once inside rival territory, the AFM would preach to members of other denominations and baptise them immediately on conversion. That new converts may previously have been under church discipline was irrelevant.[41] When Hans Nilson, head of the Rhodesian Swedish mission, Gwanda, intervened on the AFM's behalf, pointing out that 'they acted in accordance with scripture, as in the Acts of the Apostles people were baptised on the same day they confessed or accepted the faith', his words found little favour.[42]

The AFM missionaries were few and far between, their presence bolstered by a handful of Afrikaner farmers and railway workers. They had no choice but to rely on their African evangelists for pastoral work and information. Throughout the 1920s there were never more than four missionary families working in the colony at the same time. This rapid turnover of a few personnel continued into the 1930s and early 1940s. They left through a combination of exhaustion, frustration with non-recognition by the state, and lack of logistical support and understanding from Johannesburg.[43]

The Native Administration undermined both itself and the Pentecostal missionaries in attempts to limit the activities of itinerant preachers. Missionaries were blamed for the activities of the evangelists and hence not allowed into reserves. The evangelists, who could not be prevented from preaching by law, thus had a free hand. In 1943 Chief Mangwende asked a group of black AFM preachers the identity of their European leader. Enoch Gwanzura replied: 'I am the leader and have no European Minister or Supervisor'.[44] In many respects this was true. The Rhodesian AFM operated as an autonomous black church with a thin missionary coating. And it was this virtually independent section of black workers who presented a real threat to the colonial order. Not only did they undermine the regularised world of mission Christianity; they also led an assault on the other pillar of the system: traditional rulers. The resources for governance at the disposal of colonial states were not as exhaustive as those possessed by European states. Hence the colonial states also had to construct themselves through 'tradition'. Missionaries bolstered the 'thin white line' of administrators, but this was not enough. The regime imposed order and constructed legitimacy in the countryside through chiefs and headmen. Although rural patriarchy was by no means totalising, these male gerontocrats had considerable influence over women and youth, and organised the supply of migrant labour. They legitimised their rule through ancestor religion (Werbner, 1989: 79-81; Fields, 1985: chapters 1 & 2), and dispensed justice through customary law which they had helped fashion.

As soon as the AFM arrived in Southern Rhodesia's reserves, chiefs and headmen began to object, hostilities continuing well into the 1920s and 1930s.[45] In 1933 an AFM preacher named Munyengwa was prosecuted following his activities in Buhera. The Assistant Native Commissioner commented: 'The concomitant religious frenzy at this preacher's gatherings is viewed not without some concern by the elder and more responsible men. It is stated that his proselytes become possessed by some "shave" [alien spirit] and throw themselves about; rave and tear their hair and crawl about amongst the bushes.' Elsewhere in the district Munyengwa had disobeyed Chief Swinurayi by conducting a service on Dengedza Hill, the burial ground of the royal ancestors, burning a diviner's paraphernalia. Similarly, Headman Gara of Zwimba reserve reported: 'Since the AFM ... church came into my kraal there have been many disputes (*moswa*).'[46] These *moswa* or 'dissensions' occurred along lines of gender and generation.[47] As Karen Fields has shown for Central Africa, religious movements such as Watch Tower, or indeed the AFM, could have a revolutionary effect on the rural religious order. They undermined traditional legitimacy by demonising ancestor religion and destroying its sacred sites and ritual objects, they provided young labour migrants anxious to retain their wages with legitimate reasons to break free from communal demands, and they gave young women legitimate reasons to challenge patriarchal authority (1985: chapters 3-5).

Traditional leaders regarded Pentecostalism in particular as an alternative and threatening source of authority in the same way that they regarded predominantly female possession cults (Maxwell, 1999: chapter 2). This suspicion was shared by the state. On occasions idiosyncratic versions of rural Christianity emerged, which the Native Administration interpreted as direct challenges to its authority. In a fascinating report dated 1934, the Acting NC, Goromonzi District, reported the appearance of a man purporting to be Jesus who was followed by disciples, as well as 'Moses, Ezekiel, Gabriel, Luke and so forth'. A Native Messenger, Masawi, and a kraal head had encountered them and the former asked to see their registration certificates. Jesus and his disciples refused but the kraal head insisted, pointing out that Masawi was a 'police boy':

> On this, and led by one of the gathering, the crowd sprang up and surrounded both the messenger and head of kraal; they then circled the pair, gyrating faster and faster, some falling down and crawling, some moaning and some groaning like dogs. The circling natives began singing 'take off your hat' and caused their circle to get smaller and smaller in circumference until the crowd closed on the messenger and head of kraal ... unidentified members of the crowd knocked off the messenger's hat ... threw him to the ground, removing his boots and handcuffs.

Divested of his symbols of state power, and bare-headed in the presence of a black Jesus, the messenger fled. Later the group was apprehended, and the Acting NC reported that, on his attempt to interview 'Jesus', the black messiah 'ran off muttering, jumped upon a donkey, and rode back to me mouthing some gibberish and shivering'. Order was established when '[s]tern action returned him [Jesus] to his knowledge of Chishona'.[48]

Mention of 'gibberish' and 'shivering' or comparable behaviour was never far from the Native Administration and traditional leaders' description of AFM activities. The NC Gwanda reported in 1919 that the mission 'encouraged considerable emotionalism at meetings' and cited a 'trustworthy' native's opinion: 'The people [AFM] are mad. What kind of God do they serve? He must be cruel, for they lament and weep, being chastised without cause. They behave worse than those at a beer drink.'[49] Colonial governments created their own hybrid institutions such as 'native courts', but they were very suspicious of their subjects' own appropriations and inventions. Like New Guinea cargo cults, the meaning of African Pentecostalism often escaped colonial control (Shaw and Stuart, 1994: 21). Pentecostal tongues, along with pious groaning and moaning, were uncapturable discourses. Indeed, in the face of administrative intransigence AFM workers could do little more than speak in tongues in front of outraged officials.[50]

New localised syntheses of the Christian religion also challenged administrative notions of how the colonial subject's life should be ordered. First, they defied the carefully regulated life of mission converts who, under missionary supervision, went through a number of stages: probation, baptism, church membership and leadership. AFM converts could be baptised immediately and find themselves preaching a few days later. Secondly, the frenzied wailing of AFM adherents, often referred to as 'white fire', was not appropriate behaviour for a labour unit in a capitalist economy (Callaway, 1993: 51). The subject had no more utility than a drunkard did at a beer drink, which was a popular administrative phobia.[51] Such administrative prejudices persisted into the 1950s. In 1951 a particularly well-informed and perceptive Assistant Native Commissioner wrote to his immediate superior seeking to block the entrance of the Assemblies of God into Nuanetsi: 'I wish to record that I am strongly opposed to this denomination starting their activities in this district, for I consider them to be akin to Zionism. I believe that in America they are referred to as 'Holy Rollers' as their services and meetings are attended by uncontrolled rantings and contortions as the Holy Spirit descends upon them.'[52]

The 'immodest' or 'unseemly' behaviour of young women was the favourite administrative concern. Female Pentecostals were reported to roll on the ground in frenzied fits, their clothing detaching itself in the process. This was much in keeping with the widespread discourse on African female immorality that had at its root an administrative desire to maintain rural stability as part of its segregationalist policy (Jeater, 1993: chapter 9). The exaggerated reports of Pentecostal phenomena, written in appalled tones, reinforced the administration's own sense of its civilising mission.[53]

At this juncture it is important to ask whether the AFM in South Africa experienced a comparable clash with the South African state. The only significant point of conflict concerned the public health act of 1919. The legislation for compulsory smallpox vaccination ran counter to Pentecostal belief in divine healing, but AFM pressure subsequently led to a new law in 1928, which included a conscience clause. In general, relations with the South African state were good and the AFM Sending Mission was incredulous as to why their missionaries in Zimbabwe received such a poor reception. In March 1924 the General Secretary of the AFM protested to the Rhodesian Chief Native Commissioner that his movement was a 'properly constituted body of 15,000 Europeans and 40,000 Natives in the Union'.[54]

The reasons for the AFM's warmer reception in South Africa are diverse. The first lies in the African part of the movement. Elias Letwaba, the dominant figure in the black South African AFM, differed considerably from Enoch Gwanzura or Isaac Chiumbu, although he was equally, if not more, influential. Having trained with the Berlin Lutheran Mission, Letwaba had reaped the material benefits of missionary education. He knew German and was well versed in theology. Despite the fact that he outshone many of his white colleagues, he remained intensely deferential to white authority and resisted overtures from Zionists to join their movements (A. Anderson, 1992: 36-40; Burton, 1934).[55] Moreover, whilst Zionist leaders were a threat to the rural social order because of their tendency to carve out their own polities, or 'Zions', independent of traditional rule, AFM blacks had no such desire.

The main reason for AFM's acceptance by the state lay in Afrikaner politico-religious culture. Pentecostalism was less of a shock to the religious body politic than elsewhere. Lake loved to remind Afrikaner audiences that their Huguenot ancestors, the Tremblers as they were known in France, had spoken in tongues and prophesied in the spirit.[56] More recently in the late nineteenth century, through revivals and the international influence of Andrew Murray's teaching on divine healing and holiness, South Africa had directly contributed to the emergence of Pentecostalism as a global force. Thus South Africa was receptive to Pentecostal revival when it arrived with Lake and others from Indianapolis in May 1908. There was a particular openness to divine healing. In one of his sermons, Lake recounted how it held such sway among black and white soldiers in the Great War that an estimated twenty out of every hundred troops refused medical aid, necessitating the formation of a Divine Healing Corps within the armed forces (Lindsay, 1995: 130).

From the beginning, the AFM had a high profile in South Africa. Lake addressed the South African Parliament, where he advised it to adopt a policy of racial segregation similar to the American policy for Native Americans (Sundkler, 1976: 54). The wife of Prime Minister Hertzog was a staunch AFM member, and in the 1930s and 1940s South Africa was proud of the AFM's President, David du Plessis, 'Mr Pentecost', who acted as a world spokesman on Pentecostal issues. But the key reason for its smooth relations with the state was that it rapidly absorbed the dominant economic and political culture. Although the movement initially took root among marginalised Afrikaners, it nevertheless appropriated a key organisational form of the established order:

the unlimited company. AFM Pentecostalism thus staked a claim in the heartland of South African capitalism. In political terms, the movement reproduced segregational-ist and apartheid polices. Eventually some of its leading members became integrated into the white ruling class. Blacks were accorded no legal status within the AFM for over 75 years (Burger, 1995: 42; Hollenweger, 1972: 121; A. Anderson, 1992: 32-35).

The AFM and Christian Independency

In the Rhodesian case, relations between the AFM and the state did not improve but grew worse in the early 1930s. This was due to the Church's relations with Zimbabwe-an Christian Independency. In 1932 there emerged the movements of Johane Masowe in Mashonaland and Johane Maranke in Manicaland. Like the South African Zionists, both prophets had a distinctive appearance. Both wore white, carried staffs, shaved their heads and kept long beards. Both preached levitical-style taboos.

As in the case of the South African Zionists, the question arises concerning the origins of the Masowe and Maranke movements. Masowe's connections with Angli-canism, Watch Tower, and even Catholicism, have been documented by scholars (Hastings, 1994: 521; Dillon-Mallone, 1978: chapter 1). Indeed, one can speculate that his message of Sabbatarianism came from his contacts with the Seventh Day Adventist (SDA) church in Makoni (Hallencreutz, 1998: chapter 9). Once again both Masowe and Maranke's Methodist heritage proved highly formative. In this case their movements did not just take on doctrinal and organisational characteristics from Methodism but also drew from its bequest of vernacular scriptures (Daneel, 1971: 316; Ranger, 2002). The movements, characterised by their 'eschatological bibli-cism', emerged out of an ambience of popular Methodism with its strong emphasis on equipping the believer with the translated word, whether Chimanyika or Chize-zuru. African Christian prophets like Maranke and Masowe mined the Scriptures for legitimating charters for what were to become great transnational movements. In them they also read of Zion and Bethesda, sacred cities and streams, and holy mountains. These images provided the basis of a new African hymnology and the imaginative material to re-sacralise the landscape in Christian fashion. In scripture they also read of dreams and visions, exorcism and healing, and notions of provision and personal security absent from the teachings of many missionaries. But Christian independency also had direct connection with the Apostolic Faith Mission.

The key link between Masowe and the AFM was Enoch Gwanzura. By 1931 Gwanzura spent much of his time itinerating in the reserves around Salisbury. Left to his own devices he developed a version of Christianity not very dissimilar from the Zionists'. He was so renowned for preaching purity taboos, and more generally 'the laws of Moses', that he became known as 'Deuteronomy Gwanzura'.[57] AFM preach-ers also developed their own distinctive garb: white robes, shaven heads, staffs, and of course long beards. Their appearance and practices may have been copied from the Zionists who were already in the country but they were justified in terms of the rich imagery relating to kings and prophets found in the Hebrew Scriptures.[58] This AFM innovation preceded the Masowe and Maranke movements. When Masowe, also known as *Sisipensi* – Sixpence – and more often as Shoniwa, moved into the vicinity of Salisbury as a labour migrant, he became subsumed in this Pentecostal ambience.

Sometime around 1930 he met Gwanzura, who initiated him as an AFM preacher. Shoniwa eventually went his own way, taking his AFM heritage with him. The AFM tradition[59] of Shoniwa's early history bears remarkable resemblance to the internal traditions of the Masowe movement, although the latter omitted the AFM link and provided its founder with a more illustrious divine appointment.[60]

Similar links can be discerned between the AFM and the Maranke movement in the east, this time through Joel Juma. The NC Umtali reported in January 1931 that Juma now controlled the activities of the church with regard to the Africans in the district.[61] Juma, like Enoch Gwanzura, preached the laws of Moses. He also wore white. AFM tradition claims that Juma met Maranke in Umtali and baptised him in the Spirit, later accompanying Maranke as his mentor.[62] These accounts of Gwanzura and Juma could represent an act of AFM self-aggrandisement. But the Juma tradition, like the Gwanzura tradition, is shared with other non-AFM Pentecostals[63] and supported by a large amount of circumstantial evidence. The AFM was extremely strong in the Maranke reserve in the 1930s. Two of Chief Maranke's sons were AFM members.[64]

The appearance of the Apostolic or Vapostori movements of Masowe and Maranke also corresponded with internal developments within the AFM. As Iliffe (1979: 342–76) has shown for Tanganyika, and Ranger (1985: chapter 2) for Southern Rhodesia, there was a strong correlation between the emergence of independency and the Great Depression. Educational and health services contracted and missionaries were withdrawn. Those Africans seeking material gain perceived that their interests might be better advanced through association with movements like that of Masowe, which preached withdrawal from the migrant labour economy and emphasised a self-reliant life of artisanship or co-operative farming.

The AFM's experience of the Great Depression was more dramatic than that of most mission churches because it was an unlimited company (Burger, 1995: 38-9). Once the Depression set in, AFM adherents-cum-shareholders began to withdraw investment. The movement was thrown into financial chaos, and was shackled by debts incurred through rebuilding the Central Tabernacle in Johannesburg. AFM missionaries were impoverished. Their allowances were not paid and there was no money for tyres and petrol, or travel to the Annual Conference in South Africa.[65] What little supervisory power they had was now removed. In 1930, L.L. Kruger, an extremely effective AFM missionary, arrived in the country. Better qualified than his predecessors, he immediately impressed the authorities by conducting a census, which registered churches and local preachers.[66] But just as Kruger began to exert control and impose what he saw as orthodoxy, funds ran out. Now was the time to break away.

As we will see in following chapters, the appeal of these new Zimbabwean Pentecostal churches went far beyond instrumental or materialist considerations. All three movements responded to popular fears of witchcraft in the same manner. In 1932 the Mchape witchcraft eradication movement moved rapidly throughout east and central Africa. Its acolytes dispensed a medicine, Mchape, which they claimed protected people against witchcraft and killed those who practised it but did not confess. Not unexpectedly, it proved particularly effective in cleansing societies of substances associated with witchcraft. The eradication movement, like Christian independency, was given a great impetus by the Great Depression. Ranger has noted how the Mchape movement generally remained on the margins of Zimbabwe, in the east and north (Ranger, 1982: 26). This was because African Pentecostalism undercut it. Confession of witchcraft and the destruction of polluted objects often accompanied baptism.

Christian Movement	Date of Appearance	Leader
Apostolic Faith Mission	1916	Isaac Chiumbu [later Enoch Gwanzura]
Apostles of Johane Masowe	1932	Johane Masowe [Sixpence/ Shoniwa/John the Baptist]
Apostles of Johane Maranke [African Apostolic Church of Johane Maranke]	1932	Johane Maranke [John the Baptist]
Madida Apostolic Faith Mission	1945	Madida Moyo
African Apostolic Faith Mission	1945	Isaac Chiumbu
Kruger Apostolic Faith Mission	1940s	Elijah Mugodi
Ezekiel Guti Evangelistic Association [Later Assemblies of God African]	1959	Ezekiel Guti

Table 2.1 The Apostolic Faith Mission and Christian Independency in Southern Rhodesia[67]

Moreover, preachers and evangelists from Maranke, Masowe and the AFM developed a means of divining whilst in a state of ecstatic possession by the Holy Spirit.[68] Indeed it was the AFM's connection with witchcraft eradication in Wedza in 1933 that led to further restrictions being placed upon it in 1934.[69]

Official opinion conflated the AFM, Masowe and Maranke movements. Black adherents of the AFM were often placed in the same category, of subversive 'pseudo religious movements', as the followers of the two Shona prophets.[70] This was not surprising since they all looked alike, preached the same message, practised divine healing and fostered various ecstatic phenomena. Even in the minds of the adherents there was a conflation. In June 1934 a teacher and healer named Abraham was apprehended in Seki Reserve. When questioned, he claimed to be 'a teacher of the Apostolic Faith Mission under Mr L.L Kruger, and also acting leader of the sect founded by JOHANS'.[71] The rural AFM went from strength to strength in the 1930s. Black preachers were left to themselves and numbers almost doubled. Nevertheless it did lose large numbers to the Vapostori movements.[72] But there was not only movement into the Vapostori; prior to the Great Depression and the emergence of the Maranke and Masowe movements, disgruntled AFM members moved back into the Wesleyan Methodists, the SDA and the Church of Christ when the promised kraal schools failed to materialise.[73]

Missionary Orthodoxy and African Secessions

From the late 1930s, the AFM missionaries began to reassert themselves. The process began with the arrival of the Wilson brothers, Willard and Bill, from America in 1938. These American Pentecostals, affiliated to the AFM, looked and behaved like other missionaries. They restarted the school in Gwanda and in 1943 were eventually rewarded with government recognition. This second generation of missionaries placed a greater emphasis on theological training, sending some pastors to AFM colleges in Johannesburg, South Africa, or Kasupe, Zambia. They convened yearly conferences for native workers, and caucused beforehand to ensure a united missionary front. They erected church buildings to fix the movement to permanent locations. They circulated the 'AFM Form of Discipline' among Native Commissioners, and assured them that they would stamp out 'nocturnal orgies'.[74] It was highly significant that the Wilsons were Americans and not Afrikaners.

Missionary attempts to impose orthodoxy were fiercely resisted. Black AFM preachers retained links with Vapostori leaders and osmosis between movements continued. Zionist-type practices persisted well into the 1950s. One missionary noted in 1952 that his church members 'love to carry wooden crosses, sashes and gay coloured uniforms'. Black pastors outsmarted missionaries. Old hands such as Enoch Gwanzura used whites as a respectable cover while continuing to practise old-style religion in the hills at night.[75] AFM prophets roved the reserves divining witchcraft well into the 1940s. As late as 1957 some AFM adherents were under the impression that 'there was no white people in the AFM'. But the missionary grip slowly tightened. Pastors who openly preached the 'laws of Moses' were sacked. In 1957, Willard Wilson, the most remembered white AFM missionary, armed himself with a pair of scissors and initiated a campaign against long beards at an Umtali conference.[76] The gradual imposition of missionary notions of orthodoxy led to a wave of schisms in the 1940s and '50s, which created a new set of Vapostori-like churches. Madida (Moyo), Elijah Mugodhi and Isaac Chiumbu (also known as Kachembere) led the significant schisms.

The immediate causes of the schisms were varied. Madida Moyo, for instance, took great offence at the Wilson brothers' attempts to modernise the movement. Baptised in 1922 in Gwanda he had been in one of the first cohorts of AFM converts in Southern Rhodesia, and loyally served as a preacher from 1930 onwards. His split with the movement came at the 1945 annual Church Conference at Gobatema Mission. Here it was announced that missionaries had been in dialogue with the authorities concerning the possibility of opening a hospital. Given the movement's perennial shortage of resources, human and material, the plans were never realised. Nevertheless they prompted Madida to fear that his firmly held beliefs in divine healing were under assault. Far worse was the missionary initiative to rear pigs for sale on the mission farm. Holding to his literal interpretation of the Hebrew scriptures, Madida declared that the mission station was defiled and that henceforth he would have nothing to do with the 'Church of Pigs'. Although the new movement came to be known as Madida AFM, the founder intended it to be known as the Pure Apostolic Faith Mission. Madida's declared reasons for schism may well have been a *post hoc* rationalisation of a long held desire for greater autonomy. Despite dynamic preaching, Madida's rudimentary education blocked him from rising to the level of an evangelist with the requisite authority to baptise. Prior to the split he had made contact with Engenas Lekganyane, leader of the Zion Christian Church in the Northern Transvaal, and doubtless hoped to emulate him. Although Madida's new movement left AFM liturgy unchanged, Zionist and Vapostori-type practices relating to dress and the rejection of bio-medicine and schooling did permeate the movement (Dube, 1984).

The desire for greater freedom shaped other secessions. All were led by men who had been *de facto* leaders of district or national churches and who sought greater recognition and respect. But as in many other cases throughout southern Africa, the immediate reason for the split was the issue of polygamy (Hastings, 1994: chapter 11). This was certainly the case for Mugodhi, who broke away to found the Kruger AFM, claiming true descent from the figure many regarded as the pioneer missionary. Polygamy was also the cause of the biggest schism, which followed the dismissal of Isaac Chiumbu, until 1943 the head black minister. In 1943 AFM missionary O.P. Teichart was finally granted permission to visit rural areas surrounding Gatooma where Chiumbu had been working. The distance African Pentecostalism had travelled from its missionary roots disturbed Teichart, who accused the head minister of 'adultery', suggesting that he was practising polygamy. Henceforth, Chiumbu was stripped of his authority. Chiumbu, who had always operated with a high degree of autonomy, fought his case with astounding self-confidence. Petitions were sent to the Gatooma NC and the CNC in which his followers rightly asserted that he was a founder member of the AFM being dismissed by those who came after. Even a local white woman wrote to the authorities on his behalf. Once his new church was established Chiumbu managed to get himself a 'white stupa' [registration certificate] and a marriage register from allies in the Native Administration, which he used illegally to solemnise his followers' weddings. Chiumbu's new movement was known as the African Apostolic Faith Mission.[77]

Conclusion

Although Pentecostal missionaries had an inspiring global vision, the movement's appeal also lay in its capacity to take on different local forms. Missionaries and the barrage of printed literature that accompanied them transmitted its uniform doctrines and practices. But once different local communities seized upon Pentecostalism's powerful idioms, it was legitimated in local terms. The Holy Spirit was pitted against local demons and divine healing was congruent with indigenous notions of illness. In the hands of 'native' evangelists Pentecostalism moved rapidly from white to black congregations, and from cities and mines to rural locations. Adopted by labour migrants, as well carried by missionaries, its message had spread into the Rhodesias and Nyasaland within a few years. Indeed it seemed to appeal to those on the move, both physically and socially. Like other Christian movements traversing the continent at that time, Pentecostalism spoke to those experiencing the imposition or intensification of colonial rule. Increased economic exploitation through mines, farms or plantations, and extensive white settlement produced profound social, religious and intellectual disruption. In consequence, many sought a measure of security from and conceptual control over modernity by converting to Christianity because it appeared to offer a key to the new secular order so rapidly imposed upon them. Where Pentecostalism had a specific appeal was in the firm boundaries it erected between the believer and the world, its strong bonds of fellowship and egalitarian ideals from which new communities could be built. Believers experienced a new sense of empowerment derived from the newly imparted gifts of the Spirit. These religious ideas and practices had great relevance to those Afrikaners and blacks suffering the devastation of their agriculture following the South African War and the consequent travails of rapid urbanisation. Two decades later they took force among diverse communities across the southern African region during the social upheaval that accompanied the Great Depression. And as this study will show, in ever-greater detail Pentecostalism's appeal to the poor and the socially dislocated became increasingly relevant in Africa throughout the twentieth century and beyond.

In Chapter 1 Pentecostalism's rapid transmission across the globe was explained in terms of continuities. It took force along existing Protestant networks, particularly non-conformist and radical evangelical networks. Its appeal was also based on its apparent congruence with existing non-Christian beliefs and practices surrounding healing, divination and spirit possession. Chapter 2 shed more light on these processes as it explored Pentecostalism's reception in southern Africa. This chapter has also highlighted how Pentecostalism's appeal rests upon its disjuncture with African traditional religion. Pentecostals may borrow from traditional beliefs and practices but the content is re-coded within a Christian system of ideas, taking on a new form and significance. Pentecostalism thus competes for the same metaphysical domain as traditional religion but is at odds with non-Christian belief and practice pronouncing it as demonic. The Holy Spirit is pitted against alien and ancestral spirits, and conversion is immediately followed by total immersion baptism, symbolising rebirth and a break with the past. Conversion is also often accompanied by the destruction of traditional charms and fetishes, considered polluted by Pentecostals. Witchcraft and sorcery are also collapsed into the Pentecostal category of the demonic. Witches are divined through prayer and exorcised through the laying on of hands.

This adversarial approach towards African belief and practice strengthened the hand of Pentecostal missionaries and local evangelists in their evangelistic endeavours. Their message appealed to youth and women excluded from patriarchal ancestor religion. It also gave them a distinct advantage over the 'rationalist' historic mission churches that refused to recognise the very real fear of witchcraft amongst their adherents. Throughout the twentieth century Pentecostalism evolved into a new Christian personal security movement (Maxwell, 1999: chapters 2, 3 and 7). Finally, in a more instrumental sense the ruptures with tradition that conversion could bring about were central to the making of new social formations that accompanied the transition from an agrarian to an industrial and urban existence. As we shall see in the following chapters, conversion liberated Pentecostals to make the best of, or at least survive, the ravages of colonial and post-colonial African economies.

In 1959 the Apostolic Faith Mission experienced yet another secession. At the time it was no more significant than the previous secessions led by Madida, Mugodhi and Chiumbu. A young evangelist named Ezekiel Guti, accompanied by a prayer band that doubled as his choir, broke away and re-affiliated with a constellation of North American and South African missionaries. But the secession turned out to be highly significant, its agents forming the nucleus of what would eventually become the Zimbabwe Assemblies of God Africa (ZAOGA), the subject of this book. While the other schismatic movements remained collections of locally based assemblies, whose members shunned bio-medicine and schooling, ZAOGA took a very different trajectory. It is to the city of Salisbury, Southern Rhodesia, and the origins of ZAOGA, that we now turn.

Notes

[1] More recently termed African *Initiated* Churches or African *Instituted* Churches.

[2] Lehman was involved in other mission work, particularly amongst the Zulu. Ida Sackett returned home, unhealed, after a brief success in children's ministry. There is little record of Lake's (unnamed) sister.

[3] The British Apostolic Faith Church evolved into the Apostolic Church, led by D.P Williams – see Chapter 1.

[4] There were also a number of independent black churches and preachers operating under the Zion label in the late nineteenth century, pers. comm. Jeff Guy.

[5] *The Upper Room*, June 1909, March 1910, July 1910; *Confidence*, 1910.

[6] For example, *The Upper Room*, February 1910

[7] *Pentecostal Witness*, November 1908; *The Upper Room*, August 1909. [8] *The Upper Room*, June 1909.

[9] *The Upper Room*, October – November 1909, February 1910.

[10] *The Upper Room*, May 1910.

[11] *The Comforter*, February 1912.

[12] *The Upper Room*, June 1909, July 1910, September – October 1910.

[13] *Pentecostal Testimony*, ca. May 1910.

[14] S. Harris, 'Memories', nd, file, S. Harris, Apostolic Faith Mission, Lyndhurst, South Africa, (henceforth AFM); *The Comforter*, 1912; *The Upper Room*, September – October 1910; Burger, 1995: 35. No racial breakdown of the figures is provided.

[15] *The Upper Room*, October – November 1909, May 1910.

[16] *The Pentecostal Testimony*, ca. 1909. See also, *The Upper Room*, February 1911. Campbell notes the movement of Ethiopian congregations into the AFM but confuses much of the detail (2002: 234).

[17] *Pentecostal Testimony*, 1909. Other Ethiopian Churches moved under the control of British Pentecostal missionaries. Thirty-six assemblies with pastors moved under the control of the Apostolic Faith Church in 1911, *Showers of Blessing*, January – February 1911.

[18] *Confidence*, February 1909, February 1913; Lindsay, 1986. [19] Int. DM70, I.S. Burger.

[20] Minutes of the Annual General Native Workers' Council Meetings, Johannesburg, March 1947; Western Native Township, March 1950; Reinfontein [sic], March 1953, AFM.

[21] See correspondence between Hollenweger and AFM leaders (1972: 171, fn. 12).

[22] *The Upper Room*, March 1910; *Showers of Blessing*, 11, ca. 1913; Burton, 1934, chapter 9.

[23] W.F. Dugmore, AFM Johannesburg to Lord Buxton, High Commissioner, South Africa, 14 April 1919, S1542/M8, vol. 1, National Archives of Zimbabwe, Harare, (henceforth NAZ).

[24] *The Comforter*, February 1917 & March 1919. Sending Committee Minutes, 16 October 1917, AFM.

[25] Int. DM79, Jerries Mvenge. Int. DM78, Titus Murefu.

[26] Otilia Liberman to CNC 9 April 1945, S2810/4469, NAZ; Harris, 'Memories', nd, file, S. Harris, AFM; Int. DM72, Cleopas Gwanzura. John Gwanzura was also known as Johanne, Chihari, and Ezekiel.

[27] *Southern Rhodesia Pentecostal Light Bearer*, April – June 1956; Int.DM79, Jeries Mvenge. Int.TM73, Samson Gwanzura and Kuitenyi Msike; Int. DM71, Florence Goneke.

[28] NC Gwanda to Superintendent of Natives, Bulawayo, 23 September 1935, S1542/M8B vol.2.

[29] NC Umtali to CNC Salisbury, 29 January 1931, S1542/M8B vol. 1, NAZ. Harris, 'Memories', nd, file, S. Harris, AFM; Int.DM76, Kuitenyi Msike.

[30] S1542/M8B Apostolic Faith Mission, vol.1, NAZ.

[31] *The Comforter*, May 1941; *Southern Rhodesia Pentecostal Light Bearer*, April – June 1956.

[32] 'Grounds upon which recognition is claimed for the work of the Apostolic Faith Mission of South Africa', ca.1919, S1542/M8 vol.1, NAZ.

[33] F.J. Green, Glasgow Mine, Gatooma to the Private Secretary, 23 September 1919, S1542/M8 vol.1, NAZ; *The Comforter*, September – October 1940.

[34] Sending Committee Minutes, 19 January 1919, AFM. A Luttig, Salisbury to CNC, Salisbury, 4 March 1925, S138/17/2, NAZ. Sending Committee Minutes, 30 July 1918, AFM.

[35] Sending Committee Minutes, 11 February 1920, AFM. *The Pentecostal Link – Supplement to The Comforter*, August – September 1941.

[36] L Star to Superintendent of Native Affairs, 23 October 1918, S1542/M8B, vol.1, NAZ. The following year Mr Goldie died of flu. *The Comforter*, March 1919; CNC to the Secretary, Department of the Administrator, 6 May 1919, N3/5/3-4, NAZ.

[37] H. Jowitt, Director of Native Department to L.L. Kruger, Salisbury, 25 November 1931, S2810/2358/1, NAZ.

[38] *The Comforter*, September – October 1945; Harris, 'Memories', nd, file, S. Harris, AFM; NC Gwanda to Superintendent of Natives, Bulawayo, 23 September 1935, S1542/M8B, vol. 2, NAZ.

[39] NC, Sinoia to PNC, Fort Victoria, 13 November 1943, S2810/2340 & CNC's correspondence on the Apostolic Faith Church, 12 December 1923, S138/148, NAZ.

[40] Rev Holman Brown, Epworth Mission, Salisbury to NC Hartley, 5 June 1931, S2810/2358/1, NAZ.

[41] Ibid. Rev Walter Howarth, Sinoia to Director Native Education, 28 December 1931, S1542/M8B/vol.1, NAZ.

[42] Hans Nilson, Gwanda to CNC, Salisbury, 19 December 1926, S138/17/2, NAZ.

[43] Harris, `Memories', nd, file, S. Harris, AFM; B.J. Britz, 'Facts about Pentecost in Southern Rhodesia' ca.1952, personal papers of Desmond Cartwright.

[44] NC Mrewa to CNC Salisbury, 19 July 1943, S2810/2340, NAZ.

[45] CNC to the Secretary, Department of the Administrator, 19 August 1920; NC Gwanda to CNC Salisbury, 8 May 1919, N3/5/3-4. CNC Salisbury to Secretary of Native Affairs, 31 March 1932, S1542/M8B vol.1, NAZ.

[46] AssNC Buhera to NC, the Range, Enkeldoorn, 11 March 1933, S661; Statement Headman Gara before C. Bullock, NC, Sinoia, 15 March 1932, S1542/M8B vol.1, NAZ.

[47] For example: Statement, N.M. Mangama to C. Bullock, NC Sinoia, 29 December 1930, S1542/M8B vol.1, NAZ.

[48] AgNC Goromonzi to CNC Salisbury, 5 December 1934, S1542/P10, NAZ.

[49] NC Gwanda to CNC Salisbury, 8 May 1919, N3/5/3-4, NAZ.

[50] Int.TM73, Samson Gwanzura and Kuitenyi Masike.

[51] CNC to NC Selukewe, 10 August 1943, S2810/2340, NAZ.

[52] AssNC Nuanetsi to NC Chibi 1 November 1951, S2810/4424, NAZ.

[53] See S1542/M8 vol. 1 1919-32 and vol. 2, 1934-38, NAZ.

[54] General Secretary of the AFM, Johannesburg to CNC Salisbury, 25 March 1924, S138/17/1, NAZ.

[55] For Letwaba's obituary see *The Comforter*, June 1959. [56] *The Upper Room*, July 1910.

[57] Int.DM79, Jeries Mvenge. [58] Int.DM77, Constantine Murefu.

[59] Int.DM79, Jeries Mvenge; Int.DM77,Constantine Murefu; Int.DM78, Titus Murefu; Int.DM62, Abel Sande; Int.DM71, Florence Goneke.

[60] Int., Alwin Amon Negomasha, AOH/4, NAZ.

[61] NC Umtali to CNC Salisbury, 29 January 1931, S1542/M8B vol.1, NAZ.

[62] Int.DM79, Jeries Mvenge.

[63] For example, Abel Sande, co-founder of the Zimbabwe Assemblies of God.

[64] B.J. Britz, 'Facts' ca. 1952, personal papers of Desmond Cartwright;. *The Comforter*, September - October 1940. Daneel (1971: 316) rejects the idea of a strong relation between the AFM and the Masowe movement. He confuses the AFM with the Apostolic Faith Church from Bournemouth, England (see Chapter 1 & fn 5 above). Dillon Malone is more cognisant of the similarities between the AFM and the Masowe movements but does not appreciate a causal link from one to the other (1978: chapter 1).

[65] Executive Minutes, 7 January 1932, 15 January 1932, 29 January 1933, AFM.

[66] On Kruger's profile see Director of Native Development to CNC Salisbury, 18 June 1932, S1542/M8B vol.1, NAZ.

[67] The table is a summary of the key movements discussed in this chapter. There were numerous others, particularly offshoots from the Apostles of Masowe and Maranke.

[68] AssNC Goromonzi to CNC Salisbury, 10 September 1934, S1542/P10, NAZ. John Gwanzura was noted for his ability to divine witches. Int.DM72, Cleopas Gwanzura.

[69] 'Preparatory Examination' No.212, 17 August 1933, S1542/M8B vol.1. Circular Letter from CNC Salisbury, 6 June 1934, S1542/M8B vol.2, NAZ.

[70] See for example: `Meeting of Chiefs and Headmen' Marandellas, 21 April 1932, S1542/P10; CNC Salisbury, Circular Minute, no.23, ca 1939, S2810/2358/1; NC Sinoia to CNC Salisbury, 2 July 1943, S2810/2340, NAZ. AFM informants were ambivalent about the movement's links with independency, aware of its previously difficult relation with the state but also its proud tradition of autonomy and activism. Int.DM77, Constantine Murefu; Int.DM74, Samson and Laiza Gwanzura, Int.DM72, Cleopas Gwanzura.

[71] Report by Harold Jackson, Salisbury CID, 3 June 1934, S1542 M8B, NAZ.

[72] B.J. Britz, 'Facts' ca. 1952, personal papers of Desmond Cartwright.

[73] NC Wedza to NC Marandellas, 1930 & NC Rusape to CNC Salisbury, 22 December 1930, S1542/MB8 vol.1 NAZ.

[74] Int.DM79, Jeries Mvenge; Int.DM77, Constantine Murefu; Int.DM78, Titus Murefu; *The Comforter*, September - October 1945, March 1956; CNC Salisbury to NC Selukwe, 10 August 1943, S2810/2340, NAZ.

[75] *The Comforter*, July 1952; NC Concession to CNC Salisbury, 7 August 1943, S2810/2340, NAZ.

[76] Int.DM76, Kuitenyi Msike, Msana, 15 August 1996; Florence Wilson to Brother Gillingham, 10 August 1957, file, W.L. Wilson 1939-78, AFM.

[77] T.E. Rwambiwa, C/O Railway Station, Gatooma to CNC Salisbury, 3 November 1943, S2810/4469; Ottilia Libermann to CNC Salisbury, 9 April 1945, S2810/4469; AFM, Gatooma to AssNC, Gatooma, 6 November 1943, S2810/2358/1; NC Hartley to PNC Salisbury, 27 November 1953, S2810/4469, NAZ.

3

Sects & the City
Nationalism, Evangelism & Respectability
in the Making of The Assemblies of God, African
1950s–1970

The Assemblies of God, African (AOGA) officially came into being in 1968 but its origins date from the 1950s. It was founded by a group of young men and women who lived for the most part in Harare Township (since independence, Mbare). The movement emerged out of another schism within the Apostolic Faith Mission. AOGA's nucleus was a collection of young zealots: George Chitakata, Joseph Choto, Raphael Kupara, Lazurus Mamvura, James Muhwati, Pricilla Ngoma, Caleb Ngorima and Abel Sande, who formed a prayer band and choir around the charismatic evangelist, Ezekiel Guti. Their social origins were relatively humble. Chitakata and Ngorima were general hands for Springer and Amis Window Manufacturing Company and the Rhodesian Flooring Company, respectively. Muhwati was a general hand for the Rhodesia Forces Club and a messenger for Lever Brothers. Choto was self-employed selling fish. Sande sold bread on a tricycle for Pockets (later Lobels) Bakery. Mamvura was an armature-winder for Lucas. Pricilla Ngoma ran a home while her husband worked on the Rhodesia Railways. Only Raphael Kupara had anything like a white-collar job, working as an assistant salesman for the African Trading Company. Guti himself was a carpenter. In the late 1940s he had run a business in Hatfield, roofing houses in the area. City officials tore his shop down, claiming it was improperly built. He then worked for the city council before taking a job with Fisons Fertilizer Company where he lived on the compound. In 1956 he purchased one of the new middle-class houses in the Engineering Section of the New Highfields Home Ownership Scheme. He was subsequently self-employed.

One trait shared by a number of the band was that their families had a leadership role within rural society. Guti's father had been a traditional healer of some distinction. Sande's father had been a leader of the Lomagundi Watch Tower movement and Ngorima came from a family of sub-chiefs. Raphael Kupara's older brother was a rising star within the Apostolic Faith Mission, later to become its first black President. Doubtless they were pushed into the city because of the declining viability of peasant agriculture and the paucity of agricultural wages, but their own narratives suggest that they were drawn to urban life because they had great hopes and broad horizons. They lacked formal education but were determined to prosper.

The wider context for AOGA's emergence was the social upheaval within Southern Rhodesia (and the rest of the continent) stemming from the Second World War and the subsequent industrialisation and urbanisation. It was the context in which African nationalist parties emerged and multiplied. But such political movements were seldom able to effectively mobilise the peasants and workers. The masses participated in rallies and demonstrations, and, at moments, were enchanted by nationalism's millennial promises but they were never completely captured. Popular participation did not equate with popular empowerment. The proliferation of Christian ideas, helped in great part by growing literacy and vernacular scriptures, combined with the slow pace of the Africanisation of leadership within the historic mission churches, created an environment ripe for the growth of new religious movements more attuned to the popular imagination (Hastings, 1979: 69). The biggest area of growth was 'spirit-type', or Zionist, churches within Christian independency. The new areas of growth were not so much the giant movements like the Vapostori of the Masowe and Maranke but a multiplicity of smaller churches such as Madida, Mugodhi and Chiumbu. However, although AOGA arose from the same fertile soil of Pentecostalism and radical evangelicalism as these movements, it took a very different path. In the first place, it was self-consciously modernising, eventually becoming an electronic church within the global Born-again movement. Secondly, like the American Methodist Episcopal Church, and unlike the broad swathe of mission Christianity and independency, it expanded from a predominantly urban base into rural areas.

The major question this chapter considers is how AOGA grew beyond its roots in rural Pentecostalism into a modern transnational denomination when so many comparable movements failed to make this transition. Two themes predominate. First, there was a need for the movement to find its own social space. Appropriate niches were limited by an intrusive settler state and by the engrossing tendencies of African nationalism. Moreover, the historic mission churches and other Pentecostal groups fiercely contested them. Secondly, and closely related to the search for space, was the struggle for material and ideological resources. Although AOGA's leaders had antecedents in spirit-type independency, their aspirations were 'Ethiopian'. Like the ambitious young men and women who had broken away from the historic mission churches to found their own versions, they wanted what missionaries had but with no strings attached. And like those elite blacks searching for the means of upward social mobility they looked abroad for support, inspiration and models of liberation. In the 1960s these would come from black South Africans and Pentecostal missionaries. From the 1970s onwards Guti would make regular trips to the USA to procure resources himself. These resources were also important determinants of social mobility for AOGA members as they sought to turn themselves into a respectable class as well as a religious movement.

But AOGA was first and foremost a religious movement, its leaders and members animated by genuine religious impulses. Their primary concerns were their relationship with God and the search for healing and personal security, all realised through prayer. This was accompanied by a relentless drive to evangelise. Secular political concerns were secondary. The role of AOGA and the bulk of African Christianity in the era of anti-colonial struggle was one in which ordinary folk coped with rapid social change, as much a product of black nationalism and its attempts to create new loyalties, as it was a result of imperialism and colonialism. AOGA's remarkable growth throughout the period happened because it evolved doctrines and practices particularly well suited to this environment.

A New Mission Impetus within Global Pentecostalism

Before turning to religious developments within colonial Salisbury, it is first necessary to briefly revisit the American dynamo of the global Pentecostal movement, because changes in its trajectory had profound effects on Pentecostalism within southern Africa. We noted at the end of Chapter 1 that the American movement had rapidly institutionalised, often at the expense of momentum and egalitarian ideas. Of course, not all denominations fell prey to the power struggles and worldly designs of Parham, Seymour and Dowie. Indeed many American Pentecostals from humble social origins viewed its professionalisation, the growing number of adherents and higher public profile of their movement with great contentment. Nevertheless, by the late 1940s a small group of believers, increasingly uneasy with the movement's acculturation, sought its revitalisation. Led by George and Ernest Hawtin and Percy Hunt in Canada, those seeking a restoration of the Latter Rain (of the Holy Spirit) revived the rhetoric and enthusiasm of the original Pentecostal outpourings, arguing that the work of the Spirit had been lost or remained incomplete. A revival soon gripped the North American movement, having implications for both church government and the use of spiritual gifts.

Restorationists laid much of the blame for the original movement's loss of heritage at the door of denominationalism. Invoking the teachings of the Pentecostal pioneer William Durham, they argued that the New Testament advocated a strict congregational model for church government – a movement of autonomous local churches. It was the responsibility of local assemblies to recognise the ministry of apostles, prophets, teachers, evangelists and pastors within their own ranks; to set apart their own workers, commission their own missionaries and discipline their own members. The second major focus was on spiritual gifts to be discerned amongst ordinary church members, and bestowed by the Holy Spirit through the laying on of hands. This new pattern of church government not only undermined formal ordination but also created new hierarchies of Apostles and Prophets, whose spoken words often assumed the status of scripture. Restorationist Pentecostalism was therefore vulnerable to strong individuals who exercised and abused authority.

More broadly, the renewed emphasis on proclamation and spiritual gifts prompted a new wave of salvation and healing crusades, particularly overseas. These were led by magnetic personalities such as T.L Osborn, Oral Roberts, William Branham, Fred Francis Bosworth and Billy Graham. A good deal of the revival's initial success can be attributed to the promotional activities of Gordon Lindsay, of whom we shall hear more in the following chapter. While doubling as Branham's campaign-manager, Lindsay drew upon his business sense, literary skills, and ability to work across religious affiliations to turn the revival into a non-denominational movement. He organised inspirational rallies and small workshops for leaders, but of crucial importance was his *Voice of Healing*. This monthly magazine, first published by Lindsay in April 1948, had a circulation of nearly 30,000 by the end of the year (Blumhofer, 1993: chapter 9).

Restorationism had a profound effect on the Pentecostal mission, immediately increasing the number of non-aligned independent missionaries backed by local funds. Moreover, these new missionaries had a greater willingness to work with national workers within Africa and a greater respect for the autonomy of national churches. In sum, there was an increased availability of intellectual and material resources from which the likes of Guti could build a movement amongst the aspiring poor of the city.

Colonial Salisbury

As was the case in many other colonial cities, Salisbury's black population had been required to serve white needs for industrial and domestic labour, but it had never been properly planned. Prior to the Second World War, a growing sprawl of town-ships spread out on the southern swampy side of the railway tracks. Their population doubled between 1945 and 1956 to 200,000 to serve the considerable expansion in the manufacturing sector (Phimister, 1988: 252). Because the peasant option remained relatively viable for local Shona, the city drew labour migrants from Nyasaland and Portuguese East Africa who outnumbered indigenous Africans until the late 1950s. However, by the mid-1950s local Shona had come to dominate the social and political life of the city (Phimister and Raftopoulos, 2000: 295). The Land Husbandry Act of 1954 had curtailed many rural livelihoods, pushing black Zimbabweans into the urban sector in ever greater numbers; others were attracted by the possibilities of urban life. These demographic changes in turn radically altered the black city's cultural life, social structure and politics.

A rich associational life developed, reflecting the growing size and complexity of the urban African population. There were football and boxing clubs, residents' groups, entertainment parties, women's clubs, tribal dancing and burial societies. Ethnic, sporting and cultural societies were the most numerous and influential, linking urban dwellers with kin in the city and those back in the rural areas, while caring for their material needs.[1]

Church life was also diverse, enriched by foreign and local migrants who arrived in the city and replicated denominational loyalties from home. In the 1950s and early 1960s the historic mission churches still dominated but there was a growing number of what the Administration described as 'sects'. These were Vapostori, or Apostles, the Churches of Maranke and Masowe and their offspring. The growing opportuni-ties for Africans to travel, coupled with the growth of crusading activities by Western preachers, some maverick, others more orthodox, also increased the range of churches available to a complexity that perplexed Rhodesian officials. Entrepreneurial African Christians thus made links with far-flung European and American movements to create semi-autonomous movements with loose international connections. Threatened by the rising profile of these seemingly independent African movements of Christian-ity, the Catholics and Methodists increased their own public presence in the townships by holding processionals and marches.[2]

Social structure also grew more complex throughout the 1950s as a black middle class grew in size and definition. In part, this was stimulated by the state's realisation that a stabilised labour force would best serve the interests of the growing industrial sector. Housing programmes such as the New Highfields Home Ownership Scheme, begun in 1954, represented its attempts to engineer middle-class family life. But class formation was also African driven and not simply defined by access to exclusive African housing. Former mission elites entering the city, along with those who had managed to accumulate through business, worked hard to create notions of respectability based on consumption, domesticity and sociality, the development of moral discourses, and most importantly through education.

This new middle–class world was enacted in events such as weddings and formal dinners for elites gaining degrees or equally prized nursing certificates, in dances and status contests such as beauty pageants and dress competitions. The African press also stimulated class formation. Articles, letters to the editor, and advice pages in *The Daily News*, *The African Weekly*, and later, *African Parade*, provided a discursive arena in which the contours of respectability were mapped.[3] As with class, respectability was defined against others: the backward, the feckless, the uncivilised, the superstitious and the rough (Goodhew, 2000: 242). In the African press the respectable continually contrasted themselves with those who frequented municipal beer halls and participated in a culture of drunkenness, gambling, prostitution and social degeneration, people who were clearly 'a menace to the settled bourgeois family life to which they aspired' (West 1997: 646). But the respectable middle classes also contrasted themselves with whites, whose world they longed to be part of. They were frustrated by white society that placed them in the same category as the peasantry, the urban poor and labour migrants. But it was even more humiliating to suffer the same experiences of racism in the daily petty regulations of white settler society. Prohibitions from shops and pavements and the requirement to remove shoes in government offices were grievous affronts to their respectability as well as their dignity.

For a brief moment in the early 1950s it looked as if the promise of racial partnership under Federation might be honoured. But it was soon apparent to the African middle classes that their hopes for full inclusion in Rhodesian society were in vain. A new African intelligentsia began to dominate African politics, founding the City Youth League in 1956. These young men and women began to articulate a nationalist ideology. They were keen members of the middle classes but they were afforded greater respect because of their superior education. Often educated overseas or in South Africa, this group of school teachers, lawyers, doctors and clerics were frustrated by the lack of opportunity 'partnership' offered them. However, they were close enough to the frustrations of the working class to see that they could mobilise a large section of the population (Scarnecchia, 1996: 301). Under the leadership of the City Youth League, African politics changed dramatically.

Also driving African politics was the growing force of white settler nationalism, entrenched under the Rhodesian Front led by Sir Winston Field and subsequently Ian Smith. As African nationalism grew in strength so the Rhodesian state moved to suppress it, banning a succession of nationalist parties: the Southern Rhodesia African National Congress (SRANC) in February 1959; the National Democratic Party (NDP) in December 1961; and Zimbabwe African People's Union (ZAPU) in September 1962. Under state repression, nationalism split the following year with the formation of the Zimbabwe African National Union (ZANU) to rival ZAPU. African nationalism turned more radical in content and method as white settler intransigence grew stronger. Calls for racial partnership changed to demands for black majority rule, and politics itself moved from being peaceful, plural and participatory to being violent and authoritarian, then increasingly commandist. Nationalist meetings described in *The African Weekly* in 1960 began with prayers and hymn singing. A year later petrol bombs were being thrown at the homes of government employees.[4] And by 1962 even evangelistic tent meetings in Highfield and Harare Townships were targets for fire-bombing (Lungu,

1994: 57-76, 113-120). Disturbances regularly broke out where large crowds gathered for sporting and other social activities, particularly in beer gardens. Looking back in 1984, Stanlake Samkange, one of the nationalist elders lambasted for his moderation, recalled that '[l]ife in Highfields became hell on earth' (Ranger, 1995: 203).[5]

As successive nationalist parties increased their grip on the black city, so African civil society was swallowed up 'in the name of a single minded focus on national unity' (Cooper, 1994: 1516-45). In his annual report of 1962, the Director of African Administration, Salisbury commented:

> There has been a pronounced upsurge of politics on an unprecedented scale. Methods have been practised on a mass basis where the image of the ruling African Nationalist party and its political beliefs and dogmas has been insinuated into almost every facet of Township administration, and has been such that it has permeated into the lives of the whole community. Advisory Boards, Sports and Recreation, Youth Club organisations, Education, were all affected in one way or another and this was achieved by establishing unauthorised Civic and Tenants Associations. Trade Unions were similarly loaded with politics and it is a sad admission that even certain religious organisations were also subjected to political pressures.[6]

In particular, the nationalist parties subordinated more strictly urban-based movements such as the Reformed Industrial and Commercial Union (RICU) led by Charles Mzengeli. Township advisory boards, which the RICU and Mzengeli dominated, were closed down and their members were discredited as white puppets.

The neutralisation of RICU and its leader signalled the end of an older kind of patronage politics, which Mzengeli had always championed, 'where individuals and groups brought him their grievances and he worked personally to see that they were corrected'. It also brought an end to politics that were able to transcend class cleavages. The new intelligentsia who now led the nationalist movement was unable to make the same sacrifices as Mzengeli (Scarnecchia, 1993: 269). Theirs was a grudging unity concealing very real class aspirations.

By the mid-1950s the respectable classes were well entrenched, especially in the new areas of Highfield and the national section of Harare Township. Subsequent developments further divided the city. The 1958 Urban African Affairs Commission recommended new and more extensive schemes in which a higher proportion of African workers were stabilised by having a home and a nuclear family. With better housing and higher wages, permanent workers were able to join the respectable middle classes. Within this new environment, social stratification increased. Shared sporting and cultural activities within the African population gradually diminished. Indeed the historic mission churches were important vehicles of respectability, seeking to create spaces in townships free from the pollution of beer and prostitution. In his autobiography, the international evangelist Stephen Lungu tells how, as an unemployed Malawian migrant, he received no hospitality in a respectable Highfield congregation (1994: 90-91).[7]

In the coalition building that underpinned nationalist politics certain groups lost out. Scarnecchia has shown how poor women were increasingly marginalised from nationalist politics as the agenda became male dominated. Housing regulations and pass laws effectively barred these women from access to residential space. Those unable to gain accommodation through association with a man were criminalised and driven into niches of the unofficial economy. For a time these women had been able to work with the RICU to challenge state restrictions upon them. But the movement failed, and as the RICU was subsumed by nationalist politics so these women's goals were sacrificed in the interests of recruiting migrant labourers with whom they competed. Scarnecchia writes: 'Having lost the moment of real political independence and agency ... these same displaced women were now more likely to be preoccupied by the growing possibilities in formal wage employment and married life' (Scarnecchia: 1993: 269). Labour migrants fared little better. Often single males were seen as a threat to the respectable classes. They were blamed for the notorious Carter House rapes of September 1956 and were the targets of ethnic violence in the 1960s (Scarnecchia, 1996: 305).[8]

There was also great poverty in the black city. While the poverty datum line for a man, woman and two children in Salisbury 1958 was £15.13.11, the minimum male wage after 18 months of work was just £7.5.2. A year later *The African Weekly* reported that the average male worker lived well below the bread-line (Barnes, 1999: 44).[9] Infrastructure was no better. Housing was in short supply and accommodation in much of Harare Township was desperately overcrowded. In the rainy season the Old Bricks section of the township looked 'worse than a pig sty'. Again, single women and foreign labour migrants were the most vulnerable. Excluded from the official economy, single woman survived the best they could, often on the move to evade detection and removal by the police. Foreign labour migrants would often arrive with little more than a 'few rags' to wear and a cooking pot in which to prepare their food.[10]

It was from this cauldron of poverty, social upheaval, and political unrest that the Assemblies of God, African (AOGA) emerged.

Assemblies of God, African: AOGA[11]

The band that eventually became AOGA came together in the Apostolic Faith Mission assembly based in Harare Township, which had established itself in a hall by the end of the 1930s. The concept of youth ministry did not yet exist and so they were designated the usual function for young people, the choir. The initial focus of their attention was not Guti, but the powerful figure of Enoch Gwanzura, the overseer of black work within the AFM as a whole. As we saw in the previous chapter, Gwanzura was remarkably gifted in healing, exorcism and preaching and had founded many of the AFM's black churches. He had been responsible for Ngoma's conversion and Guti's baptism. Under him was the equally dynamic Langton Kupara who was the church evangelist. Finally came Guti as the lay evangelist. Guti himself had a solid Zimbabwean Pentecostal pedigree, having briefly been a member of a Vapostori church near Mutare before meeting Gwanzura. He had learnt much from Gwanzura and Kupara and was also skilled in healing and preaching. Gradually the choir came under Guti's influence, forming a prayer band to support his semi-autonomous evangelistic activities. He was one of their peers but had charisma and vision. Ngoma reminisced, 'we saw truth in him, so would follow him'.[12] Ngorima remembered: 'it was like a magnet ... people just came to him... We were attracted by his character ... his speeches, how he ministered. He would ask us to pray for Africa, to pray for our country to be civilised.'[13] The prayer band proved extremely loyal. All-night meetings were held in Ngoma's house and later in Guti's new home, Cottage 593 in Highfield Engineering. Here they sang, prayed and shared simple bread meals supplied by Abel Sande.[14] At weekends they journeyed outside the city into nearby farms, locations, reserves and towns to preach 'against all forms of sin, including drinking, smoking and ancestral worship'.[15]

They met with Enoch Gwanzura to preach at Domboshawa to the north of the city and Rufaro mission near Chatsworth. By themselves they sang and preached around the city at Beatrice, Rugare, the airport, Mufakose and Kambuzuma [see Map 3.1], and travelled to towns such as Marandellas, Rusape, Umtali and Gatooma and went into the reserves at Chiota, Chiweshe and Murehwa. Such was their desire to 'capture people from all over' they would travel as far as Mount Upton on bicycles, sometimes returning as late as 3 a.m.[16] Many of these locations were AFM sites and the prayer band soon became well known. Black AFM ministers would invite Guti to preach. Aided by Caleb Ngorima, he ran his own religious campaign in Manicaland in 1957 under the guise of the Ezekiel Guti Evangelistic Association (EGEA), while Sande cared for his family. A similar campaign was launched in Kariba in 1959 (Erwin, nd: 80–81).[17]

Some weekends Guti would stay in Harare Township preaching in the market place and in the hostels, giving the converted a letter of introduction to the Harare AFM assembly. He rapidly established a significant local following not only in Harare Township but also in Highfield where the AFM established a new church in 1956. A stream of clients would come to his cottage in Highfield in search of healing. He had a particular gift for curing infertility. His unofficial activities soon attracted the attention of missionaries and elder African pastors. There were a number of confrontations with missionaries – including Willard Wilson, George Bartholomew and a Pastor Fleuwellyn – and also with successive black pastors at the Harare Church, Wilson Chinyerere and Kuritenyi Msike. At first, the missionary overseer, Wilson, gave Guti a little black book in which he was obliged to record his activities. When this did not work there were moves to ban him and his band from AFM churches. Finally Guti's preaching certificate was taken from him. When, in November 1959, the great Zulu evangelist Nicholas Bhengu pitched his crusade tent in Highfield, Guti and his choir immediately offered their services. Effectively leaving the AFM, they placed themselves under Bhengu's authority and became part of the AOG configuration which was principally an alliance of Bhengu's Back to God team from South Africa and overseas Pentecostal missionaries.

The schism with the AFM was a result of an explosive cocktail of religious disputation, generational tension, white racism and pious ambition. The religious dispute had been structured into history of the AFM since its foundation in Southern Rhodesia. As seen in the previous chapter, the AFM was a dynamic proselytising movement led by zealous African evangelists, and followed by a handful of over-stretched but no less zealous missionaries who tried to bring it under their centralising control. Left to their own devices the movement's black evangelists and pastors created their own version of Pentecostalism, drawing particularly on the purity laws in Leviticus. AFM prophets, with shaven heads, long beards and white robes roamed the reserves with a message of repentance, divine healing and exorcism. The turning-point for the movement's relations with the state came in 1938 with the arrival of more hard-nosed AFM missionaries, Willard and Bill Wilson, willing to curb the spontaneous activities of their black brothers in return for state recognition. Missionary attempts to impose orthodoxy were fiercely resisted by black AFM preachers. Osmosis with movements of Christian Independency continued and Zionist-type practices persisted well into the 1950s. Nevertheless, the gradual imposition of missionary notions of orthodoxy led to a wave of schisms in the 1940s and '50s, of which Guti and his prayer band were just one example. Once Willard and Florence Wilson moved to Salisbury in 1951 the days of unsupervised black Pentecostal activity in the city and its environs were numbered.[18] Enoch Gwanzura was an early casualty of the new regime. Like many African Christian pioneers he had hoped for greater recognition from his missionary colleagues but it never materialised. The final affront to his dignity came when missionaries assigned his wife manual work at one of the mission stations. He increasingly withdrew from the AFM, but never founded a schismatic movement. Langton Kupara, the new leading light, was soon reassigned to work in Mrewa District. Now the band had no one to protect it.

The AFM missionaries were not merely driven by the desire for state recognition. They viewed the black AFM prophets' love of the Laws of Moses as dangerous legalism. Their attempts to curb such practices through more rigorous oversight were understood by zealous young Africans as an attempt to stifle biblical Christianity and dampen evangelistic zeal. Lazurus Mamvhura recollected how he confronted Wilson at one meeting with the following argument: 'When we read in Matthew – "Go ye and preach" we do not hear the words "but not until you are ordained". Why are you insisting on us being preachers in church. We want to go outside.'[19] Neither were all black pastors sympathetic to the band's cause. The struggle of Guti and his allies to explore their understanding of scripture merged with generational tensions within the movement. By the 1950s the AFM was beginning to lose its Pentecostal vigour and was affected by the process of 'ageing' (Iliffe, 1979: 359; Maxwell, 1999: chapter 7). The young men who had broken away from rural patriarchy to found new churches had become elders themselves. Now threatened by Pentecostalism's egalitarian potential, whereby revelation through the Holy Spirit was universal, they had begun to introduce authoritarian and hierarchical government into their churches. Recently graduated from Bible college and confident in his sense of orthodoxy, Guti's pastor, Kuitenyi Msike, was irked by the young man's propensity to evangelise in his backyard without permission. Similarly, Guti and Ngorima's 1957 campaign in Manicaland was noteworthy for its effect of instilling revival in lukewarm assemblies where 'witchdoctors' operated under a charade of Christianity. While elder pastors saw Guti's band as arrogant and disruptive, the young zealots came to believe that the elders did not believe in the Holy Spirit, or worse still that 'some had demons, and howled like wild animals'.[20]

But underpinning much of the tension was white racism. Originating in South Africa the AFM was strongly influenced by the culture of apartheid. There was a clear demarcation between English, Afrikaans, and African work in the movement and a strong Afrikaner influence over the leadership. While most missionaries in the historic mission churches were at least sympathetic to notions of racial partnership and the legitimacy of African self-government, AFM missionaries and pastors were not. The movement's magazine, *Pentecostal Light Bearer,* was a source of strident articles defending racial separation on the grounds of biology and culture. Thus in 1955, Chas du Plessis, a leading AFM minister in Salisbury wrote:

On average there is usually an appreciable difference in size when comparing the brain of a normal European with that of a native... Emotionally the white man is far more sensitive than the black. Many things that are essential to the European's happiness and fullness of living have no importance to the other race and vice versa ... few natives indeed attain to the same spiritual standards as the ordinary European Christian ... Apartheid along the lines that we have tried to point out, must always remain, in the church, as well as outside of it.[21]

Willard Wilson was no more enlightened. Band members recollected with some bitterness how when visiting his home they were obliged to remain outside on the lawn and drink tea from jam jars. Even those more loyal, such as Msike, complained about having to take his meals outside, by the 'boy's' [domestic servant's] quarters. In sum, missionary attempts to curtail the activities of Guti and his supporters were seen as yet one more strategy by whites 'to keep Africans down' and stop them from 'becoming civilised'.[22] And those black pastors who supported the missionaries were mere stooges.

Guti and his band were ambitious. And Guti, in particular, was proud. He had a strong sense of his own mission and resented any interference with it. He expected loyalty from his cohort but was unwilling to give it to anyone else. Such tendencies, although irksome to those working with the band, did have a religious impulse. The band were animated by a pious urge to evangelise, whatever the cost. They had hoped for a tent and transport from the AFM to support his preaching activities but none was forthcoming. Hence the band's encounter with the black evangelist, Nicholas Bhengu, in November 1959, was of enormous significance. He seemed to be the answer to their problems.

The Battle for Highfield

There had been earlier Pentecostal and evangelical crusades in Salisbury, many arising out of the Restorationist impulse within American Pentecostalism: William Branham in 1952; Oral Roberts in 1956; Frederick Bosworth and Lorne Fox, also in the 1950s. And American Assemblies of God missionaries, Fred Burke and John Richards, based in South Africa, conducted tent crusades in most Southern Rhodesian cities throughout the decade (Hallencreutz, 1998: 292-7). Billy Graham's 1960 Crusade happened just after Bhengu's had ended. Some of these evangelists captured the imaginations of the prayer band. Sande recollected that Branham left a 'fire burning in his heart'.[23] But they were white, and some of their meetings had been segregated. As a black man, Bhengu's effect was inspirational and unparalleled. He arrived in Highfield attended by whites and supported by an impressive infrastructure: a vast tent, public address systems and generators, trucks and Land Rovers.[24] Bhengu was the first African to make it big on the world Pentecostal scene. His southern African crusade attracted the attention of *Time* magazine in 1959 and henceforth he was feted by American and European Pentecostals. Zimbabweans had never seen an African preacher with such authority. In unpublished reminiscences Guti (or one of his ghost-writers) described the impact:

> My mind can still vividly remember Rev. Bengu [sic] - a giant among men. ... He was a great intellect and yet had a simple childlike faith in the Saviour.
> ... He was a stranger ... a South African, a foreigner, yet he was not a stranger to me after he had proclaimed the Gospel. His seriousness was clearly impressed on my mind. From the beginning of the service until the end, I gave the most respectful attention to the preacher.[25]

Guti and his band longed to have what they saw as Bhengu's freedom and authority to proselytise unfettered by structure or oversight. They were quickly disappointed. Bhengu had not simply turned up uninvited but was the guest of the AOG general council of Southern Rhodesia. This was an umbrella of Assemblies of God missionaries from South Africa, America, England, Ireland and Sweden, along with the Pentecostal Assemblies of Canada (PAOC). Thus an AOG work was already in place in Highfield, founded by a Mozambican, Shadrek Lekuku. Lekuku had a good Pentecostal pedigree, having done missionary work in his own Shangaan area of Mozambique with the great PAOC pioneer, J.W. Skinner. Also fluent in Zulu, he had subsequently worked in South Africa with Bhengu, coming to Southern Rhodesia to work with the PAOC in southern Manicaland. In the late 1950s he founded an AOG assembly at Mutasa School, Highfield. Bhengu made Lekuku overseer of the Rhodesia work, but left two other South Africans, Gumede and Sikhu, in leadership roles in Southern Rhodesia. There was no room left for Guti and his band in the township, and the families that followed them from the AFM were now under the authority of Gumede. Moreover, the band had hoped to be free of missionary control. Instead they found themselves under the oversight of missionaries from the PAOC whose finances they readily accepted but whose authority they resented. Sande summed up the new situation as follows: 'We wanted to work with Bhengu but there was Lekuku, and white missionaries. We did not want that.'[26]

Soon the township was gripped by a rather unedifying struggle as various factions vied for control. The first fracture occurred quite rapidly when Bhengu attempted to rotate Lekuku out of the leadership of the Highfield work and replace him with Gumede. Lekuku refused to go and founded his own assembly, subsequently gaining the support of the Americans who had pulled out from under the AOG umbrella in 1963. Lekuku's new church was called the International Assemblies of God. The second conflict was more complex. The Guti group had never been made particularly welcome. They had arrived under a cloud because of the circumstances of their departure from the AFM and were seen as having too many AFM-like ideas and practices. Lekuku had christened them *ma-joiners* while other black South Africans looked down upon them as 'uneducated'. The situation was further complicated by the existence of a rival local black group, led by Jeremiah Kainga, Misheck Chimsoro and D.B. Gara. These young men had joined the AOG during Bhengu's campaign and were just as charismatic and ambitious as Guti's band. They resented the arrogance and imperialism of the Guti faction, and took every opportunity to expose it at meetings and in correspondence to Bhengu and Canadian missionaries.[27]

The conflict was intense because Highfield was both the black capital of Southern Rhodesia and an important centre of Pentecostal activity. It had well developed AFM and AOG work and was the key site for international crusades and campaigns. For any ambitious Pentecostal it was too important to lose. While Bhengu initially dominated the work, his grip rapidly diminished due to declining health, distance and over-stretched resources. Highfield was also the centre of Zimbabwean nationalism and some of it rubbed off on the Guti faction, creating conflict with missionaries and 'foreign' Africans.

But given that such struggles continue into the present and figure so highly in Pentecostals' own writings, published and unpublished, it is also necessary to seek their causes in Pentecostal religion itself. Pentecostal culture, that complex mix of religious experience, teaching and doctrine, created a temperament that was not well disposed to compromise and co-operation. For many, the experience of Baptism in the Holy Spirit dispelled doubt and fostered certitude. Once set on their course, young Pentecostals such as Guti and his band were unswerving. Such was the strength of Pentecostal certainty that it 'precluded critical analysis of one's cherished convictions'. 'Certitude fostered absolutism – a propensity to see life in moral extremes.' There was little ambiguity in the Pentecostal universe and opposition was quickly equated with blasphemy. Moreover, an 'independent spirit', a single-minded desire to get on with the work of the gospel, recoiled at regularisation. But perhaps the most dangerous

Pentecostal Mission	Date of arrival in the city
Apostolic Faith Mission (AFM)	Late 1930s
Assemblies of God (South Africa)	ca. 1958
Nicholas Bhengu (AOGSA)* Pentecostal Assemblies of Canada (PAOC)*	(Bhengu Campaign, November 1959) ca. 1960
Assemblies of God, USA (AOGUSA)*	ca. 1960 (Withdrew ca.1963/4, reopened work 1968)
Independent American missionaries (loosely affiliated with the AOGUSA) Independent Pentecostals such as Alexander Warrilow*	1960s

* Initially co-operated under a Pentecostal umbrella

Table 3.1 Pentecostal Missions in Colonial Salisbury[28]

African Leader	Trajectory
Langton Kupara	Succeeds Enoch Gwanzura as superintendent of African work in AFM After 1980 leads entire movement
Ezekiel Guti	1950s Evangelist in AFM 1959 joins AOGSA (in collaboration with PAOC & AOGUSA) 1959-67 leads Ezekiel Guti Evangelistic Association 1967 leads Pentecost Assemblies of God 1968 leads Assemblies of God, African (AOGA)
Shadrek Lekuku	1940s working with Skinner in PAOC ca. 1958 sent by AOGSA to pioneer work in Highfield ca 1963 leads own independent assemblies in Highfield 1968 links up with AOGUSA 1974 disciplined by AOGUSA
Misheck Chimsoro	1960 leaves Methodist Church joins AOGSA (in collaboration with PAOC & AOGUSA) 1968 joins reopened AOGUSA work After 1980 leads AOGUSA work (AOGZ)
Jeremiah Kainga	1960 converts and joins AOGSA (in collaboration with PAOC & AOGUSA) 1978 forms Emmanuel Fellowship with two American AOG missionaries
Alfred Gumede	ca 1963 sent by Bhengu to lead AOGSA work in Highfield, eventually returns to South Africa

Table 3.2 African Pentecostal Leaders and the Emergence of African Pentecostalism in Colonial Salisbury

of all, particularly as the movement grew more successful, was 'holy rectitude', the belief that 'the perfected soul spoke with divine authority'. Thus, while Pentecostals believed that the new dispensation would end all denominations, their temperament often created the opposite effect. As Wacker observes, 'Pentecostals' ecumenism was the ecumenism of the carnivore. Everyone was welcome as long as they were willing to be devoured'(2001: 22-8, 97 &178).

There was also an organisational dimension to the conflict. Schism had been institutionalised within the Assemblies of God South Africa (AOGSA). The movement's 1938 constitution drew together a diverse collection of assemblies and leaders, black and white. It remained true to the original congregational pattern. Individual assemblies retained autonomy because the system allowed the management of racial difference. But the assemblies tended to coalesce around strong leaders. Both Bhengu and James Mullen, leader of a number of white assemblies, evolved an 'apostolic' system of government. Each sought to train by example rather than through Bible schools, gathering around themselves groups of ministers whom they knew and instructed personally. Apostleship created group cohesion, and permanence amongst the leaders, but left ordinary ministers with little influence (Watt, 1992: 38 & 93). This led self-styled apostles like Guti to resent the authoritarianism of their elders and to found movements of their own. The potential for schism was also increased by the abundance of Pentecostal mission organisations and maverick missionaries willing to support and fund breakaway movements.

Bhengu had attempted to channel the energies of the Guti faction beyond High-field. He sent Guti to the mining town of Bindura just north of Salisbury, procuring backing for him from Canadian missionaries.[29] Kupara, who had decided to minister full time, was sent to pastor a new church in Gwelo; Ngorima went to Nyanyadzi, South of Umtali. Others pioneered assemblies on a part-time basis: Choto went to the new Salisbury Township, Gillingham and Mandu to Virginia, outside the city.

In Bindura, Guti constructed a simple hut out of wood and grass helped by a new young recruit, Clement Kaseke, a painter by trade. He preached to domestic servants and to graders working in the local nickel and gold mines. Soon the small gathering was meeting at the house of Simon Nyamande who became a full-time pastor. With the help of a dedicated band of female supporters he managed to buy a building previously owned by the Salvation Army for his followers to meet in. He also spent much time in contemplation, praying on Mt Chipidura, a sacred site used for prayer and worship by the Vapostori.[30]

Bindura was the only assembly Guti ever led as pastor. His genius lay elsewhere, in his vision and the strategic deployment of his lieutenants. His auto-hagiography describes how God compelled him to march around Highfield Township on the eve of his return to claim it, as Joshua had marched around Jericho (Erwin, nd: 92). But just as Joshua had sent spies ahead of his return, so too did Guti. But by that stage he already controlled a considerable portion of the AOG work there. Although stationed in Bindura, Guti had never really left the city. Keeping his cottage in Highfield Engineering, he maintained contact with his following who were now under Gumede at Mhizha School. This small core, which included Guti's brother Nelson, was rallied by Mamvura and regularly addressed by Choto and Sande.[31] They refused to submit to Gumede's authority, complaining about the lack of new converts, and continued to look to Guti for leadership. They opened a bank account at Barclays, Chinoyi Street, to support his work and visited him in Bindura. Clement Kaseke assisted Guti's preaching activities by playing his accordion. As calls from Guti's followers for Guti's return grew louder, a frustrated Kainga attempted to expose his motives. In a November 1965 report seemingly destined for Bhengu, he wrote:

> We don't interfere with the internal affairs of Guti's assemblies, and why does he, assisted with his followers, interfere with ours? For how long is he going to be allowed to be a menace like this? If Guti has established assemblies why yet [is he] seeking to pastor Highfield? Who will look after his own assemblies? Has he accomplished making believers of all the people of Bindura that he should now look to Highfield? From this can be deduced another school of thought: That Guti thinks that he can embrace the whole work if he can only be in Highfield the centre of this work. Or that he is not quite secure because he does not have a stable base like Highfield.[32]

The struggle came to a head around 1966. Without permission from either Lekuku or Gumede, Guti returned to the city to preach in Rugare Township, Lochinvar. Over the Christmas period his group organised a convention in the AOG 'structure' – an incomplete building – in Lusaka, Highfield, again without official sanction. Frustrated by the immaturity of his African workers in Rhodesia, Bhengu wrote:

> Guti and co. have acted contrary to all accepted ethics and I cannot therefore identify myself with him. I cannot handle the situation with any satisfaction as I am not allowed to come to Rhodesia and also my age and health are prohibitive to strenuous engagements. I hate fighting the nationals of any country. Guti must be officially disciplined.[33]

The Guti group was asked to leave the AOG. Gumede and Kainga remained at Mhizah School and the Guti group began to worship at Rugare School. But the fallout was felt beyond Highfield. Guti's lieutenants stationed around the country rallied behind him, bringing their AOG congregations with them.[34] There was a protracted struggle for control of the church building in Ascot, Gwelo. It had been built by an independent American missionary, Ed Rill, and financed by him. Rill agreed to sign it over to the Assemblies of God with whom he was affiliated when they restarted their work in Rhodesia in 1968. But Kupara, now closely allied to Guti, refused to budge. Litigation between the two sides rumbled on throughout the 1970s until the Americans decided to relinquish their claims in return for part payment for the building from AOGA.[35] Bhengu seemed no match for the tenacious and wily Guti. Lionised by South African and Western Pentecostals, and perhaps the most significant African Pentecostal to date, he simply lacked the will to fight. Writing to Kainga in August 1967, he reflected: 'I have resigned and relinquished my interest in Rhodesia as a disappointed man; this I must admit. I have never been so defeated ever since I started out for my Lord over thirty years ago'.[36]

On Bhengu's departure the Pentecostal community fractured further. The Canadians persisted with their assemblies. Gumede retained links with the AOGSA. Lekuku and Chimsoro allied themselves with the revived American AOG. And Kainga eventually linked up with two independent American missionaries, loosely affiliated to the Assemblies of God, to form the Emmanuel Fellowship. For a brief moment in 1967 the Guti faction became the 'Soul Winning for Christ Crusade'. Then, for less than a year, from March 1967, it officially became the Pentecost African Assemblies of God. Finally in 1968 after an Easter Convention the group met at Sande's house in Marandellas and became the Assemblies of God, African (AOGA).[37]

AOGA: Nationalism, Evangelism and Pan-Africanism

African nationalism has often been characterised as a movement able to integrate and articulate a variety of subaltern struggles within its own hegemonic programme (Cooper, 1994; Raftopoulos, 1999). In the Zimbabwean context 'there is no doubt that unity came to be defined as the dominance over all other African associations by the nationalist movement' (Ranger, 2003: 5). For example, in 1961 Dumiso Dabengwa, Chair of the Bulawayo League of the National Democratic Party (NDP), threatened: 'Any African who remains independent and does not take part in the common cause is as bad and as sell-out as the so-called moderates ... Those who are not with us are against us.' Such sentiments were common amongst many other nationalists, including Bernard Matuma, NDP stalwart and the self-styled 'mayor' of Makoba Township, Bulawayo. In December 1961 he addressed a huge rally in the city and denounced trade union autonomy and the legitimacy of strikes not ordered by the nationalist leadership. He also instructed his audience 'to infiltrate into churches, into industry, into trade unions so that when the time comes we shall be able to effectively organise from within'.[38] It is thus pertinent to ask to what extent did the nationalist movement subsume AOGA? The question becomes more pertinent when it is recognised that AOGA and the nationalist movement had much in common. Anti-colonialism did not necessarily engender opposition to the ideals and principles of Western institutions, including Christianity. A great deal of anti-colonialism was based on the acceptance of these ideals and principles, and the insistence that conformity with them indicated a level of progress should earn African elites the right to govern their own nation-states. Nationalism, like Christianity, was essentially modernising (Ekeh, 1973; Peel, 2002).

The prayer band that became AOGA shared its Highfield birthplace with that of Zimbabwean nationalism, both emerging at the same time. It is also clear that in their schism with the AFM the prayer band was emboldened by the spirit of nationalism prevalent in Salisbury at the time. The schism came at almost the same time as the 1959 State of Emergency in Southern Rhodesia, a moment when Guti's loyal supporters had come to question the presence and conduct of missionaries in their land. It was clear that they considered missionary behaviour a subject for discussion. In one of their final confrontations with Wilson, the band told him: 'We are going to the next meeting [at Rufaro] with two certificates Guti's and yours.' A year later in 1961, Willard Wilson wrote:

> To put it plainly we have had just about all we can take from the Blacks. These days they are so arrogant and hard to deal with, this coupled with the political situation, makes it just about unbearable. There are times when I feel that my nerves will just about snap off in dealing with these people ...[39]

Nevertheless the band had no formal connection with the nationalist movement, pursuing instead a different but parallel mission. As illustrated in the previous chapter, their desire for black autonomy and sectarian purity was in keeping with their tradition of Zimbabwean Pentecostalism. Their zealous determination to preach wherever they felt called, regardless of officialdom, drew directly in inspiration and style from the linked traditions of the Masowe and Maranke movements and the AFM, all of which long predated nationalism.

74

A nationalist spirit doubtless also coloured the band's subsequent struggles with Canadian missionaries and black South Africans, a conflict that reached its peak a year after the most ferocious fighting had taken place between Shonas and Malawians in Highfield. While ZANU and ZAPU fought for political control of the black township, the Guti 'faction' fought a Pentecostal turf war with the Gumede and Kainga group for the same territory. Although social relations were egalitarian and inclusive within AOGA, it was highly predatory and exclusive in its dealings with those with whom it competed. It certainly appeared to one American Pentecostal missionary that the band's eventual choice of name, Assemblies of God *African* was indicative of 'a strong nationalistic spirit existing amongst them'.[40]

But ultimately the prayer band and the nationalist parties had distinctly different missions. The young Pentecostals were on 'social strike *from* society' whereas Zimbabwean nationalism was on 'strike *against* society' (Martin, 1996: 229; Hastings, 1976: 264). New recruits to the band converted out of the nationalist movement into Pentecostalism, believing that the lifestyle of the nationalist youth, characterised by the consumption of alcohol and marijuana, was incompatible with born-again sobriety and bodily purity.[41] While the nationalist movement focused on the community and the workplace, AOGA Pentecostals initially met under trees, in homes and classrooms, focusing their energies on individual transformation, the formation and renewing of families. AOGA pioneers aptly described the complex relation between the two movements. Mamvura explained: 'God's inspiration made us revolutionary. We were not involved in nationalist movement we worked in parallel.' Ngorima said: 'the nationalists' message was not "full freedom", just physical freedom, not spiritual freedom … We were not enemies of those people [the nationalists] because we were also grieved by land tenure …'[42]

Their band's response to formal politics was similar to that of Nicholas Bhengu. Once a member of the Industrial and Commercial Workers Union and South African Communist Party, Bhengu turned his back on formal politics when he converted. Eschewing nationalism as well as communism, he argued that the 'new nation' would be 'born from above with the likeness of God' (Balcomb, 2004). He believed that political equality with whites invited them to define the content of African aspirations. Narrow Western definitions of liberation left him unimpressed. His message of spiritual renewal, elaborated in his Back to God Campaigns of the 1950s and 1960s, had a number of strands. He put a strong emphasis on African autonomy and dignity. His preaching stressed Africa's rich Judeo-Christian heritage and its place in the Hebrew and Christian Scriptures. While he worked in association with missionaries from the Assemblies of God, he believed that Africans should be free to define their faith in their own terms. The new believer was to be honest, respectful and self-sufficient. Bhengu also encouraged church members to engage in handicrafts and penny capitalism, and to tithe in order that the church become self-supporting and free from missionary control (Watt, 1992: 40; Dubb, 1976: 8-14).

There were important areas of non-congruence with the nationalist movement. The first was *cultural* nationalism, which appealed to an essential version of African culture, embodied by the cults of great Zimbabwean ancestors such as Nehanda and Kagubi. The Pentecostals' opposition to cultural nationalism was not primarily based on the leftist intellectual objection that a revival of tradition was 'atavistic', although that was a concern. Their repudiation of such things emanated from a passionate belief that they were demonic. The other major area of non-congruence with nationalism was political violence. Although on occasions AOGA's crusading zeal nearly boiled over into Pentecostal punch-ups, the worst was usually stormy meetings. Violence was an anathema to them. As poor people, aspiring to better things, law and order were essential. 'Life was difficult enough without the added uncertainty of "confusion".'[43] Their primary objective was proselytism, usually termed evangelism, and a peaceful environment was essential for that purpose. The few occasions when AOGA meetings were broken up by nationalist youth were deeply resented.

The movement's success in eschewing connection with nationalism is best illustrated by the Rhodesian state's muted response toward it. Police officers, spies and informers attended AOGA meetings as they did all public gatherings in the townships. Missionaries complained to the authorities about the movement's illegal use of the 'Assemblies of God' label and the Kainga group complained about their illegal use of the structure in Lusaka. But these protests were to no avail. Guti was visited by police officers and taken to police stations. His details were taken but the movement's work of preaching and healing was allowed to continue, which was taken as a sign of tacit state recognition. Local authorities were dutifully approached for permission to hold rallies, and resented for their refusal to allow Guti the status of marriage officer, but otherwise the Rhodesian state hardly figured in the movement's records or official history (Guti, 1989: 11; Erwin, nd: 93, 96, 99).

Fundamentally, the movement's energies were devoted to evangelism. And in this mission the same passions and ideas behind the Revival in Azusa Street and its transplantation to South Africa animated them. They were moved by the urgent belief that they were living in 'end times', by the conviction that Christian faiths other than the Pentecostal faith were heresies, and that conventional missionary work of bio-medicine and education were dangerous diversions. The Pentecostal temperament was not inclined to compromise, even with zealous nationalists.

Indeed, so important was the primary objective of evangelism that the prayer band, and later AOGA, co-existed with strange white bedfellows. As relations began to sour with the Canadians, the prayer band drew on the patronage of an English businessman, Alexander Warrilow. He provided them with assistance for their crusades, helped roof their first Highfield church and perhaps financed Guti's study in the United States.[44] Warrilow was cast as 'European Advisor' to the movement. White patronage was also needed in representations to the state, given that all churches were still supposed to be under white supervision. Here the prayer band was assured of a smooth ride, thanks to Warrilow's friendship and business links with the Minister for Law and Order, Desmond Lardner-Burke, the ultra-right-wing member of the Rhodesian Front government.[45] While well-placed whites helped legitimate the movement in the eyes of the Rhodesian state, such associations would not have advanced AOGA's nationalist credentials. But they were highly pragmatic when it came to the work of God.

AOGA's leaders had an official strategy for evangelism. Highfield itself was first subjected to a considerable amount of proselytism. A brief account of the campaign was penned circa 1977:

> By 1969 we had pitched our tent in New Canaan, Highfields, and alternated in holding services and revivals. With me were my fellow workers Rev. Sande, Rev. Kupara and Rev. Choto. We had no external funds to support ourselves. I still remember how by night we used to share scripture with our new converts with empty stomachs.... Drunk people passing by throwing stones over our tent but we were never discouraged...
> The revival spread through Highfields. Hardened alcoholics came forward and wept their way to God...

> Conducting services became less burdensome as young men and women began to join in singing and leading services....
>
> Within five weeks we had gathered together a fair sized congregation...[46]

After Highfield, new townships such as Dzivarasekwa, Tafara and Kambuzuma were targeted (see Map 3.1).[47] Next they went to surrounding towns and cities, and finally to the rural areas. The strategy was clearly to reach the biggest concentrations of people first. Evangelistic methods were simple and straightforward. The crusade team often consisted of no more than an evangelist, usher and song leader, who would erect the tent and distribute handbills.[48] The leading evangelist was Abel Sande, a man with a remarkable gift for moving his audience to tearful repentance. Sande had an impressive pedigree in the more autonomous forms of Zimbabwean Christianity. Born in Urungwe, he had grown up in what Terence Ranger has called the 'Lomagundi Watch Tower movement', another Malawian-derived church with strong millennial credentials (Ranger, 1970: 202-15). His father had been arrested three times for preaching that 'whites would be washed away and blacks would rule'. But Sande's Pentecostal conversion in the AFM in 1949 had brought him the gift of the Holy Spirit, which made him one of the most prolific evangelists in Zimbabwe's history.[49]

Much of the evangelism, however, was spontaneous, low-key and face-to-face, carried out by ordinary church members. The sheer numbers of people in townships facilitated this as church members turned first to their kin and then to neighbours. Those who missed services were followed up and encouraged back into the fold.[50] Along with the religious impulse, the movement's growth was bolstered by both the social networks created by rural and urban Pentecostalism and the political economy that underpinned them. Prior to leaving the countryside, labour migrants mostly lived in integrated, 'loose knit' networks of relations with kin and neighbours. In town the Pentecostal convert chose to construct 'close knit' networks centred upon the church, in which most of the people were acquainted, resulting in a 'strong corporate feeling'. Elder informants reflecting on the early days spoke of the strong bond of intimacy and mutuality that was part of church life: 'It was like you could forget your own relatives because of the love'.[51] Bonds between new Christian 'brothers and sisters' replaced those with kin and one's ethnic group. And this new society was very attractive to outsiders in search of a place to belong to. 'Because of the oneness of love in these people and their great prayer-lives, souls were just magnetised [to the] church'.[52] Thus the new community became a site of 'cultural reformation' as it erected boundaries between itself and the world. In part, this took the form of rejecting 'traditional' medicine and ancestor veneration. But barriers were also erected through the rejection of popular culture, as church life became the focus of its adherents' energies (Mayer, 1961: 13-14, 200-201). Motivated not only by an evangelistic impulse but also by the desire to remain in a state of Pentecostal purity, many AOGA labour migrants returned to their villages with a strong missionary zeal. They held revival meetings in rural areas and founded rural branches capable of sustaining them in their faith. The process would usually begin with the conversion of their extended family and neighbours. Subsequently they would invite an evangelist to boost numbers and found a formal assembly (Guti, 1989:10).[53] It was in this manner, for instance, that the Manzvire Assembly in south-east Manicaland was founded in 1968. Its pioneer, Selina Chingodga, converted after being healed from an 'issue of blood'. She had been planning to divorce her husband but returned home and began

*Map 3.1 EGEA and AOGA in Colonial Salisbury c. 1950s–1970s
(adapted from George Kay and Michael Smout, 1977, Salisbury,* A Geographical
Survey of the Capital of Rhodesia, *London, Hodder and Stoughton, p.27)*

to heal people. Within 'two weeks 25 new converts gathered under a Mukwakwa tree' and soon they built a church from 'pole and mud'.[54]

AOGA also had a great appeal to foreign labour migrants. By the 1960s they felt increasingly unwelcome in the city they had pioneered. But while the new middle classes and aspiring long-term married workers saw unattached male migrants as a threat to their respectability, AOGA made them the object of proselytism. Salisbury's Director of Native Administration may well have bemoaned migrants' lack of involvement in cultural and sporting activities but AOGA offered them a new world where social and recreational activities were centred on the church, a continuous round of nightly prayer meetings and religious services.[55] Foreign labour migrants became key church members. Some, like the Lajabu family from Nyasaland, would become pillars of the Highfield church. Others such as Chitakata and Chiteka from Malawi, Simau from Mozambique, and Phiri from Zambia would subsequently return home to found AOGA branches.

Pan-Africanism was the final significant difference AOGA had with Zimbabwean nationalism. A vision that extended beyond the nation-state was nothing new in the history of African Christianity. Pioneering missionaries had an equally broad African vision, locating their mission stations on highways or natural frontiers with little concern for the region's eventual political landscape. The Universities' Mission to Central Africa Station on Likoma Island, Lake Malawi, was a prime example. Other regional Christian identities, such as the Anglican Archbishopric of Central Africa, were made possible by the existence of empire. Expanded Christian identities also developed from Africans on the move. Refugees fleeing the early nineteenth-century *Mfecane* carried their faith as far as Lake Malawi. And labour gangs from Pedi and further north in the Transvaal encountered Christianity as they moved in search of work, spreading their faith into Botswana and Ovambo (Sundkler and Steed, 2000: chapter 7). In the colonial period African independent churches exhibited a great propensity to movement across borders, often to the point of it being a defining characteristic. Initially unencumbered by large bureaucratic infrastructures and developmentalist goals, these churches could acquire a huge transnational reach. The Apostolic Church of Johane Maranke and the Apostolic Church of Johane Masowe, discussed in the previous chapter, were prime examples. By 1973 the Vapostori of Johane Maranke had spread along migrant labour routes into Botswana, Rhodesia, Zambia, Malawi, Tanzania, Angola and Zaire. Johane Masowe had witnessed the spread of his Apostolic or Korsten Basketmakers Church into eastern and central Africa as well as South Africa (Jules-Rossette, 1975: 229, chapter 7; Dillon-Malone, 1978: 106, 116-17). Closer to home, AFM evangelists had often wandered into Mozambique in pursuit of converts and Enoch Gwanzura claimed to have travelled as far as the Belgian Congo in his evangelistic endeavours.

In AOGA's case Bhengu was again important in giving the vision content and structure. In his Back to God Campaign of the 1950s and 1960s he conceived of a post-colonial Christian Africa from the Cape to Cairo. The continent was a 'sleeping giant' and its people must awake to claim their destiny (Watt, 1992: 40). Guti's auto-hagiography dates his own prayer for Africa from 1957 (Guti, 1989; Erwin, nd). Fixing the prayer to that moment may well have been retrospective, like much of ZAOGA's *Sacred History*, but he and his prayer band were certainly praying for Africa and beyond in the 1950s. At the same time Abel Sande was receiving Gordon Lindsay's *Voice of Healing* and sending donations toward his crusades in the USA and beyond.[56] Guti's revelation/realisation in 1963 that he should learn to preach in English is given prominence in both his official and unofficial hagiographies: 'The Lord spoke to my heart "Learn to preach in English; because you will go to many countries with my word"" (Guti, 1989:10; Erwin, nd: 91). Given that transnational labour migrancy was the experience of so many black urban dwellers in Salisbury, it is hardly surprising that Pan-Africanism shaped their vision so profoundly.

Not surprisingly, given the number of its nationals working in Salisbury, Malawi was the first transnational plant. The initial link with Malawi came through J.P. Chitakata, a Malawian labour migrant working for the Rhodesian window-manufacturing company Springer and Amis. Chitakata had joined the AFM Harare branch in the 1950s and was an original member of the prayer band, which he left in 1959 to join Bhengu. In 1961 he returned to Malawi and founded an Assemblies of God group in Nsanje district (Chakanza, 1983). Guti also travelled to Nsanje in 1961, and it is clear that he believed that Chitakata was working under his authority and that the Malawi assemblies were his. Indeed a typical hagiographical piece even claims Guti was the founder: 'In 1961, the Lord led Ezekiel to go to Nsanje in Malawi. He was able to build a mud church there. Many people were healed from their diseases, many were delivered from their sins...'[57] But Chitakata was Guti's kindred spirit only in the sense that he exhibited the same traits of opportunism, entrepreneurship and independence. He played the same game of manipulating external resources to build up a following,[58] and this time Guti was the victim.

In 1964 Chitakata joined with another Malawian, Lyton Kalambule, and Magnus Udd, a maverick American Assemblies of God missionary, to form the Assemblies of God, Southern and Central Africa (AOGSCA), in collaboration with Bhengu. After complaints from the 'official' Assemblies of God in Malawi, the three groupings rechristened themselves the Independent Assemblies of God (IAOG), which seems to have had a loose connection with the American movement (Chakanza, 1983: 6-7, 14-15, 30-1, 48). This new Pentecostal constellation was a threat to Guti's denominational dreams. Udd's *de facto* independence from the USA meant that he was more easily controlled by Bhengu. Malawian delegates would travel to Bhengu's conventions in East London, South Africa. Around 1967 Bhengu mooted the idea of Udd's mopping up the 'Assemblies' work in Southern Rhodesia after the South Africans had withdrawn.[59] Fearing for his fledgling organisation, Guti wrote to warn his pastors in 1969:

> We must be very careful, because the South Africans are looking to destroy our work, also the Malawi missionaries and even our residents.
> As the Lord reveals to us all the time by His spirit, I want to warn you that the big snake is coming to fight and to destroy many souls in our congregations, but we will win through the name of Jesus.

With remarkable self-confidence, Guti wrote to Udd a month later, warning him to keep away, threatening him with a curse from God for good measure:

> I have heard that you have agreed to work against me and all the work in Rhodesia which God has called me to do.
> ... what I know is that God has called me to preach the gospel to my own people and others also ...
> ... if you are coming to Rhodesia to work against me to please the south African people, (Numbers 22:6)... it is better for me to warn you that if you do that you will damage your own work in Malawi for a long time.[60]

Undaunted by the failure of its initial encounters with Malawi, AOGA would try again with more success in the 1970s, eventually 'mopping up' some of Udd and Chitakata's work.

On the whole the AOGA managed to resist the engrossing tendency of Zimbabwean nationalism and pursued its own agenda within the Pentecostal religious field. Apart from its relentless proselytism the movement focused on individual change and the promotion and renewal of the family.

Respectability on a Shoestring

At the heart of AOGA's mission was the desire for the material and moral advancement of the believer. Essentially, the movement promoted its own brand of respectability, which had profound implications for class formation. But it was not the middle-class respectability described by Michael West (1990), nor the elite Christian identity chronicled by Terence Ranger (1995) in his history of the Methodist Samkange dynasty.

Whereas growing class divisions now rendered many of the historic mission churches closed to the rough urban poor, AOGA welcomed them in, 'people in trouble', drunkards and prostitutes included. Within the close confines of the assembly, families were remade. In more abstract terms it sought to better their chances of *social reproduction*. Both Sande and Mamvura had been married on the same day in a show-case AFM wedding ceremony and 'proper marriages' became an AOGA motto.[61] New families were supported through neighbourhood networks of welfare and pastoral support. Strict moral codes enforced by the religious community bolstered marital chastity. The disciplined, ideally 'married' life of the believer looked unattractive to some, but it drew many poor young men and women in search of a stable domestic life within the city. Given that pass laws and residence requirements severely restricted the economic activities of single women within the city, a marriage certificate was a passport for personal security. Likewise, it had great appeal to male labour migrants seeking permanence in the city. In 1955 only 17 per cent of African men residing in Salisbury were in families (Scarnecchia, 1993: 176-234).[62]

AOGA members were generally the aspiring, urban poor: 'unskilled and unlearned labourers'. They had no church buildings in the city until 1968, meeting instead in schools, under trees, in 'home prayer meetings, in open fields near streams, or in tents'. Pastors went unpaid, few members owned motor vehicles, and the only musical instruments were accordions and tambourines. While on crusades in towns such as Marandellas and Rusape, band members slept in filthy conditions in working men's hostels, or upright in cars (Guti, 1989: 12). They ate 'small dried fish [Kapenta] full of sand and sack strings' and worse still, pumpkin leaves, a material and symbolic marker of poverty. Spare resources were pooled for evangelism.[63] Church members did not have access to exclusive housing or education to set themselves apart, as did the elites. Theirs was respectability on a shoestring. It worked as much through repudiation of and abstinence from the things of the world as through their acquisition. Thus while it shared a 'fixed core' with other types of respectability – 'a stress on economic dependence, on orderliness, cleanliness and fidelity in sexual relations', it differed in other aspects (Goodhew, 2000: 241). Neither was it a superficial respectability based on 'mimicking' white values and practices. The objects it defined itself against had a specific cultural import.

The movement's attitude to popular culture set it apart from the respectable middle classes. Like them, AOGA members abhorred the world of the beer hall associated with drunkenness, promiscuity and violence. But they also rejected other aspects of popular culture that began to flourish in the early 1950s, and experienced a revival in the late 1960s after the banning of the nationalist parties. AOGA members thus avoided gambling, dancing and the bioscope (cinema). Neither did they sympathise with the more liberal approach to alcohol that followed the 1957 legislation, allowing blacks to purchase wine and other light alcoholic beverages. Although consumption of these drinks was a marker of status they were nevertheless shunned as wasteful and sinful. Cosmetics and fancy jewellery were rejected too. Relative deprivation became marks of grace (Bruce, 1996: 218).

Given that worldly pleasures were questionable, multiple membership of other organisations such as sports or cultural clubs was also discouraged. AOGA was totalising in the demands it made on its members' social and leisure activities; their social world was tightly focused on an ordered life of meetings, conventions and evangelistic activities. Burial societies were a major competitor for loyalties in their levels of discipline and care and hence were a particular object of vilification.[64] In place of burial societies, the church cared for the sick and buried the dead. Neither were Guti or his lieutenants, such as Sande, Choto and Kupara, recycled elites, leading other urban organisations as well as AOGA. In spite of their considerable authority in the 1960s (and '70s) the movement's leadership remained focused on the church (Stuart, 1989).

Another facet of AOGA respectability was self-reliance. As the economy stabilised in the late 1960s there was more economic opportunity for Africans. The African media celebrated those who had made good, often valorising black Americans as templates for success. But it was keen to stress that social and economic success was due to more than mere capital accumulation. Charitable endeavour and the choice of a good wife were also important. Even greater significance was given to investment in education and diligence at work (Nottage, 2000: 31). Given that the ladder of education was not available to AOGA members, their major means of economic uplift was thrift, industry and self-reliance. Penny capitalism – the sale of cheap foodstuffs, crocheted items, needlework and firewood – was often all that was available to them. These economic strategies were already ingrained in many Zimbabweans. The Director of Native Administration, Salisbury, noted in 1952 'the Shona tribes were the Jews of Africa so well do they love to trade and so comparatively well developed is their business acumen ....'.[65] These virtues were sharpened by the teachings of Bhengu to become marks of salvation. From the outset Bhengu's lieutenant, Gumede, had encouraged female church members in Highfield to work 'talents', that is, to raise money for church growth. Through 'talents', Pricilla Ngoma and her compatriots raised much of Guti's plane fare to America. Continuing with his account of the Highfield work cited above, Guti (or more probably one of his ghost writers) wrote:

> ...I knew we could not get far in the shabby small tent...
> We encouraged the new converts to learn to work for the Lord. Many of them were poor and did not have enough to afford a living. But as they embarked on the process of working for the Lord's house the Lord blessed them tremendously, women and children sold vegetables on the township markets and each Sunday we would have a collection for the Lord's church.[66]

Thrift and sobriety also contributed to the final marker of Pentecostal respectability: the repudiation of tradition. As with the teaching of 'domesticity', the rejection of ideas and practices associated with African tradition was initially a white, often missionary-inspired, doctrine. But once again it was assiduously adopted by different categories of African society. The African press depicted tradition as a reified set of beliefs and practices, strongly associated with non-Christian rural culture, centring on ancestor veneration, possession cults and witchcraft. It was the world of 'superstition' and 'custom'. Newspaper editorials consistently taught that social progress involved a rejection of such practices and the adoption of more rational modes of thought (Scarnecchia, 1993: 203).[67] For poor urban Pentecostals the repudiation of tradition was an important strategy in helping them accumulate. Church members were discouraged from participating in family and communal rituals, or providing resources for them. Possession rituals, rain-making and first-fruits ceremonies, funeral rites, sessions of divination and beer parties were depicted as wasteful. Avoidance of such practices enabled believers to escape from at least some of the expensive demands of kin and community.

Pentecostal horror at the wastefulness of acts of traditional commensality was shared by the respectable middle classes. But AOGA members added another existential dimension to their repudiation of tradition: the world of the ancestors and alien spirits, of witchcraft and sorcery was of the devil. It was to be shunned for the sake of purity. If the body did not remain free from such polluting influences the Holy Spirit could not come and dwell in its Temple. A Presbyterian minister from Highfield could employ a traditional healer to enhance his chances of winning on the horses, or Catholics and Anglicans could perform traditional rituals at life's crises, but Pentecostals refused to compartmentalise (Lungu, 1994: 49). Here again Pentecostal faith was a totalising one. However, the dichotomy Pentecostals perceived between themselves and the world of tradition had most force on a conceptual level. Those with vivid conversion experiences immediately turned their backs on African medicine, ancestor veneration, and other possession cults, destroying sacred objects associated with such practices. But for most, the repudiation of tradition was a process, a series of acts of repentance, which continued over the years, sometimes with regressions. The pressures from non-believing kin caused some to fall back into idolatry, even if only momentarily. Relatives were targets for evangelism but they were also a potential 'door to the devil'.[68]

Unlike the more established middle classes AOGA members had not yet reached the stage of severing links with the rural world.[69] The movement grew out of the then predominantly rural Apostolic Faith Mission, with its attendant links to Christian independency. In the 1950s and 1960s farms, communal areas, and private locations remained sites of evangelism. Rhodesia's towns, like its cities, rapidly melted into countryside. Throughout the 1950s there was a high turnover of labour migrants. Analysis of the 348,000 Africans working in the city between 1953 and 1957 revealed that 70 per cent were employed for only 5.3 months before leaving.[70] And when male workers finally did settle in towns they retained a strong connection with their village communities through peripatetic wives who practised 'marital migrancy' (Barnes, 1999: 111).Urban–rural interaction thus continued unabated. To the annoyance of AFM missionaries, rural night meetings lasted well into the 1950s. Prayers in the bush and on mountaintops occurred at AOGA meetings throughout the 1960s and beyond. There were large annual conventions held in Mhondoro Reserve 1971-74 and smaller ones in sites like Bindura. At the 1969 Christmas convention at Chiringa School, Gutu, the greater Salisbury contingent arrived on a bus and camped in the bush, where they prayed all night.[71] Many of these rural locations, such as Mt Chipindura, where Guti prayed regularly, were well known sites of Vapostori/AFM activity and, at this stage, AOGA's leaders seemed keen to associate with this rural Pentecostal tradition. The conventions themselves drew not only from the AFM/Methodist-style camp meeting but also the Maranke Vapostori *pasca* [annual gathering] in terms of organisation, ecstatic 'white fire' trances, dancing, mountain-top prayer and duelling with *njuzu* (water sprites) in the baptismal pool (Daneel, 1971: 329-30; Murphree, 1969: 92 &104).[72]

Moreover, just as the first generation of urban Pentecostals retained their rural links, so too did other labour migrants, bringing their so-called traditional practices to town and drawing upon them in the travails of urban existence. Séances for the ancestors took place regularly. Infamous herbalists and faith healers lived in the townships, and those who converted were great trophies for Pentecostals.[73]

Pentecostalism did not bring about one single moment of rupture with a rural-traditional world, then, but it did accelerate the evolution of an urban consciousness (Coquery-Vidrovitch, 1991). Like other city dwellers, urban Pentecostals steadily grew apart from the rural world, their children losing touch with traditional beliefs and practices.[74] And for Pentecostals this process was hastened by their theological opposition to tradition and a growing desire to associate with the tools and practices of modernity. By the 1980s and 1990s second-generation urban Pentecostals would come to equate 'rural' with 'evil'.

Conclusion

AOGA was neither captured by the nationalists nor co-opted by the Rhodesian state. The bright young men and women who pioneered the movement were influenced by the spirit of the age. There were times when, as ambitious religious entrepreneurs, they would borrow from the techniques and practices of the nationalist youth in the townships. Indeed, as demagogues addressing crowds in cities and townships they might easily have been mistaken for nationalist politicians. But theirs was another kind of politics, the politics of social reproduction. It was a struggle to renew and ensure the survival of the family, a struggle that bound urban dwellers together just as forcefully as nationalism did.

At this stage AOGA was a fledgling movement. When in January 1969 Guti wrote to the Registrar of Buildings, Salisbury, seeking government recognition for his organisation, his claims were quite modest: '... our membership which extends to most of the principal Towns in the country, and also to Reserves and Tribal areas is in the region of 1,500-2,000 members.'

Approximate members

Highfield	130	Rusape	25	Chatsworth	100
Mufakose	50	Umtali	20	Sinoia	20
Kambuzuma	50	Nyanyadzi	200	Marandellas	30
Rugare	30	Gwelo	100	Various	300
Harare	25	Bulawayo	30		
Gillingham	35	Bindura &			
Alpha	20	District	200	Other places	
University	15	QueQue	20	Hunyani	40
Arcadia	40	Selukwe	50	Birchenough Bridge	20
Masasa	30	Gatooma	30	Melfort	25
Tafara	50	Hartley	30	Mangula	30

The movement had very few buildings to register. For the most part congregations met outside, as was the case of the 15 or so predominantly domestic servants who met in the precincts of the University College of Rhodesia in Salisbury's plush northern suburbs. The University's Senior Administrative Officer allowed them to 'hold services under a tree near the college African Staff Quarters, and during the rainy season in a corrugated iron shed near gate of maintenance yard', although the Geology Department subsequently reclaimed the facility to store its materials. [75]

AOGA was not the only religious movement to steer clear of nationalist politics. In his Annual Report for 1959, the Director of Native Administration, Salisbury, noted the existence of 'a number of religious sects and groups, which hold meetings in the open air and in school halls'. One such movement based in Bulawayo was Morgan Sengwayo's Apostolic Faith Mission (Portland, USA), of which we shall hear more in the following chapter. Another was the Jehovah's Witnesses, the respectable and now highly bureaucratised reincarnation of the Watch Tower movement. In 1955, on the eve of the nationalist period, it amassed 30,000 people for a religious rally in Salisbury. [76] AOGA would experience rapid growth in its membership and bureaucracy in the 1970s, but first Guti would have to travel to the United States.

Notes

[1]   See report by R. Howman, Under Secretary for Native Affairs, 7 March 1955, file S2805/3423, NAZ.
[2]   Annual Report, June 1954, Director of Native Administration, Salisbury, NAZ.
[3]   Stopforth's survey of Highfields showed that by the end of the 1960s over a quarter of the population read a newspaper on a daily basis and over a third read magazines regularly, Stopforth, 1972:85-86.
[4]   *African Weekly*, 20 April 1960, 4 October 1961.
[5]   Annual Report, June 1962, Director of African Administration, Salisbury, NAZ.
[6]   Ibid.
[7]   See letter from Highfield Church Association to Native Land Board, protesting against a planned beer hall. Minutes of Native Land Board, 28 May 1953, file Native Townships, 1950-1954, S2805/3918/20/3, NAZ.
[8]   There was a good deal of fighting between 'Malawians and Mashonas' in the townships in 1965. See Annual Report, June 1965, Director of African Administration, Salisbury & Rhodesia Information Services, 17 May 1965, S3330/T1/35/22/2, NAZ.
[9]   The David Betts Report four years later pointed to about a 40 per cent deficit between actual earnings of an average man and what was required to survive. Annual Report, June 1962, Director of Native Administration, Salisbury, NAZ; *African Weekly*, 14 January 1959.
[10] *Daily News*, 3 December 1959. Annual Report, June 1954, Director of Native Administration, Salisbury, NAZ.
[11] The data in this section is a composite of about 30 interviews with AOGA's pioneers, elders from the Apostolic Faith Mission and workers in the Pentecostal configuration that Guti's band eventually joined. Informants are named where they are cited directly.
[12] Int.DM53, Pricilla Ngoma.
[13] Int.DM55, Caleb Ngorima.
[14] IntsDM62 & 63, Abel Sande.
[15] Int.DM53, Pricilla Ngoma, Waterfalls.
[16] Int.DM46, Lazurus Mavhura.
[17] 'Not I But Christ', chapter 10, unpublished ms., ca. 1977, file, Histories, ZAW.
[18] *Pentecostal Light Bearer*, April-June 1955.
[19] Int.DM46, Lazurus Mavhura.
[20] 'A Brief History of Ezekiel "All Nations Evangelistic Crusade"' by R.M.G. Kupara, ca 1980, file, 'Histories', ZAW; IntsDM62 & 63, Abel Sande.
[21] C. du Plessis, *Pentecostal Light Bearer*, April-June 1955.
[22] Int.DM55, Caleb Ngorima.
[23] IntsDM62 & 63, Abel Sande.

24 J. Bond to Controller of Customs and Excise, Salisbury, 1967, file, Bhengu, PAOZ.

25 'Not I But Christ' unpublished ms., ca. 1977, file, Histories, ZAW. The prose style is not Guti's.

26 Int.DM63, Abel Sande.

27 Papers in the possession of Jeremiah Kainga, ca. 1964-8 (henceforth JK); Larry D. Malcolm, 'Development of the Assemblies of God in Zimbabwe', ms August 1981, Headquarters of the Assemblies of God, Springfield, USA, in Borrowdale, Harare (henceforth AOGZ).

28 The table is a summary of the key movements discussed in the chapter. There were other movements also at works such as the Full Gospel Church. PAOC work began in Southern Rhodesia in 1948 under J.W. Skinner. It initially focussed on southern Manicaland. (Elim Mission was given the northern part of the province). AOGUSA work began in 1952 under Fred Burke and John Richards. The movement concentrated on the Midlands, and west of the colony beginning in Gwelo.

29 James Bush, Salisbury to J. Kainga, Salisbury, 17 February 1967, JK.

30 Int.DM58, Mary Rembo; Int.DM27, Overseer Kapandura.

31 Others included the Ngoma, Mandu and Chiwanza families.

32 News Sheet, Jeremiah Kainga, November 1965, JK.

33 N. Bhengu, Johannesburg, to J. Kainga, Salisbury, ca. 1966, JK; G. Upton, Toronto to J. Bush, Salisbury, 23 December 1966, file Bhengu, PAOZ.

34 By this time Choto controlled Gillingham, Sande controlled Marandellas, and another acolyte, Sande Mhandu, controlled Virginia. J. Kainga, Salisbury to N. Bhengu, Johannesburg, 23 February 1966, JK.

35 Papers located in AOGZ.

36 N. Bhengu, Johannesburg to J. Kainga, Salisbury, 17 August 1967.

37 Until 1967 the movement operated informally as a small band known as the Ezekiel Guti Evangelistic Association (EGEA), see 'A Brief History of Ezekiel "All Nations Evangelistic Crusade"' by R.M.G. Kupara, ca. 1980, file, Histories. Then, for less than a year, from March 1967, it was officially known as the Pentecost African Assemblies of God, see Constitution in the possession of David Choto (copy in my possession). In 1968 it became the Assemblies of God, African (AOGA), see J. Choto, 'To Whom it May Concern', July 1968, file, AOGA Correspondence 1964-80. From 1972 onwards much of its transnational work has happened under the banner Forward in Faith Mission International (FIFMI), see *The Macedonian Call*, 20 May 1972, vol. 1, no. 1, published by FIFMI. In 1977 it evolved into the Assemblies of God Africa (still AOGA). And finally, after independence it became the Zimbabwe Assemblies of God, Africa (ZAOGA). Executive Minutes, 6 December 1977 and 26 May 1981, ZAW.

38 *Bantu Mirror*, 6 May 1961 & 2 December 1961, cited in Ranger, 2003: 5.

39 W.L. Wilson, Mabelreign to Brother Von Rensburg, 9 March 1961, file, W.L. Wilson, 1939-78, AFM.

40 Paul Wright, Salisbury, to E.L. Philips, Springfield, USA, 6 November 1968, file, Correspondence 1968-78, AOGZ.

41 Int.DM4, Christopher Chadoka.

42 Int.DM46, Lazurus Mavhura. Int.DM55, Caleb Ngorima.

43 Goodhew, 2000: 264, citing E. Genovese, *Roll, Jordan, Roll! The World the Slaves Made*, London, 1975: 115.

44 Int.DM62, Abel Sande.

45 J. Bush, Salisbury to John Bond, Pretoria, 15 April 1967, PAOZ.

46 E. Guti, 'Highfields' ca. 1977, file, Histories, ZAW.

47 File, British South Africa (BSA) Police, 1960s and 1970s, ZAW.

48 Executive Minutes 1979, ZAW; Minutes of Workers Meeting, Nyanyadze, 8 July 1968, file, AOGA Correspondence 1964-1980, ZAW.

49 Int.DM62, Abel Sande; File, CNFI 1970s and 1980s, ZAW.

50 Int.DM66, Mateus Simau; Ida Chikono, Anniversary celebrations, Mt Pleasant, 12 May 1996, fieldwork notes.

51 Mrs Chesa, Anniversary celebrations, Mt Pleasant, 12 May 1996, fieldwork notes.

52 Report on Highfields 1977, file, AOGA correspondence 1964-80, ZAW.

53 Short descriptions of the crusades are given for the Christ for the Nations Native Church Project, file, CFNI, 1970s and 1980s, ZAW.

54 Ezekiel Guti, Manzvire, Final Report, 21 April 1980, file, CFNI, ZAW.

55 Annual Report, Director of Native Administration, June 1954 & June 1957, NAZ.

56 Int.DM62, Abel Sande.

57 'Biography of Rev. E.H. Guti', nd, file, Histories, ZAW. An earlier unpublished history reports that Guti went as part of a team stationed at Port Herald on the Shores of the Lake, 'Not I But Christ', file, Histories, ZAW.

58 Int.DM41, Bartholomew Manjoro.

59 J. Bush, Salisbury, to G. Upton, Canada, 1 December 1966; G. Upton, Canada, to J. Bush, Salisbury, 12 December 1966, file, Bhengu, PAOZ; Nicholas Bhengu, 'Suggestions for Rhodesia', ca. 1968, file, AOGA correspondence 1964-80, ZAW.

60 E. Guti, '*Ku Vafundisi Vese*' (trans. Erica Chikodo], 11 January 1969, file AOGA correspondence 1964-80; E. Guti to M. Udd, 27 February 1969, file, AOGA correspondence 1964-80, ZAW.

[61] Int.DM46, Lazurus Mavhura.

[62] Here AOGA stood in the same trajectory as the Mai Chaza Movement, which, contrary to the accusations of the Methodist Church and the African Press, *did* place a premium on marital chastity. Annual Report, Director of Native Administration, June 1955, NAZ.

[63] *The Macedonian Call*, published by FIFM International, vol. 1., No. 1, May 1972. Pumpkin leaves are usually a last resort, often eaten in times of drought.

[64] Minutes of Deeper Life Conference, 13 November 1974, file, Deeper Life, ZAW.

[65] Annual Report, Director of Native Administration, Salisbury, 1952, NAZ.

[66] E. Guti, 'Highfields' ca. 1977, file, Histories, ZAW.

[67] See for instance the *African Weekly*, 16 October 1960 with its critique of traditional systems for the appointment of chiefs.

[68] Deeper Life Meeting, 13 November 1974, file, Deeper Life, 1974-1996, ZAW.

[69] Kileff, 1975. Though even amongst these elites there was a different response to obligations towards kin, and the real change was most apparent in their children's attitudes.

[70] Annual Report, Director of African Administration, Salisbury, 1957, NAZ.

[71] Int.DM49, Anna Mturi, with Perpetua Mkodzansi & Stella Dembedze; Diary extracts, Mrs M. Chesve.

[72] The ZAOGA anniversary each May also borrows from the Maranke *pasca* in its emphasis on the founder's life history. It would appear that full immersion baptism offers traditional spirits, represented by *njuzu*, the opportunity to win back a convert. The baptiser is also vulnerable (Malone, 1978: 152). The similarity of early ZAOGA activity to Vapostori practice was clear from testimonies given by older church members at the anniversary celebrations, for example: Solomon Goko, anniversary meeting, University of Zimbabwe, 12 May 1996, fieldwork notes. See also, file, AOGA Correspondence 1964-80 & Executive Minutes, 23 June 1973, ZAW.

[73] Int.DM15, Debson Chizivano; Diary extracts, Mrs M. Chesve.

[74] This occurred as early as 1953 amongst the children of those who considered themselves 'permanently urbanized'. Annual Report of Director of Native Administration, Salisbury, June 1953. Stopforth's survey of Highfield in the 1970s is a better indication of social trends. In his findings, 71 per cent reported that their children learnt progressively less about 'custom' (Stopforth, 1972: 69).

[75] Ezekiel Guti to the Registrar of Buildings, Salisbury, 3rd January 1969 & Senior Admin Officer, University College of Rhodesia, 23rd May 1969 to Ezekiel Guti, file AOGA correspondence, 1964-1980, ZAW.

[76] Director of Native Administration, Salisbury, Annual Report, June 1959, NAZ. *African Weekly*, 12 October 1955.

4

'Pooma Satani'
Chasing out the Demons of
Sin, Sickness & Poverty
Church Growth in the Decade of National Liberation
1970–1980

In 1970 southern Africa appeared a world apart from Africa north of the Zambezi. White supremacy seemed overwhelming. Black opposition had been effectively curtailed in South Africa and Rhodesia. European economic sanctions had failed to break the Rhodesian Front's Unilateral Declaration of Independence and guerrilla insurgency had made little impression. Apartheid not only continued but was also consolidated by an economic boom and the establishment of cordial relations with Malawi and Lesotho. Military alliance with Rhodesia and South Africa strengthened Portugal's position in Mozambique and Angola.

Yet African nationalism was gathering pace. In Rhodesia the force of opposition to the proposals agreed upon by Sir Alec Douglas-Home and Ian Smith in 1971 for a new white-dominated constitution showed that popular desire for black majority rule was far from dead. The level of support for the African National Council, a new body led by Methodist Bishop Abel Muzorewa to fight the proposals, was immense. Meanwhile in Mozambique the liberation movement Frelimo was making significant progress. By 1971 it was operating south of the Zambezi close to the Rhodesian border, and was soon able to provide bases for the Zimbabwe African National Liberation Army (ZANLA), the insurgent wing of ZANU. And ZANU and ZAPU were strengthened through ideological connection with Communist China and the Soviet Union respectively.

Within this broad panorama of political change AOGA continued to blaze its own distinctive trail. The movement's mission of evangelism and divine healing continued unabated, carrying it across new frontiers into Mozambique and Botswana. It also looked beyond the continent. In 1971 Ezekiel Guti travelled to the USA in search of a place to study and funds for church expansion. The resulting American connections brought changes to the movement: buildings, bureaucracies and new types of respectability. And Guti's travels helped him to evolve his own idiosyncratic responses to poverty and cultural nationalism. The 1970s would prove crucial in the movement's growth and consolidation.

An African Christian Encounters America

With no solid plan but a good deal of faith, Guti's American encounter began in Pittsburgh where an AOGA member had a relative, his only American contact. Unable to find a place of study in the city he quickly moved on to Berean College, Dallas. The College operated on a faith basis whereby its members pooled their wealth and lived collectively. After five months it fell apart. In later years Guti would turn this experience into a parable that justified his authoritarian style: 'I could see that if leaders were not careful the Devil could creep in and destroy a big organisation. I have learned to be careful in my ministry with three things: money, women and pride. These can destroy an organisation easily' (Erwin, nd: 106). In the meantime, however, study and qualifications seemed to be eluding him. Sande came to the rescue. A loyal reader of Gordon Lindsay's *Voice of Healing Magazine*, now re-titled *Christ for the Nations*, Sande had read in 1970 of plans to start an Institute by that name in Dallas. Acting on Sande's advice Guti made contact with Christ for the Nations Institute (CFNI) and was admitted.[1]

Lindsay was a pivotal figure in American Pentecostalism. His formation had begun working alongside Pentecostal pioneers such as Lake and Parham. He had witnessed the founding of denominations and played a leading role in the subsequent Restorationist critique of them in the 1950s. In CFNI he looked forward to the growing charismatic movement – a non-denominational enterprise in which Pentecostals actively collaborated with Evangelicals who were open to Gifts of the Spirit (Blumhofer, 1993: 216-17).

At Christ for the Nations Guti took a diploma in 'Charismatic Orientated Biblical Studies'. The course was vocational rather than academic. Evangelism, Church Growth, Charismatic Gifts and Worship were the major priorities. There was a strong focus on reaching different social categories associationally through Prison Ministries, Hospital Work and Youth, Women's and Student Ministries. Scriptures were learnt rather than interpreted and examinations took the form of simple multiple-choice questions. Much of the learning was done through listening to audio-tapes, although students were expected to read Gordon Lindsay's tracts and booklets including some of his more idiosyncratic interpretations of Old Testament prophets, who he believed foretold the invention of the television set and the motor car. Credits were gained through attendance rather than examination, and these were measured with a time clock and swipe card. There were penalties for tardiness.

The institutional ethos valued *experience* of God as much as intellectual and vocational development, emphasising the cultivation of Christian character. Formation was shaped by regular sessions of corporate prayer, worship and Bible study but more broadly by the promotion of the appropriate manners and mores. The regime decreed a separation of the sexes through curfews and strict rules on visiting. Codes of conduct were also directive with regard to appearance. Dress was for faith and not fashion. Female students were advised:

> Modesty, femininity and good taste are the guiding principles ... short dresses, brief shorts, low-necked dresses or blouses or blue jeans are not permitted ... Masculine-type clothes are not acceptable for women. One-piece swimming suit with cap is required for swimming....

And men were informed: 'Beards are not acceptable. Moustaches should be trimmed above the corners of the mouth. A moderate haircut is required. *Hair must not hang over the shirt collar nor completely cover the ears.*' 'Bad habits' such as 'smoking, drinking, and cursing' were 'not allowed in any of the student apartments at any time'.[2]

Those who remembered Guti at CFNI observed that he did not stand out among his peers. He never really mastered spoken English and the shy retiring part of his character manifested itself. He did not impress his teachers as Benson Idahosa had done. Idahosa, an accountant from Nigeria, and later a renowned Pentecostal leader in that country, had the distinction of being one of the 'sharpest looking' foreign students CFNI ever had, someone 'very, very careful about his appearance'. He was also unrivalled in the extent to which he 'circulated', preaching wherever he got the chance in Texas and beyond. If anything it was Bartholomew Manjoro who followed Guti from ZAOGA to CFNI in the 1980s, who made more of an impression, cut from a similar cloth to Idahosa (F. Lindsay, 1976: 263-5). But Guti was the first Zimbabwean to go there and that secured his position as AOGA's leader.

Ezekiel Guti: Patron and Prophet

Guti held the loyalty of his prayer band in the 1950s. In the 1960s his disciples got their first real taste of power and status as they were dispersed around the country to work under the AOG umbrella. They developed their own followings and sensed the possibilities for expansion that could come with missionary resources. Indeed while Guti commanded their respect, a loyalty honed from years of struggle and sacrifice, there were others who were not so impressed with him. Mastery of the English language was an important mark of status and sophistication but Guti's spoken and written English remained poor, even after his study in Dallas (Ranger,1995: 53). More significantly, his marriage had failed and he had lived for much of the 1960s as a single man with continual doubts cast upon his morality. While Guti had charisma and vision, Sande was by far the more successful evangelist, founding numerous assemblies throughout the country and beyond. And Kupara was patrician, educated and gifted in administration. Both of these men had their own access to missionaries and both had been discussed as possible leaders of the African AOG work in Southern Rhodesia just prior to the schism that created AOGA. Indeed Guti may have brought things to a head to stop this happening.

Once Guti returned from the United States power relations within the movement were dramatically altered. Black Zimbabweans, like their South African counterparts, increasingly and somewhat uncritically viewed America as a place of sophistication and equal opportunity (Campbell, 1995). As Britain's formal empire steadily declined, an informal American economic and cultural imperialism was taking effect in southern and central Africa. Throughout the 1960s American film and music had also been filtering into the country. Highfield residents had a regular diet of John Wayne, Burt Lancaster, Rock Hudson and Elvis Presley at the Cyril Jennings Hall. This had considerable effect. Young men mimicked the attire of cowboys and later the comrades modelled themselves on American gunslingers (Lungu, 1994: 45; Ambler, 2001).[3] Even those Zimbabweans of a religious disposition who rejected such 'worldly influences' were aware of the growing American missionary involvement with Southern Rhodesia. Its impact had steadily increased through organisations such as the American Methodist Episcopal Church, the American Board, the Church of Christ, the Evangelical Alliance Mission, and more recently the Assemblies of God. The impressive campaigns of globe-trotting evangelists such as Oral Roberts and Billy Graham in the 1950s and '60s only served to underline that growing influence (Dodge, 1987).

To get to America was to make it big. Academic or not, Guti's American diploma sounded impressive . In 1965 as few as 1,000 Zimbabweans held college degrees (West, 2002: 65). Indeed his return from CFNI was recorded in *The Rhodesia Herald*, the national daily.[4] Along with his new-found status, Guti's American encounter had furnished him with a huge pool of material and ideological resources with which to build AOGA. In June 1973 he addressed the first Executive Meeting since his return. Full of millennial fervour he informed them of his plans to put up church buildings, preach to whites and convert rich people.[5]

Gordon Lindsay, the founder of CFNI, died in 1973 but under his wife Freda it became a dynamo for charismatic Christian advance, not only in America but also Africa, Asia, and Latin America. Guti was on good terms with Mrs Lindsay and travelled with her to Israel in 1977. American resources soon flowed into the movement. Of particular importance was the CFNI's Native Church Crusade whereby the American Bible School found sponsors to pay for the roof of a building if indigenous Christians found resources to build the four walls. Locally made bricks and labour were cheap and readily available. It was the asbestos or corrugated iron roofing and steel supports that were expensive and CFNI donated US$500-1,000 per building. The scheme cemented Guti's position as unrivalled leader of the movement. Never revealing the source of his largesse, he alone appeared to have fixed the movement into the landscape, giving it a denominational presence it had previously lacked. Church structures were soon built in Salisbury's townships and other towns and cities including Fort Victoria, Gwelo and Chiredzi. CFNI's approach to mission was well suited to AOGA's aspiration for autonomy. One of the Institute's administrators explained in a letter to Guti in 1974, 'in essence we submit ourselves to the local church to use the tools they have as they think fit'.[6] The Institute provided easy money with few strings attached, obviating the necessity of working with missionaries.

Funding also came for a Bible school in Glen Norah on the edge of Salisbury. Requesting money from Native Churches Crusade in Dallas for a 'spirit-controlled Bible School', Guti wrote: 'We are burdened with thousands of dying souls. We need trained men and women to take the good news to them.' The school was completed in 1978 and initially named Christ for Rhodesia Institute, after the Dallas prototype.[7]

The American connection also exposed Guti to new networks from which resources flowed. He returned from Dallas with another strange white bedfellow, a Scotsman, Alistair Geddes, who had previously been a member of the Rhodesian police force.[8] At Mrs Lindsay's behest, Forward in Faith Mission International (FIFMI) backed Guti and Geddes. This organisation, with an American address and board of advisors, appears to have been a hastily convened front to raise money for AOGA's expansion into surrounding nations.[9] Guti acted as FIFMI's Mission Director and Geddes its International Director and National Supervisor. At times, Geddes also represented AOGA to the Rhodesian state, proving useful in fronting applications for church sites in townships, and in attracting donations from white farmers.[10] Guti grew to dislike Geddes' oversight and soon the two parted ways, but the CFNI connection had furnished him with a host of well-intentioned whites willing and able to help his fledgling movement. In 1974 he convened the movement's first international Deeper Life Conference, an idea borrowed directly from Dallas, and invited Mrs Lindsay as his main speaker. Numerous other Americans would follow in the coming years. Lastly, Guti exploited the growing network of the Dallas school's alumni by arranging for Choto and

Sande to study at Benson Idahosa's All Nations for Christ Institute in Benin City for nine months in 1978.[11]

Building Bureaucracy and Bourgeois Respectability

Drawing from his American experience, Guti refined AOGA's model of respectability, in particular the teaching and practice of domesticity. The notion was well established by the 1950s and '60s. It derived from a long and varied tradition reaching back to the 1920s encompassing 'native education' embodied in Jeanes teaching, domestic train- ing and the 'homecraft' movement, and women's clubs. As Michael West has observed, 'the cult of domesticity was not … simply a missionary or government imposition on Africans. Both female and male members of the emerging middle class voluntarily sub- scribed to it' (West, 1990: 2, 3, 102). The historic mission churches organised compre- hensive programmes of meetings and talks for 'Home and Family Weeks'. The bloused African women of the Methodist *Ruwadzano* – Fellowship – groups actively promoted the idea of a regulated domestic world (Burke, 1996: chapter 2). The message of order and cleanliness had been central to Bhengu's teaching and found its way into AOGA practice in the 1960s, but Guti made additional strictures when he returned from the ordered and conservative world of Christ for the Nations, Dallas. Keen to demonstrate his new sophistication, he taught manners and mores, diet and hygiene to his pastors and their wives at the first Deeper Life Conference. These socially aspiring followers were taught how to 'make a party', how to organise a bank account, and how to be chiv- alrous towards women. Under the last heading AOGA husbands were encouraged to give up their seat for a woman, to give their wives pocket money and not tell them dirty jokes. Taking a leaf out of Idahosa's book, his sartorial advice to pastors was that they have a 'black suit and a white shirt for Holy Communion and burying the dead'. These were key features of bourgeois respectability but in AOGA's case they were ini- tially tempered with a deference to middle-class blacks whose souls and cheque-books they strove to win. Pastors and their wives were given lessons in how to approach 'higher people', such as nurses.[12]

Guti's new-found sophistication helped him bureaucratise the movement. Soon after his return from Dallas the movement began to pay more attention to keeping records. And in these records, particularly the executive minutes, he dominated, continually dis- coursing about rules, procedures and structures: the tasks of a pastor; the registration of property; the importance of a pension fund. The process of bureaucratisation began at the local level, where assemblies were instructed to appoint secretaries and treasurers and organise distinct groups for women, youth and children. Annual conventions for the first two of these social categories were taking place in 1974. These cross–cutting bonds of fellowship based on age and gender helped integrate members who were beginning to be separated by geography and class, and maintained the intimacy and intensity that animated the early movement. Guti also decentralised the Rhodesian movement into five provinces, each with its own overseer and headquarters.[13] By 1977 each provincial office channelled pensions, tithes and wages into a financial department at the head- quarters in Salisbury. The following year Guti told his executive 'we are going to look at what Europeans do, they know that their minister is going to have such an amount of money through the year and they put it aside for him. Our work is going that way'.[14]

All assemblies were also made to conform to a formal liturgical pattern of weekly and monthly meetings.

Before Guti could dominate AOGA, however, he needed to resolve his own conundrum of respectability. His first marriage had never been happy and it was irreparably damaged once he had joined Bhengu. His wife had been a great AFM stalwart. While evangelising in the hostels of Harare Township he had met an ambitious young trainee nurse, Eunor Sithole, and on arriving back from the USA he announced he would divorce his first wife and marry Eunor. Given the importance of marriage and settled family life as a badge of respectability, there was a good deal of internal dissent. But once again American connections helped Guti to win his struggle. He arrived home with the blessing of 'faithful spiritual leaders' in the USA (Erwin, nd: 111). As a nurse, Eunor Sithole represented the stratum of people the movement sought to win. By marrying her, Guti arrived at bourgeois respectability, and to mark that transition his executive built a house for him in Marimba Park, the new suburb for elite blacks.[15]

But if Guti, like many prophets, was a contradictory character, often breaking his own moral strictures, his lieutenants were no less contradictory in their support for him. Although he kept them divided, often seeing them individually and playing them off against each other, they remained loyal in his struggle with the AFM and later in the battle with the leadership of the AOGSA configuration. They even helped raise money for his trip to the USA. Once the furore concerning his marriage was over, they threw themselves behind him with remarkable zeal. The movement's Executive Minutes record his growing stature. Along with dictating events, his discourse was peppered with elliptical statements and prophetic rebuke of his former peers:

> You delay me to what God has told me to do with you, to put you on God's place. God is after lifting His work, not for us to live in the flesh. I am not free to say to you this and that…
> Some people ask me why I work like this. [It is] Because I don't have a helper. [16]

In 1974 Guti was given the praise name 'the Lord's anointed man'. By 1979 he was no longer an ordinary Pentecostal brother but 'the Servant of God'. By then he ruled with remarkable self-confidence. In that year's Executive Meeting he declared: 'Many ministers and pastors don't know their ministry; they need someone to tell them…'. To which his board assented:

> Rev Maoko said 'my vision is to listen to the Servant of God to what he told me to do and I must follow and see things moving'. Rev Nyamnande said, 'I just follow what the Servant of God said, I know that many people will follow Him, what I think is just to agree with Him'. Rev Sande said, 'I just follow what the Servant of God told me to do'. Rev Muhwati said, 'I just follow what the Servant of God told me to do'.[17]

AOGA's government was recast around Guti. In the 1974 Deeper Life Conference he observed:

> All churches who want unity of churches have no progress. The churches which are progressing in number regardless of holiness are: Roman Catholic, Watch Tower and brother or rev. Sengwayo's churches. So if these can have a strong membership without company it shows that we can do without company.[18]

These movements were highly sectarian and authoritarian. Indeed, in Sengwayo's

Apostolic Faith Mission Guti found a local model of growth and government. Seng-wayo (properly known as Morgan Sithole) had struck out on a similar trajectory a few years prior to Guti, modernising his Bulawayo-based Pentecostal movement through connection with the AFM Portland, USA (see Chapter 1). Guti shared the same Ndau ethnicity as Sengwayo and often visited him in Bulawayo, adopting his leadership style of aloofness and mystique.[19]

But the desire for a 'big' Christian leader also came from Guti's peers and from below. Sande had exhorted Guti 'to make the organisation strong', while Choto 'wanted people to know that this is a "Man of God". That if you go to him you can get help'.[20] As in other African Christian movements, a rich and powerful man was believed to be more able to secure property for the church and thus put it on a sure economic foundation. A strong leader was believed more effective in representations to the government, and able to rectify the injustices and dispossessions visited upon his people by the white man (Sundkler, 1961: 129-30; Campbell, 1995: chapter 1). Guti was *beginning* to fill the vacuum left by the likes of Mzengeli as a community leader. Hundreds of urbanites flocked to him for guidance.

Personal Security and Racial Vindication

External funds strengthened Guti's position within AOGA and furnished the move-ment with the image of success. Nevertheless the membership remained ignorant of the source of Guti's funding. By 1977 the movement was producing its own pro-motional literature comprising brief histories, testimonies and sermons. One of its earliest tracts read: '[AOGA] does not get money from overseas but the members do the work themselves. The organisation of Rev Guti believes on nothing else but the power of the Holy Spirit to whom it puts its faith. It has no money from banks but does everything using faith.'[21] This statement was somewhat economical with the truth, but it served to underline how self-reliance had become central to what the movement stood for and why it appealed to Southern Rhodesia's urban poor. Fundamentally, AOGA helped provide them with personal and collective security.

The movement had always expected members, particularly women, to engage in penny capitalism – small-scale production of foodstuffs and clothing – to enhance church finances. In the 1970s this practice was bureaucratised as a biannual event under the leadership of Pricilla Ngoma. Highfield members alone raised $8,000 in 1977 for the extension of their famous Revival Centre though 'sewing, selling things and vegetables'. Large amounts of money were raised within the movement for church buildings, pastors' wages, crusades and motor vehicles. Church accounts reveal that Talents alone raised the following approximate amounts:

Mashonaland	$23,000
Matabeleland	$17,000
Victoria	$8,000
Midlands	$7,000
Manicaland	$4,000
Total	**$59,000**[22]

These sums were remarkable, given that Rhodesia was then embroiled in war. Although Talents money went into church coffers, it did create a culture of industry and entrepreneurship that sustained members, as we shall see in later chapters. The collective dimension of giving was also important. It was bound up with what James Campbell calls 'racial vindication': the notion that exemplary new lives embraced by believers would hasten their full inclusion in white-dominated Rhodesian society (Campbell, 1995: 26-7, 64). Although the movement sought autonomy from whites, 'whiteness' remained strongly associated with sophistication – knowledge of the tools and practices of modernity. Whites set the standards to which Africans aspired, and Guti would remain fixated with them, conducting his affairs in a similar manner and achieving similar levels of progress. Physical markers of progress were important. Given that most AOGA members were poor, significant consumption was only possible on a collective scale. The continual bragging about buildings and vehicles and their costs in the movement's literature served not only as a concrete reminder of how far the movement had come, but also signalled its independence from external control. Gayle Erwin's account of the dedication of the Tabernacle built for the movement's Bible school illustrated the potency of this struggle for vindication:

> Zimbabwean native men do not walk around with their hands in their pockets ... They keep their hands out of their pockets, because they believe that to put them in your pockets means that you have money or some reason to put your hands there. This makes pocket hands a signal of wealth or position. Being mostly poor people they consider it arrogant to place their hands in their pockets... The speaker, a leading businessman, who led the dedication, at the close of his message told the hands in the pocket tradition, then he said 'Now we have something. We are rich. I want everyone to walk around at the front with their hands in their pockets' (Erwin, ca. 1997: 6-7).[23]

Tithing was another defining part of church life. In 1977 the movement collected approximately $81,000 from tithes, $2,500 from a crusade fund and $3,500 from donations.[24] A 1979 newsletter carried the following testimony of a Mr Mandienga:

> When I accepted Jesus as my personal saviour, I was indeed very poor. I was living in one room, sleeping on a mat. We had only two blankets for me, my wife and two kids. I had one shirt and one pair of trousers. My wife had only one dress, my children went naked. Winter was spent in misery.
>
> I was working as a garden boy, earning $30 a month. We just did not have enough. We have gone for many nights without food. Poverty was dominating. One day I heard Rev. Guti preaching on tithes. He was preaching on Malachi 3:10. I started to act upon the word of God. I started paying my $3 as my tithe. The Devil told me that I would be the poorest in this Church and worse still, previously I used to live on $30, now that I am tithing, I must live on $27 which is less! My wife also started giving tithes of sugar and mealie meal and all the groceries...
>
> God started to move in. After 3 months, I got a better job, I worked as a night watchman at a factory. My pay was then doubled. So also I doubled my tithes. By this time tithing was not burdensome but a joy. After 2 months there was a job for a supervisor at a factory. I applied for the job and I got it. Now my pay is four times as much. I am staying in a four roomed house at Glen Norah. The house rents are being paid by the firm. Our wardrobe is full of clothes. Our children look healthy and well dressed. We have a beautiful bedroom suite. This I say to testify that I have proved God according to his word and God is faithful.[25]

Although the message was not as explicit as versions of the prosperity gospel that would appear in the 1980s and '90s, the clear implication was that giving brought greater material blessings from God.

Some AOGA members certainly did experience a redemptive uplift, rising in social status and managing to accumulate. As the movement began to create respectable urban dwellers, it also attracted them. A second generation of more literate and professionally accomplished young men such as Bartholomew Manjoro, Cuthbert Makoni, Bill John Chigwenembe and Jason Marowa grew in prominence in the 1970s and would have a profound effect on the movement's direction. Prosperity coming through giving was not so contradictory when it was accompanied by the adoption of a puritan work ethic of sobriety and industry, and a rejection of what were seen as wasteful cultural practices like consorting with traditional healers. In June 1979 Guti preached to a Big Sunday gathering in Salisbury:

> Many people are bound by evil spirits, for example, the spirit of poverty. Poverty is from the Devil. There was one very poor man who went to Chipinga to find the best magician who could make him rich. So he consulted the magician, who gave him a magic tickey [3d. coin]. He had to pay twenty dollars to have that magic tickey. This magic tickey was supposed to produce a thousand more.

> The man was excited. He was instructed not to open the suitcase in which the magic tickey was until he reached his destination. So he went off home happy and excited. He imagined a lot of money produced, and already the suitcase was very happy. When he reached home he called his wife and asked her to close the door behind her. He carefully opened the suitcase, and to his disgust, only found an empty suitcase and the magic tickey.

> This is an example of the evil spirit of poverty, which was binding this man. He sought his help from men instead of God. Come to Jesus, He can set you free from all kinds of evil spirits.[26]

The teaching of tithing, Talents and the 'spirit of poverty' would be refined and systematised in the 1980s to become a defining part of the movement's doctrine. Rooted in struggles for survival in wartime Rhodesia, it would have widespread appeal.

Divine healing had always been central to AOGA's doctrine, and space was provided for it in almost every service. It was another vital factor drawing the urban and rural poor into the church, intricately bound up as it was with deliverance from poverty and demonic possession. Contemporary printed histories and testimonies offer great insight into its practice. Healing was broadly concerned with maladies ranging from cancer and mental confusion to asthma and ascites (a distended abdomen). Cures were both miraculous and mundane. The dead were raised to life and headaches dispelled. The alleviation of sickness benefited the individuals concerned and their families. Previously sick parents could now nurture children, and money wasted on healing practitioners, traditional and bio-medical, could now be invested in clothes and education. The following account of a woman from Chiredzi previously 'bound by asthma for seven years' captures many of these themes:

> Her husband was one of the most miserable men I ever saw. When he would go home from his job, he had to start cleaning the house, do the laundry, washing the dishes and to cook for his children and then hurry to hospital to catch up with the visiting time – to see his wife in severe asthmatic attacks. The hospital bill for his wife's sick bed was so high that he could never manage to pay the children's school fees. Poverty, misery, and sickness were dominating in the family – the Devil himself. But praise to God! This woman, Mrs Stephen, was completely delivered

from chronic asthma through the power of Jesus' name. You would marvel to see such a change in the family.[27]

African Pentecostals rejected traditional healing wholesale, consigning both the malevolent spirits afflicting the sick and the practitioners mediating with them to the realms of the Devil. Believers were also ambivalent about bio-medicine. Like many from a humble class position they resented paying expensive fees to quacks whose remedies were by no means always efficacious. More importantly, 'missionary medicine reached far too few people and excluded too many problems to fulfil the needs of the common man' (Hastings, 1979: 72; Wacker, 2001: 191-2). Early missionary medicine often had been personal, practised in a mission dispensary by a Catholic Brother or Sister or Protestant minister with little formal training but a breadth of experience and enough charisma to draw clients from afar. But by the 1960s missionary medicine had become bureaucratised, practised by doctors with little understanding of local language and culture, who took an impersonal clinical approach. Rituals of healing were of primary importance in traditional society and Pentecostal religion, like Christian independency, resonated with them, making available the 'power of the Holy Spirit to counter all other spiritual agencies' (Ranger, 1982: 339-41). What was revelatory about divine healing was that it released the sick from dependence on the benevolence of lesser spirits and instead connected them through prayer with an omnipotent God concerned with the intimate details of their small lives, a God who 'saves, keeps and satisfies'. The appeal of divine healing was enhanced through demonstration at crusades and rallies. In the same June 1979 Big Sunday mentioned above, six people previously affected with paralysis of the limbs 'jumped for joy' and eleven previously 'barren women' testified, some 'holding up babies for all to see'.[28] Healing of infertility remained central given that 'barrenness' placed marriages at risk and threatened the security of women (Scarnecchia, 1997).

Evangelism and War

Evangelism remained AOGA's supreme goal, even in wartime. While the activities of the historic mission churches were curtailed during the liberation war, particularly in rural areas, AOGA rapidly expanded (Hallencreutz and Moyo, 1988; Bhebe and Ranger, 1995). As missionaries were forced to leave the country and mission stations were closed or their activities restricted, AOGA's programmes of formal evangelism continued. Abel Sande led most of the crusades, preaching in both towns and rural areas. There was 'heavy revival' in Wankie, Bulawayo, Gwelo, Masvingo, Marandellas and Umtali (see Map 4.1). He even preached in protected villages [keeps] where converts were baptised in large oil drums filled with water, and he was proud that both freedom fighters and security forces came to his preaching and healing rallies.[29] The crusades acted as catalysts, creating or strengthening a core of believers who continued with the work of evangelism and teaching, seeing the process of church building through to the erection of brick structures. The following account written for the CFNI Native Churches Crusade Programme outlines a typical example of the process:

It was in 1975 when brother Abel Sande pitched his tent in Dangamvura, Umtali. Over 300 people were converted and became strong believers.... As these went from house to house witnessing

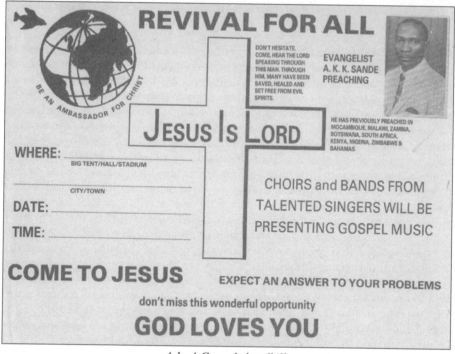

4.1 A Crusade handbill

many were added to [the] church and they grew to be 600...
In 1979 women began to grow and sell vegetables in order to get money for building the church.
The men who were working gave all their wages as little as it was for some earned $20 a month.

Often assemblies continued to grow because of the agency and inspiration of ordinary church members. In Chapter 3 there was a brief account of the founding of Manz-vire Assembly in south-east Manicaland by Selina Chigona. In 1977, the community, which had met under a mukwakwa tree, was moved into a protected village. Nevertheless they continued to worship together and began making their own bricks and selling vegetables to raise money for a church building. A brief progress report for CFNI recounts what happened when American funds for roofing arrived:

> After the news was circulated that the sheets were coming they waited at the gate of their dense, protected village, singing and praising the Lord. The local people and authorities were delighted to see how much these people loved their church and cared for it better than their own huts... [they] paid for the rest by picking cotton ...
> The Lord is blessing these people abundantly they have better huts and better clothing than their fellow men in the protected village.[30]

When the liberation war did get a mention in reports for American donors and in contemporary printed testimonies it usually provided the backcloth to a story about a miraculous deliverance from persecution or death. The stories illustrated both the protective hand of God and the faith and endurance of AOGA members in the face of danger. Two short testimonies illustrate these themes. In the first, 'a female pastor and her whole congregation escaped death just by the grace of God, when bullets were fired into the church where they were praying ... not even one was hurt. God protects his own.' In the second, a 'terrorist' sought to kill a young pastor by making him eat crushed glass. The terrorist was suddenly 'caught by a deep sleep'. When he woke up he forgot all about the crushed glass. The next morning the young preacher was to be shot dead. Again in the middle of the night, 'God gave the ter[rorist] guards a deep sleep and he escaped home safely'.[31]

War was only one of the themes of the movement's canonical history of the 1970s. Self-reliance continued to be a dominant motif figuring alongside other types of perseverance. AOGA expanded in the face of opposition from angry spirits, Moslems and even the forces of nature. Insects, though, were open to aiding evangelical activity, as the following account of the construction of Chisumbanje Church reveals:

> The women fetched water from the Sabi River and the Lord protected them from being killed and eaten by crocodiles for 18 women, non Christians, were killed and eaten during that period ... [God] ... made the bees to chase away the soldiers who wanted to take away a place ... cleared for the house of the Lord.[32]

Such stories contain a good degree of preacher's licence but they nevertheless offer insight into the movement's remarkable growth. By 1977 its membership had increased more than twenty-fold, with 40,000 members in Rhodesia alone. It now had 185 branches across the territory, 34 of them in Salisbury. It could boast 15 church buildings with another six in progress. If anything the war stimulated expansion. With few church buildings in rural areas, ordinary AOGA members continued to meet and pray in their homes, usually unhindered by guerrillas. Mission churches were hampered by their perceived associations with colonialism and the more immediate withdrawal of expatriate personnel, but AOGA expanded from township to township, for the most part spread by ordinary church members. Indeed AOGA's perceived autonomy became a marketing strategy aimed at impressionable youth. A young pastor working with the Pentecostal Assemblies of Canada at Enkeldoorn, Chivu, lost many of his flock when they were told that he had been 'bought by missionaries'.[33]

A similar pattern of growth was taking place in Mozambique, which had eclipsed Malawi as AOGA's second largest transnational offshoot. By 1977 there were 50 assemblies in Mozambique, 32 in Malawi, five in Botswana and four in Zambia.[34] Movement of migrant labour from Mozambique into Rhodesia continued apace in the early 1970s. English was not the *lingua franca* but ChiShona sufficed in the central Manica Province. Guti began the Mozambican work with a brief campaign in 1969. He drove from Umtali to Machipanda and from there preached in Tete and Gaza provinces. He visited churches in Beira, Chimoio and Maputo and 'many people who were crippled, blind and those who had suffered from body diseases were healed in Jesus' name'.[35] The following year Guti sent Mateus Simau back to Mozambique to found a church in Chimoio. Simau had come to Salisbury as a labour migrant in 1960, found accommodation in Dzivarasekwa and worked as a carpenter. In 1963 he was converted by a relative and joined an assembly led by Joseph Choto. Choto encouraged his lively faith and soon he was ordained.

Once back in Mozambique, Simau worked in much the same manner as his Zimbabwean brethren. Towns and cities were targeted first, rural areas later. Congregations in cities such as Chimoio and Beira were built through a combination of door-to-door

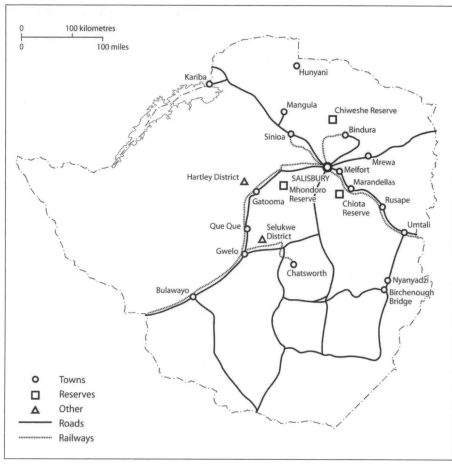

Map 4.1 EGEA and AOGA in Southern Rhodesia c. 1950s–1970s

work and small-scale open-air meetings. Sande conducted crusades in 1971 and 1972. As with AOGA's inception and numerous other nascent Pentecostal movements considered in this study, converts were attracted by powerful manifestations of the Holy Spirit. Prayer for the sick and deliverance for the demon-possessed were central. By 1972 a number of local pastors had joined Simau, but with them came pressure to re-affiliate to the better-funded International Assemblies of God. Some left, taking their churches with them. In 1974 Raphael Kupara, AOGA's administrative genius, entered Mozambique to register the movement as the Assemblee De Deus Africana (ADDA). By 1978 it had spread along the two main arteries into Rhodesia: the Beira and Tete corridors. But evangelism was never straightforward in Mozambique. Under the Portuguese, Catholicism had a near monopoly, while the Marxist Frelimo government, coming to power in 1975, was hostile to all religions. Simau was imprisoned three times between 1978 and 1981. Reflecting on this period, he revealed how the scriptures had sustained him: 'I was strengthened by the struggle of [King] David who fought the bear, then the lion and then Goliath.'[36]

Other Mozambican pastors were more fortunate. In Vila Fontes, on the Tete corridor, Pastor Nyakanyanza came to an understanding with local chiefs and party workers, possibly because his mission against 'witch doctors' was in line with Frelimo's attack on 'obscurantism'.[37] Low-key, localised evangelism, done mostly on foot, was crucial to the movement's success. Its public profile remained low as it gradually expanded its cell-like structure across townships and villages. As in Zimbabwe, its independence from missionary control saved it from the Marxist slur of association with 'capitalist imperialism' and made it difficult to dislodge.

Transnational expansion went forward in other neighbouring countries but with less vigour. The Malawian work continued to be animated by faction and ambition especially as Guti's nemesis Chitakata remained on the scene. In 1969, after power struggles, Chitakata split from the Independent Assemblies and founded his own African Assemblies of God, re-affiliating to Guti's AOGA (Chakanza, 1983: 6-7).[38] But fission and fusion continued, stimulated by missionary and African ambition and a broader political culture of Malawian nationalism. One Malawian assembly appealed unilaterally to Rhodesia against Chitakata, another affiliated to escape missionary authoritarianism. Between 1973 and 1974 AOGA reinvented itself as Forward in Faith International in Malawi, claiming only *affiliation* with the assemblies there. Relations with Chitakata deteriorated when he established connections with Guti's former white patron, the Rhodesian businessman F. Warrilow. Links were finally severed in 1977; loyal assemblies coalesced around D. Chiteka, a Malawian with strong Rhodesian connections, who was faithful to Guti. Alongside the transnational realpolitik, local evangelism continued: Chiteka founded assemblies in Ndirande, and F.S. Phiri returned to Blantyre from Rhodesia to found churches in Ntcheu and Chikwawa. Other Malawian assemblies moved under the control of AOGA's Mozambican arm in 1977.[39]

Two other transnational outgrowths, although much smaller, emerged through the same processes of labour migration and missionary activity. Zambia's linchpin was Pastor Mwanza. He had grown up in AOGA, Salisbury in the 1960s and 1970s, while his father worked for the Rhodesian railways. Guti sent him back to Zambia and work began, getting a small boost in 1977. While on a tour through central and east Africa, Guti persuaded two Zambians working with other Pentecostal movements to join AOGA's Zambian team. Another impressed Zambian promised a house. By the end of the year, however, the house had not materialised and one of the pastors had not joined. Guti sent a prominent elder from Rhodesian AOGA to help organise the work, but it remained small until after independence.[40] In 1974 Appiah Manjoro felt called to preach in Botswana. Her spell in Gaborone laid the foundations for a small number of assemblies. Later in the same year Abel Sande was sent there to encourage them.[41] Botswana's poor relations with the white minority regime in Rhodesia made movement between the two states difficult. The work there remained small but well organised, led by a local businessman–cum–pastor, Last Fundira.

Nationalism and Liberation

While printed testimonies and funding applications referred to the war in miraculous terms, the movement's Executive minutes and unpublished histories reveal there was no official engagement with its politics. The only formal reference to the war came in the context of a debate about whether 1977 Talents needed to be deferred because of the state of the economy. In the event it went ahead. The social and economic chaos the violence caused appeared but a mild inconvenience to the movement's leadership. Travel to neighbouring countries became more difficult and Guti was arrested returning from Mozambique in 1975 (Guti, 1994:17). Conventions previously held in rural areas were relocated to farms closer to Salisbury.[42] Otherwise it was business as normal. Ordinary AOGA adherents from Zambia, Malawi and Mozambique continued to travel into Rhodesia for annual conventions between 1974 and 1977. The movement's guidelines for the Ten Days of Prayer at the beginning of 1977, a period when the war was becoming more intense, remained completely focused on matters of holiness, personal transformation and church growth. There was no mention whatsoever of the political violence in the list of intercessions.[43]

In some respects the movement's leadership exhibited a naivety toward nationalist politics. While the liberation movements aligned themselves with strong anti-Western, anti-imperialist causes, AOGA's leaders appeared unashamedly impressed with the United States, keen to invite American speakers to their conferences and make full use of their resources. In the movement's publications, guerrillas were referred to as 'ters' in the same pejorative manner adopted by the Rhodesian authorities. If any of the socially mobile members were politically aligned it was to the pro–capitalist, pro–Western leader of the American Methodist Episcopal Church, Bishop Abel Muzorewa, although this was not an alliance one would readily admit to in independent Zimbabwe. For the most part, ordinary AOGA members persisted with a sectarian disregard for politics honed in the era of open mass nationalism, 1957-64. One prominent Highfield elder observed: 'As a Christian I could not be involved in politics. It was associated with violence, abuse and drink. And political meetings and rallies were held on Sundays.'[44]

However, AOGA's leadership was not unaffected by the spirit of the age. Its Pan-African vision and search for black autonomy grew stronger. In 1977 the movement changed its name from the racially bound and diminutive Assemblies of God Afri*can* to the expansive Assemblies of God Africa.[45] And Guti began to work out his critique of African cultural nationalism and mission Christianity, rooting the African Church in a rich Judaeo-Christian heritage. His visit to Israel in 1977 influenced him profoundly. He did not adopt the Christian Zionism espoused by CFNI but was prompted to re-read the Scriptures through African spectacles. In June 1979 he told a gathering of 3,000 people:

> Let me speak a little to my fellow Africans. Jesus is God. Jesus is not a white man. You might have seen a picture of a white man representing Jesus. I would like to tell you that in the days of our Lord Jesus, there were no cameras. Some clever fellow, who must have been white, has painted Jesus like a white. …
>
> If you go to Israel … you would be astonished to see a black Jew, you could easily mistake him for a black Rhodesian. So who can assume Jesus was white, he could easily have been black? And you know that when he was a baby Joseph and Mary brought him to Egypt, an African country – for security reasons.

The critique continued in September when Guti began to assert an African monotheism. He shared with his audience of 7,000 that:

> When I came from Israel I came with a burning heart wanting to tell people that he is our GOD.
> 1. In the Bible people paid lobola [bride price] but Europeans don't.
> 2. African people - Blacks pay lobola.
>
> In the olden days our people used to have the feast of harvest. Is it not there in the Bible? The person who brought the Bible should have explained that we worship the real God.

Many of these ideas about the African roots of Christianity would also be expanded and refined by Guti in the 1980s and 1990s. But when it came to the meaning of liberation he had a standard response that would remain foundational. Proselytism and personal transformation were the central objectives. The September Big Sunday of 1979, the last one before Independence, had a triumphal ring about it. It was held at the National Sports Centre, and eight pastors took turns in baptising 1,111 new converts while Guti preached. His main text was taken from Proverbs 14:34, 'righteousness exalteth a nation, but sin reproveth the nation'. Formal politics were rejected and in their stead he advocated an inner spiritual transformation:

> Everybody wants to belong to a righteous nation. But who can make a good nation? From the knowledge of the word of God, it is only God who can make us a good nation. No one can enter into someone's heart and make him good…We have all got to come to God. He is the only one who can change things.[46]

A New Indigenous Player on the Pentecostal Field

By 1980 AOGA's membership probably stood somewhere around 45-50,000. It had become a significant player in the Pentecostal field, recruiting members from rival movements such as the Apostolic Faith Mission, the Pentecostal Assemblies of Canada and the Assemblies of God (USA). The latter had initially represented a new challenge to Guti's movement. In 1968 AOG (USA) missionary Paul Wright and his wife transferred from Malawi to Salisbury to reopen American work there. They drew up a new constitution and doctrinal statement and invited a number of Pentecostal ministers to join. In the event the new denomination was based substantially on the work of Shadrek Lekuku (see Chapter 3). The revamped AOGUSA thus operated in Guti's backyard, with assemblies extending out from Highfield into adjacent townships in a similar pattern to AOGA. But AOGUSA had the advantage of external resources. In 1970 it organised the Impact 70 Good News Crusade with high-profile meetings in Rhodesia's major cities. In Salisbury it hired the Gwanzura Stadium, attracting as many as 6000 people to evening rallies.

But by the end of the 1970s the AOGUSA comprised no more than two ordained ministers, one licensed minister and only eight congregations. In 1981, Larry Malcolm, an American Assemblies of God missionary sent to revive the work, reflected on the lessons to be learnt from the previous decade. The big campaigns had failed to translate into conversions and church membership. Large meetings 'impressed' but did not 'win people'. Missionaries and ministers had not followed up the thousands who had responded to the preacher's message. What worked better was 'where a missionary worked with the local pastor on a small scale ... in the local church meeting place, a rented hall, in the open air, or a small tent'. And in this context it was crucial that 'the [African] pastor was active and did some of the preaching'. The movement had also been too American in its literature and programmes. Its training had been too academic and intense. Potential ministers had been required to submit to a four-year programme based on the US curriculum. A simplified training in an evening Bible school would have been sufficient. Worse still, as the war had intensified, missionaries had proven a liability. 'Black pastors did not want to be seen with white missionaries or have them visit their churches for fear of reprisal.' The war also made mass evangelism impossible except in local churches in the cities, and travel to conferences and meetings had been difficult. Missionaries had put up buildings and 'not let locals do their share' and hence congregations did not feel they owned their place of worship. Missionaries had created the impression that 'a building was necessary to develop a strong church'.

The manner in which the AOGUSA had rebuilt its work by grafting itself onto existing assemblies had also stored up problems for the future. Many of the pastors and members did not share the standards, doctrines and methods of the new organisation and resented them being imposed in a hierarchical manner. Lekuku continued to act as *de facto* leader, refusing to submit to church discipline when he erred. Between 1974 and 1978 the church was embroiled in eight different court cases with him. The litigation was an expensive drain on resources. Its coverage on the front page of Rhodesian newspapers was disastrous, causing half of the movement's pastors and congregations to leave. The most successful aspects of the AOGUSA programme had been the elements for youth and women. The latter had 'responded well to Bible studies, handicraft projects and fund raising'.[47]

Malcolm's report is a useful summary of AOGA's best practice. The movement's emphasis on African autonomy, grass roots organisation, local evangelism, self-reliance, even strong discipline, were key to its remarkable growth. But this was only half the story. AOGA also provided personal security, a dimension best brought to life through the remarkable testimony of Debson Chivizano, a long-standing member of the Highfields Revival Centre:

> I was born in Chiweshe in 1950 but by the 1970s I was living in Highfield Engineering. I was very sick. My skin leaked blood. I played the Mbira [finger piano]. My half-brother was possessed and

made me learn it so that his *mudzimu* [ancestor spirit] could speak to the family. Many members of my family were possessed by demons. My first and second sisters were mediums and my first brother had such a strong spirit that he lived in the forest chained up. At times we had to flee him.

One evening in 1975 as I was returning from Chiweshe I came across Bill John Chigwenembe preaching alone at the Terminus. I was going to the pub. I had just 6 cents left and was on the way to Katanga Beer Hall. I liked dancing to Jiti music on the Jukebox. It cost 5 cents a record. I could also play music on the banjo. I often fought over women but usually lost because I was so weak.

I went across to listen to Bill John. I did not repent but I asked him if he could heal me. I was stopped from listening because of ancestral spirits. I was playing the Mbira all night to those who were possessed. Bill John took me to see Manjoro. We knelt in the church that Saturday night. Rev Fundira laid hands on me and I was healed.

I went home and received a message to go and play Mbira for a girl who was possessed. I followed three men. Evil spirits led us to the house because we had no address. I started to play but the spirit did not come. So at 10.00pm we departed. They gave me a small clay pot full of beer to drink.

That night I dreamed that I was baptised in the Holy Spirit. The Holy Spirit wanted to chase sickness from my body. The Holy Spirit was shouting 'Go Away Satan'. The Holy Spirit was a person dressed in white, like a *Mupostori* [apostle of Maranke or Masowe]. I woke up and a voice said go to that church. I bathed and ran to the church. I sat as normal for the first time. The Reverend Sande was preaching. He called people to receive Christ. But I did not understand. It seemed that I was in another country.

After I was healed I was still a loafer. On the following Tuesday Chigwenembe said to me: 'This week you will have a job'. The Holy Spirit was speaking to me in *Chilapalapa*. It was chasing my demons away in *Chilapalapa* like the Vapostori [apostles] do. The Vapostori use *Chilapalapa* when speaking in tongues. They say 'Pooma Satani'. I went to Henry Sholts in Southerton [Township] the following Thursday with no NIC card. I had sometimes worked as a labourer with a man who had one. I got a job as a painter.

That second week I dreamt of an iron ironing lice out of a blanket. The lice represented poverty. My poverty had gone away. I also dreamt of being cleansed in the body. I had been very ill. Sometimes I leaked so much blood that I could hardly stand. My skin felt dry. I could not go anywhere.

I started working for the church. The church started building a Bible college near Mhondoro [Reserve] but it was too far out. So we brought AMFCC [Africa Multination for Christ College] nearer town. The church got richer and bigger. Buildings started to come. And with Talents we began to buy cars for Overseers. In the 1970s the church was renting schools [meeting in classrooms] or was in houses. But we built in Kambazuma and Tafara [Townships]. I was a dagga boy [builder's mate] when we built.

The church helped me a lot. I was not seeing clearly or hearing clearly. My body was like a guitar with just two strings left on it. I had a poor memory. The Holy Spirit pushed me to read the Bible from 10.00pm to 6.00am. I joined a prayer band. We were going outside to Bacaster to open ground to pray. To begin with I did not memorise stories but just understood them. Today I can memorise them. I stopped drinking, fighting, visiting prostitutes and playing the Mbira.

These days we can just play the Mbira for God like the guitar. I am filled with the Holy Spirit and am asking a friend to buy an Mbira for me. The *Vadzimu* [ancestors] have been chased away by Pentecostal churches.[48]

This testimony differs from others cited in this chapter. It is not an abbreviated story printed for the purposes of publicity or proselytism but a personal reminiscence collected during interview. Like many testimonies, it built on Biblical narratives, in this case the Gospel account of the Gerasene Demoniac (Luke 8: 26-38), but it combined with a personal story in a way that animated the movement's history over the preceding two decades. Chivizano's personal trajectory mirrored that of the movement: a story of progress and prosperity. The testimony shed light upon the early appeal and subsequent development of AOGA. A labour migrant caught up in the Highfield popular culture of drink, dance and womanising, Chivizano encountered the movement through an evangelist preaching where people gathered at the bus terminus. At this stage the movement was a small community with a close-knit group of pastors who were able to draw him into a network of care. His personal transformation was holistic, embracing a range of issues related to his personal security, rather than just a straightforward conversion. His remaking was more a result of the ministry of hands and the power of dreams than the initially incomprehensible words of a preacher. Indeed conversion was never mentioned.

First Chivizano was healed. His sick body, which he compared to a partially strung guitar, was mended. He could attend church with a healthy body, a sound mind, and properly clothed. Next he found work. Only slowly, as his ancestral spirits were defeated, did he come to understand Christian doctrine. Initially his new religion was a religion of power encounters in which the Holy Spirit was the major player. God the Father and Christ the Son did not figure. The battle was cast in dualistic terms between the Holy Spirit and Satan. The Devil was appropriately ordered out of his body – *Pooma Satani*, in *Chilapalapa*, the lingua franca of Southern Africa's labouring poor. Chivizano was liberated from the world of the ancestors and drawn out of the destructive township culture of drink, violence and promiscuity. At the same time he was drawn into a community of prayer and Bible study. His literacy and intellect increased. He was better able to comprehend both the physical and spiritual dimensions of life. He memorised scripture and began to rebuild his life upon it. As Chivizano moved forward so too did AOGA. It constructed church buildings and a Bible school, projects in which he participated. It purchased vehicles for its Overseers. The story looked backwards to one of the movement's religious antecedents and looked forwards to a future development. There were suggestions of the movement's shared heritage with spirit-type independency. Chivizano had a good deal of familiarity with the practices of the Vapostori. And, like the Vapostori, AOGA adherents continued to pray together on open ground.

The testimony finished with an anecdote about the culturalisation of traditional religion. By the mid-1990s, when the interview was conducted, the movement had moved so far from its roots that the *Mbira* had lost its associations with possession cults and had become a simple musical instrument, a harmless symbol of an indigenous Zimbabwean culture. It could be embraced and used as an instrument of worship.

Conclusion

In the 1970s AOGA began the slow transformation into a denomination. There was a growing concern for property and place, the training of ministers, and the attainment of official recognition. There was also an effort to establish bureaucratic procedures and a desire for the things of the world. But the new bureaucracy was patrimonial, dominated by Guti. The absolute sharing and equality that characterised the movement in the pioneering sectarian phase of the 1950s and 1960s gave way to practices of structured generosity and a concern for status. Collective entrepreneurship remained important in the practice of Talents but there was a growing emphasis on individual social mobility and personal accumulation. All of these processes would continue into the 1980s and 1990s (P. Werbner, 1990: 327-8).

In other respects the movement remained highly sectarian, proud of its separation from politics and disparaging toward ecumenism. Evangelism and divine healing remained central. Its appeal and strength lay in its synthesis of Christian traditions. AOGA's emphasis on healing and exorcism stood it in the tradition of both indigenous and missionary Pentecostalism. Its teachings on industry and self-reliance drew from both Ethiopianism and the spirit-type independency of Masowe and Maranke. But in its structures and procedures it eagerly sought to 'do what missionaries did'. Indeed AOGA's love of tented crusades placed it firmly within the Evangelical/Pentecostal tradition. In the 1980s and 1990s AOGA would evolve further by borrowing from the global Born-again movement.

The external funding Guti drew into AOGA was not the key to its success. The movement's growth lay in its ability to address the aspirations and desire for personal security of ordinary Southern Africans. Nevertheless, American resources were important. They reinforced Guti's position as unassailable leader, but more significantly, they provided a basis for sustaining AOGA's autonomy from Zimbabwean nationalism. Here the church followed a strikingly similar trajectory to that of the trade union movement. Indeed the individual abuses of power and rivalries that came with the injection of outside funds into the union movement would visit AOGA in the 1980s (Phimister and Raftopoulos, 1997: 82-9). However, on the eve of independence AOGA was like a coiled spring ready to take full advantage of the new dispensation.

Notes

1 Int.DM62, Abel Sande.
2 'Biography of Ezekiel Guti', ms, ca. 1985, file, Histories; 'CFNI 1972-73 Enrollment' & Courses, file CFNI, ZAW; Int.DM110, Howard Reents. Int.DM102, Randy Bozarth; Int.DM107, John McLennon.
3 See *Kuwadzana*, produced by Highfield Township Management, September 1964–May 1970. The December 1968 edition records 'over 70 000 of us attend cinema once a year'. The figures appear to refer to Highfield alone.
4 *Rhodesia Herald*, 14 May 1973.
5 Executive Minutes, 23 June 1973, file, AOGA Correspondence, 1964-80, ZAW.
6 S.B. Stevens CFNI to Ezekiel Guti, 16 January 1974, & correspondence relating to The Native Church Crusade 1973-1996, file CFNI, ZAW.
7 Ezekiel Guti to Brother Hodges, CFNI, 25 May 1977, file, AOGA Correspondence 1964-80; Executive Minutes, 6 August 1977, ZAW.
8 Freda Lindsay, 1984, *Freda. The Widow who took up the Mantle*, Dallas, Christ for the Nations, Inc, 228-32.
9 *The Macedonian Call*, vol.1, no.1, 20 May 1972, published by FIFM International. This appears to have been the only issue of the journal ever published.
10 Files, CFNI & AOGA Correspondence 1964-80, ZAW.
11 Report on Deeper Life Conference, November 1974, file, Deeper Life 1974 –96, ZAW. See correspondence between Guti and Idahosa, February 1975-May 1978, file CFNI, ZAW.
12 Report on Deeper Life Conference, November 1974, file, Deeper Life 1974 –96 & Executive Minutes, 8 May 1979, ZAW.

[13] Easter Youth Conventions were held at Rainbow Farm, near Salisbury, press cutting (name not included), April 1974, file Press Cuttings. The Provinces were: Abel Sande, Mashonaland; Caleb Ngorima, Manicaland; Lazarus Kataya, Victoria; Joseph Choto, Matabeland; Raphael Kupara, Midlands; Mateus Simao, Mozambique, cutting ca. 1974, press cutting, (name not included) file, Press Cuttings, ZAW.

[14] Report on Deeper Life Conference, November 1974, file, Deeper Life 1974-96, ZAW; Executive Minutes 16-19 February 1978, ZAW.

[15] Report on Deeper Life Conference, November 1974, file, Deeper Life 1974 –96, ZAW.

[16] Executive Minutes, 8 May 1979, ZAW.

[17] Ibid.

[18] Report on Deeper Life Conference, November 1974, file, Deeper Life 1974-96, ZAW.

[19] Int.DM16, Joseph Choto; Int.DM87, Wilson Dube.

[20] Int.DM62, Abel Sande; Int.DM16, Joseph Choto.

[21] 'Rev Guti's Organization' ca. 1977, file, Histories, ZAW.

[22] Report on Highfield, 1977, file, AOGA Correspondence 1964-80; Executive Minutes, 2 December 1977, ZAW.

[23] G. Erwin, ca. 1997. *That Reminds me of a Story*, 6-7.

[24] AOGA Balance Sheet, 30 November 1977, file, Finance 1976-96, ZAW.

[25] The Ezekiel Evangelistic Crusade Newsletter, May 1979, file Histories, ZAW.

[26] Ezekiel Guti, Big Sunday, 10 June 1979, file, Histories, ZAW

[27] 'Not I But Christ', ms., ca. 1977, file, Histories, ZAW.

[28] Ibid.; Big Sunday 10 June 1979, file Histories, ZAW.

[29] Int.DM62, Abel Sande.

[30] Progress Reports for Native Churches Crusade, 21 April 1981, 1 August 1978, file CFNI, ZAW.

[31] 'Miracles During Times of War', ca. 1980, file, Histories, ZAW.

[32] Chisumbanje, Final Report, Native Church Crusade, 29 January 1982, file, CFNI, ZAW.

[33] Int.DM87, Wilson Dube.

[34] 'Not I But Christ', ms., ca. 1977, file, Histories, ZAW.

[35] Ibid.

[36] 'Mozambique (and Malawi)' ca. 1978, file, Mozambique: Missions, ZAW; Int.DM66, Mateus Simau; Sermon, Deeper Life Conference, 6 February 1996.

[37] 'Mozambique (and Malawi)' c. 1978, file, Mozambique: Missions, Africa, ZAW.

[38] Special meeting of the Chiloni Church, Blantyre, 1969, file, Malawi: Missions, ZAW.

[39] Correspondence, 2 February 1972, 31 December 1972, 4 January 1973, Minutes of Meeting, Blantyre 6 January 1973, correspondence 12 July 1973 and 16 May 1974, file, Malawi: Missions; Executive Minutes, 23 June 1973, file, AOGA correspondence 1964-80, 'Mozambique (and Malawi)' c. 1978, file, Mozambique: Missions. Executive Committee Minutes, 6 September 1977, ZAW; Int.DM23, Ezekiel Guti.

[40] Executive Meetings 6 August and 2 December 1977, Executive Minute Book, ZAW.

[41] Int.DM41, Bartholomew and Appiah Manjoro; E. Guti, 'To Whom it May Concern', 7 September 1974, file, AOGA correspondence, 1964-80, ZAW.

[42] Int.DM50, Luxford Muchenje.

[43] 'Ten Days of Prayer and Fasting', letter from Ezekiel Guti to Congregations, 16 December 1976, file, AOGA correspondence, 1964-80, ZAW.

[44] Int.DM50, Luxford Muchenje.

[45] Executive Committee Minutes, 2 December 1977, ZAW.

[46] Big Sunday, 10 June 1979, 9 September 1979, file, Histories, ZAW.

[47] Larry Malcolm 1981, 'Development of the Assemblies of God in Zimbabwe', mimeograph; John Elliot, 1990, 'History of General Council and Other A/G Groups'; Files, Formative Period & Personnel 1968-71, AOGZ; *Pentecostal Evangel*, 28 May 1971, 18 July 1971.

[48] Int.DM15, Debson Chizivano.

5

'A Sleeping Giant'
Religious Globalisation, History & Identity
in the 1980s

Introduction

In the late 1970s there were two parallel and somewhat contradictory responses to the military advance of the liberation forces. The first was an Internal Settlement aimed at sidelining the radical Patriotic Front of ZANU and ZAPU and their military wings by electing a more moderate African leader. An agreement signed in March 1978 paved the way for the election in April 1979 of Bishop Abel Muzorewa as the Prime Minister of what was called Zimbabwe-Rhodesia. But white Rhodesian Front politicians retained a disproportionate influence in the new government, and Muzorewa, who lacked popular legitimacy, was seen as little more than a white puppet. The guerrilla war continued. In 1979 Britain led a more concerted international effort to bring peace, culminating in the Constitutional Conference in Lancaster House, London in September 1979. The Conference took place with considerable participation from Zimbabwe, including the Patriotic Front, making possible relatively free and fair elections in March 1980. ZANU/PF swept to power to form Zimbabwe's first independent government, bringing significant changes to the lives of ordinary black citizens. Under the statesmanship of Robert Mugabe,the new government concentrated on 'reconstruction, reconciliation and redistribution under an apparently socialist banner carefully tempered by pragmatism'(Hammar and Raftopoulos, 2004: 4). Donor assistance, both capitalist and communist, flooded into Zimbabwe as the most recent and most favoured addition to the international community, enabling the rise of another independent African developmentalist state. Its priorities were to extend healthcare and education to the African majority, reverse racially based inequalities in land and asset distribution, and ensure fundamental civic and human rights for all its citizens. Great strides were made in many of these endeavours, excepting land ownership, which remained predominantly in the hands of several thousand white farmers.

The new political climate accompanied by the end of relative isolation also had a profound effect on Zimbabwean Christianity. It allowed for the greater movement of people, ideas and resources, enabling Zimbabwean Christians to engage more fully with a rapidly globalising Born-again movement. The global Born-again movement presented ZAOGA with both threats and opportunities. There was a vast proliferation of new ministries and fellowships enhancing the range of sources to which Guti could turn for money to build his movement and his own network of patronage. But ZAOGA's continued growth caused growing dissent amongst Guti's lieutenants, who wanted a greater share of the movement's resources and who were tempted by the possibility of founding rival organisations in a vastly diversified religious field. The Born-again movement also had strong homogenising tendencies in terms of doctrine and the styles of preaching, proselytism and worship propagated by an increasingly vital electronic media. There was a danger that ZAOGA would lose its distinctiveness to a generic Born-again culture. The solution to these problems of factionalism and boundary maintenance lay in sacred history: the construction of identity through the repeated narration and enactment of a part real and part imagined past.

There was also the more immediate problem of establishing a *modus operandi* with a new regime that jealously guarded its legitimacy. But Guti sought more than the establishment of cordial relations with the state to safeguard ZAOGA's future. He wanted recognition for his own achievements within his increasingly prominent movement. ZAOGA would cast aside its sectarian outlook and enter the political arena.

Encounters with the Global Born-again Movement

Independence exposed ZAOGA members to a rapidly changing religious landscape, increasingly shaped by the USA. The Born-again movement was gathering pace and within it the Charismatic strand was in the ascendant. And as Charismatic and Pentecostal Christianity increased in significance it began to change in nature. There was a move amongst 'spirit-filled' believers from cultural alienation to the sanction of Christian alternatives. Charismatic Christianity radically cut across denominational boundaries, drawing together all those open to the Gifts of the Spirit. Renewed Catholics and Protestants (usually Evangelicals) found themselves in close communion with Pentecostals, with whom they shared a belief in the practice of tongues, divine healing, prophecy and exorcism. The Charismatic movement did not subscribe to all Pentecostal doctrine. For instance, it rejected Baptism in the Holy Spirit as an essential post-conversion experience. Nevertheless Charismatics stood squarely in the trajectory of the Restorationist Pentecostalism discussed in Chapter 3. Those seeking a restoration of the Latter Rain (of the Holy Spirit) had raised expectations of sympathetic leaders within radical Evangelical circles and the historic denominations. The global salvation/healing crusades conducted by the likes of T.L. Osborn and Oral Roberts had 'created a variety of non-denominational agencies and institutions that helped sustain and channel interest in charismatic worship and spiritual gifts'. And the ministry of David du Plessis, an Assemblies of God pastor and international spokesperson for the movement, 'gave Pentecostalism visibility, first among ecumenical leaders of mainstream denominations and then Roman Catholicism'. New Christian unity amongst 'spirit-filled' believers prompted new non-denominational organisations of which the Full Gospel Business Men's Fellowship International (FGBMFI) was the most prominent (Blumhofer, 1993:223-4). The Charismatic movement also created its own devotional literature and new styles of worship. Songs, choruses and gospel music accompanied by bands with electric guitars and keyboards replaced or supplemented hymn singing, encouraging youth participation. Finally, there was a renewed drive away from denominationalism, which spawned a host of new independent and semi-independent churches with aspirational names such as Highway Assembly or Abundant Life Centre, led by a charismatic pastor and his wife. Amongst these, the Pentecostals might retain a loose connection with Assemblies of God or the Pentecostal Holiness Church, and the Charismatics might participate in a loose network of like-minded movements, but their autonomy complemented the broader American culture of free-enterprise and individualism. The movement was propelled forwards by a new generation of Bible schools of which Christ for the Nations Institute, Dallas, was a prime example.

Although Pentecostalism's engagement with Charismatic and Evangelical culture prompted a plethora of new organisations, there were countervailing homogenising forces that bound these different strands of Christianity into a broader Born-again movement. There was a common pool of techniques of preaching and proselytism, shared forms of organisation and leadership, and a corpus of songs and hymns. New practices in divine healing and deliverance spread rapidly around convention circuits, carried by the latest Born-again celebrities.

America was the dynamo of charismatic renewal as it had been in the birth of the original Pentecostal movement and its restoration in the 1950s and 1960s. But the USA was not the only source of religious change. David du Plessis was South African by birth and had risen through the ranks of the Apostolic Faith Mission. Another influential figure was the British Assemblies of God pastor Donald Gee. Moreover, new ideas and practices spread rapidly, aided by air travel and the electronic media. West Africa, particularly Nigeria, was the first part of the continent to embrace Charismatic Christianity. The movement started among university Christian groups in Ibadan in 1970 and graduates were soon founding their own organisations. It spread in a similar manner in East Africa as the Fellowship of Christian Unions (Focus), which linked student groups in several nations, facilitating renewal across borders (Ojo, 2001: 3-6).

Because the charismatic movement drew its constituency from members of the historic denominations and from among more socially mobile Born-agains, it was more inclined to engage with contemporary culture. Televangelists such as Jim and Tammy Bakker and Jimmy Swaggart influenced the process enormously. Secular popular culture was 'sanitised' by adding 'Jesus language'. Christian media 'marketed everything from Christian rock and soap operas to Christian exercise videos, sex manuals, and diet programs'. Theological shifts both mirrored and legitimated this cultural change. Stress on Christ's imminent return was dampened by a growing emphasis on the celebration of the Spirit and on blessings, usually material in nature. The religious experience that had led to social ostracism among first generation Pentecostals now 'seemed a ticket to health, prosperity and general well-being'. In a fluid, 'Spirit' orientated culture, Pentecostal and Charismatic preachers, writers, and artists drew from a secular vocabulary of self-help and individualism. They moulded a new faith congruent with the values and technology of Middle America (Blumhofer, 1993: 256-60), a faith that would appeal to African elites in the neo-liberal world of the late 1980s and 1990s.

Technological and cultural change within the USA and Europe revolutionised and revitalised its missionary enterprise. As Born-again Christianity grew in significance it radically altered conceptions of mission. Long-standing missionary organisations such as the British Baptist Union and the American United Presbyterian Church continued to send workers overseas, but recognised that Africa's vibrant church did not need evangelists so much as lecturers in theology, medics, Bible-translators, and development workers. But the Born-again movement persisted in its evangelical activity. In the 1980s, Zimbabwe, like many other African countries, experienced an increase of almost 250 per cent in the number of Protestant missionaries, many of them American and Born-again. Some of the wealthier independent American ministries or fellowships could afford to send their own missionaries, or even set up their own Bible colleges and eventually found new denominations. Financial constraints on other Born-again Christians caused them to channel their missionary impulses through a host of new non-denominational bodies such as Youth With a Mission (YWAM) or Campus Crusade (Gifford, 1994: 519; 1998). Some Christian leaders saw work in Africa as no more than an adjunct to their teaching ministries based in the United States or Europe. The new free-market, Spirit-orientated culture brought forth a new generation of religious consultants who touted their religious wares on business cards and letterheads:

Pulpit Supply Seminars and Bible Studies with transparencies
Benefits of the Cross
End-time Events & Prophecy
Marriage & Family
New Age, Acts etc

Ordained pastor and international evangelist in spirit, word and song.

These consultants preached the same message to respectable middle-class audiences in Houston and Harare, Pittsburgh and Pretoria.

While the new generation of Born-again missionaries and teachers were animated by a similar desire to evangelise and share gifts of the Spirit that had motivated previous generations, they were nevertheless influenced by wider cultural changes. Notions of sacrifice that had inspired the Pentecostal pioneers to offer decades of missionary service were diluted by a desire for instant results. For the price of a few hundred dollars a month in sponsorship, a small American ministry could attach to itself a sizeable African denomination, gaining a successful mission outreach at minimal human cost. A good deal of the new mission work was virtual mission. Roving American preachers and evangelists returned home with videos of themselves addressing large African gatherings. These films were shown to local audiences and accompanied by published accounts of mass conversions and baptism in the Holy Spirit, peppered with numerous miracles of healing and exorcism. Printed and electronic media circulated amongst Born-again brethren in sister organisations, creating the impression of a vibrant missionary enterprise. But, beneath all this religious hype, vast movements such as ZAOGA retained firm control over the work of church building and leadership. External resources profoundly influenced the structures and politics of leadership but Western doctrines were quickly appropriated and localised.

Some Born-again missionaries trained in institutions like the Fuller Theological Seminary, Pasadena, or Wheaton College, Illinois, were better informed about shifts within world Christianity and interpreted their vocation as supporting vibrant national churches in Africa or Latin America. But a well-intentioned desire to work with the indigenous leaders of local organisations that remained unaccountable also strengthened large movements such as ZAOGA, whose leadership continued to consolidate itself with injections of outside funding into its networks of patronage.

'Strong Fat Churches': Expansion and Professionalisation

Evangelism and church growth remained ZAOGA's priority, and the social and economic change that accompanied independence made it easier to achieve these goals. With an end to segregation, more socially mobile members moved into new areas of Zimbabwean cities. Within Salisbury, now renamed Harare after the renowned African Township, ZAOGA adherents migrated across the railway lines, first to former coloured suburbs such as Waterfalls and then to the margins of the former white suburbs, such as the Avenues area north of the city centre. Those prosperous enough to live in the plush northern suburbs were still few, but church members who were domestic servants swelled their numbers. Others were low-paid manual workers and general hands who lived in servants' quarters, or who rented (often shared) rooms from richer church members in larger suburban houses. A growing body of ZAOGA members who were students at the polytechnic and university joined them. Enhanced communication, increasing social mobility and the state's new developmental agenda swelled the ranks of the proselytisers. Nurses, teachers and civil servants in rural areas joined returning labour migrants in spreading ZAOGA's message beyond the towns and cities.

The movement also evolved formal evangelistic strategies to complement the expansion that accompanied the movement of people. The plan was two-fold: first, to reach geographical areas formerly untouched by the movement; secondly, to reach new social categories. Beyond that, there was a desire to adopt a 'born-again' style – a discourse, an organisational outlook and a positive approach to the media and related technologies. Such a style was not only more suited to outreach but also facilitated the movement of people and resources from the global Born-again movement.

The locations of unevangelised peoples were plotted on a map and the church was organised into twelve provinces so that expansion could be more effectively co-ordinated. It was seen as a priority to expand from urban areas into the reserves, now called communal areas.[1] New enlarged crusade teams were created, such as those led by Paul Saungweme and Bill John Chigwenembe. Sande and Guti had tutored these men, but their operations were slicker. Zimbabwean Pentecostals learnt from Reinhard Bonnke's Christ for All Nations crusades, held in the country during 1980, 1984 and 1986 (Gifford, 1987).[2] But the younger evangelists also drew stylistically from preachers like Jimmy Swaggart, Jimmy Bakker, Benny Hinn and John Avanzini, whose video- and audio-tapes were available locally. Gospel music was now used to draw crowds, and the teams developed impressive musical line-ups: male vocalists with sharp haircuts and smooth voices, and backing groups of pretty girls in sleek satin dresses accompanied by musicians on electric guitars and the ubiquitous Hammond organ. These crusade teams often followed ordinary church members back into rural areas to boost fledgling churches. The movement's musical culture was further enriched from the mid-1980s with the growth of regional choirs. Each had its own uniform and range of songs, some locally composed, and did its best to outclass rivals in exciting singing competitions. Greater utility was made of the print and electronic media. The movement began to print its own tracts to supplement preaching. In 1982 Raphael Kupara was the first ZAOGA member to speak in the nightly slots on TV.[3] The leadership also began to use press releases to raise its own national profile. In 1983, for instance, it released the following statement:

Zimbabwe Assemblies of God Africa International Resolution to Change Title

At a meeting of the ZIMBABWE ASSEMBLIES OF GOD AFRICA National Executive, held at Harare recently, it was resolved that the TITLE "PRESIDENT" in respect of REV Ezekiel H. Guti founder of the largest indigenous church organisation that covers Southern, Eastern and Central Africa, should now be void and that the TITLE "ARCHBISHOP" now take its place. [4]

As ZAOGA grew, it developed a rich associational life of 'ministries' for wives, husbands and youth out of existing local church fellowships (Guti, 1999: 129). Such associations not only served to mitigate the potential dullness and alienation of institutional church life but also acted as new modes of evangelism and church expansion. Intended to be non-denominational, they were aimed at those unwilling to set foot in normal church services. Given that they were clearly founded and dominated by ZAOGA members, they came into conflict with the leaders of the historic mission churches, who saw them as vehicles for sheep-stealing.[5] Names and styles were lifted directly from organisations encountered by Guti and his wife Eunor but their practices were subsequently Africanised. The most significant association by far was the Gracious Women's Fellowship, officially founded in 1986 for the purpose of evangelising women and saving their marriages. Its aims and structures were lifted directly out of the famous American Women Aglow Fellowship but were re-written ZAOGA-style. Its government was to be more hierarchical, centred on a National and International President based at ZAOGA head office. Weekly studies of the Bible were to be replaced by study of internally produced Gracious Study books. There was a stronger emphasis on giving and the procedures for the handling of money and more emphasis on restoring family relationships, including those with in-laws. Lastly, there was to be more evangelism and hospitality.[6]

Guti first had a vision to reach 'high' and 'educated' people during his training in Dallas in 1971; a decade later it was still unrealised. His first solution was a new drive for order and dignity in the church. Services had to be conducted with reverence. There had to be proper teaching on giving, and announcements had to be made before and not after the worship. Weddings, funerals and Holy Communion had to be conducted with solemnity. There was also a renewed emphasis on financial propriety. Accounts had to be audited and property registered and money banked before it was spent. 'If the church is not dignified', Guti told a 1983 Executive Meeting, 'we will lose all the high people. Everything must be done in order.' It was the specific task of the Overseer to 'reach the high people of the city'. In a coded message to some of his co-founders, he chided those Overseers who did want to study, warning them that 'in future the church will have many educated people'.[7]

An effective Bible school was now crucial to the movement's growth and survival, not only because it needed a more sophisticated pastorate to meet the needs of educated members but also because the movement was growing so quickly. By 1985 ZAOGA had more than 700 assemblies in Zimbabwe alone. There were simply not enough pastors to go round. In the meantime Guti kept alive the pattern of small meetings in homes, led by a deacon or elder, that had animated the movement in its early days. '[In] many places the church relies on the pastor but we want a strong fat church ... No one should backslide because the leader knows his people.'[8]

Guti looked to the United States for personnel to get the school established, believing Americans to be 'better organised than Africans'. His first appointment was Paul Grier, a Texan, who also studied with Guti at CFNI in 1971. Another Texan, Wiley

Perry, followed, then Bruce Coble and Ronnie Meek from Tennessee. Each of these acted as Director of the school in charge of curriculum, timetabling and other matters of administration. Culturally the school retained a strong African input with an African Principal, Jason Marowa, who worked alongside the American Director, in charge of staff and student concerns. Given his prior experience of AFM missionaries, Guti was careful to appoint Americans sympathetic to ZAOGA's vision. Perry did clash with Guti over conditions in the Bible school that had led to a strike,but on the whole the Americans were loath to criticise Guti's authoritarianism, interpreting it as merely cultural. Moreover, they were only too aware of the excesses of their own American church leaders, most notably the televangelists mentioned above. All saw their position in the Bible school as a remarkable evangelical opportunity.

Another sympathetic American was Gayle Erwin from California who would eventually become one of Guti's biographers. The two had first met at a national renewal conference in Salisbury in 1978 where Erwin's teaching on 'Servanthood', and his simple narrative preaching style, had been very popular. They met again in South Africa in 1980, after which Erwin was invited to Deeper Life Conferences until 1986. Salisbury in the late 1970s reminded Erwin of Mississippi, where he had spent his childhood in the 1940s and '50s. Erwin admired Guti for the way he had led his people in the face of racism and poverty, and helped him recruit Coble and Meek. He subsequently provided Guti with hospitality and preaching itineraries to raise money for the college. The preaching circuits usually comprised independent charismatic assemblies, Calvary Chapels and Assemblies of God Churches too small to attract famous American speakers. Nevertheless, they enjoyed the novelty of African preachers: their story telling, powerful testimonies, English [sic] accents, and gifts of healing and exorcism. And such preachers could be rewarded richly with love-offerings ranging from US$200 to US$2,000. Some Africans such as Nevers Mumba or George Chikowa were immensely popular, but most needed fresh itineraries each year so as not to wear out their welcome.[9]

In his travels through the USA and, to a lesser extent, Europe, Guti also developed a host of sympathetic contacts with small semi-independent churches operating in a congregational AOG-type framework. Such churches were looking for a 'mission' connection and donated sums of between US$500 and US$1,000 towards ZAOGA's work. If such donations were paid into an American account registered to an American office in Plano Texas, taxes could be saved. In return, donors received personalised or circular letters offering Christian greetings and news of crusading activities, conversion figures, and stories of repentance and deliverance. There were also some fairly big donors such as Dan Duke from Florida, and Paul Grier, Doyle Davidson and Mrs Lindsay, all from Texas. Their gifts were used to build dormitories and a chapel at the Bible college. Other donations were used to buy cars and trucks for overseers and evangelists.[10]

Donations also continued to come from CFNI's Native Churches Project. In 1984 Guti received US$6,700 to roof four buildings and in the following year US$10,400 for ten more. The movement had 55 church buildings by around 1982 and some 75 three years later. By this stage the Archbishop's ministry was used to legitimate CFNI's mission. A 'product' of the Dallas Institute, he and his wife were cited in the organisation's hyperbolised promotional literature as having 'helped start some 2000 churches in Zimbabwe … plus neighbouring ones in African countries'. In return for his good services Guti got to act as a 'gate-keeper', vetting applications to study at CFNI and for various types of financial support.[11]

In the eyes of his people Guti was a hero. He had built an organisation over which no white man ruled. And because he continued to mask the external sources of funding, it appeared as if ZAOGA was solely the result of tenacious African self-reliance. His leadership began to take on a cultic appearance, with members praying to the 'God of Ezekiel'. His wife Eunor came to realise that her position within the organisation hinged upon her husband's reputation, and so she did much to encourage the cult, regularly exalting 'the Servant of God' in Executive Meetings. In May 1981, citing Judges 10:2, she observed: 'it's good when we teach about the Servant of God. On this chapter God revealed to me that the generations to come may not know what God did in the beginning.' Other board members were soon competing to outdo each other in their flattery. A year later the following discussion took place on the Executive:

> Rev. Manjoro 'the work has grown all over Africa, I have a suggestion that our President get the title of ARCHBISHOP.' After discussing this point it was agreed [that the title of Archbishop would be adopted].
>
> Mrs Guti 'May I also suggest that we apply for a doctorate?'
> Rev Sande 'How do we go about it?'
> President 'It is an honour given to people with outstanding work. It comes from the University.'

Not wanting to be upstaged, Manjoro went on to suggest that ZAOGA purchase 'a small plane for the President [Guti] as he travels about the provinces'.[12]

The plane proved unrealistic but Guti did change his title to Archbishop. Moreover, and in spite of Erwin's wise counsel, he set his heart on an honorary doctorate, eventually procuring one from Northgate Graduate College in Washington DC. The ceremony took place in October 1983 in a hall booked at the University of Zimbabwe, leaving some with the impression that Zimbabwe's leading university was itself the awarding body. A month before the ceremony Mrs Guti urged the Executive to 'give thanks to the Lord concerning our Father [Guti] for having been successful for having all these degrees', at which all members stood up to pray and praise God.[13] Guti actively boosted his own status by embracing his new titles – the Servant of God, Apostle Archbishop, Dr – and directing his colleagues on the appropriate moment to deploy each one.[14] By the end of the decade Executive discussions about who would accompany him became so heated that roles had to be carefully delineated on paper:

> After much discussion the executive resolved that Pastor Muhwati and Pastor Mathebula would always escort the Servant of the Lord to stand from the Tabernacle throughout the conference and whenever there would be such other meetings. Pastor Ngorima and Pastor Gun would escort him to and from residence and conference campus. Pastor Manger and Pastor Christmas would sit next to the Servant of the Lord to enable him to send them in case of anything cropping up. Pastor Ndongwe would be in charge of freewill takings. Pastor Christmas or Pastor Muhwati to carry the Servant of the Lord's Bible to the Pulpit.[15]

The Archbishop had by then effectively edged out his colleagues and co-founders, replacing respect with fear. 'Do not backbite the king,' he warned his Executive, 'for heavenly birds will come and tell him'.[16]

'Sifting and Schism': Church Politics [17]

There has been a tendency within Pentecostal movements for pioneers to be driven out of the denominations they founded after two or three decades (see Chapter 1). In most cases the subsequent denominational histories rationalise the reasons for expulsion as dogmatic deviations, autocratic tendencies and moral failures. There was often an element of truth in these charges because they corresponded with an underlying developmental process that required the removal of the charismatic founder. After twenty to thirty years the denomination develops bureaucracies that demand a new type of pastor with administrative skills; this type of leader inevitably comes into conflict with the charismatic pioneer of the first generation (Hollenweger, 1972: 477; B. Wilson, 1961: 39-50).

In the case of ZAOGA, Guti avoided his own demise by harnessing the very forces that threatened his position, deploying them against potential rivals in a wave of purges that spanned the 1980s and early 1990s. Not surprisingly the ejection of many of ZAOGA's co-founders and other rising stars receives little coverage in the movement's canonical history. Even the schism caused by the departure of Abel Sande in 1987, which hit national headlines, received only a few rudimentary lines: '1987 was the year of shaking for ZAOGA Forward in Faith, which resulted in Marondera being snatched by the enemy ... The shaking sifted many people. Some fell but the church continued to grow' (Guti, 1999: 103). This spiritualised account mystified forces that animated the movement throughout the 1980s and which are manifest in the polemics of those involved in the schisms. The first set of tensions related to the demands of bureaucratisation. The process of institution building did indeed require a new leadership with technical skills and administrative ability, but Guti skilfully marshalled a younger cohort against his charismatic peers Sande and Choto and hence avoided his own demise. A new generation of ambitious pastors happily colluded in the removal of elder pioneers.

The second set of tensions revolved around the politics of succession. While Guti grew increasingly unassailable, at least some of his peers hoped to succeed him. But as the Archbishop's position was consolidated so too was that of his clients and allies. His brother, Nelson, and son-in-law from his first marriage, Michael Maoko, already in the ascendant in the late 1970s, increased their influence. With them rose the unremarkable figure of James Muwhati, Guti's cousin. Another more distant relative, Langton Mpanduki, rose quickly in the 1980s and later Guti's nephew, Joe, would receive a good deal of favour. But the person who stood to benefit most from the Archbishop's largesse was his wife Eunor. In 1983 she was made Vice-President of the movement. Eunor's rise was accompanied by the growing prominence of two businessmen, both initially church elders who subsequently became Overseers. These were Elson Makanda and Christopher Chadoka, whose wives were close friends of Eunor. Along with others such as Martin Chesve they had risen to prominence as governors of the Bible college and members of the Finance Committee. Chadoka was an immensely forceful character who would become third in line to the throne, cementing his position through the marriage of his daughter to Joe Guti. The first consequence of Eunor's rise was that she usurped Pricilla Ngoma as 'Mother' of the movement. Ngoma had often fed and cared for Guti after his first marriage ended, and the initial meetings of the prayer

117

band that eventually became ZAOGA were convened in her home. Furthermore, as 'Guti's bank' she had organised annual and biannual Talents events, raising money for the Church's expansion. After Guti's second wife took on these functions Ngoma was marginalised, and moved out of her large house in Greendale to a smaller stand in Waterfalls. As other co-founders saw the spoils of leadership going to Guti's kin and new allies, so they perceived that their hopes of succession would never materialise. In turn, even rising young modernisers like Bartholomew Manjoro would see their own aspirations blocked, and would leave.

Worldly and religious ambitions combined to create the third set of tensions. While the co-founders wanted a larger share of the resources coming into the movement, like Guti they also craved greater recognition for their sacrifices and achievements. All possessed considerable skills in leadership and the work of church building, and all experienced a growing sense of frustration with an increasingly hierarchical movement. When they finally struck out on their own they were driven by the same impulse of thwarted creativity that had given rise to the Christian independent movements discussed in Chapter 2. In this case African patriarchy replaced missionary racism and paternalism as the cause of schism (Murray, 1999; Englund & Leach, 2003). But the major difference from the early waves of independency was the greater availability of external resources. Guti cast his seceding co-founders as being 'bewitched' by American money, but this was only one of a number of factors that caused them to found their own organisations. None were ever as successful as Guti at raising external funding. External resources simply helped make the initial break manageable. As well as illustrating the tensions shaping ZAOGA's development in the 1980s, the schisms also shed light on the forces extending the Pentecostal spectrum in Africa.

There had been a simmering discontent since the late 1970s, as Overseers jostled for position while Guti convalesced in Marimba after an illness. At the time of independence the Highfield Action Party caused Guti to relocate temporarily to Mutare. Inspired as much by the radical politics of African nationalism as by the egalitarianism described in Acts of the Apostles, this collection of young church members protested about the rising prominence of Guti's family and businessmen within the movement. The growing affluence of some was affecting local patterns of leadership. In 1981 Guti was compelled to preach against the awarding of church positions simply on the basis of who paid the most tithes.[18]

Raphael Kupara was the first co-founder to leave the movement in 1984, departing after coming under considerable pressure from Guti and his allies. He was the first obvious target. Although never as popular as Sande, he had immense gravitas and considerable administrative skills. He managed the movement's bureaucracy, particularly its transnational expansion, and had helped launch the Bible school. His pedigree was excellent. His brother, Langton, was already the leader of the Apostolic Faith Mission. He was widely perceived to be the movement's number two, embodying many of the modernising forces that unhinge charismatic founders. The charges laid against him included the acquisition of property without permission. But perhaps more significant was that he began to speak out against the growing cult of leadership surrounding Guti, preventing choirs singing about the Servant of God and discouraging prayer to the God of Ezekiel. For this he was 'sold out' by those loyal to Guti who used it as evidence of his rebellion. Other co-founders, Choto and Sande along with Manjoro, were willing accomplices in Kupara's demise. The Archbishop told Choto: 'Kupara is fighting me and wants to kill me. He is my enemy … Kupara wants to plant a landmine.'[19] In a similar manner to the way Guti had been treated by AFM missionaries, Kupara was grounded, and was unable to preach without invitation. When no invitations were forthcoming he wrote his letter of resignation and left to found United Assemblies in Africa. According to Sande, the promotion of Eunor to Vice-President in early 1984 may have been a clever ruse to frustrate Kupara's ambitions. After his demise the post was abolished. [20]

Kupara's departure was accompanied by that of ZAOGA's fastest rising star, Cuthbert Makoni. Originally a clerk for Guardian Assurance, he had taken up full-time ministry in the church in 1976. He had helped raise money for church building in Kambazuma and had success in Chiredzi. By 1978 he was on the Executive and was Overseer of Mutare, where he had seen to the construction of the Dangamvura Revival Centre and had put up buildings in Nyanyadzi, Chisumbanje and Manzvire. Back in Harare he had overseen the construction of the chapel at the Bible school and raised a successful following at Waterfalls. Makoni had been too independent and too successful. Much to Guti's chagrin he had found an American donor to pay for his flight back from CFNI, Dallas, in 1981 to attend his mother's funeral. Pressure was brought to bear upon him by Guti and his lieutenants. At Deeper Life 1984 he was publicly humiliated, called to repent for being 'too conceited and proud' and for 'justifying' himself. He was subsequently summoned to a meeting at Braeside, reminiscent of Guti's own disciplining by missionaries. There, according to Choto, the Archbishop – 'shouting and shivering' with rage – rebuked him by reading a piece of scripture in front of assembled witnesses: Sande, Ngoma and Maoko and a delegation of senior leaders. Beside Guti stood his wife Eunor, file in hand, listing reasons for the suspension. He had built too big a church at Dangamvura; had returned from the USA to attend his mother's funeral without permission; had built a church at Tafara without permission and preached in Waterfalls without approval. And in Waterfalls he had purchased a piece of expensive property without Guti's signature. Makoni had 'made a name for himself' and was grounded for the next six months. When his wife had a vision of a large angry black snake blocking their way on the road, Makoni took this as a sign to leave ZAOGA. Starting with small prayer cells in homes, he founded a new movement. Christ Ministries, eventually building a college and church in Belvedere, Harare, funded by tithes and Talents. The property he had bought in Waterfalls subsequently became ZAOGA's Headquarters, celebrated as such in the movement's canonical history (Guti, 1999: 103).

Guti had always skilfully kept his lieutenants divided, meeting them alone, playing them off against each other. Choto and Sande had been willing accomplices in the removal of Kupara and Makoni but it was soon their turn to feel the heat. Choto had pioneered Matabeleland Province more or less from 1970 to1987, overseeing the construction of numerous churches. A powerful preacher, he had built up a considerable popular base there and when in 1980 Guti replaced him with Manjoro, who did not speak Sindebele, there were immediately demands for his return. As will be illustrated in the following chapter, Choto managed to expand the movement into South Africa from his Matabeleland stronghold. He also facilitated the movement's entrance into Britain, which won him headlines in both the Zimbabwean and British press. In 1987 Guti came to Bulawayo with a group of young pastors to condemn him in a meeting. On 22 September 1987, after a number of further public denunciations, he was told to leave the movement.

Kupara, Choto and Makoni all went quietly, the first two pacified with church houses. Nothing would prepare Guti for Sande's defence. Sande was never obvious leadership material like the patrician Kupara but he was charismatic and enormously popular. His remarkable preaching gifts meant that he had pioneered a large number of the movement's assemblies. Newcomers to ZAOGA usually met Sande well before they encountered Guti, and many of the pastors had been converted or trained by him. It was Sande rather than Guti who represented the old-time religion of hymn singing and long meetings. He had resisted many of Guti's innovations. Like Choto, he too had a strong base, this time in Mashonaland. But Sande's claims to succession were severely dented when he was accused of a sexual misdemeanour in 1982 and placed incommunicado for six months. When the need for a Vice-president was first mooted in early 1984, Sande felt compelled to nominate Mrs Guti, in addition to standing himself. Despite that, he still lost only by a narrow margin of five votes to Eunor's seven.[21] Faced with mounting pressure in 1987 Sande's assemblies in Marondera stood by him, attacking Guti's car when he arrived for a meeting and declaring, 'if you chase him we'll chase you'. The disturbances spread to Mtoko and received coverage in the national press; 13 people were arrested for violence and disorder. Serious litigation ensued when Sande's followers refused to leave the church they had built, declaring it was their property because they had built it. Eventually, elders and deacons were expelled from the local leadership and Sande was forced out after his phone and electricity were cut off. Sande proceeded to hire lawyers to claim his share of the organisation he had worked so hard to build.[22]

For a while, Choto and Sande worked together. They called their new church Ambassadors for Christ, after Paul Grier's organisation, in the hope that he would fund them. In the event he gave them a few hundred US dollars to cover their first few months and funded one or two crusades, but then withdrew his help for fear of risking his relationship with Guti. The local leader of Family of God Church, Andrew Wutuwanashe, proved more helpful to Sande and bought him a truck. Sande and Choto quickly fell out in a struggle over control of the organisation, each remaining leader of their half of the church. ZAOGA's canonical history describes the conclusion of the Sande affair as follows:

> The repossession of the Marondera Church, which had been snatched by the enemy was a miracle. That is why David said 'God arise and let your enemies be scattered.' When God arose no one raised their heads again. Many of them were arrested and punished for trespassing. The Marondera church is full of joy as if nothing ever happened (Guti, 1999: 103).

But Sande did not go quietly, and the fallout would affect ZAOGA for some time to come.

Other rising stars such as George Chikowa, Aaron Muchentgeti and Kennedy Manjova left ZAOGA in the 1980s and early 1990s, each founding a new church. These were schisms of a lower order, but they represented a considerable loss of skilled leadership from ZAOGA's ranks. The last conflicts of major significance were the departure of Manjoro and marginalisation of Marova. Both had impressed American church leaders during periods of study at CFNI and had a train of potential sponsors willing to support them while they founded their own movements. But both preferred to believe they had a future in ZAOGA. Manjoro had been like a son to Guti, caring for him in Cottage 593, Highfield, acting as his secretary and accompanying him on preaching expeditions. He had helped build the work in Mutare after Makoni, and then replaced Kupara as the movement's administrative guru. As we shall see in Chapter 7, he had established a good number of the Church's transnational connections. Many had viewed Manjoro as Guti's successor but his path was clearly blocked by Eunor Guti. In 1993 he left to found Faith World Ministries, building a 5,000-seat church in Belvedere. Initially the church was supported by an American, Doyle Davidson, but as it became established it deployed local fund-raising techniques as used by ZAOGA.

Guti's confrontation with Jason Marowa was the most public clash. Marowa's potential challenge was multi-faceted. First, he was the best educated of ZAOGA's leadership. Having trained at CFNI, he returned to a college in Florida to study for a doctorate in Contemporary Christianity. Secondly, as Pricilla Ngoma's son-in-law he represented an alternative and threatening lineage to the Guti family with its own legitimate claims to succession. Worse still, it had been prophesised in a Deeper Life Conference that he would succeed. Thirdly, he was immensely popular and had a strong power base within the movement. He had spent most of the 1980s as Principal of the Bible college responsible for a generation of gifted young pastors who regarded him as the movement's best preacher. Beyond the Bible college he had a wealth of connections into the movement forged through his training with Sande. His time in the USA, coupled with American friends teaching at AMFCC, gave him an international network of support that rivalled Guti's. His mistake was to cast doubt on the competitive nature of church fund-raising events at a public meeting in Highfield. Guti was soon phoned by the regional overseer and told: 'Jason is working against Talents'. For having supposedly undermined the movement's income-raising activity, Guti immediately barred Marowa from teaching at the Bible college and then summoned him to Mutare. There, he was watched and tested as he was made to lead a crusade. Meanwhile the students at the college went on strike. When Marowa returned they ran from morning prayers to embrace him. He addressed them and pleaded for peace but once again he was sold out. Guti was telephoned and told that when Marowa 'arrived back the students were told the President has come'. The very next morning the Archbishop arrived for prayers dressed in his iconic striped jacket, the one he had worn in his early days as a hot young evangelist, a jacket for 'fighting his wars'. On the platform he announced: 'those who want a new President, Marowa, stay here. Those who want me as President go into that room'. The students, who had never envisaged such a choice, opted for Guti. Henceforth Marowa was grounded and sidelined, given a meaningless desk job at headquarters. Police Commissioner Chihuri spotted him and appointed him Chaplain-General to the police force. Marowa thus remained in the movement as an ordinary church member, untouchable because of his powerful connections. Subsequently the Archbishop's nephew became Principal of the Bible college.

Although none of the schismatic movements were ever as successful as ZAOGA itself, most were in part a reaction against the cult of Guti, a cult they had helped to create but which was consolidated and disseminated through a printed history.

'History is Strength by Always Narrating': Power and Identity in the Written Word

Apart from the threats to his leadership, imagined as much as real, Guti had to fight off challenges to the movement itself from a homogenising global Born-again movement that threatened to dilute ZAOGA's identity and entice away its best leaders. His salvation lay in the production and dissemination of a canonical history. This *Sacred History* influenced ZAOGA's evolution in a number of ways. First, it tidied up the movement's historical reputation and silenced any challenges to Guti's authority from the movement's co-founders. Secondly, it melded ZAOGA as a homogenous Pentecostal community with its own distinctive identity. Thirdly, it sought to influence the movement's future direction.

The project of constructing an official written history of ZAOGA began in the early 1980s, marking an important period of transitions for the movement. The first transition was a general one affecting the whole of Zimbabwean society: the move from the colonial to the post-colonial period. This was a time when Zimbabweans grasped their agency in the making of independence in 1980, accompanied by a good deal of writing and rewriting of the recent past, with the new elites constructing their victors' narratives. The second transition was specific to ZAOGA. Guti's interest in history coincided with the beginning of his purges of co-founders and other leaders, reflecting his concern to establish his legitimacy. Ezekiel Guti's history was that of an archetypal victor.

The Archbishop had a fundamental grasp of the legitimating power of history. In one of his 'Third World Mentality' sermons he told his audience:

> If you go to Zimbabwe ruins you will see what was built by blacks But the white man came and looked for a book, then he said that no blacks did this, they [the builders] are people from Phoenicia. But we are putting it in writing that we are the ones who built it ...I want to challenge all members of ZAOGA if you do not write books today the white people will write books, saying we did this. In America I saw three books written about this ministry and Ezekiel Guti. They did not ask me to write that book. If you do not write a book for your organisation you are in trouble.[23]

During his time at CFNI, Dallas, Guti encountered the cheap and widely circulated spiritual autobiographies of key Pentecostal pioneers and forebears described in Chapters 1 and 3: John Alexander Dowie, founder of Zion City, Chicago; John G. Lake, founder of the Apostolic Faith Mission of South Africa; and Gordon Lindsay, a leading architect of the modern charismatic movement. From studying these historical tracts Guti learned that contemporaries and later generations often equated those who wrote down their movement's traditions with their foundation. Like Lindsay in his later life, the Archbishop increasingly devoted his time to writing history and doctrines, realising that it is the best means of influencing a movement with an increasing transnational reach.[24]

Guti's version of ZAOGA's history was recorded in a booklet entitled *The Sacred History of ZAOGA Forward in Faith to the Leaders and the Saints*. It was first printed in 1984, updated in 1989 and 1995, and reproduced in a glossy paperback cover under a slightly different title in 1999. *The Sacred History* was supplemented by two other sources: first, what initially appears to be a brief biography entitled *African Apostle: The Life Of Ezekiel Guti* written by an American, Gayle Erwin ca. 1986; and second, *The Remained Unspoken of the African Apostle* by Robert Takavarasha ca. 1988. Of these literary productions, *The Sacred History* was the main testament of the church. Taking the form of a spiritual autobiography of Ezekiel Guti, its 52 pages and 85 sections were a canonised history recounting the origins and evolution of his ministry. Drawing on both biblical and 'local religious traditions' it described in simple, often ungrammatical English, Guti's visionary experiences, his moments of divine commissioning, and his ministry of the miraculous. In places it strongly resembled *From the Bush to the Pulpit*, the testament of his friend and mentor Morgan Sengwayo.[25]

In many respects, Guti's written testament corresponded to standard Pentecostal histories. Keen to restore the supernatural powers of the first-century apostles to the twentieth-century church, Pentecostals have sought historic legitimisation by claiming the contemporary restoration of the apostolic age. Thus, in various passages, Guti's account of his ministry read like the 'reincarnation of the book of Acts' (Neinkirchen, 1994: 122). For example, a young man was healed by contact with a handkerchief prayed over by the Archbishop, reminiscent of Acts 19. More generally, the miracles provided proof of Guti's calling as an apostle: the numerous accounts of his healing ministry revealed him as an anointed instrument through which the 'power of God' flowed; the maladies and afflictions from which people were cured, such as 'withered arms' and 'flows of blood', mirrored those found in the Gospels.

The spiritual autobiography also used biblical narratives in a number of paradigmatic ways. His description of his ministry was authorised by lifting it almost verbatim from Luke's Gospel: Christ's self-justification to John the Baptist's disciples becomes Guti's justification (Luke 7: 22). 'Soon after that the Lord began to use me in a mighty way, healing many sick people, making the blind see, the crippled to walk, the deaf to hear, leprosy cleansed, the dead were raised, and those who were possessed by spirits of madness and poverty'. Biblical precedents legitimated his actions, his struggle to capture and dominate Highfield finding a biblical precedent in Joshua's capture of Jericho (Joshua 6). Unfortunate and potentially ungodly episodes were sacralised by biblical parallels; Guti's expulsion by missionaries was no different from the experience of the blind man who was healed by Christ and put out of the temple for speaking the truth (John 9: 34, 35). Sometimes the Bible was used 'analogically, in order to clarify novel situations in terms of familiar ones' (Peel, 1995: 596). Thus the Archbishop's intercessions on behalf of the Zimbabwean nation during the 1991 drought were reminiscent of Elijah's spiritual clash with the prophets of Baal over the moral well-being of Israel (1 Kings: 18). In some passages the scriptural references were included, while in others, such as that describing Guti's transfiguration in the Highfield cottage, the reader was simply left with the resonance.

But *The Sacred History* also drew upon another source of legitimisation: apart from drawing on apostolic and biblical roots it located itself within the Zimbabwean Pentecostal tradition of divine calling and prophetic utterance. The text made connection with this missionary-inspired but relatively autonomous tradition of Zimbabwean Pentecostalism by two means. First, Guti placed himself within a lineage of prophetic forerunners such as Maranke and Masowe through his connection with Enoch Gwanzura, the Head Pastor of the Black Section of the AFM (Swartz, 1994: 144). Secondly, his testament employed some of the same literary devices used in the written traditions of Maranke and Masowe. Like these two prophets, Guti asserted an encounter with God that was not mediated by a church or white missionaries. Moreover, all three traditions claimed further encounters with the divine, following extensive periods of praying and fasting on mountains or in the bush, places often referred to as the 'wilderness'. Such encounters, often accompanied by temptations from the Devil, led to instances of special commissioning and blessing once the Devil had been defeated. Here, too, the devices these churches used to signify the commissioning were the same. All three sets of traditions played on the symbolism of stars as signs foretelling the eventual size of their movements. Like Masowe and Maranke, Guti was claiming a unique encounter with God to assert the 'authenticity' of his calling and the 'indigenous' nature of his church.

Nevertheless *The Sacred History* did differ from the Maranke and Masowe traditions. The desire to assert indigenous roots is often simply the first stage of the developmental process of a religious movement, which can be followed by a gradual shift to an assertion of universal credentials. Here, Gayle Erwin's *African Apostle* acted as an important supplement to the official testament of the church, emphasising the modern, international character of ZAOGA. More prominence was given to Guti's first meeting with Nicholas Bhengu in 1959: 'When they shook hands, it was such a powerful experience for them that their hearts were melted together.' Bhengu was the forerunner of later, high-flying African religious executives like Benson Idahosa from Nigeria, Mensa Otabil from Ghana and Nevers Mumba from Zambia. Guti laid claim to that tradition too. Erwin also gave greater emphasis to American connections. The closing section of the *African Apostle* reproduced a glowing endorsement of the Archbishop by Dr Judy Florentino of Zoe College in Florida, given when she arrived in Zimbabwe to award him his second honorary doctorate in 1989. Like other biographies of Born-again figures, the narrative culminated with the hero becoming sophisticated and 'international' (Lungu: 1994: 106).

As this study has shown, beneath ZAOGA's respectable sacred history lay a less impressive secret history of ambition, faction, and manipulation. The movement's emergence was animated by two fierce struggles that were only hinted at in its public history. The first struggle was the Pentecostal turf-war for control of Rhodesia's black capital, Highfield, and other significant townships in Salisbury, Gwelo and Umtali. The second struggle took place within the movement, as Guti purged or marginalised its co-founders and rising stars, replacing them with his kin, members of his ethnic group and businessmen. Biblical precedents abound for these events; for example, the anarchy and search for leadership described in Judges, or the accounts of factionalism and feuding recounted in I and II Kings. But these were not the precedents found in *The Sacred History*. Instead, more congenial scriptural analogues were selected to redeem the chequered past of the Archbishop, and to a lesser extent that of the movement. Thus the turbulent conflict with Sande became no more than a supernatural act of 'sifting' whereby 'enemy' elements were shaken out to leave a pure remnant. But, more than that, the texts consolidated Guti's position within the movement by means of suppression. *The Sacred History* and two supplementary biographies flattened and stripped the historical landscape so that Guti loomed large as the sole agent of God's advance. There were no references to the considerable contribution of his co-founders and others in fund-raising, teaching, evangelism and administration. The few who did appear on the historical stage did so only when they had the effect of legitimising Guti, or when their political loyalty was undoubted.

There were also remarkable inversions. The stream of American Bible teachers who administrated and taught at the ZAOGA Bible school in the 1980s were depicted as foreigners who came to sit at Guti's feet to learn about the movement: 'Every month there used to come groups of people from overseas and other different places to learn. Even today they are still coming from USA, Denver Colorado, Chicago, Arizona, Australia, Jamaica, Israel, Nashville Tennessee, Texas, South America, Canada, California' (Guti, 1999: 106). Just as European missionaries stripped African agency from their accounts of the Christianising of the continent to boost their own heroic status, so too in the post-colonial context Guti silenced white voices and minimised white agency in ZAOGA's testament.

Nowhere was evidence of Guti's calculated approach to the past more apparent than in ZAOGA's own archives. Amidst the assortment of papers was a file entitled 'Histories'. In this file lay, first, a collection of alternative histories, probably written by other co-founders. Some of these texts resembled the Archbishop's narrative and were perhaps written to flatter him, or were even solicited by him. However, they were not to his liking. The texts included many more names and made much of the golden age in the late 1950s when they were all members of an evangelistic band in which Guti was only first among equals.[26] Other 'factual' accounts of the past were written in preparation for the litigation over property caused by Sande's departure from the movement.[27] But all of these accounts remained unpublished and unknown. With them were a series of editorial comments on Erwin's *African Apostle*. Here, Guti's intent to suppress was clear:

> p. 19: Langton Kupara—omit the names introduced [sic] to his younger brother [Raphael]
> p. 22: Omit name Langton Kupara. First black superintendent of that denomination [AFM].
> p. 25: Omit the names of persons.
> p. 30: Where Ngoma is put another lady.
> p. 31: Omit Canadian and American missionaries and put two missionaries one in Mutare and one in Harare.[28]

A whole section describing the seven-year period of Guti's stormy relations with Bhengu and the Assemblies of God, South Africa, from 1960 to 1967, was deleted. Given Guti's editorial powers it comes as no surprise that the project was never conceived of by Erwin as a biography. Erwin's final text was originally entitled *African Prophet: As told to Gayle Erwin by Ezekiel Guti*. Guti maintained strong editorial control over the various drafts and ZAOGA's press produced the final version.[29] *African Apostle* was yet another autobiography, or more appropriately, auto-hagiography. In March 1989, shortly before the second printing of *The Sacred History* in tract form, Guti conveyed to his Executive the importance of anniversary celebrations:

> It is very useful to say out the history of your church. You can ask for some speakers ... we must use the book. Testimonies are important. . History of your leader is very important. The names of other people are not important. Know your leader and the HISTORY. ...We must not talk about those who left the church...

Thanking the Archbishop for his contribution, another board member observed:

> HISTORY is strength by always narrating.[30]

Thus *The Sacred History* is more than just a text. It is also liturgy and ritual. The testament's preamble states:

> This book must be read every second Sunday of May so that it might be a remembrance to those who will follow this ministry, that they might know whence they came from and whence they are going, that they may not be misled by many who will rise up and say: 'I am founder of this church'.

> And Joshua said unto them, pass over before the ark of the Lord your God into the midst of Jordan, and take ye up every man of you a stone upon his shoulder . . . and these stones shall be a memorial unto the children of Israel for ever. Joshua 4:5,6,7.

Once a year the testament is read in ZAOGA assemblies. It is an event that demands public participation. The hour-long reading is punctuated by instructions and refrains placed in significant moments in the narrative. Guti's transfiguration is followed by: 'Let all the Saints rise up and say "Halleluya! Halleluya" Amen.' And the passage concerning the foundation of the church in Bindura finishes with the instruction: 'Let all the people stand up and shout praises and give glory to God.' The anniversary coincides with the Archbishop's official birthday, ensuring that the man and the movement become one.

From the outset, ZAOGA's co-founders fought Guti's hegemonic history. As the Archbishop sought to dominate the church, the issue of what constituted the official version of the past became a heated debate within the movement's executives. When the idea of an anniversary was first mooted in 1982 a vigorous discussion ensued concerning the date of the movement's founding:

> Rev. Sande: Do we take the date when we had our constitution?
> President: I[t] can be that date or it may be the 12th of May 1960, the day when the Lord told me to go to Bindura. That's the time when this organization was started. We will discuss it on [sic] a General Conference.
> Rev. Sande: This is the Highest Board in the Church, so what we agree upon here will be handed.
> President: Let's hear what the board says, either 12th May or Easter 1967 [The date of the constitution].
> Rev. Mrs. Ngoma: The important date is 5th December 1960, that's when God started.
> Rev. Ngorima Proposed and Rev. Muhwati seconded. The house agreed on anniversary day to be 12 May.[31]

Some of Guti's peers could already see the writing on the wall.

Zimbabwean Nationalism meets American Spiritual Imperialism

By the end of the decade Guti had gained the personal accolades he thought he deserved. He was now President and Archbishop of the movement, honoured with two doctorates. His life was celebrated in print and liturgy. But his personal gains were not mirrored by public recognition of the movement. Throughout the 1980s he consistently failed to translate ZAOGA's growing denominational significance into the equivalent political capital. Managing relations with the state would not prove as easy as managing his reputation.

Like the main-stream denominations, ZAOGA initially trod very carefully in its relations with the new ruling party, ZANU/PF. Zimbabwean cultural nationalism had cast the church as a retrogressive agent in colonial Southern Rhodesia, associated with land expropriations, racial segregation and cultural imperialism. When independence came, church leaders felt at a moral disadvantage and threw themselves behind state-led development to prove their good will (Maxwell, 1995). It was clear that partnership in development was what the state required of the church. In a speech in March 1987 at the opening of a new ZAOGA church at Mucheke, the Governor of Masvingo, one of the few high-level political connections the movement made in the 1980s, told those assembled: 'FAITH WITHOUT works is dead, but what you have done is to prove that you have both faith and works... If you "churches" work hard the government's work will be less. ..... You who are grown up do like Nyerere not like Banda.'[32] Hence one of Guti's first directives was to order assemblies to co-operate with the newly formed Ministry of Women's Affairs. Two years later he told his Executive: 'Christianity is to have a burden for the country and help people with needs.' A senior pastor was selected to liaise with the government over development issues and ZAOGA initiated its own development projects as well as donating to state-led enterprises.[33]

ZAOGA's engagement with development sprang in part from the realisation that there were new resources available from religious and secular NGOs. By the 1980s, Western donors influenced by a neo-liberal agenda grew ever more doubtful about the ability of states to deliver aid, looking instead to churches and other elements of civil society. Churches appeared to be even-handed and efficient institutions able to provide services in health and education where states were failing to do so. But the movement's new-found social concern was also shaped by its enduring sectarian tendencies. 'In our constitution we have a clause saying no beer drinking, no ancestral songs or political songs because we just support the government', Guti told his Executive.[34] Nevertheless ZAOGA was evolving and realigning itself ideologically. It had always promoted black autonomy and self-reliance. And, whereas it had previously rejected Zimbabwean cultural nationalism because of its associations with ancestor religion, it now selected from what it saw as the more benign aspects of African culture. In 1981 Guti announced to the church leadership, 'we don't just take from western culture'. Appreciating the value of an 'African authenticity' the mbira, a musical instrument previously associated with spirit possession, was encouraged in church services. The Christ for Zimbabwe Institute was renamed Africa Multination for Christ College. Formal links with CFNI Dallas decreased as the movement recruited white American Bible teachers for its college from small independent or semi-independent assemblies that could not threaten the autonomy of his movement.[35]

The state's agenda also provided the broader context for the movement's canonical history. ZAOGA's testament was intended to resonate with the prevailing nationalist ideology. As we have seen, the first edition stressed that Guti's primal encounter with God happened without the mediation of missionaries and it made connections with seemingly indigenous traditions of Zimbabwean and South African Pentecostalism. In line with ZANU/PF's stress on self-reliance, ZAOGA emphasised penny capitalism and its financial autonomy from external sources. American connections were played down despite their very real substance.

Despite ZAOGA's conversion to the language and practices of development and its sympathies with cultural nationalism, relations with the ruling party were not good. Given that the state initially loved the church for its body, ZAOGA did not have much to offer because it remained so steadfastly committed to proselytism. It did by the end of the decade have a number of orphanages and needlework schools but even these had an evangelistic dimension and were insignificant in comparison with the vast medical and educational infrastructures of the historic mission churches. A request in 1983 for representation on the advisory board of the Army Chaplain's Corps was turned down because it was not perceived to be one of the 'main and well known denominations'.[36] But ZAOGA did appear threatening to a young government jealously guarding its legitimacy. ZAOGA's highly effective and locally rooted organisational structure gave it a remarkable capacity for rapid multi-ethnic mobilisation, a capacity that the new Zimbabwean government seemed to fear as much as its colonial predecessor feared Christian independency. Moreover, ZAOGA's organisational character, its acronymic name and growing leadership cult made it look like a political party. Its predominantly urban character meant that, like the ruling party, it could regularly gather its member-ship together in sports stadiums for large rallies. And in its control over youth it rivalled the ZANU/PF Youth League. Worse still, like the newly constituted Zimbabwe Coun-cil of Churches (ZCC), ZAOGA suffered from appearing to have the wrong political connections (Hallencreutz, 1988).[37] The flight or out-manoeuvring of the movement's co-founders throughout the 1980s served only to reinforce the movement's image of being dominated by the Ndau – an ethnic group that maintained strong loyalties to the rebel nationalist leader Ndabiningi Sithole and his ZANU Ndonga party. This impres-sion was reinforced by the fact that the Archbishop's wife, Eunor, was related to Sithole. Finally, because its sectarian tendencies were never fully transcended, ZAOGA chal-lenged ZANU/PF's authoritarian version of nationalism that was itself founded on intolerance of pluralism.[38]

ZAOGA's leaders attempted to steer a neutral path, sticking to Gospel rather than government in high-profile events. Guti publicly chided three speakers from Trinidad attending the 1985 Deeper Life Conference for mentioning politics. But trouble still came. The first major clash with the government happened because of the Zimbabwe-an Born-again movement's connections with the American Religious Right. In 1986, ZAOGA, along with other Pentecostal, Charismatic and Evangelical churches, sup-ported Reinhard Bonnke's Christ For All Nations Pan-African Crusade. Following the Crusade, Ralph Mahoney, one of its American personnel, published a right-wing tirade against Zimbabwe (Gifford, 1991: 66-7; Maxwell, 2000: 257-8). Although the Zimba-bwean Born-again community effectively rebutted Mahoney's misinformed rhetoric in a letter to *The Herald* as 'an insult to our sovereignty as a nation', the incident did alert ZAOGA to the dangers of close association with the American Religious Right.[39] From the mid-1980s onward the movement began to realign within the spectrum of American Christianities. Guti cultivated links with black Pentecostals whose doctrines on prosper-ity, black pride and self-actualisation amplified his own teaching against the third world mentality – an attitude of fatalism, and deference to whites (see below).

Although this realignment within American Christianity was partly intended to make ZAOGA appear less vulnerable to right-wing causes, the movement had other ideo-logical and material motives. Guti had not always been at ease with whites teaching in his Bible college in the early 1980s. Whilst he was busy building a denomination, the likes of Erwin and Grier had been strongly influenced by the Restorationist critique of clerical bureaucracies. Others had little time for his assumption of the title 'Archbishop' and his wearing of clerical garb. The American Assemblies of God maintained a strong populist tradition within which it valued the 'socially "humble" person as more receptive to the gospel'. They were also deeply suspicious of the prosperity gospel and the search for respectability.[40]

Black American and Afro-Caribbean Christianity was characterised by glossy magazines, high-profile conventions in plush hotels and a strong reliance on the electronic media. According to Gayle Erwin, the Archbishop's desire to connect with it represented an attempt to enter what Guti perceived as the big league.[41] In ideological terms, the realignment also signalled the beginnings of a shift towards the right, which would take on a greater significance in the post-Cold War era. While these new American friends had a black theology more conversant with ZAOGA's own historical experience, they nevertheless preached a prosperity gospel that increasingly aligned the movement with the values of liberal capitalism. Whatever subtle ideological shifts were taking place, the leadership continued to defend African autonomy. Mindful of the force of American cultural imperialism, US influences were increasingly brought under the centralising control of the leadership, who policed transnational connections through a separate office staffed exclusively by Guti's family and friends. Visiting speakers were always chaperoned and those who taught at the Bible school had their preaching activities restricted to certain churches.

The next clash with the government happened over a prospective 'big league' event. In February 1988, Nathan Shamuyarira, the Minister for Foreign Affairs, banned ZAOGA's rally at the National Sports Stadium, and the Ministry of Home Affairs deported the invited black speakers. The rally had been widely advertised on radio and television. Shamuyarira sent Guti the following rebuke:

TRANS-DENOMINATIONAL RALLIES OR ASSEMBLIES

When you hold trans-denominational public gatherings that go beyond usual church services in their scope and organisation, and when they involve preachers from other countries, especially from the United States of America, you should seek the permission of this ministry to do so. There may be international repercussions to such occasions, which go beyond preaching the word of God.[42]

Undaunted by the government ban, ZAOGA's leaders fasted, prayed and then took the Commissioner of Police to court, gaining an order to restrain him from banning the rally. The rally went ahead and Guti preached a message of personal repentance and black pride:

... our people want to be servants of white people. They trust whites better than our own people. This is what we call third world mentality ... Don't go to Europe and learn their ungodly things. Learn what they used to do before [they were backslidden] ... One day I saw another man carrying his car battery and asked him where he was going and he said, 'I am taking my battery to trustworthy white people.' You see! We must change our minds and be faithful to one another. ... We will trust our skin. Only righteousness can change our minds. Without righteousness we will live in a country telling lies to each other.[43]

One month later Guti wrote to Shamuyarira demanding an apology. In a blunt rebuttal to state power, he pointed out that his movement had gained approval from the Ministry of Home Affairs for the rally and complained about the 'confusion and misunderstanding' between that Ministry and the Ministry of Foreign Affairs. Guti also complained about the ad hoc warning he had been given pertaining to the ban: 'after advertising through the radio, local paper and TV wasn't it the duty of the minister to

129

let us know in time. If the minister was too busy doesn't he have secretaries or deputies to assist him?' Drawing together the rhetoric of black pride and cultural nationalism he threw them back at Shamuyarira in a stinging rebuke:

> Are whites to be honoured more than blacks? We couldn't understand whether the move to deport blacks was in the interest of our Government ...
> We pray that God may not put into authority Zimbabweans with Rhodesian minds.[44]

While Marxism-Leninism had lost much of its rhetorical effect by the late 1980s, ZAOGA leaders recognised the continuing force of cultural nationalism as among the most powerful arguments for criticising the government and holding it to account (Alexander, McGregor and Ranger: 2000).

In seeking to ban the rally, the government may have been influenced by two incidents preceding it. First, the movement was still suffering from the fallout from its bloody public schism caused by Sande's departure. Given Sande's undoubted popularity, the Ministry of Home Affairs may have feared a Pentecostal punch-up at the rally. Secondly, the leader of ZAOGA's Zaire assemblies appeared to have been using his church identity and transnational connections to facilitate arms dealing.[45] But these two factors were not necessarily at odds with the ruling party's overriding concern that ZAOGA undermined its project of nation building. As a movement that commanded strong loyalties, which transcended loyalty to the Zimbabwean state, ZAOGA evoked notions of citizenship very different from ZANU/PF's hegemonic project for the nation.

But ZAOGA's confrontation with the government came at a pivotal moment in church-state relations. The signing of the Unity Accord between PF/ZAPU and the ruling party on 22 December 1987 brought about a rapid change in the political climate. 'People were able to direct their attention to the real issues and could air their views without being mistaken as supporters of ZAPU or dissidents, hence being labelled as enemies of the government' (Ncube, 1989: 309). In this new environment of openness, the ruling party's legitimacy rapidly began to wane. ZAOGA's leaders doubtless sensed this in their confrontation with the government in 1988. In his sermon at the National Stadium Guti did preach loyalty to the government, but while the language of his address – sin, backsliding, righteousness – was not overtly confrontational, he did put forward an 'argument of accountability', a moral critique of the status quo. Recovering from its moral disadvantage in the early 1980s the Zimbabwean church now represented new sources of legitimate authority, in contrast to the diminishing authority of the state (Werbner, 1995; Maxwell, 1995). On the eve of 1990 ZAOGA was well placed to gain the public recognition and political capital it had failed to secure in the first decade of Zimbabwean independence.

Conclusion

On the final pages of Gayle Erwin's *African Apostle* there is a record of the speech given by Dr Judy Florentino of Zoe College, USA, when she awarded Guti his second honorary doctorate on 11 February 1989. As a celebration of the Archbishop's achievements it is a useful summary of ZAOGA's growth in the 1980s. By the end of the decade the movement claimed 300 church buildings and houses; 1,000 pastors, evangelists and teachers; Bible schools in Zimbabwe and Mozambique; an Orphanage Centre in Mutare, and a host of ministries for School Children, Students, Wives and Husbands. Florentino stressed the international dimensions of Guti's work (Erwin, nd: 144-6). Transnational expansion was the most significant aspect of ZAOGA's development in the 1980s and it will therefore be considered separately in Chapter 7.

Many resources for ZAOGA's growth did come from overseas, but very little came with strings attached. By dealing with carefully selected organisations and individuals, Guti managed to maintain autonomy over the movement. Rather than bringing about dependency the external resources were extraverted, used to develop and consolidate Guti's power base. Moreover, as we shall see in following chapters, the larger part of the movement's wealth resulted from the generosity and industry of its own members. As ZAOGA's successes multiplied, so Guti's heroic status metamorphosed into a leadership cult. Admiration turned into adoration, respect into fear and sycophancy. His life was celebrated in liturgy and sacred history and his position was maintained through a network of informers and henchmen. The leadership cult would evolve further in the 1990s.

As the Zimbabwean movement left its sectarian roots there were other signs of re-engagement with the world. Mirroring the leadership struggles within the movement's hierarchy, positions of leadership were being allotted to the powerful and wealthy rather than the spiritually gifted in local assemblies. As *braais* [barbecues] and parties became popular social events for husbands' and wives' ministries, so the movement was compelled to remind members that the consumption of beer was forbidden.[46]

Despite the great strides both Guti and his movement had made in the 1980s, ZAOGA still lacked public recognition within Zimbabwe. Deploying one of Nicholas Bhengu's powerful metaphors, Guti captured both the movement's growing secularity and its unrealised potential in a 1989 sermon: 'ZAOGA is a church like a Big Giant sleeping with its strength. We must recognise our strength. The church is becoming so big, bigger than the people in it. It is like a Rich man's son who does not know the life of a poor person. There are some people who lack God.'[47]

Throughout the 1980s ZAOGA moved considerably from its roots in Christian independency and mission Pentecostalism toward an international type of church situated within the global Born-again movement. Yet ZAOGA's appearance and progress remained profoundly influenced by the force of Zimbabwean nationalism, causing it to emphasise 'authentic', 'indigenous' roots and to exercise extreme caution when forging foreign connections. Local and national forces proved as transformational as international influences. ZAOGA's growing worldliness would be a dominant theme of the 1990s and beyond. Its relations with the ruling party would improve considerably in the early years of that decade, though a warmer relationship with ZANU/PF would not prove to be as satisfying as initially imagined.

Notes

1. Executive Minutes Book, 28 April 1983 & 8 September 1983, ZAW.
2. Int.DM64, Paul Saungweme; Int.DM9, Bill John Chigwenembe.
3. Executive Minutes, n.d., 1982 & 21 September 1982, ZAW.
4. Press Release 1983, file, Histories, ZAW.
5. Conflicts arose with the Scripture Union, which already had a well-established ministry in schools, and also with leaders of the Anglican Mothers' Union.

[6] Ezekiel and Eunor Guti to Kathryn Purks, Foreign Missions Board, Southern Baptist Convention, Virginia, USA, 2 October 1989, file, Non-Denominational, USA, 1989, ZAW. The constitution of The Gracious Women's Fellowship appears to have been based upon that found in 1978, *The Advanced Leadership Training* manual produced by the Women Aglow Fellowship. An annotated version of this is located in the Gracious Women's file, ZAW.

[7] Executive Minutes, 21 September 1982, 28 April 1983, 25 September 1984, ZAW.

[8] Executive Minutes, nd, 1982, ZAW.

[9] Int.DM104, Bruce Coble; Int.DM108, Ronnie Meek; IntDM105, Gayle Erwin.

[10] Files, CNFI 1973-1996, Non-Denominational USA 1989, Executive Minutes, 28 April 1983, ZAW.

[11] Correspondence between Ezekiel Guti and Shirley Childs, file, CNFI, Church Projects and Literature Projects, 17 June 1983, 5 November 1984 and passim. Int.DM102, Randy Bozarth; Int.103, John Carver; IntDM106, Sally Horton; Int.DM110, Howard Reents; Int.DM111, Bernice Watson.

[12] Executive Minutes, 27 May 1981, 21 September 1982, ZAW.

[13] Eunor Guti to Director of Central Services, University of Zimbabwe, ca. 1983, file, Non-Denominational, USA. Executive Minutes, 8 September 1983, ZAW.

[14] Minutes of Executive Fellowship and Business Meetings throughout Deeper Life Conference 6–17 Feb 1989, file, Deeper Life, ZAW.

[15] Executive Minutes, 8 February 1989, ZAW.

[16] Executive Minutes, 25 January 1989, ZAW.

[17] This section is drawn from a synthesis of interviews of the leading protagonists in the drama, Ezekiel Guti, his co-founders and other leading members of the movement in the 1980s. Interviews are referenced only when an informant is cited directly.

[18] Executive Minutes, 26 May 1981, ZAW.

[19] Int.DM16, Joseph Choto.

[20] Int.DM62, Abel Sande.

[21] Executive Minutes, 8 February 1984, ZAW.

[22] File, Mashonaland East, ZAW.

[23] Ezekiel Guti, 'Third World Mentality', Mutare, 11 November 1989, file, Sermons, ZAW.

[24] Ezekiel Guti, 'South African Conference', 3 June 1995, file, Sermons, ZAW.

[25] M.J. Sengwayo, nd, 'From the Bush to the Pulpit', Gen P - Sen, NAZ.

[26] For example, file, Histories, R. Kupara, (nd), 'A Brief History of Ezekiel All Nations Evangelistic Crusade', ZAW.

[27] These were written ca. 1988, file, Histories, ZAW.

[28] File, Histories, list of corrections, ca. 1985, ZAW.

[29] Int.DM105, Gayle Erwin.

[30] Executive Minutes,17 March 1989, ZAW.

[31] Executive Minutes, nd, 1982, ZAW.

[32] 'Governor of Masvingo's Speech', 7 March 1987, file, Relations with Government, ZAW.

[33] Executive Minutes, 26 May 1981, 28 April 1983, ZAW.

[34] Ibid.

[35] Executive Minutes, 26 & 27 May 1981, ZAW.

[36] Army HQ, Chaplains to ZAOGA, Harare, July 1983, file, Relations with Government, ZAW.

[37] In the ZCC's case it suffered from an association with Abel Muzorewa.

[38] A useful comparison with the post-independence situation between UNIP and the Lumpa movement in Zambia can be made here. See van Binsbergen, 1981: chapter 8.

[39] *The Herald*, 19 March 1986.

[40] On the USA AOG see Paul Freston, 1995: 124; Edith Blumhofer, 1993: chapter 11. Int.DM108, Ronnie Meek & DM105, Gayle Erwin.

[41] Int.DM105, Gayle Erwin.

[42] N. Shamuyarira, Minister of Foreign Affairs to Archbishop E. H. Guti, 15 February 1988, file, Relations with Government, ZAW.

[43] 'Lift up a Standard for the People', National Stadium, Harare, 7 February 1988, cited in Guti, 1989: 23-7.

[44] Ezekiel Guti to N.M. Shamuyarira, 14 March 1988, file, Relations with Government, ZAW.

[45] Chimpaka Lawanda Penge, Lusaka, to the Minister for Foreign Affairs, Zimbabwe, 13 February 1987, file, Relations with Government, ZAW; Int.DM22, Ezekiel Guti; Int.DM48, Simon Monde.

[46] 'Braes and Parties', Gracious Women's Fellowship International, 5 January 1990, file, Gracious Women, ZAW.

[47] Executive Minutes, 25 January 1989, ZAW.

6

Managing Ministry
Mission, Money & Memorialisation, 1990s–2000s

In 1999 ZAOGA's *Sacred History* (1989) was updated and republished in a glossy colour edition re-titled *History of ZAOGA Forward in Faith*. More than double the length of the original *Sacred History*, the new version raced through the movement's evolution over the previous decade. A number of themes predominated. The first was the increasing professionalisation of the movement's personnel: Mrs. Guti became Zimbabwe's first woman marriage officer; ZAOGA pastors were invited to participate in radio and television broadcasts and to become police and army chaplains. The second theme was the unabated material expansion of the movement: the first church building in South Africa was constructed, forty local Bible schools were founded to train ordinary church members; the movement moved to new headquarters in Waterfalls, Harare, and the Archbishop's office moved uptown to the city centre. Thirdly, bureaucracy increased: a committee was formed to relieve Guti of his administrative load, and the movement was decentralised to provincial offices. Fourth, a rich associational life continued to develop through ministries and fellowships such as the Gracious Women's Fellowship, the Men of Integrity Fellowship, Forward in Faith College and High School Ministry, the Teachers' Fellowship, the Post-Graduate Fellowship, and many others. Fifth, the new edition drew attention to the growing international status of the movement and Ezekiel Guti as its leader. In 1993 Myles Munroe, the Bahamas-based Pentecostal leader, declared Guti 'the Spiritual Father of Third World Christian leaders'. The Archbishop's international itinerary was cited at various points in the text, including his preaching in Jerusalem and Holland in 1993. On one of his many visits to the United States in 1992, he was given the freedom of the city [sic] of South Carolina. A final theme was the centrality of the Archbishop to the nation's post-war experience. It was related how his own prayers broke the 1991 drought, and how, during a 1993 International Conference on Christian leadership, Vice-President Muzenda went down on his knees before him to repent of the regime's violence in Matabeleland.

As an official statement of what ZAOGA's leadership considered important about the 1990s, the *History of ZAOGA* provides a useful foundation for this chapter. The main themes tell a story of a large organisation that had become integrated into wider Zimbabwean society. The movement's numerical growth had continued unabated, matched by a plethora of new managerial structures and associations. Its expansion went beyond the new South Africa into Europe and America, enabling the Archbishop to maintain an impressive international preaching schedule. As the movement grew so did the stature of Ezekiel Guti and his wife Eunor. They were finally able to make much coveted political connections with the likes of Vice-President Muzenda and even President Mugabe himself. But what the official *History* failed to mention is that ZAOGA increasingly experienced the problems of large organisations – authoritarianism, bureaucracy, impersonality and specialisation – which can be called 'disengagement' (Iliffe, 1979: 358). These problems were compounded by the movement's authoritarian direction, which manifested itself in an ever more elaborate and extensive leadership cult surrounding Ezekiel Guti. Although subscribed to by many of the movement's ordinary adherents, the Archbishop's kin and ethnic group who had most to gain from his patronage actively promoted the cult. Complaints about the loss of fraternity and fellowship within ZAOGA merged with accusations of nepotism, tribalism and corruption from a dissatisfied collection of pastors, professionals and students. Nevertheless, the movement continued to grow as it helped ordinary Zimbabweans towards personal security and taught them how to make the best of modernity.

ZAOGA's transnational expansion will be the subject of Chapter 7. This chapter will consider the movement's development within Zimbabwe. Both the national and transnational fortunes of the movement were contingent upon Zimbabwe's changing political economy.

Zimbabwe's Shifting Fortunes

The ruling party's legitimacy suffered its first major setback in 1988, following a series of scandals, particularly the famous Willowgate debacle in which government ministers used their privileged position to buy motor vehicles cheaply and re-sell them at inflated prices. The major turning-point, however, came when ZANU/PF adopted neo-liberal economics to secure loans and debt relief. From 1990 the World Bank and the International Monetary Fund (IMF) increasingly directed fiscal policy with Economic Structural Adjustment Programmes (ESAPs), forcing Zimbabwe to cut public expenditure. Unemployment mushroomed as public sector jobs were cut. The removal of protective tariffs on imports through trade liberalisation caused a 40 per cent decline in local manufacturing and added to the army of unemployed. Meanwhile, the growing shortage of foreign currency limited the growth of new private enterprise. Real wages declined by approximately 50 per cent between 1982 and 1994, and by 1995 61 per cent of Zimbabwean households lived below a level sufficient to provide basic needs. Removal of subsidies on basic foodstuffs left an unemployed underclass malnourished and prone to sporadic rioting.

It was in this economic context that the opposition movement grew. The formation of the Movement for Democratic Change (MDC) in September 1999 was part of a wider process of the revival of an assertive civil society that began in the late 1980s. The labour movement was central to the process. In 1987 the Zimbabwe Congress of Trade Unions (ZCTU) elected a new leadership led by Secretary General, Morgan Tsvangirai, and was no longer willing to act as a compliant wing of the ruling party. The ZCTU immediately experienced a growth of affiliates and a stabilisation of membership. After 1990 the ZCTU developed a strong critique of neo-liberal economics and extended its remit into a campaign for democratisation. Alliances were formed with the student movement, women's groups and various other civil society organisations. Faced with this broad coalition of opposition movements and its increasingly effective strike actions the government grew more authoritarian and coercive.

By contrast, when in 1997 the Zimbabwe National War Veterans Liberation Association (ZNWVLA) lobbied for greater compensation and political recognition, Mugabe gave in to their demands. Frightened by their legitimacy and mobilising power, he gave each veteran the sum of Z\$50,000 and a monthly pension. The compensation was given without any fiscal planning and did enormous damage to the economy. Mugabe decided to raise the money by placing a levy on tax-payers. Although the levy was subsequently dropped it precipitated the biggest general strike in Zimbabwean history in December 1997, followed by mass stay-aways in 1998. Workers, professionals and even employers took part in the industrial action. The ZCTU also began to extend its reach into the rural areas, smaller towns and mining centres. The membership expanded to 200,000. But, although the labour movement had extended its constituency, it was frustrated that this had not been translated into greater influence over the economy. So, early in 1998, the leadership set its sights on broadening its alliance and seeking a political solution to the growing economic crisis. The ZCTU became a central player in the launch of the National Constitutional Assembly (NCA) along with other civic groups such as the Zimbabwe Council of Churches, NGOs, and lawyers' organisations.

The NCA's mission was to lobby the public for a broad, popular process of constitutional reform. Its effect was almost immediate. It forced ZANU/PF into establishing its own Constitutional Commission and there ensued an intense debate over the process and content of constitutional reform. This was followed by the February 2000 referendum when the government sought national acceptance of a draft of its new highly authoritarian constitution. The constitution was comprehensively rejected by a now highly conscientised public. The constitutional debate propelled the labour movement, and particularly its leader, Morgan Tsvangirai, into opposition politics. The debate had also broadened the opposition. The NCA had grown to 96 organisations comprising women's coalitions, churches, cultural and students' groups along with the labour movement. Out of the NCA emerged the MDC opposition party with Tsvangirai as President.

The popular rejection of the draft constitution was the first explicit electoral challenge to ZANU/PF ascendancy in twenty years of government. To maintain power the party-state revived the 'land question', always popular with the land-hungry peasantry, encouraging invasions onto mainly white-owned commercial farms. War veterans initially led the occupation of farms but soon party-trained youth militias and state security forces came to their aid. The violence was subsequently extended to attacks on members of the opposition MDC, their families and those suspected of being in sympathy with its aims. The violence included arson, false arrests and incarceration, beatings, torture, rape, deliberate starvation, disappearances and murder, all of which intensified around elections, especially the parliamentary elections of June 2000 and the presidential elections of March 2002. The MDC and its allies were accused of sabotaging the final phase of the nationalist, anti-colonial revolution, the so-called *Third Chimurenga* – War of Liberation (Raftopoulos, 2001; Raftopoulos and Hammar, 2003).

Evangelism and Church Growth

The early 1990s were a good time for ZAOGA. The purges, schisms and generational struggles of the 1980s brought to the fore in the 1990s a new cohort of bright young men such as Oscar Murindagomo, William Rupapa, Steve Simango and George Rwizi. Some were related to the Archbishop by blood or marriage but all were motivated by an ethic of Christian service and loyalty to their church. Rwizi, a graduate from the University of Zimbabwe, eventually worked at the Bible College. Prior to that he was assigned to the headquarters, where he made an immediate impact by requiring regular reports from the provinces. The reports point to new patterns of growth and administration. The movement had expanded into communal areas in the 1980s. In the 1990s it extended to the very margins of the country: Nkayi in Matabeleland North, Gwanda in Matabeleland South, Dande in Mashonaland and Katerere in Manicaland. In these areas ZAOGA often became a church of the very poor led by a handful of professionals: nurses, teachers, civil servants originally from the city. The majority of the rural salariat adhered to the historic mission churches that had created them through schooling and now employed them in health, education and development work. ZAOGA's appeal was thus strongest amongst the most marginal: widows, divorcees, former sex workers and their children; people who rarely felt respectable enough to attend mission churches but nevertheless aspired to a modernising gospel that was often absent in Christian independency (Maxwell, 1999: chapter 7).

Growth continued in the cities. In the high-density suburbs, formerly known as townships, there was a multiplication of churches. Existing assemblies were split when they outgrew their buildings and new ones were established in schools and community centres managed by a system of pastors and regional pastors. The movement also increased its presence in the low-density suburbs, most of which were limited to whites in the age of colonial segregation. In City Assembly in Harare's Avenues, where new sites were difficult to secure, the overseer resorted to 'hot-seating', a series of services like the sessions of teaching deployed in some of Zimbabwe's over-extended schools. In Harare where the movement was strongest, ZAOGA divided its work into 24 regions. A similar process took place nationally when in 1995 the movement increased the number of provinces from 12 to 21. Some of the new provinces, for example Chitungwiza, the second largest conurbation in the country, arose from the need to manage large concentrations of members *in situ*. Other provinces, such as Gokwe, a region much neglected by church and state in Zimbabwe's Midlands, were target areas.[1] Expansion was possible with the vast numbers of pastors graduating from ZAOGA's Africa Multination for Christ College (AMFCC) each year. In 1994 alone, 177 students graduated. Such numbers dwarfed the total of ordinands at Harare's Anglican College in Mount Pleasant, which often did not reach double figures. Nevertheless the Anglican training would have been more academically rigorous, and in a continued drive for respectability Guti once again looked to the United States for ratification of AMFCC's programme. In Friends Christian University he found the perfect institution. Self-consciously 'not a missionary organisation' but 'sensitive to needs of Third world organisations' it simply credited them for 'teaching their theology their way' in return for a fairly sizeable fee. Thus ZAOGA gained academic respectability but retained autonomy.[2]

136

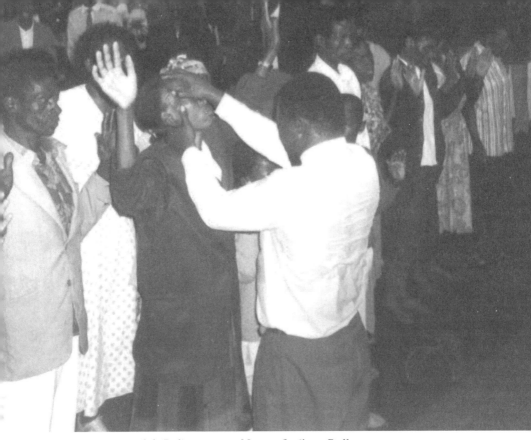

6.1 *Deliverance at Mutare for Jesus Rally*

6.2 *Gospel Artist, Lawrence Haisa*

At the beginning of the 1990s ZAOGA went electronic (Guti, 1999: 113). Grasping the appeal of Gospel and Christian rock music to the nation's youth, Guti instructed his Executive that all mother churches should have PA systems and good instruments. Soon the movement would have its own recording artists of national renown -- Lawrence Haisa, Biggie Tembo and Xechs Manatsa – who could draw large crowds at conferences and crusades. Guti also grasped the potential in the electronic media for boundary maintenance and the boosting of his authority. Overseers were told to record his sermons when he came to preach in their provinces and students at the Bible college were to have a tape-recorder so that they could listen to them. By 1993 most of the movement's offices had computers.[3]

Both the computers and the regular receipt of reports meant that the movement could begin to collect and collate statistics on church adherence and assets. This data, collected by the Archbishop's nephew, Elisha Manzou, not only proved useful for potential donor applications but also acted as insurance against schisms and avaricious pastors. In 1994 the Zimbabwean arm of the movement recorded 2,454 assemblies, 186 houses, 140 church buildings, and 125,889 'tithe-paying members'. Given that perhaps only a third of regular adherents in an assembly paid tithes, and gained full membership, the movement probably had between 300,000 and 400,000 people pass through its doors on a regular basis. The following year Manzou filled in a Target 2000 Survey. On the Archbishop's instruction he recorded the movement's total membership as 1.5 million. Although the figure was meant to include members in other countries it was a significant exaggeration, doubtless because the survey hinted at funding. What was more noteworthy about the survey was the data on evangelism. Under the question on 'key evangelists' just about everyone in the movement was listed: 'evangelists both local and national, elders, pastors, church members, group leaders, overseers, youth, deacons'. 'Church planting methods' were equally broad: 'local teams from assemblies, local church crusade teams, door to door witnessing, personal witnessing, home bible fellowship, family fellowship, youth fellowship, mass evangelism, open air preaching points, revivals by youth'.[4] The relentless proselytism conducted by ordinary adherents remained an important factor in ZAOGA's growth.

Manipulation and Memorialisation: The Cult of Ezekiel Guti

There is a danger in devoting too much attention to ZAOGA's leader, Ezekiel Guti. This study has continually attempted to deconstruct the church's official narratives to highlight the agency of other leaders and members in the making of the movement. Nevertheless, by the mid-1990s Guti and the movement appeared synonymous. The Archbishop, aided by his kin and clients, engineered the cult that was responsible for this impression, though there was also popular subscription to it. It is important to analyse the cult's evolution in the 1990s and consider how it appealed to ordinary ZAOGA adherents. Moreover, the cult gave the movement a very specific character, helping to define it over and against rival movements.

By the start of the 1990s Guti was subject to a great deal of reverence and adoration. He was addressed in praise names: Apostle, Servant of God, and the Man of God. Women, church veterans, and ordinary members celebrated his life in song. Everywhere ZAOGA members looked or went they would encounter his photograph:

the Waterfalls headquarters; regional offices; the Bible college; local churches; needle-work schools and pastors' homes. His booklets and tracts were replete with pictures of him in different costumes, poses and contexts. His omnipresence was reinforced at every Bible study, prayer meeting and church service where he was always remembered in prayer. His movements and his needs, whether spiritual or temporal, significant or insignificant, were relayed down the hierarchy of regional overseers to local pastors and the faithful. God was called upon to strengthen Guti not only in his cosmic strug-gle with territorial spirits of poverty but also in the more mundane – though trying – struggle with the Post and Telecommunications Corporation to have an extension put into his home. More than that, ZAOGA members prayed to the 'God of Ezekiel', believing that mention of his name would give their prayers added potency.

Often the adoration became misdevotion. At the 1996 Deeper Life Conference, Overseers Elson Makanda and William Rupapa both 'preached the man', choosing to expound Guti's tracts rather than the Scriptures. The former finished his sermon in tears:

> Father [Guti] ... Please pray that we have that connection, a better connection with you, that we may know what your God wants. We have come. Where shall we go? Pray for us. Your God will answer. Look at the thousands of people. We have come to hear from you. There is no one else.[5]

The episode was reminiscent of the Apostle Peter's recognition of Christ's divinity recorded in the Gospel of John 6: 68. Indeed, many of the public utterances made about Guti by his followers, and even some of his self-characterisations, resonate with the accounts of Christ in the Gospels. His wife Eunor told the pastors gathered at their Annual Conference that her husband would put *his* 'spirit in them' (Ezekiel 36: 27). Stones he had touched and sheets he had slept in were a source of blessing. Criti-cism of his policy was dismissed as 'blasphemy'.[6]

While at pains to emphasise that he was a 'humble servant' of God and to deny that he was the Christ, Guti actively built his own personality cult, exalting himself as a special mediator of God's word (Guti, nd-e: 18; 1989: 4). God's vision for the church quickly merged with his life-story: 'God gave a revelation through Jesus Christ. And Jesus Christ gave it to the Angel. Then the Angel of God was sent to me. Now I am giving you the vision. This is not my vision. It is his vision but he gave it to me to give to his church' (Guti, 1995 (d): 24). His writing and preaching were full of scriptural analogies comparing himself with great figures of the Old Testament: 'When follow-ing the man of God sometimes other Christians will try and discourage you. The sons of the prophets were jealous about Elisha but Elisha told them to hold their peace' (Guti, 1992d: 21). His habitual self-references resembled those of Christ: 'You will always have these people but you will not always have me'; 'my Pastors are in me and I am in them' (John 14: 11, 15: 7).[7] Guti sought to be associated with every success of the movement. Evangelists and Overseers were rebuked if they did not mention his name in media interviews. Alternative sources of revelation were discouraged. The movement's bookshops were noteworthy for the absence of books, videos and audio-tapes other than those produced by ZAOGA. Media produced by a few other selected non-ZAOGA preachers and leaders were sold, but externally donated books and tapes often remained in boxes at the headquarters. The Archbishop castigated those he dis-covered writing to America for literature and recorded sermons.[8] ZAOGA members were dissuaded from studying theology abroad or even at the University of Zimbabwe.

All pastors and teachers had to spend some time at the Bible college where the curriculum was strictly controlled and there were virtually no library holdings. Such was Guti's holy pride that those who dared to criticise him were sinful or 'backslidden'. Those who left the movement were dismissed as opportunists in search of material gain (Guti, 1994d: 18).[9] But like other prophets Guti broke his own rules and ignored his own shortcomings: 'some leaders don't accept correction from others. If you are like that you will end up with big problems in your life...Toleration is the greatest gift of the mind' (Guti, 1994d: 86).

Memorialisation was central to the extension of the cult of Guti in the 1990s. The movement's official history was inscribed into the landscape as sacred sites complemented sacred texts. The cottage in Highfield from which Guti directed his early ministry became a museum. International guests were taken there to see where the Archbishop was transfigured. On the site where Guti pioneered his first church under gum trees in Bindura a three-thousand-capacity cathedral was constructed. The cave on Mt Chipindura above the cathedral where Guti used to pray was turned into a shrine, a place of pilgrimage, prayer and fasting. Hundreds of ZAOGA members were transported to the mountain during the movement's anniversary and during special weeks of prayer. Members of the *Vapostori* who shared the sacred mountain with Guti were chased away. Finally, each new assembly building, even in Mozambique and South Africa, was supplied with a foundation stone reminding members that Guti was the founder of ZAOGA. All of the new sacred buildings and spaces were illustrated in colour in the updated *History*. The Archbishop stands in front of each in his iconic stripy evangelist's jacket.

The growing prominence of the Bindura site illustrates the role of both popular and official agency in the making of the leadership cult. There was a sacralisation of the landscape from below (Ranger, 1987) and a process of memorialisation from above. In 1985, soon after the first attempts to celebrate ZAOGA's anniversary, handfuls of ordinary church members came to the site of Guti's first church. The following year those in the Bindura congregation started caring for the gum tree. By 1990 the anniversary had grown in significance and numbers coming to the site were growing. In 1992 a group of 84 elders and deacons from Seke travelled to the mountain shrine in search of blessings for their region. As they prayed at the cave the Holy Spirit came down, reminiscent of *Vapostori* mountain vigils and Methodist camp meetings. Another miraculous event took place when two pastors and a doctor visited the site during a rainstorm and never got wet.[10] Guti made his way to Bindura in May 1993 and held a large healing service. He went again in 1995. By that stage Overseer Kapandura was in charge of the Province. A ZANU/PF stalwart, Kapandura used his contacts with the ruling party to gain control of state land where the original church was sited and then to obtain permission to construct the cathedral at the cost of Z$3.5 million (approx. £270,000). This process of religious memorialisation actively borrowed from the Zimbabwean state's attempts to remember the liberation struggle. The cathedral was built from natural stone like the National Heroes' Acre in Harare and was indeed located near the provincial heroes' acre. From the outset it had been Guti's idea to have a place of national gathering for the anniversary, the conferences and provincial councils.[11] As we shall see below, borrowing from civic ceremonial displays added impetus to the cult.

Well before the construction of the cathedral the Archbishop grasped the importance of physical memorials. In December 1988 he told his Executive: 'we need to build a museum so as to put all our things from old times. 593 [Guti's cottage in Highfield] should not be sold but kept for other people to see as they also read about it. History of the church strengthens the church.' The Rev N.K. Guti, the Archbishop's brother, added: 'We need to help. All our people who go to these places will first come to Harare and be trained on what to say.' It was to be an officially sanctioned version of the past 'realised and enforced from the top down, at considerable cost in material, social and cultural resources' (Werbner, 1998: 78). [12] Overseers and flying squads from the headquarters ensured that the anniversary and other ZAOGA doctrines were practised within two or three years of a new assembly's foundation. [13] Video and audio media were used to bring about the 'delocalisation' and homogenisation of annual celebrations. High-profile celebrations, usually involving the Archbishop, were captured on tape and circulated among the membership (Marshall, 1998). [14]

Beyond text and memorial, Guti's public persona was managed with great precision. Hierarchy and mystique were maintained. The Archbishop's attendance at events was stage-managed so that he was the last to arrive and the first to leave. Audiences waited with great expectation for his chauffeur-driven silver Mercedes to draw up outside the church or convention centre. As he entered he was accompanied by a host of overseers and pastors bowing and scraping before him. Some stirred the audience by whistling and with shouts of acclamation, others fussed around him as he was accompanied to the best seat. A stocky bodyguard lurked behind this mass of courtiers. Rarely did ordinary ZAOGA members get to rub shoulders with him. Those who came to see him at the headquarters were made to wait in dimly lit corridors. An overseer especially assigned to manage his itinerary controlled access to him. Increasingly his family and kin sought new ways to reinforce the leadership cult, seeking to enhance their own legitimacy. Eunor Guti cast herself as her husband's acolyte, transcribing his prayers and prophecies before relaying them to his followers.

Leading overseers competed to upstage each other in acts of sycophancy. One such event held on 10 December 1995 at the Conference Centre was a special Big Sunday in appreciation and recognition of the Archbishop's Apostleship. The organiser, Elson Makanda, sought to bestow upon Guti multiple confirmations of success and honour. The event was an amalgam of wedding, graduation and royal pageant. The hall was decked out in different national flags and banners covered with scriptures concerning prophets and apostles. On stage a large band played an assortment of keyboards and electric guitars, and also traditional *mbira* and *hwamanda* (antelope horns). Young girls danced in bridesmaids' outfits accompanied by young men and boys dressed in black ties and dinner-jackets, blowing whistles in time to the music. Around them were bouquets of flowers and large iced cakes. Amid the cacophony of sounds and symbols entered Guti and his retinue, dressed in academic gowns and floppy felt hats, wearing floral garlands around their necks. As they neared the stage the audience waved small flags in bright yellows, reds and greens. There then followed a celebration of Guti's life in speeches and song. Speakers often expounded key passages from *The Sacred History* to make points about the Archbishop's courage, selflessness and vision. His Apostleship was marked in other ways, too. Visitors from the Friends Christian University, USA, awarded him another honorary doctorate (in Christian Ministry). He was given a number of gifts intended to associate his achievements with longevity: a map recording the locations of ZAOGA assemblies within Zimbabwe; an engraved commemorative plaque said to last 100 years; and a large German clock encased in American oak. Not long after the event Makanda was edged out of the movement. He had become too ambitious and had overreached himself.

The sycophancy of certain overseers was matched by adoration from below. Along with the formal birthday and Christmas offerings collected by the provinces, the Archbishop also received hundreds of spontaneous gifts by letter and parcel from ordinary church members seeking his prayerful intercession on their behalf. In 1992 for instance, the Archbishop and his wife received approximately 40 letters containing sums of money ranging from twenty dollars from individuals to many thousands from Assemblies and Ministries. Sometimes the letter specified the use to which the money should be put, such as new bed sheets, or margarine and Milo (a milk drink) for 'Baba'.[15] Other gifts were ferried to the headquarters by overseers when they attended executive meetings. This tribute from the provinces included goats, sofas, vacuum cleaners, soap, and crocheted items. Some sent gifts as thanks for answered prayers. Others simply wrote to express their gratitude. In 1993 one couple wrote to thank him for the birth of a new child: 'We consider it a marvellous privilege to be your children. To us it is beyond Parents in the Lord, you have done everything that our own fleshy parents could not ... your God continues to faithfully assist us as we participate in his work.' Many believed Guti had privileged access to God. In the same year another correspondent wrote, 'I would like to thank you for revealing to me the power of the living God. I was lost in every way but now I know the truth because of your communication and obedience to God.' Many sent gifts in the hope that they would encourage the Archbishop to pray to *His* God on their behalf.

Yet others sent simple letters requesting prayer on a host of matters. In 1994 the Archbishop and his wife received 480 letters. About 30 per cent of the correspondents requested prayer for emotional and material needs: for marriage partners, healed and stable marriages; for healing from ulcers, depression, toothaches, headaches, stomach problems and AIDS; to pass exams, to find work, to gain promotion and for success in business. This letter from a church member in suburban Harare was fairly typical:

Enclosed is a gift as a vow to my prayers. Please pray for me:
1. For Sekai to hear and speak
2. For me to have total healing of my body and spirit
3. For my husband ... and son in law ... to be saved
4. That I may prosper at work and home
5. For Catherine to have a baby
6. For my children to have perfect marriages and prosperity.[16]

Some letters came as a last resort from those who had not found relief through the ministry of their local assembly. One such correspondent was the man who suffered from an unpleasant body odour:

I have so far spent more than a thousand dollars buying some deodorants and all sorts of cosmetics thinking it can help alleviate the problem ...but it could not help. I have been praying and fasting constantly for all these years but nothing changed. Most pastors and overseers have prayed over this issue but never yielded fruitful results ... The Devil has tormented me long enough.

Some correspondents requested direct help from Guti himself, usually for employment in the church as a cleaner, pastor or musician. Others simply wrote for 'counselling' about intended business ventures or for advice about the purchase of property, obtaining work permits and procedures to work abroad. Guti was perceived to have great understanding in matters of finance and law, great personal resources and immense spiritual empowerment. A church member wrote to thank him for his prayers of protection during the 1992 drought and for advice on his own personal ministry:

> Dad on behalf of [the region of] Gokwe I would like to thank you for your prayers especially through hard times. Man of God we managed to come out of drought with all our believers, even though we had some who went without food. Your God preserved your rural people.

But it was not just Guti's prayers that were seen as efficacious. When he visited the eastern town of Chipinge in 1991, the hundreds who turned out to visit him laid down their coats and jackets for him to walk on. The event was staged like the Biblical account of Christ's triumphant entry into Jerusalem. The cult of Guti evolved in symbiosis with ZAOGA's relations with the ruling party. In the 1990s, ZAOGA gained the political recognition it had long desired. Before analysing the movement's brief rapprochement with the government, it is worth considering how Guti conceptualised politics.

Politics Pentecostal Style

By the late 1980s Guti had clearly rejected the sectarianism that framed the movement's initial encounters with African nationalism. ZAOGA would not make a chiliastic withdrawal from the world. Indeed on the theology of the millennium – the last 1000 years before the return of Christ, often the source of Pentecostal otherworldliness – Guti took an idiosyncratic stand, grounded in African realities:

> We used to preach about rapture. Oh yes, we used to say the church will be caught up before the tribulations, but I don't preach it again in this country but in America they are still saying that the church will be caught before tribulations, but in Africa we no longer say that, why? Because we went through some tribulations. Our people were hung in trees and burnt alive. Others were forced to kill their parents … Some of the tribulations we read in the Bible have been seen in Africa (Guti, nd-a: 4-6).

His preaching and writing on politics was initially weak in terms of analysis and ideology, lacking a coherent theology of the state or economics. Economics clearly defied him. In one of his earliest tracts, *Where is Heaven*, written in the mid-1980s, he instructed the reader on the 22 'marks of the beast' – the anti-Christ. In a passage which resonates with some of the global Satanic conspiracy theory of Gordon Lindsay (see Gifford, 1991), Guti pointed to worrying shifts in economic systems:

4.   There is now privatisation. Privatise means to transfer from state to private ownership.
5.   But you can be surprised that no company wants to stand on its own.
6.   Now from private to co-operative.
7.   From co-operative to world government.
8.   Why world governments? It is because co-operative invites foreign investments in any country (Guti, nd-a: 2).

Guti left such conspiratorial material behind; it hardly featured in his later writings or sermons. By the 1990s he had developed a more explicit 'political theology', an idiosyncratic programme, which attributed Africa's crisis to a shifting combination

6.3 *Archbishop Guti in trance at 1996 Deeper Life Conference*

6.4 *Archbishop Guti preaching at 1996 Deeper Life Conference.*
His son-in-law, Pastor Steve Simango, translates into English

of external agency, moral failing and Satanic influence. This theology was first articulated at ZAOGA's International Christian Leadership Summit For Africa, in the
Harare International Conference Centre, February 1993. A number of Guti's sermons
preached on this occasion were later published in a short book entitled *The Church and
Political Responsibility* (1994a):

> All of these problems we are facing in Africa, most of them are not our own but its outside
> influence which causes us to fight one another. So that they can sell more guns and kill each other.
> They are earning their living through selling guns...

> Preaching alone without involvement in the development of the nation it can only help spiritually,
> but people are living in poverty. That's why the politicians are not worried about the indigenous
> churches...

> The signing of the Economic Structural Adjustment programme has caused African countries to
> release exports in order to get Foreign exchange. By doing that we have sent all our good things
> for little profit, trying to get foreign currency from devalued local currency ... why is it that the
> American Government borrowed billions, trillions but their money never devalued, why? You
> must think. Their people never suffer .[17]

Guti's political thinking had shifted to a hybrid of evangelical morality, liberation
theology and cultural nationalism. On one level it described, and proposed political
remedies for, the structural condition of the majority of ZAOGA adherents, many
of whom filled the seats of the Conference Centre. On another it was rhetorically
effective showmanship for a constituency outside the movement. The speech was
what Herbst calls 'symbolic politics', mirroring the ruling party's rhetoric on South
African regional dominance and American imperialism (1991: 233-4). The context
of Guti's utterances was important for understanding their significance. The Leadership Summit was a huge public relations exercise to impress local politicians and
enable Guti to make his mark on the International Third World Leaders Association
(ITWLA) which he had recently joined, and was soon to lead.

The style of political posturing adopted by Guti took its form directly from
ITWLA. It was a form of politics highly conducive to the neo-patrimonialism that so
often characterises the practice of African states. It functioned through personal ties
between religious and political elites under the pretext of reforming the political process: 'Our major thrust is to become a catalytic agent for unity among Christian leaders,
statesmen, churches and Ministries who desire to share a common bond of commitment to the Kingdom of God'.[18] Conducted by high-flying religious executives, this
politics of influence happened at state banquets, presidential prayer breakfasts in
international hotels and Christian conventions. Save for its emphasis on 'marriage'
and 'morality' and the virtues of liberal capitalism, Guti's political thinking essentially
lacked an ideological content that could be readily transformed into a political programme. His politics drew from an elite political culture that capitalised on its 'Third
World' origins but ignored the third world's problems.

Guti was most astute when he came to practical engagement with politicians: the
potential benefits for church growth were never off his mind. He believed that politicians needed to be saved and to be encouraged to attend church like anyone else.
According to the Archbishop, most politicians had not heard good preaching and had
sadly been dismissed as 'terrorists' by missionaries. Thus Guti taught that politicians

should be respected, as the Apostle Paul instructed in Romans 13, but not feared. Church leaders had to 'bless them' and give them 'good advice'. The church leader should model himself on Billy Graham, who 'prays with any government that comes in and advises any government that comes in because he doesn't take sides'. Where his analysis was most poignant was on church-state relations in post-colonial Africa. Free from missionary guilt for a chequered colonial heritage, Guti was never awe-struck by the party of liberation (Maxwell, 1995): 'The church has been intimidated by the governments, yet the greatest blessing of the state is the church. In some third world nations, it seems like the government is the light of the world.' The church was to disciple the nation, the nation was not to disciple the church. The church had to train doctors, lawyers and judges 'not just to go to heaven' but to 'run the earth'. But Guti had a specific agenda for his own church, which in this context he cast as 'indigenous' rather than 'international':

I believe African Governments should support the indigenous churches because this will help them not to be afraid of foreign invasion or super power invasion. Some indigenous churches which have no outside link have no ambition or power, because they are satisfied with what they are doing – building the nation by teaching productivity, praying for the government and preaching peace and unity through Jesus Christ (Guti, 1994a: 32, 44–8, 14–15).

The Archbishop was aware that 'indigenous' movements like ZAOGA needed to overcome past passivity and a narrowly defined sense of mission:

The problem of indigenous churches is that they lack influential power to influence nations. Therefore indigenous churches should look at life in a much broader horizon than to only think of future blessings ... preaching alone without participation in the development of a nation can only help while people live in poverty without financial resources to spread the gospel. That is why politicians are not bothered about indigenous churches because they do not have a realistic approach.... (Guti, 1994a: 64).

As with much of his preaching and writing, Guti's approach to politics finished where it started: 'spreading the gospel' for the salvation of individuals. Even his famous sermon to the nation, 'Lift up the Standard For the People', in February 1988, finished with an altar call. Ultimately it was 'righteousness that exalts a nation', a righteousness that comes from 'receiving Jesus Christ the son of the living God' by being 'born again by the Spirit of God'. Political involvement was the handmaid of evangelism. Citing 1 Timothy 2:1-2 he instructed church members to pray for their leaders because 'good government allows the gospel to be preached freely' (Guti, 1989: 27; 1995e: 12-13).

ZAOGA and ZANU/PF: 'The Politics of the Belly'

ZAOGA's chances of winning public recognition improved significantly when the ruling party's legitimacy began to wane. By 1988 ZANU/PF was dogged by corruption scandals, a poor human rights record and economic downturn. Support from the older historic mission churches was declining. Various agencies within the Catholic Church started to voice their concerns. The Catholic Commission for Justice and Peace began to campaign for democratisation and accountability, while the radical Catholic monthly, *Moto*, revived public concern over the 5th Brigade's ethnic-based violence against the Ndebele (1982-87). Silveria House, an engine for Catholic social teaching, began to critique the newly adopted Economic Structural Adjustment Programme. Other mainline churches followed suit (Maxwell, 1995). As these churches publicly distanced themselves from the ruling party, in the continuous search for respectabil- ity and advantage over religious rivals, ZAOGA's leadership seized the opportunity to make friends with it and get ahead. But this religious realignment was more than an instrumental move on ZAOGA's part. Its religious leadership was taking its place amongst Zimbabwe's dominant elite, participating in the culture of patrimonialism and prebendalism. On the state's part 'it was inevitable that ... [it] should attempt to absorb religious personalities who are suspected of having the ability to control the youth, and instil them with an alternative model of society' (Bayart, 1993: 188).

From the early 1990s ZAOGA began to court the leadership of ZANU/PF. Party leaders and their spouses were invited to conventions and conferences, graduation cer- emonies and the opening of new churches.[19] Donations were made to Sally Mugabe's Zimbabwe Child Survival and Development Foundation; ZAOGA lent out its confer- ence centre for state events; and the famous ZAOGA Kambuzuma choir regularly entertained the President (Guti, 1999: 129-30).[20] Key moments for feting government ministers and other party dignitaries included high-profile dinners in plush hotels hosted by the Husbands' Agape and Gracious Women's Ministries. At such events ZANU/PF leaders embraced ZAOGA's conservative doctrines on divorce and sexu- ality, using them to bolster its '"indigenous" authoritarian nationalism' against the growing rights-based discourse of opposition groups within civil society (Hammar and Raftopolous, 2003: 17).[21] Moreover, when President Mugabe made anti-feminist or homophobic statements, ZAOGA members marched in support of him. ZAOGA's September 1995 press statement on homosexuality made a point of stressing the movement's 'solidarity with his Excellency The President of Zimbabwe' following one of Mugabe's famous outbursts on the subject (Guti, 1999: 81-3, 120-22).[22] Although much of ZAOGA's public activity was pragmatic, there was a good deal of ideological agreement between the movement and the ruling party in this instance. The updated version of ZAOGA's *History* proudly declared:

> as members of the Gracious Women's Fellowship were no longer claiming unreasonable equality in the home, other women organisations which are pro-Women's liberation and extreme feminists misunderstood the vision of Gracious Women's Fellowship. They rose in fierce public opposition but God turned it out for the good … when the President of the country heard about the vision of the fellowship he acknowledged the good work and called it 'The Anti-Divorce Group' (Guti, 1999: 119-20).

ZAOGA's leadership was more instrumental in its political engagement when it lent legitimacy to Robert Mugabe in the presidential election of 1996. One of Mugabe's first formal campaign engagements was a meeting for Born-again leaders involved in the Benny Hinn Healing Crusade. This was an event controlled by ZAOGA and con- vened at ZANU/PF headquarters. The meeting was brought to a close with a prayer led by Benny Hinn. Along with others on the platform, Mugabe raised his hands as Hinn prayed. This moment of presidential charisma could be interpreted as a gesture of sheer pragmatism. Mugabe had long cast himself as a sober atheist and had never been known for acts of ecstatic activity. Nevertheless, he may well have been captured by the passion of the moment. Other government ministers have certainly been moved by ZAOGA events. As guest of honour at the 1993 International Leadership Conference, Vice-President Muzenda turned his address into a lengthy sermon punctuated by 'Amens' and 'Alleluias'. William Gumbochena, the Deputy Minister for Education and Culture, was deeply moved by testimonies of former street children given at a ZAOGA Youth Rally.[23] Other ministers such as Florence Chituaro, Minister for Home Affairs, and Olivia Muchena, Deputy Minister for Lands, were well-known Born-again Christians sympathetic to ZAOGA.[24] In his conversion to Pentecostal practice President Mugabe may well have been moved by another sort of passion: his second wife, Grace, was a ZAOGA member related to one of the movement's overseers. Moreover, Mugabe's sister taught Sunday School at ZAOGA's Chispite Assembly. Familial relations are crucial determinants in contemporary Zimbabwean politics.

The day after the ZAOGA-ZANU/PF rally, Zimbabwe's national daily, *The Herald,* displayed a picture of Mugabe and Guti on the front page.[25] 'Catch the Cockerel before dawn', a senior pastor told his faithful a few days later when encouraging them to vote (the cockerel being the ZANU/PF symbol). In their encounter with ZAOGA ZANU/PF grasped the civic virtues of Pentecostalism. They admired ZAOGA-style Pentecostalism for its discipline and social control. It was a movement that took young people off the streets, and gave them a moral framework and a desire to work.[26] Moreover, in the post-Cold War era the prosperity gospel and bourgeois values propounded by ZAOGA's leaders were consistent with the regime's abandonment of Marxism-Leninism and engagement with economic liberalisation and structural adjustment. Through this 'reciprocal assimilation of elites', ZAOGA was able to enhance its primary objective of evangelism (Bayart, 1993:150-79; Freston, 1996). Guti used his personal connections with Mugabe to aid the movement's transnational expansion: he gained a letter of recommendation to President Moi to aid the movement's registration in Kenya and a visa to visit and preach (clandestinely) in China.[27] More generally, good relations with the government, especially the Ministries of Foreign Affairs and of Trade and Commerce, facilitated the movement of money, people and equipment necessary for transnational crusades and international conferences based in Zimbabwe. By the mid-1990s American evangelists such as Benny Hinn were no longer seen as a threat, but as a political opportunity.

The 'emergent political hybridity' from this new-found reciprocity was 'a two way process' (Werbner, 1996: 16-17). Mugabe lifted his hands to become momentarily a charismatic Christian, gave his testimony at prayer breakfasts and appropriated the language of moral and spiritual renewal to replace the discredited rhetoric of Marxism-Leninism. In return Guti borrowed some of the ruling party's clothes. Like President Mugabe, the Archbishop's authority was boosted by civic ceremonial displays: the motorcade, the staged entry and exit, the birthday gift. It was celebrated in women's songs and reinforced through the dissemination of his photographic portrait. Before each working day commenced at the ZAOGA HQ in Waterfalls, Harare, devotions were held during which a reworked version of the former Zimbabwean national anthem was sung:

God bless Africa
exalt its name
hear our prayers
God bless your family

God bless ZAOGA
exalt its name
hear our prayers

God bless your family

God bless Ezekiel
Uplift His Spirit
Hear our prayers
God bless your Servant

In a literal illustration of what Richard Werbner calls 'cross dressing', Eunor Guti would arrive at church events, like royalty, dressed in gold and silks, adorned with a crown-shaped brooch, wearing a brightly coloured turban (1996: 16-17). The ruling party also provided ZAOGA's leadership with an excellent blueprint for church politics: the leadership cult; the purges of the pioneers and other influential leaders; and the growth of patronage along lines of ethnicity, kinship and faction. And Guti made much of his association with Mugabe to boost his status. Photographs of Guti accompanied by the President visiting the Bible school adorned the walls of the headquarters and were included in the 1999 version of the *History*.

At times ZAOGA's leadership sounded more like chest-thumping politicians than men of God. In a surprisingly *un*-pastoral statement to his 1995 Pastors Conference, Guti taunted his church leaders: '[some of you] are with me because there is nowhere else to go. Others are with me because I have overpowered them ... they cannot do better things. They do not love me but they have nowhere to go.'[28] The assimilation of ruling party practice also legitimated the rapid movement of resources up the church hierarchy through the processes of gift exchange and clientage, thereby increasing the inequalities between ordinary pastors and a charmed few who surrounded Guti. In August 1996, Overseer Christopher Chadoka, the movement's number three, was called upon by the popular monthly *Parade* to defend the leadership's increasing tendency towards nepotism and tribalism. He chose to do so, not by drawing on Biblical precedent, but on the practice of patrimonialism: 'if we look at these companies, are there no managing directors' relatives?... And if you buy bread, do you give it to other people leaving your relatives hungry?'[29] In a graphic illustration of what Bayart describes as the 'politics of the belly' (1993), Chadoka enlightened the 1996 Deeper Life Conference on the virtues of giving:

> I did not know that you can call money saying 'Money come, come, come' [beckoning gesture]. Many times in my house if we did not have eggs I would walk up and down [praying] because I am pastor and you would see the eggs coming ... One day my kids told me the meat in the fridge was getting finished. I said 'I am not going to buy, it will come'. One region would bring a goat or a sheep. If Mrs C... was here -- she was filling my deep freezer with meat. When I was in Norton preaching, raising money ... somebody ran away and brought a goat. Now the boy who is working at my home is getting tired of killing because the God of Ezekiel supplies.[30]

There is a danger of exoticising African religion and politics by analysing them in terms of local idiom. ZAOGA developed out of a synthesis of local and global cultural forces. The Guti family also legitimated their hold over the movement by observing that Christ For the Nations, Dallas, was now run by the widow 'Mrs Gordon (Freda) Lindsay' and her son, Dennis. Moreover, American evangelical leaders, such as Jerry Falwell and Pat Robertson, have attempted to influence the political process. Similarly, successive American presidents have not fought shy of calling themselves 'Born-again' or appropriating the Christian language of moral and spiritual renewal. However, in

Zimbabwe religious and political interactions are localised and specific. Given the relative strength of the church and the limited size of the dominant elite, church leaders can exert a direct and personal influence on politicians in a way that the complexities of the American political system would not allow. These personalised politics stand in contrast to the highly organised politicking of the US Christian Right.

In Zimbabwe, as in the USA and Latin America, the Born-again engagement with politics has not always produced the desired results. Politicians such as Mugabe have consorted with the church in moments of crisis only to abandon the counsel of leading clerics when it is no longer required. Within ZAOGA much was made of the fact that Guti was hand-picked by President Mugabe to sit on the 1999 government-appointed commission to redraft the constitution. But what was just as noteworthy was that he was only one of 395 appointees, chosen alongside numerous other church leaders and representatives of interest groups. ZAOGA was but one of a range of sources of legitimacy ZANU/PF sought to exploit in its attempts to undermine the National Constitutional Assembly.

Often, the 'noisiness' of ZAOGA's arrival on the political scene was just that. Contemporary Pentecostalism is characterised by a good deal of hype and choreography (Freston, 1996: 164). Commonplace events are turned into the miraculous in order to convince members that they are part of a unique and anointed movement. The movement's canonised history casts Guti as central to the nation's post-civil war experience. The reader is told that, during the International Leadership Summit in 1993, Vice-President Muzenda went down on his knees before Guti 'as the apostle of God prayed for the country to be healed' (Guti, 1999: 128). Yet Muzenda himself had preached a message about individual cleanliness and was coaxed into receiving Guti's blessing by the Ghanaian master of ceremonies, Kingsley Fletcher. A disaffected guest speaker at the Summit complained that in spite of its high profile there were in fact very few national or international leaders present at all. The conference centre had been packed out with ZAOGA women. Moreover, the unpublished minutes of a debriefing meeting shortly after the event recorded 'the vice President was prayed for and was afraid that a demon may be cast out'. It would seem that ZAOGA had as little respect for political leaders as politicians had for the church.[31]

In essence the state has never been ZAOGA's 'critical referent' (Marshall, 1993: 216). ZAOGA's leadership were simply accomplished in what Paul Freston describes as 'time serving', 'the art of keeping oneself close to power, regardless of ideology or principle, in order to receive benefits' (Freston, 1994: 563). Even in the 1990s, ZAOGA's energies were primarily directed at constant internal restructuring and domination of the religious field. The leadership's rhetoric and practice were chiefly concerned with *religious* struggle. Having just purchased the former Dutch Reformed Church in Waterfalls, the jubilant ZAOGA Overseer Chadoka told a crowded suburban gathering:

> We will choose which building we need and not waste time. God said we are going to move the names of other churches and put ours in its place ... The God you will see in this organisation is different. Others come to our Big Sundays to take what we teach to their churches ... this is the Royal family in the Kingdom of God.[32]

Thus, in spite of its ideological sympathies with ZANU/PF on the family and sexuality, black autonomy and self-reliance, ZAOGA's leadership were quick to shift their loyalties once the relationship no longer suited them. As ZANU/PF's legitimacy grew ever more tenuous and it resorted to political violence to stave off the MDC, so ZAOGA's love affair with the government came to an end. Given that the bulk of its membership in the townships were terrorised by a coalition of war veterans, police and the army who saw them as potential MDC supporters, ZAOGA could not ignore their voice. But there were strong ideological reasons for realignment. Political violence and instability made the movement's primary goal of evangelism far more problematic, while inflation and the shortage of foreign currency hindered transnational expansion. Economic stability was crucial for other ZAOGA activities and doctrines. The collapse of the economy undermined Talents, the possibility of a respectable family life and the gospel of prosperity. Mugabe had lost his chance. From 2000 onwards, leading overseers advised their flocks to vote for the MDC, and ZAOGA joined other churches in Manicaland in two public statements condemning ZANU/PF-directed political violence.[33]

The Gospel of Money

By the 1990s ZAOGA had become a victim of its own success. It had engendered social mobility, creating and attracting a middle-class membership while retaining its original township base and expanding into the rural areas. It had become a microcosm of wider society, embodying all its tensions. The need to create a large bureaucracy to manage such a large movement had alienated many of its longstanding adherents. A question-and-answer session at the Annual Pastors Conference held in the early 1990s illustrated how far the movement had evolved. The Conference provided a powerful contrast to a similar session held almost twenty years earlier shortly after Guti had returned from Dallas (see Chapter 4). At that stage the movement was a sect whose timid members were conscious of their poor education and low social standing, and uncertain of their relation to rival movements such as burial societies. They looked to Guti for advice on matters relating to table manners, bathroom decorum, and the correct form of address to people of high social standing. Two decades later their concerns were quite different. Some of the questions, submitted anonymously, concerned the aloofness of their overseers and their bias towards the rich when it came to the distribution of positions within local assemblies. Others raised the issue of women wearing trousers, or asked whether *Kwasa Kwasa*, a type of music associated with a highly sexualised form of dancing, should be played at weddings. In the 1970s the consuming passion of ZAOGA's pastorate had been evangelism; now the pastors' primary concerns related to their material well-being.[34]

In spite of the continued effervescence of Pentecostalism in the Southern hemisphere, little research has been conducted so far on those who have 'walked out' of the movement. Early indications suggest that one of the most vulnerable social categories comprised the children of the pastorate. This was recognised in 1991 with the foundation of a new ministry for pastors' children called Sons and Daughters of the Prophets (SADOP) (Guti, 1999: 123). At their first conference of that year the children had a question-and-answer session with the Archbishop. Their questions, submitted anonymously, pointed to similar concerns about their material circumstances, about fashion and popular entertainment. Other questions suggested a strong resentment about the way their leisure and love affairs were scrutinised by their parents' assemblies. Finally there were questions that suggested disdain for their poorly qualified parents and other leaders. SADOP members, particularly the children of overseers and other high ranking leaders, had had their horizons widened by higher education, travel abroad and the comforts of a middle-class existence. They were more aware than others of what the world had to offer, that life could be ordered in ways other than those ordained by ZAOGA. Leaders' children were also painfully aware of the pressures and double standards by which the church leadership operated. Some children had lost allegiance to ZAOGA when abroad; others had developed bitterness toward their parents. Others still had channelled their religious enthusiasm into other Pentecostal and charismatic churches with a more sophisticated leadership, a subject discussed in more depth below.[35]

In interviews, ZAOGA's leaders repeatedly stressed that their emphasis on money was necessary if they were to maintain and expand the movement's numerous ministries. ZAOGA did not have permanent and wealthy overseas donors like the historic mission churches. Nevertheless, wealth and growth had brought unforeseen problems. For Pricilla Ngoma the movement's evolution had become a morality tale: 'We used to pray for prosperity from God because the church was poor. We prayed for people who are educated who could repent and help us financially. However the blessing has become the gospel of money ... the church is full of rubbish, with people made leaders who are not saved.'[36] Many others alleged that certain businessmen had been promoted despite private lives that fell short of Pentecostal expectations. After recitation of the *Sacred History* during anniversary celebrations, there was space for ordinary members to testify. Longstanding members used it as an opportunity to highlight how hierarchy, wealth and power had replaced the equality and intimacy that characterised early gatherings: 'there used to be lots of love in ZAOGA. Everyone was the same in the eyes of the people and of God.'[37]

ZAOGA's dominant elite had come to espouse the values of liberal capitalism: the rationale of the market, the acquisition of consumer goods and real estate, the centrality of the nuclear family, the virtues of education, cleanliness and sobriety. The resulting class divide had been clouded by the movement's promotion of a civic consciousness: an emphasis on citizenship, obeying the law, respecting property and challenging corruption. This consciousness had been fostered in the 1970s and 1980s by the gathering of the movement at Deeper Life Conferences, National Big Sundays and rallies for the various ZAOGA associations. By the 1990s, ZAOGA had expanded to such a degree that it was forced to decentralise. Big Sundays were now restricted to regions and districts. There was only capacity at Deeper Life Conferences for church elders, not even deacons. Tensions of class, generation and ethnicity increasingly came to the fore.

Social divisions were most manifest amongst the young pastors and Bible school students who had the greatest sense of the inequalities of power and wealth within ZAOGA. There was a perception that the Archbishop, his overseers and the favoured few administrators had lined their own pockets at the expense of pastors and membership. Guti and his henchmen had fallen foul of a moral economy operating within the movement that was a 'reinvention of traditional cultural constraints' on accumulation (Burke, 1996: 187; Marshall, 1993: 230). Believers were not supposed to be 'stingy' nor were they supposed to be greedy. The legitimacy of leaders rested on keeping their accumulation in balance with the fortunes of their members. There was a widely felt sense that the leadership had overstepped the mark.[38] While Guti received millions of Zimbabwean dollars from the church in Christmas and birthday gifts, many pastors were as poor as church-mice on allowances of Z\$200-500 per month (£15-37.00). Those in suburban locations led churches which could collect as much as Z\$20,000 (£150) each month in tithes. Moreover, the Archbishop's taunts were true. Many of these young men (and women) did indeed have nowhere else to go. Often they were from the streets or a poor background and possessed few qualifications. They relied on the church for their training, wages, accommodation and bride price. They were a long way from the spoils of power seen to ascend rapidly through the church hierarchy. One church worker ruefully cited the scripture, 'don't muzzle an ox while it threshes', and protested that he had certainly not been delivered from the spirit of poverty. Others made ethnic jokes, complaining that they had not progressed within the movement because they did not marry an Ndau – a member of Ezekiel and Eunor Guti's ethnic group. Another mused that he had only been promoted once he had started buying bread for his overseer. While the gifted, well-connected and sycophantic were promoted to richer churches with the opportunity of extensive gifts from their flocks, most remained poor, serving in rural areas and high-density townships. Ordinary pastors remained liable to 'capture from below' (Campbell, 1995: 142). Dependent on local assemblies for their survival they were drawn into local struggles for housing, health and employment. A good deal of their time was spent meeting the material needs of their flocks.

Compromised by their dependence on the senior leadership, young pastors and Bible school students 'toy[ed] with power rather than confronting it directly' (Mbembe, 1992: 122). While a senior pastor saw it fit to tell his flock to 'catch the cockerel before dawn', a younger pastor told his congregation a joke about an American tourist who confused ZANU/PF headquarters, emblazoned with the symbol of a cockerel, with the fast-food chain, Chicken Inn.[39] Many of the young pastors shared in the widespread delight of the much publicised by-election victory of the rebel politician Margaret Dongo over the official ZANU/PF candidate in late 1995, and embraced the MDC's formation in 1999. Like the youth in South Africa's Zionist churches, they were none too impressed by the political connections made by their elders (Kiernan, 1994: 79-81).

The pressure from below occasionally manifested itself in outright challenges to clerical power. One assembly in a Harare high-density suburb, who described themselves as 'some of the poorest people in Zimbabwe', organised a petition and delegation to ZAOGA HQ against a greedy pastor (and relation of the Archbishop). They complained that he appeared bent on humiliating church members because of their poverty rather than seeking the betterment of the whole religious community. Moreover, within the 'free space' of the local assembly, democratising forces ran counter to the growing hierarchy and authoritarianism of the movement (Martin, 1990: chapter 12). A great attempt was made to conduct elections for posts of deacons and elders with scrupulous honesty, in marked contrast to the corruption and filibustering that characterised ruling party politics. In January 1996 there was some disquiet over the elections in the main Highfield Assembly. The election had happened too quickly and some of those in office had been dropped without warning, or a chance to stand again. On 14 January a flying squad of two elders from assemblies outside Highfield arrived to officially nullify the results and re-run the election. Having lectured from the *Rules and Policy* booklet and checked the credentials of those standing, they oversaw an orderly vote. When new officials were elected in accordance with procedure, a leading female member of the assembly summed up: 'we are not like ZANU/PF, we have a good spirit here'.

Another source of egalitarianism lay in the movement's student and post-graduate associations. Their educated elite membership was well travelled and widely read, and had experienced other models of church government with which to compare ZAOGA. They were also influenced by Western-derived rights discourses, which were more than simple rhetorical devices in the hands of political elites (Monga, 1996: 46–54). Confident in their authority and social standing, they spoke out in assemblies against erroneous abuses of power. At a gathering in one of Harare's plusher suburbs the female master of ceremonies suggested that if those present purchased a red carpet the Archbishop might be persuaded to visit. A student member groaned loudly in disgust. It was widely accepted that Think Progressive ZAOGA (TPZ), a troublesome pressure group within the movement, had its base amongst students and post-graduates. In 1996 TPZ went to the popular monthly *Parade* to expose nepotism, tribalism and authoritarianism within the leadership.[40]

The aspirations of ZAOGA's dominant elite came to be expressed in theological terms in a prosperity gospel that endorsed the acquisition of wealth and conspicuous consumption as a sign of God's blessing. It was a doctrine that also explained poverty and misfortune in terms of a lack of faith and generosity rather than the inequalities created by capitalism. The theological shift was apparent in the Archbishop's writings and preaching. His earlier publications had countered prosperity teachings by emphasising the place of suffering in the Christian life. One tract in particular, *Human Beings Cannot Change without Pressure*, described a God who chastens and a Christ who suffered. And Guti drew upon the significance of trials and temptations in his personal development. 'One time I went into the bush saying to God, I must die, because of the pressures which were like fire on me ...' (1992d: 5). This early theological emphasis on suffering and perseverance gradually gave way to the 'gospel of money'. In an address to the Pastors Conference in 1997 he warned those gathered:

> If you don't want to die or leave and get poor, or have little kids mock you in the streets, then stay and grow rich. People who have left do not prosper, they lose their blessings. When they get old they will have nothing. It takes time to build a church and to start making money.[41]

His address was entitled 'The Crucified Life'. Guti's wife Eunor was equally explicit. Urging people to give towards the costs of the 1996 Benny Hinn Healing Crusade, she told crowds gathered at the Rufaro Stadium, Harare, that they remained poor because they lacked generosity. In the early 1980s ZAOGA had taught that giving was 'a natural expression of loving God' and that it respected 'each individual's right to be responsible in his giving'; by the 1990s tithes were something that *had* to be paid to ensure full church membership.[42]

Opposition to the prosperity gospel was expressed in theological terms. The most effective critique came from the older populist Pentecostalism that animated the movement in the 1960s, and emphasised suffering as a necessary part of the believer's life. Pastors who had joined ZAOGA in its infancy when it was rooted in township culture maintained this holiness tradition (see Chapters 1 and 3). These older hands expressed bewilderment and disquiet at the preaching of the new 'soft and smooth' Christianity. Others made a theological critique on the basis of more orthodox evangelical doctrine and were particularly critical of the personality cult that merged Guti's identity with that of Christ.

Finally, protest took the form of migration. The smaller schisms of the 1990s that led to Mike Muwani's Bible Believers' Church, Cleopas Chitapa's Cornerstone Fellowship, and Sam Manyika's Living Word Ministry were as much about doctrine as power. These smaller churches, and to a lesser extent those founded by other ousted pioneers, aimed at restoring theological orthodoxy. There were alternative routes out of ZAOGA taken by students and young professionals who simply changed churches, joining smaller charismatic churches they had encountered at college. These movements such as Richmond Chundidiza's Glad Tidings Fellowship or Ngwisa Mkandla's Faith Ministries were founded by graduates and were more sophisticated in their teaching and appeal.[43] Other professionals who had established themselves in Harare's plush northern suburbs simply moved into white-dominated charismatic churches such as Rhema and Vineyard.

Instruction on Modernity

While some of the ZAOGA pastorate grumbled about hypocrisy and inequality, most of them remained within the movement. Likewise, graduates and professionals disliked the theological and authoritarian direction of the leadership, but most stayed. The vast majority of the movement overlooked the shenanigans of their leaders or chose to forgive them. Like Christians across the globe, many ZAOGA members found contentment in daily contact with their religious communities. Their life of prayer, worship and ministry will be the subject of Chapter 8. But the last section of this chapter will consider how ZAOGA's leadership faced problems of disengagement and attempted to address the needs of ordinary adherents.

First and foremost Guti was a religious leader. His first tracts written in the late 1980s and early 1990s addressed issues of worldliness within the movement by asserting classic Pentecostal teachings. His booklet *Principles of the Doctrine of Christ* read like a Pentecostal catechism (1993c). Drawing heavily from the Epistles it first established the nature of the Church and a pattern for church government. It subsequently discussed key Pentecostal practices and doctrines: prayer and fasting; worship and praise; and the gifts of the Holy Spirit. Guti's writings always placed a strong emphasis on individual spirituality. His *New Believer's Guide to Christian Success* initiated the new convert into the importance of Bible study, prayer, and being filled with the Holy Spirit (1992a). Given that the nature and works of the Holy Spirit were central to Pentecostalism, the subject recurs throughout his writings and preaching. The tract *Saved, Baptised and Filled* was devoted to the subject (1993b). The Archbishop saw prayer as crucial. It was a means by which the believer built a personal relationship with God, and the engine of church growth. Finally, in spite of the leadership cult there was a strong Christocentric element to his preaching. The redeeming work of Christ underpinned all that the Church stood for (1995c, 1992b, 1995d: 45–51).

The Archbishop was also acutely aware of some of the excesses of the broader Pentecostal movement. Pentecostals had come to place too much emphasis on the Holy Spirit as a source of empowerment at the expense of virtue, obedience and self-discipline. Thus he restated the Holiness roots of the Pentecostal movement: 'We have been misrepresenting scriptures ... The Bible says apply instruction in learning but we have given everything to the Holy Spirit. We have tempted the Holy Spirit because of our laziness and saying the spirit will do everything for me' (1995c: 12).

Commenting on the failed marriages among believers, he observed: 'The problem is that people are praying for power and binding the Devil instead of asking God to give long suffering which is very needful to any married couple.' Instead of naively relying on the Holy Spirit as some sort of spiritual palliative, Guti argued that believers should strive to develop their character built upon 'courage' and 'refusal to fail'. Guti stressed that Pentecostal Christians should be agents in the making of their own lives. Christians grew through self-discipline and obedience (1994b: 52-4). Guti believed that self-control, particularly the power of positive thinking, was the key to success:

[F]irst of all we must be able to control our minds because the battle ground of the devil is in the mind. Proverbs 25: 28 'Like a city whose walls are broken down is a man who lacks self control'. When you overcome your mind you will enjoy life. [Y]ou cannot dream yourself into character. You must hammer it yourself through self-discipline' (1992d: 12, 15; nd-i: 6; 1994d: 86).

Equally important were his teachings on the family and modernisation. While the ideology informing his engagement with the state was fairly limited, he did have a politics of social reproduction. His vision for the individual extended to the family and its immediate surroundings, but not much further. A stable nuclear family was a central concern in Guti's preaching, the most important theme after doctrine and spirituality. He penned three short booklets on the subject: *Hearing and Listening is a Problem even in the Home* (1993a); *Does Your Marriage Look Like This?* (1994b); and *Shut your Mouth!* (1995b). In these publications he advanced a clear patriarchal basis to social life beginning with the nuclear family: 'Here is the order: single then marriage, then family, after family is community, then society; then nation. All this builds on the male man' [sic] (1994b: 26). Guti's model of male headship required a benign patriarchy, a husband willing to stay at home and take his responsibilities seriously. Such an emphasis was well-placed because male desertion, violence, promiscuity and alcoholism were some of the key forces threatening the survival of women and children (B. Martin, 2001). Guti taught that for the African family to function properly the male had to be re-socialised and domesticated:[44]

[T]he Devil has a plan to destroy the young man, putting him on drugs. To put him in jail, to put him in violence, to put him in crime, why? If he can destroy the man, he can destroy the society. If you want to have a strong nation, a strong society, bring the man back to God. ... Men go out into your cities, take the young boys off the streets. Bring boys back to God. Bring men back to God and save the families of the nation (Guti, 1994b: 10-13).

A Christian husband was to be a *responsible* husband able to provide for his family. If the family did not develop it was *his* fault. The Archbishop counselled women not to marry men who were unemployed. The husband was expected to honour his wife, to be sensitive to her needs, to buy her flowers when she was alive and not just for her grave. He was expected to know about diet and not get sick or overweight ((1993a; 1994b). He was also to be a good lover. In *Shut your Mouth*, Guti instructed the husband on the physiology of female genitalia and the importance of satisfying his wife's sexual desires (1995b). He bemoaned the liberal USA where spanking a child was viewed as abuse. It was the task of parents to instil respect into their children:

'It is hard for the people to respect the government … unless they learn obedience in the home and family' (1994a: 32-3, 37). Therefore 'a responsible husband [was] a responsible citizen'. A strong family was the start of God's plan for a strong nation. It also made sound economic sense. A wife was the best possible business partner. Guti wrote: '[d]ivorce is not the answer and divorce is not losing your spouse only, but your dignity, respect, money, trust, family and house' (1994b:v., 22; 1993a).

Guti's writing on social reproduction flowed into advice on modernisation. His reflections on the importance of regulation and planning, organisation and self-control, discipline and virtue began with the church, but had intended consequences for the domestic sphere and the world of work. The Archbishop's vision for a modern well-run church is found in his copious writings on church life. He asserted that pastors should be trained: 'The days of self-made leaders are gone'. They had to set a good example to their flock and crucially not to have 'credits' – debts. A good pastor was not to have the same 'burdens' as the people (nd-h: 4-5). Church meetings were to be ordered. The pastor should know how to chair a meeting and deal with questions from the floor. While having the appearance of spontaneity, praise and worship had to be properly organised. Pastors and their acolytes were given clear directions on how to choose songs, set up instruments and use a microphone. Pastors had to do their homework for weddings, acquainting themselves with the law regarding 'marriage, custom and tradition'. They also had to acquit themselves well in public. When visiting a hospital the 'pastor should carry some form of identification … [and] take time to introduce himself to the head nurses' (1995d: 40; nd-f; 1991: 37, 23). They were instructed to study 'ethics and etiquette and dressing'. Eating when walking along the road was wrong because 'the Bible says man looks on the outward appearance' [1 Samuel 16: 7; Titus 2: 10; 1 Timothy 3: 7]. When visiting friends or new believers, the pastor was to stay for just a short time. He or she should 'clean [the] bathroom after bathing' and 'flush [the] toilet after using it'. And pastors were to speak quietly when talking. The worst sins were poor time-keeping and disorganisation. A good leader did not turn up late to church, kept his appointments, did not spend too long preaching, dwelt too long in the bathroom and toilet, or spend too long dressing. The pastor who had his passport stolen in the same place every year when attending the annual conference was a particular object of the Archbishop's scorn. There was a similar range of instructions for elders (1991: 48; 1994d: 70-80; 1994c).

The significance of a well-ordered church was not lost on the Archbishop. He reminded pastors that if they learnt to put together a pastoral strategy for their church they could also 'plan for [their] school children, for Christmas, for life, for holidays'. His advice addressed issues beyond the church. Young couples had to learn to budget, and everyone had to learn 'modern ways of eating'. Fatty and sweet foods were to be avoided. Believers had to guard their health by taking rest (1995c: 32; 1994b: 67-76; 1995d: 40-41).Family planning was also essential. In a version of his Third World Mentality sermon, he chided his audience: 'Some black people today complain. They have got black children and they only earn $100. They complain "I have got many children. My money is little". Who bore the children?' [45] Finally, believers had to change their attitudes towards work. Husbands had to work hard for their families but also for their companies. If a believer was promoted to foreman he should leave later than workers.[46] And work was to be done to a high standard. Speaking the language of hard-nosed black and white bosses, he told one audience: 'We do not want "chop-chop things". The work should be done properly. When you are repairing my car do not put temporary wires in it. You should take your time and do a good job.'[47] The theme of personal responsibility runs though much of Guti's teaching and in his approach he shares a good deal with the highly respected Ghanaian preacher Mensa Otabil with whom he appears to be on good terms (Gifford, 2004, chapter 5).[48]

Guti's writing and teaching were all the more credible because they were replete with modern images. Marital relations were modelled on management structures. 'Before God, man and woman are equal. But God has given us different responsibilities. Just like in the company, one is a director, one is secretary or deputy director.' And when encouraging pastors to use their imagination in preaching he drew from a range of examples spanning business, politics and the media. 'Advertising men, Salesmen, Radio Broadcasters, Television Producers, Business Executives, Educators, Presidents, Prime Ministers and Military Leaders all relied on the power of imagination.' Similarly, he reminded young preachers of the power of statistics, and cited research from psychology on the power of visual representation (1994b:77; 1991: 14, 29, 33).

Finally, Guti's words were compelling because his writings and teachings were patterned on his accessible and widely circulated autobiography, *The Sacred History* (1989). His early life was noteworthy for its representativeness. He was the archetypal modern Zimbabwean man. From a humble background he came to the city and struggled to find permanent work and residence, education and respectability. He struggled against racism, not just at work but in the church as well. He succeeded, and built a life of dignity and prosperity. Moreover, his later life as a globe-trotting African ambassador of the Born-again movement was an achievement many aspired to. Church members recognised their lives and aspirations in Guti's narrative, and perceived in it how they could begin to change them. As J.D.Y. Peel observes: 'Narrative empowers because it enables its possessor to integrate his memories, experiences, and aspirations in a schema of long-term actions' (1995: 587). While not endorsing all of modernity's values, Guti had mastered its institutional and technological tools and sought to help others toward a similar mastery. 'He has brought his people a long way' was a common refrain among ZAOGA members.

ZAOGA members also progressed towards modernity through membership of the numerous ministries that proliferated within the movement in the late 1980s and early 1990s. After independence a small but growing class of professionals and businessmen had driven the movement forward. This group had moved out of overcrowded accommodation in the former townships into luxurious houses in the former white suburbs of Zimbabwe's towns and cities. They had also moved into positions of leadership in business and the civil service, rubbing shoulders with whites and international visitors. This rapid social change was accompanied by significant shifts in gender relations in the work-place as legislation and education opened up new areas of work for women. There was a good deal of popular concern with how to manage this rapid social change, as reflected in the debates and advertisements in Zimbabwean monthlies like *Parade* and *Horizon*. Some of ZAOGA's ministries acted as 'finishing schools', teaching 'propriety and domesticity' and the means to advance economically within a Born-again framework (Mate, 2002: 552). One of ZAOGA's most prominent new ministries in the 1990s – the African Christian Business Fellowship – served this purpose exactly. Founded by Guti and officially opened by the Minister for Industry and Commerce, Cde Simon Kaya Moyo, the Fellowship met every lunch hour for prayer at a venue in Harare's central business district. Guti was a regular speaker, instructing those gathered on how to conduct their affairs in a godly manner and without recourse to witchcraft, particularly the use of body parts for powerful medicine (Guti, 1999: 110-11).

The Gracious Women's Fellowship also initiated members into the modern world. Evolving out of local women's meetings of the 1970s, it continued to teach industry and entrepreneurship through Talents, enabling women to develop their business activities. The simultaneous teaching of domesticity helped them grasp the demands of a bourgeois life-style. There were also new activities such as lavish dining events in international hotels. Co-organised with the Husbands' Agape Fellowship, these events enabled ZAOGA's elite membership to turn out in their finery to be entertained by choirs and public speakers at events suitable for the fêting of government ministers and other dignitaries.

Rekopantswe Mate has argued that the function of the Gracious Women's Fellowship was to enable Born-again married women to manage modernity while retaining a Christianised version of patriarchy. It encouraged women to excel professionally and economically while ensuring that they submitted to their husbands when they got home. Thus patriarchy was never rejected but simply 'bargained with' and reintroduced through the Christian notion of female submission to male headship (Mate, 2002: 565-6). There is some truth in Mate's analysis. Male headship was a key doctrine within the Gracious Women's Fellowship, but Mate's model of the patriarchal Christian household is too simplistic because she fails to consider how Pentecostal movements can domesticate and re-socialise men into responsible providers. The central aim of the Husbands' Agape and Gracious Women's Fellowships was to maximise the opportunities of social reproduction for both men and women alike.

The women's ministry as 'finishing school' made most sense among elite women, professionals and wives of senior church leaders who attended meetings in Harare's low-density suburbs and city centre where Mate conducted her fieldwork. In these areas, events such as 'baby showers', *braais* and parties for brides-to-be socialised women into a middle-class existence. Indeed some of these women referred to the 'School of Talents'. But for most Gracious Women who lived in Zimbabwe's townships and communal lands a comfortable lifestyle remained an aspiration. These women joined the Fellowship for female solidarity, which came through prayer, hymn-singing and Bible study. Like numerous Christian women's groups before them, Gracious Women were the foot-soldiers of the church. Their vital contribution to evangelism and teaching was recognised and institutionalised in 1989 with the formation of the sub-ministry, Go Quickly and Tell. If there was any patriarchal plot within the movement it was that groups such as Gracious Women and Go Quickly channelled female religious enthusiasm away from the centre of church life where it could pose a threat to male authority (Campbell, 1995: 44-51). By the 1990s it was clear that women's work through Talents was the financial backbone of the Church. In 1995 their income-generating activities enabled the movement to purchase 18 new trucks for provincial overseers and two lorries. The millions of Zimbabwean dollars they raised far exceeded external donations.

While ZAOGA's rich associational life taught children, schoolteachers, blind people and widows useful organisational skills, the ministries were essentially evangelistic. Thus the Post-Graduate Fellowship founded in 1992 was to keep young professionals within ZAOGA, and 'to win other graduates for the Lord'. In promoting the corporate interests of each group and providing them with intimacy, the various ministries proved vital in ameliorating the worst effects of alienation experienced in large organisations such as ZAOGA (Hastings, 1994: 592-604).

Conclusion

In the mid-1980s, Archbishop Guti explained to a ZAOGA gathering, using his characteristic turn of phrase, that part of his 'Ministry' was 'to bless the poor so that they can come up ... to raise people from the ash and polish them and make them well accepted in the Country'. But respectability brought a host of new problems.[49] David Martin identifies a tension inherent in expanding Pentecostal movements: 'Much depends on the balance, which Pentecostalism maintains between its ability to expand among the masses, by remaining of the masses, and its ability to advance their condition. If the former remains powerful the latter must operate at the margin' (Martin, 1990: 232). By the 1990s that tension was very apparent. The class divide within the movement was most antagonistic within the pastorate where the majority grew ever more resentful at the lifestyle of a chosen few who comprised Guti's kin, tribe or business allies. Ironically it was a group of successful church members, the young professionals, who put most pressure on the leadership. These university-educated men and women with a greater theological sophistication and liberal notions of human rights objected to ZAOGA's authoritarian government and the excesses of the leadership cult. Though influential, these groups represented only a minority of church members. Most members remained content with their leadership. They perceived Guti as a Christian prophet with special powers to ensure their personal security in relation to healing, fertility, defence from demonic possession and the avoidance of absolute poverty. His ability to act as a mediator between his people and God also guaranteed the loyal support of some professional elites. 'As a bringer of divine blessing' he was 'believed to be able to change the course of nature, to sway the will of God, and thus to affect the predestined movement of the universe' (P. Werbner, 1996: 105). If these elites succeeded in business, built successful marriages for themselves and their children, passed examinations, secured well-paid work and obtained promotions – many interpreted this as a sign of God's blessing conferred on them via the man of God. Guti's own vast riches were similarly regarded. His wealth and that of other ZAOGA leaders was seen by most as a 'chief political virtue' rather than an 'object of disapproval' (Bayart, 1993: 242). 'For those at the very bottom of the social order, the material prosperity of their betters is not itself reprehensible so long as they too can benefit materially from their association with a patron linking them with elites' (Chabal and Daloz, 1999: 42). 'A man of wealth who is able to amass and redistribute becomes a "man of honour"' (Bayart, 1993: 242). As in other African Christian movements, a rich and powerful leader was believed to be more able to secure property for the church and thus put it on a sure economic footing. A 'big' Christian leader was also viewed as more likely to be effective in representations to the government, and able to rectify the injustices and dispossessions visited upon his people by the white man (Sundkler, 1961: 129-30; Campbell, 1995, chapter 1).

Many ZAOGA members did not give much consideration to the excesses of their leaders. Despite what *The Sacred History* taught, ZAOGA was the church they had built through their evangelism, and through their tithes and Talents. As we shall see in Chapter 8, life in the worshipping community of the local assembly had a satisfying dynamic all of its own. And for those who wanted more there was a rich variety of ministries. In essence, for all its problems, ZAOGA remained a vital Pentecostal movement. At the end of the 1999 version of *The Sacred History* were included 17 pages of miracles to supplement the ten pages of wondrous happenings found in the original. Some were of visions, prophecies and signs explicitly pointing to ZAOGA as the 'true church of God'. Most were accounts of healing. Amongst these were remarkable stories of people raised from the dead, and people cured of being deaf, dumb, blind and insane. But most numerous were the accounts of women healed of infertility. The movement continued to address the personal security of its poorer members who remained its largest constituency (Guti, 1999: 130-47).

But divine healing was the movement's second priority; evangelism still ranked first. Although there was a growing concern amongst the leadership with its memorialisation and to increase the movement's public visibility through the construction of cathedrals, the purchase of large buildings, and high-profile public events, the desire to win souls remained central, driven as much from below as from above. Events within Zimbabwe at the end of the 1990s simply changed the nature of the movement's mission. From ZAOGA's beginnings the imperative to win souls had orientated the movement beyond the nation-state. As the possibilities for evangelism and church building diminished with the political violence and economic downturn that accompanied Mugabe's *Third Chimurenga*, so ZAOGA once again turned its attentions beyond Zimbabwe's borders. It is to the subject of the movement's transnational expansion that we now turn.

Notes

[1] Files, General Reports, ca.1980-96, Newsletters, 1981-96, ZAW.
[2] Newsletter, 21 March 1994, file, Newsletters, 1981-96; Edward Michaelson to Ezekiel Guti, 9 June 1994, file, Sponsors, ZAW; Int.DM109, Edward Michaelson & Charles Bullock.
[3] Executive Minutes, 5 December 1988, 25 January 1989 & 17 March 1989, ZAW.
[4] I have been unable to ascertain which organisation was behind the Target 2000 survey. File, Statistics, ZAW.
[5] Elson Makanda, Deeper Life Conference, Glenora, 8 February 1996, fieldwork notes.
[6] Zambia National Executive to Ezekiel Guti, 21 November 1989, file, Missions, Zambia, ZAW.
[7] Ezekiel Guti, Edgware, London, 13 August 1995 and Annual Pastors Conference, Glenora, 9 November 1995, fieldwork notes.
[8] Ezekiel Guti, 'Awake Sleeping Giant', 7 February 1989, file, Sermons, ZAW.
[9] Jean Henderson, annotated notes, Pastors Conference, Autumn 1996.
[10] M.T. Timbe, Seke Region Progress Report, 14 March 1992, file, General Reports, 1980-96, ZAW; Guti, 1999: 143-4.
[11] Int.DM27, Overseer Kapandura.
[12] Executive Minutes, 5 December 1988, ZAW.
[13] File, General Reports 1980–96, Report from Nyamaropa/Katerere Region, 10 May 1994, ZAW.
[14] Executive Minutes, 17 March 1989, ZAW.
[15] File, Locals, 1992, ZAW.
[16] File, Locals, 1994, ZAW. The names have been changed.
[17] Ezekiel Guti, International Leadership Conference, 9 February 1993, file Sermons, ZAW.
[18] 'Introducing the Third World Leaders Association' nd, file, International Third World Leaders Association 1993-6, ZAW.
[19] Files, Gracious Women; Sponsors, 1981-96, ZAW
[20] Mrs S. Mugabe to Eunor Guti, 5 August 1991; Speech Made at Gracious Women's Fellowship and Husbands' Agape Fellowship in the Presence of Mrs W.Z. Duri, MP, file, Gracious Women, ZAW.
[21] Speech made by the Mayoress to Gracious Women's Fellowship, 21 October 1990, file, Gracious Women, ZAW.
[22] 'Homosexuality', ZAOGA Press Release, September 1995, file, Relations with Government, ZAW.
[23] Int.DM113, William Gumbochena.

[24] Int.DM115, Olivia Muchena.

[25] *The Herald*, 29 February 1996.

[26] Int.DM113, William Gumbochena.

[27] For Kenya, Archbishop Ezekiel Guti to President Robert Mugabe 24 May 1994, file, Relations with Government, ZAW. For China, sermon preached by Ezekiel Guti, South Africa, 3 June 1995, file Sermons, ZAW. In this sermon Guti extolled the virtues of supporting the government. He told his audience of his difficulty in getting travel documents and then remarked: 'we have a very good President. If we have any problems we just go to him.'

[28] Ezekiel Guti, Pastors Conference, AMFCC, 9 November 1995, fieldwork notes.

[29] *Parade*, August 1996.

[30] Overseer Christopher Chadoka, 'Better Giving', AMFCC, 10 February 1996, fieldwork notes.

[31] Int.DM85, Phineas Dube, Harare, 1 March 1996; Minutes of Meeting for Leadership Conference, 3 March 1993, file, General Reports, 1980-96, ZAW.

[32] Overseer Chadoka, Mt Pleasant Big Sunday, University of Zimbabwe, 5 November 1995, fieldwork notes.

[33] Churches in Manicaland Public Statements, *Daily News*, 28 December 2001 & 10 December 2002.

[34] Pastors Conference Discussions, ca. 1992, file, Sermons, ZAW.

[35] General Conference Questions, ca.1991, file, Sermons, ZAW.

[36] Int.DM54, Pricilla Ngoma.

[37] Anniversary Celebrations, City 1 Assembly, Baines Avenue, 9 May 1996 & University of Zimbabwe, Humanities Theatre, 12 May 1996, fieldwork notes.

[38] *Parade*, August 1996, September 1996.

[39] Students at the Bible college regularly referred to ZANU/PF headquarters as 'Chicken Inn'.

[40] *Parade*, August 1996 & September 1996.

[41] Jean Henderson, annotated notes, Pastors Conference, Autumn 1996.

[42] Eunor Guti, Rufaro Stadium, 28 February 1996, fieldwork notes; 'Ministry Finance' (ZAOGA) ca. 1980, file, General Reports, ca.1980-96, ZAW

[43] Int.DM94, Ngwisa Mkandla.

[44] See also Mukonoweshuro, 1993; ZAOGA Tract: *Husbands' Agape Fellowship.*

[45] Ezekiel Guti, 'Third World Mentality', Mutare, 11 November 1989, file, Sermons, ZAW.

[46] Ezekiel Guti, Sermon to General Conference 1984, file, Sermons, ZAW.

[47] Ezekiel Guti, 'Awake Sleeping Giant', file, Sermons, 7 Feb. 1989, ZAW.

[48] Otabil wrote the foreword to Guti (1994d).

[49] Ezekiel Guti, The Last Workshop, ca. 1986, file, Sermons, ZAW.

7

Taking up the Missionary Mantle
Transnational Expansion
in a Post-Colonial World
1980s–2000s

Economic meltdown and political violence thwarted ZAOGA's ambitions within Zimbabwe. But the movement had always maintained a vision that transcended the nation-state. From the 1980s its transnational character took on new significance in an era of globalisation. The movement had begun life in the 1950s as a small prayer band cum evangelistic team that actively eschewed missionaries. It had struggled to create distance from the historic mission churches dominating Salisbury's African townships and it fought to retain autonomy from younger Pentecostal missionary organisations. Its expansion had come mostly through labour migrants returning home. By the 1980s, aided by resources from the global Born-again movement, ZAOGA had taken on the missionary mantle, commissioning its own Shona emissaries of the gospel. It continued to define itself in opposition to a caricatured version of mission Christianity while its workers reproduced some of the excesses of missionaries past and present.

Mission and Missiology ZAOGA-Style

Throughout the 1980s ZAOGA's pan-Africanist vision was sharpened into an ideological critique of dependency and Western Christianity, offering instead a powerful assertion of Africa's mission. Western churches, once the cradle of Christianity, were now apostate. Africans had become the bearers of Christian truth. In his famous 1988 sermon, 'Lift up the Standard', given at Zimbabwe's National Stadium, Guti told his audience:

> One of the problems we have in the third world is that of copying what backslidden western people are doing instead of copying the good things they were doing before they backslid. These nations used to have many churches and many of their leaders were Christians ... but when they prospered they forsook God ... I believe this is our time. It is time for black people and their nations to rise up. Don't go to Europe and learn their ungodly things. Learn what they used to do before ... . (1989: 23-7).

In another sermon, 'Third World Mentality', the Archbishop elaborated on the West's malignant influence. Europeans and Americans had engendered 'the spirit of admiring white men', 'the spirit of division', and 'the spirit of fear'.[1] These forces crushed black self-confidence, encouraging a culture of dependency and deference to whites:

How can you write a letter asking for tapes from back-slidden preachers in America. ... It is because you hate the blackness of your own skin ....

When a black man decides to do something other black people say oh no only a white can do that. This is why independence took 16 years to come.

I have seen a black man respecting and admiring a white man more than his fellow blackman. You can see this in business and some banks. It is because of the mentality that has been put in us by some people, who have bewitched us, that we may not trust one another.[2]

According to Guti, Africans were imbued with an aid mentality, vulnerable to structural underdevelopment and neo-colonialism:

[F]oreign donors are the new colonialists. In the third world countries our people are just waiting for handouts and some of them do not want to work anymore but only to receive...Why are our people hungry yet we live in rich countries? Africa is said to be stagnant. Yet her lakes breed fish and her forests all kinds of trees. Africa is still importing fish and toothpicks from outside countries in large quantities. The fish goes out to be tinned and then they sell it back to us in cans... There is a problem of external powers which came into Africa and other third world countries, to stir civil wars, causing us to fight among ourselves so that they could make profits by selling firearms whilst causing division (1994a: 68, 70, 78).

In his sermons and books the Archbishop laid a good deal of the blame for this dependency at the feet of Western missionaries. In places his rhetoric echoes the speeches of African nationalists and the slurs of Western secular liberals. Guti asserted that, although missionaries were to be praised for bringing the gospel, they had nevertheless acted as unwitting 'agents of colonialism', which used Christianity as a 'tool for the western domination of Africa'. After independence missionaries had 'spoiled Africans, who got to depend on the leadership and handouts from abroad ... [and had] despised their own skin and sunk into apathy'.[3] Missionaries had built churches for which Africans felt no responsibility. Thus he taught his people to build their own churches so that no one would 'kick them out' (1994a: 82; nd-i: 5-6). On other occasions his critique of missionaries verged on insult. He accused them of greed and incompetence:

Almost half of Africa has been taught that Pastors should eat all the money from their churches. Probably this fact was brought about by Missionaries.

When I went to America they said "We never sent a good preacher to Africa. All the good ones are here." When someone starts a church there they announce that they want to send people [here] and they choose the backbenchers. And the backbenchers are willing because they are promised money.[4]

In place of a divisive third world mentality and a deadening Western cultural imperialism the Archbishop advocated a pan-Africanism. His famous 'Lift up the Standard' sermon recorded in the movement's *Sacred History* finished with a prayer for 'one Africa from Cape to Cairo' (1989: 27). And elsewhere he fleshed out his vision:

We are praying for Africa to have one currency so that it will be easy to travel and proclaim the gospel of Jesus Christ our Lord, which will help bring peace among the nations of Africa. It will be easy to import and export ... Let us pray for Africa to be a united states of Africa for that will help in stopping the enemy from invading the nations of Africa, dividing Africa and causing endless wars (1994a: 74).

His sense of unity was founded on a vigorous Afro-centrism confidently rooted in scripture *and* church growth statistics:

> Jesus was born in the Middle East not in Europe ... we all know that the gospel came to Africa first before it went to Europe. ... Most of the good things started in Africa. Civilisation started in Africa in Genesis 50: 2-26. There were doctors or physicians. In Egypt and Ethiopia there is one God, 600 years before the Hebrews, what they call MONOTHEISM. They also knew about banking before Christ ... 'AFRICA WILL BE SAVED'. ... Church based statistics show that in the years to come sixty percent of the world's 3 billion Christians will live in the third world with Africa recording the highest (1994a: 52-5, 80-81).

Such teachings were both a powerful antidote to missionary cultural imperialism and a foil to cultural nationalists who assert a monolithic traditional religion centred on ancestor veneration:

> If you are a true African you cannot deny God. When an African says that there is no God it is because he heard or read from backslidden nations. Black people from the beginning trusted God. They knew God before the Bible came, just like Abraham, Isaac and Jacob who worshipped God before the Bible (1989: 26).

Here Guti also asserted a theology of race. Blacks were descended from Cush, a great and mighty nation that lost its blessing because of carelessness. The world's races are descended from the sons of Noah: Ham, Shem and Japheth. Each race reigns for 2,000 years. Black people, the descendants of Ham, have had their turn, as have the descendants of Shem. Now it is the turn of Europeans, the descendants of Japheth, to run the world. But as the world nears the millennium and the reign of Christ, black peoples can be blessed again. Moreover, with a post-colonial redefinition of mission Guti argued that it was time for Africans to bless Western nations with the 'true Gospel', which they had now lost (1994a: 51,80–81).

As previously discussed, some of Guti's teaching on cultural imperialism, dependency and pan-Africanism was mere rhetoric. Nevertheless, his writing and teaching did have practical missiological effect, honed through decades of evangelistic activity by the likes of Sande, Choto, Kupara and those that followed them. He believed evangelism was most effective when it was local and small-scale: 'If you want a big church you must have small groups to disciple and to evangelise.' '[A] society can only be reached by the people living in that society.' The lessons of the missionary encounter with African societies had been well learnt. The evangelist needed to know the 'real needs of the people': their 'occupation, culture, history and traditions' (nd-b: 9–10; 1991: 49, 14). At the heart of his strategy was a critique of the large crusades that drew a good deal of popular (and academic) attention but did not have the enduring success of low-key local work. In a 1987 sermon preached in the wake of a Reinhard Bonnke Crusade and Ralph Mahony's tirade against the Zimbabwean state (see Chapter 5), Guti told his audience:

> [T]he problem is that after all these big evangelists have gone everybody and everything disappears. You remain with the decision cards but no people... ZAOGA does not send an evangelist to a village until we know local people able to take over when the evangelist is gone. Evangelists gather

people, then send teachers in, then a pastor will come and take over. Never open a new place without preparing who is going to pastor these people. ... [We] don't want to go into a place and leave people alone. Some pastors they burn all their charms, all their witchcraft and they go and leave them in fear. Their people go back again to their charms and the second time they will not listen. ... We win people from small groups they are more strong than people from the tents because you win them in the home and you see them all the time. At crusades you only have names and you try to visit them and they are all Christians ... Big crusades give a good bump to the area but you need to build a church from small groups.[5]

The breaking of traditions, whether traditional or Christian, is a key theme in the Archbishop's preaching and a powerful weapon in shaping a distinctive movement. Those coming with the mindset of established churches must either leave or submit to re-education. Far better are those converts with no prior Christian experience. These initiates are more open to ZAOGA's idiosyncrasies, the cult of Guti, and teachings on Talents and Spirit of Poverty, which distinguish it from the homogenising global Born-again movement. In 1985 Guti instructed the leaders of the movement's embryonic Forward in Faith Mission International (FIFMI), South Africa: 'When you start a church appoint a ten-member committee – it will be temporary because first and second committee will go. First committee will run the church like a Methodist church – first and second people are coming from tradition – it is better to have people who have never been to church.'[6]

By the 1990s the movement's leadership had learnt to wrap up these principles in the language of 'Church Growth' to enhance its appeal to donors. Small cottage meetings became 'Home Groups' then 'Cells', and their spread across townships became 'The Chain of Multiplication'. And the importance of attending to the varied needs of congregations across the region came to be expressed in the language of indigenous authenticity (1991; 1995c). Such principles have underpinned the spread of Christianity in Africa throughout the twentieth century but in ZAOGA they have become institutionalised.

Marriages of Passion and Convenience: Networks Old and New

In spite of Guti's teaching on dependency, America remained an important source of resources for transnational expansion. ZAOGA did, however, begin to look elsewhere for material support and inspiration. As African Pentecostalism took off during the 1980s, so Guti joined an exclusive club of like Born-again 'big men' preaching in conferences and conventions across the continent. New allies were Nevers Mumba from Zambia and Stanley Ndovi from Malawi. Guti's real kindred spirit, though, was Mensa Otabil from Ghana. But within Africa ZAOGA's networks were mostly orientated south of the Limpopo. The fall of apartheid in 1994 allowed interaction with a range of new charismatic churches, black and white. Important collaborators were Fred Roberts from the Durban Christian Centre, and Rhema Ministries, based in Johannesburg. Because of its relative wealth, South Africa offered rich pickings, but America remained the central focus in terms of Guti's travelling and correspondence. The majority of contacts were white Americans from the mid-west but the movement's guests were increasingly black Americans and Afro-Caribbeans. Most of these were members of the Third World Christian Leaders Association which, despite its

name, was dominated by leaders from the northern hemisphere and had little practical commitment to Africa.[7] The American connection was cemented when in the
early 1990s the Gutis' daughter Fiona married Pastor Paul Arthurs, son of Dr Carlton
Arthurs, leader of the Wheaton Christian Center, Chicago. At the 1996 Deeper Life
Conference Dr Arthurs observed, 'I feel that the church in Zimbabwe and the church
in Wheaton are almost married and it is a good marriage.'[8]

The networks were most apparent to ordinary ZAOGA members at the annual
Deeper Life Conference, when international friends were invited to speak alongside
the movement's rising stars. For the most part, however, they were given substance
through the exchange of letters. Aided by word processors and a small number of
trusted family and friends, Eunor Guti produced a regular newsletter. This described
ZAOGA's recent crusades and missions, and the Gutis' international itinerary. Mrs
Guti also added a few personal words to many of the missives, often in response to
ministries abroad. Such communications did much to stimulate a shared sense of
mission, though for the most part the networks remained an elite affair. Ordinary
ZAOGA members rarely rubbed shoulders with foreign visitors and had little sense of
the resources foreigners brought with them. As we shall see in the following chapter,
the concerns of worshippers in suburbs, townships and rural areas were little affected
by global Born-again culture and a vast amount of money was raised locally, far more
than from foreign donors.

Foreign connections did, however, bring immediate benefits to the movement. White
Born-agains in Cape Town helped bankroll FIFMI South Africa in its early stages.
And American donations paid for bicycles for Malawian pastors and a pick-up truck
for the Mozambican Church, and helped with the construction of its Bible school in
Beira.[9] As ZAOGA's transnational expansion gathered pace, it took on a dynamic of its
own. One connection could lead to another. Thus money raised by Forward in Faith
Mission International, London, funded the first crusade in Tanzania.[10] Moreover the
networks were not unidirectional. The Zimbabwean Church had provided a training
ground for Paul Arthurs and was subsequently a site of overseas mission experience
for ordinary members of the Wheaton Christian Center. By the 1990s there appeared
to be an informal re-denominationalisation of non-denominational Christianity as
small independent churches in South Africa, Britain and Australia looked to Guti as
their 'Shepherd' or 'Spiritual Father'. This re-organisation was driven in part by the
leaders of small movements who felt the need for pastoral oversight and accountability. It was also a pragmatic way of retaining autonomy. There were limits on how
much influence the nominated Spiritual Father could assert. However, transnational
connections were not simply instrumental. As we shall see, African Pentecostalism
could enchant Westerners.

In sum, ZAOGA's foreign links were cautious and low-key. The movement's evolution had been shaped by continued struggle for autonomy from external agents, and
its leaders were all too aware of the force of cultural nationalism and the damage neo-
colonial associations could do to their image. Apart from policing foreign connections,
the leadership took advantage of a growing tendency amongst international agencies
to preserve and promote 'images of local specificity', and sought out international
organisations, which participated in this globally constructed localism (Miller, 1995:
9; Robertson, 1995). Donors and visiting missionaries were told that the movement was
'indigenous', run by 'indigenous workers who know how to handle the situation in their
country'.[11] Thus, while southern African Pentecostals have an existential and ideological

7.1 Archbishiop Guti anointing South African visitors to Deeper Life

aversion to 'tradition', they nevertheless foster specific notions of authenticity in particular contexts to gain resources and political capital.

Christianity without Frontiers: Transnational Mission to Africa

ZAOGA's post-independence transnational expansion stood in continuity with much that had gone before. Low-level, personal evangelism carried out by ordinary church members continued, as did the crusading activities of evangelists like Abel Sande. War and social unrest remained an important force, shaping church growth in Mozambique and South Africa. But independence did herald a new era. With an end to sanctions and the restricted movement of people and information across borders, the possibilities for mission increased greatly. Freedom to enter and leave Zimbabwe provided an immense boost to ZAOGA, bringing its leaders into contact with ambitious and entrepreneurial Pentecostals beyond the national borders. Bartholomew Manjoro made many of the initial connections, his rise to prominence as the movement's key administrator having been hastened by Kupara's departure in 1984. Like Guti, he had studied at CFNI, Dallas, which boosted his status and expanded his horizons beyond Zimbabwe. Links with Zaire came in 1981 while he was visiting ZAOGA's Zambian work. On the Copper Belt he met Francis Penge, a Zairian, who subsequently invited a ZAOGA team to his country to form the Assemblée de Dieu au Zaïre, Afrique (ADAZA). Manjoro was also responsible for beginning the work in Tanzania. While in Zambia again in 1985, Manjoro met an energetic Tanzanian, Stephen Nzowa, who was on a preaching tour. Nzowa invited him to visit his church in Mbozi, Tanzania, and the church was integrated into ZAOGA's empire.[12] The Kenyan churches came via the Tanzanian connection. They were founded by a Kikuyu named Paul Kimaruh, who learnt of FIFMI from Nzowa while participating in a Tanzanian crusade and was invited to the 1990 Deeper Life Conference in Zimbabwe. Henceforth he decided to put his churches under the oversight of a 'Spiritual Father' and 'Apostle', Ezekiel Guti.[13] Mission work in West Africa began after Manjoro had a chance meeting with some Ghanaian pastors at the Bonnke Harare Fire Conference in 1986. Contacts with Rwanda were first made through Central African Pentecostals who had been given Manjoro's business card. Joseph Choto forged the South African link in 1984 having come across Pastor Wilson Mabasa, working for the Pentecostal Full Gospel Church in Soshanguve. Mabasa was invited to ZAOGA's Pastors' Conference and encouraged to join the movement. Choto had helped to found the Bulawayo assemblies, the initial negotiations for which were conducted in Sindebele.[14]

Zimbabwe's location at the crossroads of central and southern Africa aided transnational expansion enormously. Shared languages and continuous flows of labour migrants created important bonds between Zimbabweans and their neighbours. Assemblies in Manicaland were assigned to support those in Mozambique in monthly and bi-monthly Big Sunday meetings. In a similar manner ZAOGA members in Bulawayo were encouraged to look to Botswana. Harare and Matabeleland South were made responsible for South Africa. Other Provinces were twinned with Zaire, Zambia and Malawi.[15]

Once links had been established, Zimbabwean evangelists, teachers, administrators, and even Guti himself, went to help local people expand their embryonic movements. Both Saungweme and Chigwenembe made extensive visits outside Zimbabwe with their crusade teams. Saungweme took groups to Swaziland and Zambia in 1991 and Mozambique in 1995; he was also part of a smaller contingent led by Manjoro to Zaire in 1986. Chigwenembe led teams to South Africa in 1992 and 1995 and also to Botswana, Zambia and Malawi. Both evangelists were part of a large teaching and preaching team led by Overseer Elson Makanda to Tanzania in 1988.[16] Their reports detailed numerous conversions and powerful manifestations of the Holy Spirit such as healing miracles or victories of deliverance over local spirits. Apart from Manjoro's visit to West Africa, the journeys were all made by road. Chigwenembe was eventually to lose his life in a car accident while returning from a crusade in Harare. The Zimbabweans recounted in detail the travails they had experienced on their journeys: breakdowns, accidents and near-misses, shortage of foreign exchange, the trials of border controls, and the search for accommodation.[17] Their accounts of transnational encounters resembled those of pioneer Victorian missionaries. Beset by difficulties, they were making conquests in the wilderness beyond, in the name of civilisation (Comaroff and Comaroff, 1991: 1972).

Transnational crusades demanded great sacrifices from those involved. While the Zimbabwean movement prospered, members of the crusade teams felt marginalised in a church that had moved from mission to maintenance. In 1995 they were paid just Z$300 (£23) a month. Their lifestyles could not have been further removed from those of American televangelists, and their satisfaction was derived from a deep sense of Christian service.[18] Saungweme, like his mentors, had that 'burning desire to preach'. Soon after his conversion in the late 1970s he went out on his own in eastern Zimbabwe armed with a gas lamp, a sleeping bag and a Bible.[19]

In spite of all the costs, ZAOGA did make transnational strides. Zimbabwean leaders offered technical expertise on bureaucratic matters and advice on strategies for church growth. Crusade teams brought encouragement and inspiration, often helping to initiate a local church. But, as with ZAOGA itself, much of the real work was done by local agents. To begin with, Wilson Mabasa stayed in his job with the South African railways preaching on trains on his way to work. At the weekends in Soshanguve he concentrated on a Sunday School for young people, sending them home to evangelise their parents, followed by his own visits, praying for the sick and needy. The church spread to Mamelodi and Soweto.

In Mozambique, other remarkable men and women helped Mateus Simao propel the church forward. Jorge Joachim Matus joined the church in Nampula in 1983 after his wife was healed. In 1987 he left his profession as a tailor and became a full-time pastor. After a vision he moved to the far north of the country to start the church in Cabo Delgado Province. Settling in Pemba, he moved from house to house preaching and healing the sick, slowly building a church.[20] Violence and social dislocation continued to shape Assemblee De Deus Africana (ADDA). By 1980 the counter-revolutionary movement Renamo was wrecking the hopes of independence. Simao was abducted by Renamo in December 1981 and only escaped by hiding in a pit-latrine. Yet throughout the 1980s the Mozambican movement grew steadily. By 1986 ADDA was present in eight provinces with 52 pastors and 94 buildings. The take-off came in 1988 with the construction of a Bible school. By 1995 the movement claimed 120 pastors, 300 buildings and 100,000 adherents.[21]

Of all ZAOGA's transnational connections Mozambique stands out as the pre-eminent success story. Accounts of crusades and meetings, and a brief spell of fieldwork suggested the country was experiencing classic Pentecostal revival, as described in Chapters 1 and 2. Heartfelt crying and confession of sin, holy laughter, exorcism and ecstatic possession by the Holy Spirit animated Church meetings. The ongoing violence and dislocation is an important explanatory factor. ZAOGA's attraction across southern Africa lay in its cell-like organisation, which made it difficult for hostile states and political movements to dislodge it. Its attraction also lay in its tendencies towards peace and social reconstruction. Its message of sobriety and industry, its taboos on alcohol, marijuana and tobacco and its focus on stable married life offered a powerful contrast to the 'Kalashnikov culture' prevalent amongst many young men (Martin, 1996: chapter 2).

As in Southern Rhodesia in the 1930s, Mozambican Pentecostalism also functioned as a movement of witchcraft cleansing (see Chapter 2). Throughout the 1990s, when ADDA was growing fastest, Pentecostal services were regularly accompanied by the destruction of polluted objects and the conversion of traditional healers. In one brief crusade in Beira over 50 kilograms of charms were burnt within three days. A similar picture emerged in Pemba, where such phenomena were witnessed in ADDA meetings and those of other Pentecostal movements – Assemblies of God, Evangélica and Assemblies of God International. When Fernando Sumunitato, an ADDA elder from Pemba, began to evangelise the Makonde on the Mueda Plateau in 1990 he met with immediate results. Wycliffe Bible Translators working there reminisced that the movement spread like 'wildfire', offering deliverance and protection against demonic possession and restoring families riven by domestic violence and alcoholism.[22] Pentecostal growth mirrored a succession of witchcraft eradicators who crossed the province at the same time. These men, both of whom went by the name Ningore, divined and destroyed medicines and charms, and extracted public confessions from their owners who tended to be rich and powerful, and were popularly perceived to be using witch-craft to gain an unfair advantage in matters of business, politics and sexual relations. Those most frequently exposed were Frelimo party members, businessmen, priests and pastors from historic mission churches, and Muslim leaders (*Shehes*). Neo-liberal economics combined with donor-aided party and church patronage, had intensified inequalities of wealth and power and heightened popular fear of witchcraft. Thus Mozambican Pentecostalism complemented and competed with more traditional forms of eradication (Harry West, forthcoming).[23]

While growth was less spectacular in other countries, its patterns were similar to the Zimbabwean movement's evolution. Having established itself in the city, the Malawian church turned rural areas into a mission field. Work started in Chikwawa District in 1987, producing three assemblies and 380 adherents by the following year.[24] By 1991, Lusaka Province had 25 assemblies and seven trained pastors. The Copper Belt had three assemblies. In Petuke, a 'witch doctor' of great renown converted, abandoning his '*mashabe*' dance and numerous Mozambican clients to found three assemblies. Guti had advised the movement that a strong urban membership would put the church's finances on a surer footing and aid rural expansion.[25] Having rapidly established the movement in Dar es Salaam from its base in Mbozi, Nzowa founded churches in Mbeya District.[26]

'Bags of American Money': Extraversion & Competition in a Global Religious Market

ZAOGA's transnational mission proved extremely successful in the decades following independence. But along with church growth came the replication, even intensifica-tion, of some of the Zimbabwean movement's more worldly characteristics. In 1981 Guti told a Zambian audience of his frustrations with their Malawian brethren:

> In Malawi people were in trouble because of what they use[d] to say or do when someone comes from America. They went to join him because of money. Now if the money is finished they left him and join someone else whom they know had bring [sic] another bag of money. They were not after God but after money.[27]

This pattern of fission and fusion continued in Malawi and elsewhere. Six Malawian pastors left to found their own ministries but were welcomed back into the movement in 1989.[28] Fission was prompted as much by a desire to maximise the opportunities of extraversion as by a sincere search for purer forms of religious expression. After receiving an exceptional amount of resources from Zimbabwe and England and train-ing at the Zimbabwean Bible college, Nzowa decided to go his own way in 1995.[29] The Zambian church seemed to reproduce the character of the dominant socio-politi-cal culture. In 1990 an irate pastor wrote to Zimbabwe complaining of nepotism and favouritism. Only a select few preached at the richer churches where the rewards were great. Church positions were bought with bribes and pastors preferred to conduct their own business rather than care for their flocks. Other reports alluded to the misuse of church funds and tribalism in the distribution of scholarships to the Zimbabwean Bible college.[30]

When it came to corruption, Zaire was in a league of its own. It appeared that Francis Penge was using his church identity and transnational connections to further his personal business interests. Unlike Muslim traders in West Africa, Penge did not use his Christian networks as a guarantee providing strict rules of conduct to boost the confidence of those that he dealt with (MacGaffey and Bazenguissa-Ganga, 2000: 14–15); instead he plundered these connections for resources. Soon Simon Monde, another Zairian, educated in Zimbabwe and more loyal to ZAOGA, was petitioning the Harare headquarters for Penge's removal. His letters claimed that Penge had committed numerous crimes: not paying pastors' salaries; hiding the bank book, correspondence, the church stamp, letterheads, post-office keys; selling invitations to Zimbabwe to Nigerians; falsely promising bales of clothes in return for cement for church buildings. Before he was removed, Penge wrote a damaging letter to the Zimbabwean Ministry of Foreign Affairs claiming that Monde was secretly involved in the arms trade.[31]

To counter the fissile and destructive tendencies within both the Zimbabwean movement and its transnational plants, ZAOGA's leaders resorted to a combination of bureaucratic control and the promotion of its own distinctive brand of Pentecostalism. The leadership actively went out to export its doctrines and style of government but also drew newcomers into its centre so that they could experience these things at first hand.[32] Soon after a transnational connection had been made, or in Mozambique's case when it was safe enough, flying squads, often accompanied by crusade teams, would visit the country. Leaders such as Makanda, Manjoro, and occasionally Guti himself would instruct local members on how to achieve self-reliance through tithing and penny capitalism. Leaders of the Gracious Women and Gracious Single Women Associations, such as Liniah Rusere, would advise on entrepreneurial activities such as sewing and cooking. They also taught domesticity, leadership skills and ways of strengthening marriage. Once local money was being generated, direction was given on its appropriate management. Tithes were to be receipted and the money deposited in bank accounts controlled by properly constituted boards. Pastors were to be paid regularly to stop them from 'running away due to lack of food'.[33] Once the women's movements were functioning, the youth and men's work was encouraged. As in Zimbabwe's case, this proliferation of associations created a multiplicity of cross-cutting bonds of fellowship which ran across ethnicities and regions, reinforcing the movement's cohesion. They also provided forums for its key teachings on the family.

In the case of the Zambian, Malawian and Zairian assemblies, Manjoro or Makanda were called in as trouble-shooters to sort out financial misdemeanours, sexual improprieties and general mismanagement. Zimbabwean 'missionaries' were also sent out to help 'kick-start' new foreign works. In 1991 Pastor Mpanduki went to South Africa and Pastor Christmas to Botswana. These missionaries were sent to establish bureaucracies and administrative procedures. Others like Maggie Ndlouvu, also sent to South Africa, had specific gifts in evangelism and youth work and, more importantly, the local language. Crusade teams also demonstrated Zimbabwean capabilities. In 1990 they were sent to Lusaka and Pretoria as a show of force after various assemblies had defected.

Finally, the Zimbabwean leaders would also instruct surrounding nations on the movement's *Sacred History*, the canonised narrative of the spiritual autobiography of Ezekiel Guti. Copies of this history in short tract form were distributed, and for Zaire it was translated into French. New assemblies were encouraged to participate

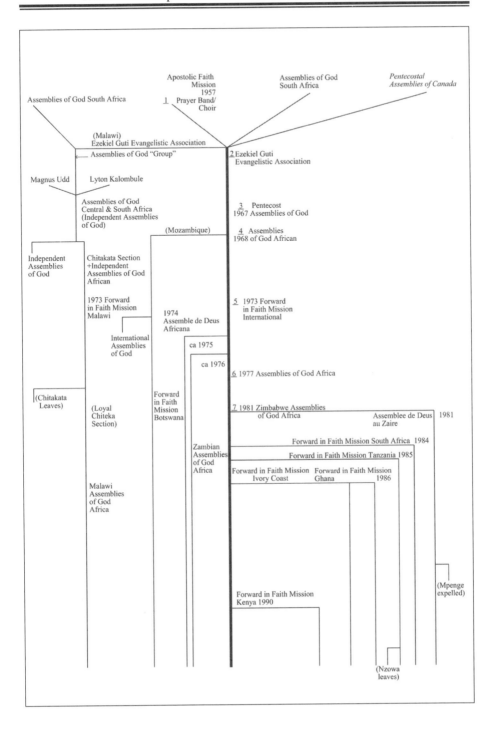

Table 7.1 Fission & fusion in the making of a transnational Pentecostal movement

in its synchronised annual recital to enhance the imagination and embodiment of the transnational community in text and performance. Foreign leaders were taken on pilgrimages to memorials in Zimbabwe that marked key moments in Guti's life. Simon Monde argued that Guti would ultimately prove more successful than the great Zairian prophet Simon Kimbangu because 'he wrote things down'.[34]

Schisms often resulted directly from sheep-and-shepherd-stealing. Foreign pastors and their flocks transplanted into ZAOGA came with different mentalities and sometimes found the movement's doctrines and practices too exacting. While the leaders of ZAOGA's transnational branches could not be 'home-grown', they could at least be drawn into the movement's Zimbabwean core for re-formation. Thus the favoured Zairian leader, Monde, and the South African leader, Mabasa, were brought in for a year's training at the Zimbabwean Bible school and for placements at the headquarters and Harare churches. Once established in Zaire in 1988, Monde set about founding fresh assemblies by convening small worship meetings in homes. 'Now we have started the real ZAOGA', he wrote to Manjoro.[35] Many other foreign leaders and pastors experienced this formation process. The Bible school with its rigorous diet of doctrine, prayer and worship, general work and placements in pastoral or evangelistic teams was a powerful homogenising force. In 1989 it was reported that three Zambian pastors who had defected would be allowed back into the movement if they first consented to go to the Bible school for the 'refreshing of their minds'.[36]

More temporary, but no less vivid, experiences of the Zimbabwean movement were offered through the annual Pastors and Deeper Life Conferences which drew hundreds of foreign delegates to the movement's impressive 3,000-capacity conference centre, with its television relay to overspill tents. The Deeper Life Conference combined the traditions of the Vapostori *pasca*, the Methodist Camp Meeting and the Born-again convention, offering visitors a week of teaching from international and Zimbabwean speakers, and high quality music and worship, culminating in a final communion service. Core ZAOGA doctrines were continually expounded by Zimbabwean speakers, while high-profile African and American guests emphasised links with the global Born-again movement. National and ethnic cultures were celebrated with flags, dress and evening festivities: thigh-slapping Zulu dancing; Tanzanian drumming; the award-winning Zimbabwean Kambazuma and Marlborough choirs and a host of other traditions. It was at once an affirmation of global and African Christian identities and an assertion of the movement's strong Zimbabwean character.

Other homogenising forces were the locally produced audio-visual and print media. Key sermons and events were recorded for circulation within the movement. Those unable to afford electronic media could buy ZAOGA's cheap and widely circulated tracts on doctrine and history. A flying squad visiting Accra assemblies in 1995 showed new Ghanaian members video recordings of the ZAOGA style of worship, and a Guti sermon on repentance.[37]

'Into the Darkness': ZAOGA/FIFMI & Mission to Great Britain

Most of ZAOGA's transnational expansion came through labour migrants returning home to Zambia, Malawi and Mozambique. These foreign workers founded cells or cottage meetings in their own towns and villages. When small gatherings had grown into more formal assemblies, an evangelistic team would be sent from Harare to encourage the faithful and increase their number. A ZAOGA missionary or administrator would then be sent, succeeded by delegations and visits from the Archbishop and his wife to introduce specific teachings. There would be a gradual imposition of orthodoxy as the transnational plant took on the distinctive ZAOGA hue. To some extent the expansion of the movement to Britain in the guise of Forward in Faith Mission International (FIFMI) stands in a similar trajectory, but there have been significant differences. First, Zimbabweans in Britain are not returning home but seeking incorporation into a new host society. Secondly, FIFMI members understand their presence in Britain as a God-given opportunity to missionise the West. The religious imperative is conceptualised differently from proselytism among African peoples; it is regarded as re-missionisation, the conversion of a country which was once the crucible of the missionary enterprise but is now back-slidden and ungodly.

There is an important and rapidly expanding body of research on the African Diaspora in Europe and America (Khoser, 2003). Of particular significance is the growing interest in African churches as a means of creating active citizens while simultaneously reinforcing ethnic identities (*Journal of Religion in Africa*, 2004, 34, 4). This section will engage with such issues but it will also consider the hitherto much neglected question of reverse missionisation. ZAOGA/FIFMI's presence in Britain provides a rare opportunity to consider the encounter of African Christianity with the West.

It is clear from Guti's missiological writing and preaching that ZAOGA's missionary impulse to Britain is primarily driven by the desire to reach a nation that has lost its Christian birthright. However, the West's condition is seen as more than post-Christian. It is viewed as spiritually dead, in need of remoralisation, described in terms very similar to those used by Victorian missionaries writing about Africa. In August 1994 Guti told one of his London assemblies: '... if you buy me a beautiful house in London I would say no thank you. I am afraid that I would die spiritually ... there is a darkness, a heaviness over London ... If I found a church with over 200 people in it that is a big church for London.' He proceeded to tell his audience of a church he had attended in Frankfurt, Germany, the previous Sunday: '... it was a beautiful church but God was not there, just people ... to me it was a warning that you can have the Bible of God without the God of the Bible'.[38] But mission to the West is intertwined with mission to Africa. Within Africa there is a growing appeal of things 'international' among the continent's aspirant youth and middle classes. There is a cachet in belonging to a church with a reach beyond the nation-state, with connections to America and Europe. Movements such ZAOGA/FIFMI make much of their international credentials at conferences, on letterheads and in publications which celebrate the latest missionary triumphs abroad. At the same meeting of August 1994 described above, the master of ceremonies introduced ZAOGA as 'the biggest church in the world with its name in 18 countries including Australia' with a leader who 'has preached all over world'.

There is also a range of more instrumental reasons for mission to the West. First, it is a source of foreign exchange to subsidise other dimensions of the movement's transnational enterprise. In a similar manner to the way ZAOGA once aspired to evangelise Zimbabwe's middle classes to boost tithes, now it seeks to convert wealthy Westerners. Secondly, the movement's British mission fields are an extension of Guti's neo-patrimonial system of government. Service abroad is a precious reward for those loyal to him. More generally, ordinary ZAOGA members view time in Britain as a much-needed opportunity to enhance social reproduction. Work in Britain generates valuable remittances able to sustain families coping with inflation and unemployment back in Zimbabwe. And, prior to the visa restrictions of 2002, relatives were continually visiting, procuring commodities for profitable resale in Zimbabwe.

Opposing tensions animated ZAOGA/FIFMI's encounter with British society. The desire to have tight boundaries to maintain control over members was in conflict with the need to extend connections into the world to provide webs of solidarity for immigrant members. As in Africa the threat was from a rival homogenising force, the global Born-again movement, from which ZAOGA/FIFMI draws resources but which it also resists for fear of losing its members. Another tension was between the urge to convert Britain and the need to create a place for Zimbabweans to feel at home.

FIFMI began in Britain from two families. The first was that of Joshua and Mabel Samasuwo. Joshua had come to Britain in 1972 to train as a nurse and had subsequently become a maths teacher, settling in Edgware, north London, with his wife, also a nurse. Both had strong evangelical credentials with a Scripture Union background. Joshua had been brought up a Methodist in Mhondoro Reserve outside Salisbury where his father had been the headmaster of Sandringham School. But once in Britain their commitment to the church had waned. The link with ZAOGA came through Mabel's sister, Miriam, who had studied in Britain in 1978. Subsequently she cultivated links with the movement in Bulawayo where she had become acquainted with Joseph Choto. Miriam returned to London again to train as a nurse and Choto visited her in 1983 on route to Dallas. Through Choto the Samasuwos were baptised in the Holy Spirit and grew interested in the Zimbabwean movement. Choto returned to plan a crusade in 1984 and then brought a small team of preachers and musicians to London in 1985. *The Times* was soon reporting on their work in 'darkest' London, using all the clichés of evangelical discourse. However, the church they planted in East Ham did not last. Its membership was mostly Afro-Caribbeans culled from those previously involved in the New Testament Church of God, and they proved uninterested in ZAOGA's doctrines and style of government. Moreover, the Samasuwos could not afford regular travel to that part of London. This attempt to unite the two black Diasporas failed, and the church was allowed to die. A new one was founded in Edgware in the Samasuwos' large extended council house. This time, tried and tested methods were used to evangelise: the cell division honed in Zimbabwe's townships. Soon the cells were numerous enough to come together for monthly Big Sundays.[39] Trusted Americans encouraged the fledgling church – Gayle Erwin in 1986, Shirley O'Dell from Oklahoma in 1988 – and the Gutis became regular visitors. Then came the missionaries. The first was Chris Sande who came in late 1985 and washed up in a fish and chip shop to raise money to hire a hall. Tedius Mhike and Consult Chirambadare followed him.

FIFMI gradually replicated ZAOGA practices. A regime of nightly meetings was introduced for prayer, Bible study and fasting. The ministries were introduced, first Gracious Women and then Husbands' Agape. ZAOGA tracts, tapes and videos were imported. And members were drawn back into Zimbabwe through attending the annual Deeper Life Conference, pastors' training events and special meetings for the ministries. Converts were initiated into the story of Guti's prophetic vision. By 1994 FIFMI was teaching members about the Spirit of Poverty and how to work Talents. There was a very strong emphasis on tithing and other offerings. By that stage assemblies had been founded across London, in Tottenham, East Ham, Peckham, Brixton, Edgware and Radlett. There was even an embryonic church in Glasgow. Although a handful of Nigerians, Ghanaians, Ugandans, Zairians, and Afro-Caribbeans attended meetings, it was a Zimbabwean, even a Shona, movement consisting of dynamic young men and women who had come to Britain as students, nurses, teachers and airline staff. Worship was punctuated with song and testimony in Shona with continual reference to Harare, the Zimbabwean Jerusalem. This highly bounded movement of small and intense meetings proved very attractive to Zimbabweans looking for a home from home.Some without any previous connection to ZAOGA were also drawn in.[40]

Whites were also recruited. By 1996 about 30 had passed through the movement's doors but none of them had stayed. Like many converts in the early Christian history of Africa they tended to be drawn from marginal sectors of society. Two groups were particularly distinctive. The first was a collection of predominantly single women of widowed and divorced backgrounds who were articulate and confident, but financially struggling to raise families. They had originally been Anglicans but were edged out as they embraced Charismatic renewal. The second small group came from Drum Chapel, a deprived area in Glasgow, and had testimonies of conversion from drink and drugs, and struggle with periods of poverty and unemployment. The movement paid for their travel to London for national Big Sundays. The warmth, self-confidence and exoticism of the Shona Christians attracted them. The constant reference to the Prophet Guti and the home church in Africa appealed to one informant like 'the smell of lamb roasting in the oven'.[41] Zimbabwe seemed like a real Holy Land. These groups of whites and others were given much attention. They were thrust into leadership positions, funded to go to Deeper Life in Zimbabwe, invited to study at AMFCC and to train as pastors and missionaries to their own societies. Most of them embraced the movement with great enthusiasm, some spending as much as twelve months training in the Bible college and working in local churches. The added hardships of climate, a meagre diet, poor accommodation and a highly circumscribed existence of endless meetings were initially mitigated by the excitement of fellowship and friendship with Zimbabwean Christians and aspiration to missionary service.[42]

Yet initial enchantment turned to disillusion. The white converts complained about ZAOGA and its African missionaries in much the same ways as African converts have often complained about European ones: 'You have to lose your identity to join the church. We did a lot of that in colonialism but they are doing it now.' ZAOGA are 'no different from missionaries. They are unable to separate African culture from message.' This reaction against ZAOGA's doctrine and organisation mirrored that of elite members within Zimbabwe. Initially impressed with the Archbishop, white members quickly grew disillusioned with the cult of Guti and double standards. They objected to the excessive hospitality he received in Britain, and to his special bank account into which was deposited 'the tithe of tithes'. They objected to the lack of transparency about money, the prosperity gospel, the volume of meetings, the hierarchical leadership, the overseers, and poor time-keeping, and worried about the tax implications of working Talents.[43]

The whites had hoped for a personal transformation of the spirit; they had found 'a crushing of personality'. Some of the disillusion stemmed from cultural difference. The Archbishop's joke about mean Scotsmen was not well received by his downtown Glasgow audience, neither was testimony given by a speaker at Deeper Life who spoke of his hatred of whites. A number of whites felt reduced to the status of objects, or 'trophies', that validated FIFMI's mission. But these cultural gaffes were not as significant as a more general inability to understand the white psyche. After a period of study at AMFCC Phil Austin returned to Britain with his new Zimbabwean bride Norah Lajabu to work as missionaries in Glasgow. Even before he had arrived, plans for the Glasgow work had already gone awry when the other white couple intended to work there had left the movement during training in Zimbabwe. Isolated from the main body of the church in London and dogged by a lack of results, Austin found himself slowly edged out and replaced by a Zimbabwean lecturing in one of the city's universities. This new cheerful leader appeared unable to discern worrying personality traits in those whites who joined him. Austin observed that 'these people [Zimbabweans] just don't understand depression and mental illness, they just get on with things'.[44]

But the Zimbabweans were equally disillusioned with whites. Their new brethren had neither built new churches nor raised lots of money. In fact whites had been subsidised! The Zimbabweans had a variety of explanations for their failure. Guti wrote to his London Overseer: 'It's the white people's behaviour all over the world. They don't feel adequate to be led by Blacks.' More generally, whites' hard-hearted response to the gospel was explained by legacies of bitterness in the British collective mentality created by the slave trade and the Second World War. And too many bitter Nigerians lived among them. Other Zimbabweans perceived whites as spoiled by liberalism, possessing 'too many human rights'.[45] Moreover, initial attempts to reach Afro-Caribbeans had also failed. Worse still, London's streets were not paved with gold and there was no new income to subsidise ZAOGA's transnational expansion in Africa. Like other immigrant groups, the Zimbabwean Pentecostals settled in inner-city London. Apart from the recurring problem of having their meeting-places occupied by squatters, the movement mainly seemed to attract African students, who had little money and no private accommodation to host meetings.[46]

ZAOGA's mission to the West was eventually overtaken by events. The great Zimbabwean Diaspora that entered Britain between 2000 and 2003 resolved its failure. A combination of asylum seekers, teachers, nurses and social workers swelled FIFMI's existing assemblies and helped found new ones in Leeds, Leicester and Manchester. Within a very short space of time the movement in Britain became self-reliant and almost entirely Zimbabwean. National Big Sundays in London were attended by as many as 1,000 members in 2003. In these services collections of £15,000 funded new buildings in Malawi and the maintenance of the movement in Zimbabwe. By then Guti was spending much of his time outside of Zimbabwe and placing less emphasis on the Zimbabwean nature of his church. Prompted no doubt by the state's economic decline and political violence, he announced that ZAOGA was now big enough at its source and had to grow internationally. By 1999 ZAOGA had established itself in Germany, And the movement's *History* showed Guti baptising a white woman (1999:28).

ZAOGA's Transnationalism: Appeal and Limits to Growth

ZAOGA's success in surrounding African countries, and beyond, has derived from several sources. Its appeal is rooted in general Pentecostal practice, an emphasis on gifts of the Spirit. Throughout southern Africa in the twentieth century Pentecostal pioneers, both Zimbabwean and non-Zimbabwean, have consistently stressed 'signs and wonders' in moments of foundation. Public confession of sin, the destruction of polluted objects, deliverance, divine healing and possession by the Holy Spirit have animated fledgling assemblies and drawn adherents. This ministry of the miraculous helps explain ZAOGA/ADDA's remarkable expansion in Mozambique, where it had a good head start establishing itself long before the Pentecostal take-off in the 1990s. But there are other more specific reasons for the success of Mozambican Pentecostalism. Here, as in Latin America, Pentecostals benefited from the break-up of the age-old monopoly exercised by state religion (Martin, 1990: 279). Assaults on religion by Frelimo ripped open the sacred canopy of Catholicism, creating free social space into which Pentecostal churches could move. While zones of popular Catholicism existed throughout the war, and subsequent rapprochement with Frelimo helped the Catholic Church to maintain its favoured position with the state, Catholics were acutely aware of the Pentecostal threat. Within Cabo Delgado the Catholic hierarchy conspired with Frelimo to limit the activities of big-time Pentecostal preachers such as Peter Pretorius, and even local agent evangelists working for ADDA.[47] Among the coastal Mwani people Pentecostal advance at present appears blocked by another 'totalising' religion, folk Islam.[48] War and political violence also created conditions that augmented ADDA's appeal in Mozambique. Pentecostalism's general emphasis on a peaceful temperament, its particular capacity to re-socialise the young male through the disciplining of the body, speech and sexuality, gave it added force in Mozambican society, while ADDA's cell-like structure of organisation ensured an enduring local influence in townships and villages. In many respects ADDA's growth in the face of political violence replicated ZAOGA's trajectory in the 1970s. A similar, though less pronounced, pattern was also discernible in South African townships in the late 1980s and early 1990s.[49] However, the specific reason for Pentecostalism's mass appeal in 1990s Mozambique lies in its capacity to cleanse people from witchcraft when public fear of the phenomenon had a high profile, stimulated by the growing inequalities of power and wealth that accompanied the neo-liberal age.

The prevalence of other well-established Pentecostal movements was always going to limit ZAOGA's appeal in South Africa. As we saw in Chapter 1, South Africa was a key player in the global Pentecostal movement from the very beginning. The Zimbabwean movement was never going to successfully compete alongside the major denominations such as the AFM, AOG and Rhema. Allan Anderson has conducted an in-depth survey of Soshanguve, ZAOGA's prime South African site. His work showed that ZAOGA was just one of many vibrant Pentecostal churches operating there (1992). The existence of competing Pentecostal movements throughout the rest of the continent meant that ZAOGA had to be sufficiently distinct to appeal to potential converts. In other African states, appearing to be an impressive operation enhanced its appeal. It owned fleets of trucks, lorries and cars all identified with the ZAOGA logo. It had hundreds of church buildings, a Bible school and a conference centre. It held conventions in plush hotels and its international connections allow the movement of people and resources across Africa and beyond. It was run by well-dressed, dynamic young pastors, gifted evangelists and overseers, and boasted musical soloists with national, even international, reputations. At the helm was an Armani-clad Apostle, Ezekiel Guti, chauffeured in a silver Mercedes. ZAOGA's success impressed Africans and missionaries. It appeared to bear the logic of its own teachings on self-reliance and black autonomy. Many new adherents, used to missionary largesse, confessed to being enchanted by a movement of black missionaries.[50]

ZAOGA's expatriate workers were indeed missionaries. In one sense they were the heirs of the Shona missionaries of the Masowe and Maranke movements, but with the sophistication of the global Born-again movement. In another sense they replicated the missionaries of the imperial age. Their accounts resemble the narratives of Victorian pioneers and their printed histories likewise stripped their subjects of any agency in the mission process. And Guti's self-confidence matched any nineteenth-century missionary, animated by vanity, Zimbabwean nationalism and material success. The Archbishop's sermons to foreign assemblies often digressed into bragging. In 1982 he told a Zairian assembly: 'I know how to work with all tribes in the world. I cannot make a mistake.'[51] Thirteen years later he lectured a group of newly established South African assemblies on the virtues of his movement:

When I was in Scotland I wanted to buy a car for the pastor ...I was a black man trying to buy a car for a white man... I have millionaires in my church ... Where ever I go I like to have Zimbabweans because they are well trained they help support the church. We have got [Zimbabweans] in Swaziland. Without a Zimbabwean there is no money. Some other tribes have not yet understood.... some other tribes expect money from the white man ... This year we don't want anyone in the office who can not write one million because millions are coming in....

In my church I have got white people. Next year I am sending a black pastor to lead white people ... Many people from overseas admire our Rules and Policy. Even white people are coming to borrow this book. So if there is a statement in the book which does not fit in your country show me. According to our study the book fits anywhere in any country, in any nation.[52]

Moreover, like Victorian missionaries before them, the Zimbabweans' endeavours began with a firm material foundation. Their relative economic strength gave them an advantage in the informal hierarchy of nations that operated in southern and central Africa. Up to the late 1990s, the Zimbabweans could boast a stronger economy, better infrastructure and a more valuable currency than most of their neighbours. Some nineteenth-century missionaries preached a gospel inseparable from capitalist imperialism; ZAOGA's was inextricable from the language of development. Orthodox Pentecostal doctrines and ZAOGA's more idiosyncratic teachings were interspersed with references to 'upgrading'. Sermons and meetings were littered with references to cars, lorries, houses and bank accounts. For those below Zimbabwe in the hierarchy of nations the ideology could create dependency. Malawians, Zambians and Zairians asked repeatedly for Zimbabwean leaders to help sort out their problems. Monde of Zaire wrote: 'I am not in the state of looking to the east or the west but to our lovely JERUSALEM, HARARE.' 'May you clear the Bishop of Macedonia to come to us. Rev. B. Manjoro.'[53]

Those above or equal to Zimbabwe in the hierarchy presented other problems. Those in Botswana resented the repatriation of tithes and offerings to Zimbabwe and openly criticised the leadership cult and the continual reference back to Harare. The South Africans proved even less deferential, demanding an updated version of the *Sacred History* which would celebrate their own agency. While the Zimbabweans' crusading capabilities impressed many, South Africans, raised on a diet of Born-again megastars like Bonnke and Pretorius, offered only a muted response, as they struggled with sermons poorly translated into Afrikaans.[54] Others spoke out against the activities of Zimbabwean missionaries who seemed to prefer exporting knitting machines to curing souls.

Finally, there was a limit to the extent to which the Zimbabwean centre could dominate distant mission fields. Travel beyond the country's borders could be perilous, and not just for Zimbabweans. In 1985 Monde wrote: 'It was war with the Devil to enter Zaire. We arrived in Lumbashi with not a cent left.'[55] The most effective form of communication with Zaire was via a white lorry driver who transported eggs into the Copper Belt. In Cabo Delgado Province, Mozambique ADDA members organised an anniversary to celebrate the life of their own local founder, Joaquim Matus, and appeared only vaguely aware of the distant Ezekiel 'Goot' .[56]

In Britain ZAOGA/FIFMI's failed mission to whites means that it remains a movement based on the Zimbabwean Diaspora. Although the potential for growth is limited, the Zimbabwean character of the movement does enable it to maintain a homogenous identity. FIFMI's tight boundaries provide members with a secure place in which to feel at home, while the bonds of trust and transnational connections facilitate the vital transfer of resources and people between Zimbabwe and the former metropole. At present the leadership is able to marshal its Zimbabwean membership, encouraging them to moonlight as cleaners or factory workers to boost the income needed to maintain growth within Africa. Nevertheless, like elite members in Zimbabwe FIFMI, the wider Born-again movement influences members in Britain. They watch the God Channel, listen to United Christian Broadcasters and Premier Radio and read the *Kingsway* newspaper. Some FIFMI members study at Bible colleges in Hampstead or Kensington, and others join parachurch organisations such as Women Aglow. Many attend the conferences and crusades of Morris Cerullo or Kenneth Hagan. These influences give the British arm of ZAOGA a distinctive local colour. Those returning from a Kenneth Hagan rally espoused a Christian Zionism rarely encountered in Zimbabwe.

Conclusion

This chapter has analysed the specific, contingent and changing character of ZAOGA's transnational growth as it expanded from its Zimbabwean base. It provides new insights into the protean nature of post-colonial Christianity. It is also a powerful counter to externality theories about contemporary Pentecostalism, showing how ZAOGA expanded as a movement of Africans evangelising other Africans. The analysis also sheds light on the nature of Pentecostal/Born-again Christianity: on one level it is a fairly unified set of doctrine and ideologies, of styles of proselytism and organisational techniques that allow for Western domination and homogenisation; on another level it is a series of overlapping networks that offer movements such as ZAOGA resources to create autonomous versions of Pentecostalism suited to different contexts.

The chapter also sheds light on the nature of post-colonialism. Some critics use post-colonialism as a description of the activities of cosmopolitans, whose writing and reflection is animated by the anguish of alienation from their lands of origin (Bhabha, 1994). These cosmopolitan elites are taken to represent the Third World Diaspora living in the West. In reality most such Africans are ordinary economic migrants and refugees living in inner cities, earning a living from poorly paid manual work. Many are sustained not by intellectual endeavour but by the life of religious communities. This religious activity also challenges prevailing notions of the post-colonial. There is a widespread assumption that movement to the West is essentially radicalising. Gyan Prakash writes: 'The third world, far from being confined to its assigned space, has penetrated the inner sanctum of the first world. It has reached across boundaries and barriers to connect with minority voices in the first world: socialists, radicals, feminists, minorities etc' (1990: 403). FIFMI and movements like it will no doubt contribute to replenishing and renovating the church in Britain but in a socially conservative manner. In its pursuit of the values of liberal capitalism and its approach to issues of gender and sexuality, this 'returning' missionary movement of black Christianity certainly does not make alliances with radicals and revolutionaries.

Notes

1 Ezekiel Guti, 'Understanding Third World Mentality', 10 April 1987, file, Sermons, ZAW.
2 Ezekiel Guti, 'Awake Sleeping Giant', 7 February 1989 & 'Understanding Third World Mentality', 10 April 1987, file, Sermons, ZAW; 1994a: 80.
3 Ibid. Published Interview with Ezekiel Guti, *Africa Arise*, c. 1993.
4 Tanzanian Forward in Faith Ministries Church Board, 23 October 1988, file, Tanzania, Missions, ZAW; Ezekiel Guti, Speech to Malawi Assemblies, ca. 1989, file, Finance, ZAW.
5 Ezekiel Guti, 'Understanding Third World Mentality', 10 April 1987, file, Sermons, ZAW.
6 Ezekiel Guti, 'RSA', 3 June 1985, file, Sermons, ZAW.
7 Guti expressed disappointment at the failure of many of the leading members of ITWLA to attend his Leadership Summit held in Harare in 1993, despite the fact that their participation had been advertised. ITWLA Minutes, 15 March 1993, file, International Third World Leaders Association, ZAW.
8 7 February, 1996, fieldwork notes.
9 Ezekiel and Eunor Guti to Charles Trombey Ministries, Oklahoma, 25 July 1989; Dan Duke Ministries International, Florida to Ezekiel Guti, 7 August 1989, file, Non-Denominational, USA, 1989, ZAW.
10 FIFMI, Edgware, Middlesex, Financial Report, April-June 1989. Letter, 7 September 1987, files, England and South Africa, Missions, ZAW.
11 For example, Friends International Christian University, which validates ZAOGA's Bible courses. Circular letter to donors, FIFM, Mutare, file, 'Sponsors 1984-85', ZAW.
12 Int.DM41, Bartholomew & Appiah Manjoro.
13 Int.DM30, Paul Kimaruh.
14 Int.DM16, Joseph Choto; Int.DM35, Wilson Mabasa.
15 Executive Minutes, 24 May 1989, ZAW.
16. Int.DM64, Paul Saungweme; Int.DM9,Bill John Chigwenembe; file, Missions, ZAW.
17 Int.DM64, Paul Saungweme; Int.DM41,Manjoro; Int.DM9, Bill John Chigwenembe.
18 Int.DM39, Innocent Makwarimba.
19 Int.DM64, Paul Saungweme.
20 Int.DM45, Jorge Joaquim Matus; Int.DM67, Fernando Sumunitato; DM93,Benjamin Leach.
21 'All Pastors and Buildings 1986', file, Mozambique, Missions, ZAW; Int.DM66, Mateus Simao.
22 Saungweme Report, 3 October 1995, file, Mozambique, Missions, ZAW; Int.DM67, Fernando Sumunitato; Int.DM1, Joaô Almeida; Int.DM93, Benjamin Leach.
23 Int.DM81, Bacai Casimba.
24 Correspondence, Isaac Phiri, Blantyre, 6 December 1988 and Mabviko Phiri, Chikwawa, 29 December 1988, file, Malawi, Missions, ZAW.
25 Report Zambia Assemblies of God, ca. 1991, file, Zambia, Missions, ZAW.
26 B. Manjoro, ZAOGA to Ministry of Home Affairs, Registry of Societies, Dar es Salaam, 29 May 1985, file, Tanzania, Missions, ZAW.
27 AOGA Zambia Committee Meeting, 22 August 1981, file, Zambia, Missions, ZAW.
28 Ezekiel Guti to Pastor and Mrs Owiti, Kisumu, Kenya, 19 July 1989, file, Kenya, Missions; correspondence to Pastor J. Mabviko Phiri and Pastor B.M. Pondamali, 26 August 1988, file, Malawi, Missions, ZAW.
29 Tanzania Forward in Faith Ministries Church Board with its Financial Committee, 23 October 1988, file, Tanzania, Missions, ZAW.
30 Correspondence and reports 1989-1992, file, Zambia, Missions, ZAW.
31 Letters from Simon Monde to Harare, 5 March 1987, 28 March 1987, April 1993, file, Zaire, Missions; Chimpaka Lawanda (Francis) Penge, Lusaka, to the Minister for Foreign Affairs, Zimbabwe, 13 February 1987, file, Relations with Government, ZAW; Int.DM22, Ezekiel Guti; Int.DM48, Simon Monde.
32 File, Missions, ZAW, particularly years 1988-97.
33 Minutes of Makambako Committee Meeting, 7 October 1988, file, Tanzania, Missions, ZAW.

34 Int.DM48, Simon Monde.
35 Simon Monde to B. Manjoro, 4 January 1988, file, Zaire, Missions, ZAW.
36 Report, Zambia Assemblies of God, Africa to Ezekiel Guti, 21 November 1989, file, Zambia, Missions, ZAW.
37 Isaac Frimpong Mintah, Forward in Faith Ministries International, report, Ghana, 25 January 1995, file, Ghana, Missions, ZAW.
38 Ezekiel Guti, Sermon, London 13 August 1994, fieldwork notes.
39 Int.DM61, Joshua & Mabel Samasuwo; Int. DM16, Joseph Choto; *This is That*, no. 1. September 1986, *Alive*, vol., 1.no. 2. August 1989, file, Missions, London, ZAW.
40 File, Missions, London, 1985-96, ZAW.
41 Int.DM2, Phil Austin.
42 Jean Henderson, account of time in Zimbabwe, 19 November 1993 to 14 May 1994, in my possession.
43 Int.DM25, Jenny & John James; DM25, Jean Henderson; Jean Henderson, notes on Pastors Conference November 1996, in my possession.
44 Int.DM3, Phil Austin. Int.DM25, Jenny and John James; Int. DM24, Jean Henderson.
45 Ezekiel Guti to Joshua and Mabel Samasuwo, 13 October 1989, file, London, Missions, ZAW; Fieldwork notes, Deeper Life Conference 1996.
46 Chris Sande to Ezekiel and Eunor Guti, 14 May 1989& Consult Chirambadare to G. Rwizi, 14 November 1994, file, London, Missions, ZAW.
47 Int.DM96, Father Amaro Valeiro. According to ADDA evangelist Fernando Sumunitato the Catholic Church initially conspired to have arrested as a Renamo agent. Int.DM67, Fernando Sumunitato.
48 Wycliffe Bible Translators, Mwani Strategy Document, ca. 1994, in my possession.
49 Int.DM35, Wilson Mabasa; R. Mabasa to Ezekiel Guti, ca. 1991, file, South Africa, Mission, ZAW.
50 Int.DM48, Simon Monde; Int.DM66, Mateus Simao.
51 Report of meeting, 4 August 1982, file, Zaire, Missions, ZAW.
52 Sermon to RSA, 3 June 1995, file, Sermons, ZAW.
53 S. Monde to E. Guti and Bishop Nduna, 30 April 1991 and 25 April 1992, file, Zaire, Missions, ZAW.
54 Int.DM35, Wilson Mabasa.
55 Simon Monde to Ezekiel Guti, 24 March 1985, file, Zaire, Missions, ZAW.
56 Fieldwork, Pemba, Mozambique, June 1996.

8
'Priests for our Families'
Poverty, Prosperity & Pentecostal Spirituality in Neo-Liberal Zimbabwe

Introduction: Neo-Liberal Zimbabwe

The end of the Cold War did not bring about a cessation of external intervention in Africa, but rather a change in its nature. Neo-liberal economics exemplified by privatisation and state contraction spread across the continent in the 1990s, inaugurating a new era. Western-dominated international institutions such as the World Bank and the International Monetary Fund dictated financial policy, insisting that government revenue be used primarily to pay overseas debts, thereby elevating private initiative over public responsibility. In the face of Economic Structural Adjustment Programmes (ESAPs) state provision of services rapidly diminished (Birmingham, 1998). In Zimbabwe health care and education deteriorated, unemployment increased, while the population expanded with many young people migrating to towns and cities. By 1998 many Zimbabweans were only eating one meal a day. [1] Nevertheless a few benefited from the changes. These elites were able to secure their families' health and the future of their children's education through the growing private sector. Other winners were those who ran private security companies. As poverty increased, so did crime, and law and order could no longer be guaranteed by a retrenched police force. Multinationals and their senior employees increasingly paid for their own protection.

The decline in food security led to a large increase in child labour as poor, usually rural, people put their children into the custody of their richer, usually urban, relatives. These children often worked as unpaid labour in exchange for food and accommodation. They might also end up assisting their parents and relatives working on commercial farms, mines and quarries. Orphans and those unable to cope with the demands of their hosts often opted for a life on the streets. By the mid-1990s growing unemployment and declining state provision for education meant that schooling was no longer the social lever it had been before. Once-prized exam certificates were increasingly worthless, rather like Zimbabwe's currency. Without jobs, many youths faced a future of being 'just seated'. They had become a statistic, worse still a social problem, often viewed with suspicion by a state which was only too quick to brand them as 'thugs'. The ZANU/PF government became increasingly remote and detached from the lives of ordinary Zimbabweans. The enormous and expensive out-of-town mansion, constructed by the President as a gift to his new wife Grace and popularly known as 'Gracelands', came to symbolise how far removed he had become from his people. It was built at a time when public sector wages were falling rapidly behind the rate of inflation and civil servants were forced to strike. Growing industrial unrest from the mid-1990s onwards reflected a growing trade union militancy that would eventually lead to the formation of the MDC.

Zimbabweans increasingly experienced their state as violent, bankrupt and immoral, a context that provides the background to this chapter, which is concerned with the world of ordinary ZAOGA members. It begins by considering how Zimbabweans are drawn into the Pentecostal community by processes of rupture. Later sections consider how other schemes of discontinuity such as ascetic codes and acts of exorcism maintain adherents within that community. The core of the analysis centres upon a lexicon of key words, phrases and narratives drawn from Pentecostal music, preaching, testimony and prayer. It shows Pentecostalism as a quintessentially popular religion, able to satisfy existential passions and to aid those struggling for survival. In particular it demonstrates how Pentecostal religion addresses the personal sense of abjection created by shattered hopes of independence, and offers security in the face of state retrenchment, the capriciousness of global capitalism and growing levels of violence and crime. Beyond providing them with security, the Pentecostal community captures adherents and offers them stability and hope as they strive toward something better.

Altar Calls and Calls to Alter:
Ruptures and Discontinuities in the Making
of the Pentecostal Community

Pentecostal discourse is replete with images of rupture and discontinuity. Although some believers point to a moment of conversion, membership of the Pentecostal community has been marked for many by a series of breaks, which may have included recommitment and rehabilitation as well as conversion (Robbins, 2004). For some, such as Debson Chivizano whose testimony was discussed in Chapter 4, entrance into the Pentecostal community came through a holistic set of transformations that delivered personal security and the opportunity of becoming more modern. This opening section considers how discontinuity is conceptualised and marked through rituals such as baptism and the destruction of polluted objects. Schemes of transformation are most apparent when a person converts. Other schemes such as ascetic codes and disciplines are important for maintaining discontinuity and will be discussed in later sections.

Emphasis on discontinuity is most marked at Pentecostal crusades, events explicitly aimed at winning the 'heathen' and led by evangelists skilled in the art. Most Pentecostals are not initiated into faith in this manner. Friends, family or neighbours introduce them to the church. Others turn up at services independently, searching for relief from poverty, sickness or family problems. Others attend out of curiosity. All Pentecostal pastors are to some extent evangelists. They work closely with full-time revivalists, their services usually finish with an altar call and they emphasise dualism in their preaching and ritual practice. However, the crusades are the frontline, and professional evangelists spend longer reflecting on their practice than normal pastors. Crusading techniques will therefore be discussed as a means of illuminating some of the transformations involved in joining the Pentecostal community. I followed two of

ZAOGA's key evangelists as they engaged in their trade, filmed their rallies and used the playback facility on the camera to gain their reflexive commentary. I attended the campaigns of Paul Saungweme at a rural growth point near Charter in Manicaland, and in the low-density suburb of Chisipite, Harare, and those of Bill John Chigwenembe in the high-density urban location of Sekubva, Mutare and the medium-density urban area of Braeside, Harare.[2]

The evangelists worked as part of a team. Occasionally someone with a special ministry would assist them in the work of deliverance but the co-workers were predominantly musicians and vocalists. The music group was essential to draw visitors into the tent and keep them there long enough to hear the message. The entertainers were young and good-looking. They wore fashionable clothes and had sharp haircuts, which attracted an audience. Their job was to create an atmosphere of 'rejoicing' and 'liberty', because it was not possible to 'feed sad people'. The music and dancing were mostly upbeat for the sake of the young people in the audience who usually made up the majority, but there were occasional quieter songs for elders. Once they had an audience the evangelists saw their task as one of 'building faith', which involved 'breaking links' with doctrines, traditions and spirits that held people back. As Saungweme put it: 'an evangelist's work is power. The evangelist has to exert power to show people that the Word is living … Evangelistic work is warfare. The Devil cannot give you these people on a silver plate. It is a struggle.'[3]

The Devil was countered with words and displays of power. Song was a key means of building faith and Pentecostal classics such as 'There is power in the blood of Jesus' were sung repeatedly. The audience was also told to 'expect miracles', that they 'would never be the same again'. To reinforce the message of transformation, converts from the night before were encouraged to give their testimony. But most important were the words of the evangelists. Their sermons addressed the problems people experienced in their daily lives: matters relating to health, demon possession, marriage and poverty. The evangelists were down-to-earth and frank, especially on matters of sexuality. Their intention was to 'touch the heart'. They sought to 'paint a picture of a crushed person, a person who needs a solution because that is why he has come into the tent'. Examples of failure and heartbreak were varied for different audiences, depending on age, class and location.

Where Pentecostal crusades differed most from the work of evangelical preachers such as Billy Graham was in the displays of power that accompanied the sermon. Most important was the destruction of charms and fetishes brought by those who had repented the night before. Beads, cloth, knobkerries and pouches filled with magical substances were burned in a wheelbarrow as the musical group danced and sang *'tinomatsika madhimoni nezita raJesu'* – 'we step on demons in Jesus' name'. The public destruction of these polluted substances was intended to encourage others to break links with tradition. It was important for the preacher himself to exude power and confidence as he preached. Both Saungweme and Chigwenembe were prone to gymnastic displays. They jumped up and down, contorting their bodies and sweating profusely as they exhorted their audience toward repentance. When the altar call was given, those who came forward were made to wait in lines, encouraged to focus on their problems and the miracles they wanted through Jesus Christ. Some would repent but many simply wanted prayer for healing and deliverance. Once again the evangelist and exorcist threw their bodies into this cosmic struggle with the Devil, often delivering the supplicant of his or her demon with loud shouts and violent shaking. Those possessed would sometimes fall to the floor and struggle as the evil spirit made a last-ditch attempt to remain with its host. Converts were encouraged to return to the crusade throughout its duration to build their faith. They would be introduced to a ZAOGA pastor, drawn into the Pentecostal community and baptised.

Prayer and Preaching: The Word and the Lexicon

The preaching in ZAOGA assemblies was not expository. There was little detailed reflection on a specific passage, placing it in context and drawing out its significance through discussion of key words and phrases. Most preachers were untrained, and pastors who had been to the Bible college had only been given a practical training in evangelism, demonology and deliverance and church management. They were taught Bible knowledge but not how to engage with Scripture critically. Sermons were usually a composite of passages and verses woven together with a limited commentary. Major points and key words and phrases were repeated over and again, the preacher raising his or her voice to emphasise their significance. And there was a good deal of story-telling. One pastor confidently explained that 'in ZAOGA we don't preach theology, but contemporary issues'. Indeed, because the vast majority of the preachers were 'of the people', not separated from their congregations by ethnic or class barriers and sharing the same neighbourhoods, their sermons were extremely effective, summoning up ideas and images that sustained and inspired their flocks (Gill, 1990: 711). It was often possible to record, even video, services because Pentecostals do this as a matter of course themselves. When it was not possible to make use of electronic media it was fairly easy to take accurate notes because Pentecostals attend services with pen and paper ready for inspiration from their brethren.

Fearlessness and Security

City Assembly 1, Baines Avenue, 1 October 1995

By 10.30 the hall was full of about 100 smartly dressed people, in their twenties and thirties. The second service began with forty minutes of church business, all of which was about money. This was longer than usual but the biannual Period of Talents had just begun. During Talents, members buy, sell and make things in order to raise money for the church. Thus a woman discoursed at length about her own enterprise of gown-making. This was followed by a time of pledging as members made promises about how much they would raise. Members were then asked to pledge financial gifts for the pastor's wedding and the Archbishop's Christmas Gift. The Church Secretary recorded these pledges in a book. Members were reminded that a new month had begun and tithes were due. A freewill offering was then taken up. There was a brief praise session, with vibrant singing mostly in ChiShona, and then the sermon began.

A young man preached for about 30 minutes on Esther 6. The context of the passage was the time of Exile when the Israelites were under Persian rule. The passage itself was the story of Esther and Mordecai's triumph over Haman, who was bent on the destruction of the Jews. The story's denouement is the execution of the evil Haman on the gallows he had intended for the murder of Mordecai. The story was read and then retold by the preacher with much gusto and good deal of licence. For the entertainment of his audience he pranced around the front of the hall waving his arms, injecting as much energy as possible into the story, particularly the execution. His interpretation was simple but very effective. He explained that Christians were descendants of the Jews, their history was the continuation of the Jewish story. Thus he concluded:

'God is on the side of Jews ... As long as you are of Jewish origin, i.e. of a Christian background no one will touch you. Witches will come but they won't touch you. The blood of Jesus is a durawall [a proprietary brand of pre-cast concrete walling in Zimbabwe]. God intervenes like a strong wrestler in touch wrestling.'

The image of wrestling evoked a good deal of laughter. The weekly bouts of the sport organised by the World Wrestling Federation (WWF) were shown regularly on Zimbabwean television and the likes of Hulk Hogan were enormously popular amongst Zimbabwean youth. Mention of the sport was made in a number of sermons, always to good effect, although some of the more thoughtful preachers were ambivalent about its effect on the peaceable Pentecostal temper. But far more profound was the equation of Christ's blood with a durawall. As in many other cultures, blood is a potent image for Zimbabweans; it is associated with life, sacrifice and cleansing (Lan, 1985: 91-8). Christian imagery resonates with all of these associations by linking blood with Christ's sacrifice on the cross. Pentecostals tend to focus on blood's specific protective quality in their ongoing struggle with the Devil and his emissaries in this world. Thus a few months later in the pre-meeting prayer session at City 1 Assembly I overheard a young male student praying the following words and phrases repeatedly like a plain-chant:

Father we worship you. We thank you for your presence, your anointing, we worship you alleluia, we thank you [*glossalalia*] *eli eli li elikai, eli e likai* ....

Holy, Holy, Holy art thou ... we worship you. We thank you for your word which is going to change our lives ... We thank you for your anointing... many people will come today with spiritual, financial, sickness problems we pray that you will help them. I pray God for your anointing ... anointing.... anointing....

We pray that this area will be a no-go area for demons, for spirits of criticism, spirits of reasoning ... cover it with the blood of Jesus . . . the power of the blood.[4]

The equation of blood with a durawall powerfully evoked that protective quality, concretising it in one of the most prescient images of the 1990s. Made from large concrete slabs and pillars, durawalls surround most factories and low-density housing in Zimbabwe's towns and cities, providing them with rudimentary security. The level of protection is increased by security guards, stationed by their gates and regularly patrolling their perimeters, and enhanced by the presence of live-in domestic servants often resident in shacks or cottages in the grounds of plush suburban homes. Many rank-and-file members of ZAOGA do these jobs, or at least started out doing them. The durawall also conjures up another potent, though more ambivalent, image of survival for many urban dwellers. In the southern part of Harare, on the edge of the industrial area and high-density suburbs, lies the Walled City. This market area surrounded by slabs of concrete wall is a place where Zimbabweans can buy and sell on the black market. Contained within are street kids, hawkers and petty entrepreneurs ready to help the visitor procure any item, including parts from his or her truck stolen the night before. As such it is a vital part of the informal economy providing many on the edge of starvation with the means to survive.

The image of security and protective barriers pervaded many sermons and was often imaginatively rooted in Scripture. One visiting preacher at City 1 cited Job chapter 1, where Satan taunts God for protecting his servant by putting a hedge around him and his household. The preacher declared 'God builds a wall around believers as he built a wall around his people.' During the 1996 church anniversary celebrations the pastor at City 1 chose to speak on a God who 'endures with his people', taking as his text Psalm 46:

> God is our strength and refuge an ever-present help in trouble …
> There is a river whose streams make glad the city of God, the holy place where the Most high dwells.
> God is within her, she will not fall …
> The Lord almighty is with us;
> The God of Jacob is our fortress.

His commentary was brief but rousing, the audience urging him on to greater rhetorical heights with ululation and shouts of 'Yes!' and 'That's right!'. Beginning with the premise that 'the church is a refugee camp, a place where God protects his people', he quickly moved to a more triumphal note. Drawing liberally from the Psalms, he pushed his audience to applause, declaring: 'Some trust in chariots and some trust in horses but we trust in the name of the Lord' [Psalm 20: 7].[5] The image of fortifications was most powerfully evoked in a special Youth Big Sunday at Highfields Revival Centre in October 1995, intended to draw together all the young people attending the ten assemblies in the suburb.

> The formal service began with victory shouts that worked rather like a modern antiphon. The Master of Ceremony would exclaim: 'There is Power in the name of …' to which the audience would reply 'JESUS!' The shouts would continue 'All devils tremble in the name of …. JESUS' 'There's deliverance in the name of …. JESUS', etc.

> After a series of these shouts the Master of Ceremonies elaborated 'Jesus is not a noun but a verb! We say rise up in Jesus name'! Then a preacher spoke about the 'spirit of fear' prevalent amongst young people: 'fear of – tsotsis [thieves], dogs, cats, fear of being kidnapped, fear of witches'. He cited Psalm 127: 'Unless the Lord watches over the city, the watchmen stand on guard in vain. In vain you rise early and stay up late, toiling for food to eat – for he grants sleep to those he loves.' Then he referred to Deuteronomy 27 and 28 where Moses addresses the Israelites at the point of their entry into the Promised Land. The Israelites will be God's people, they will have a land of milk and honey and enemies will flee them if they obey His commands. The preacher proceeded to tell an excited audience about their God-given Spirit of Power. 'This is God's Church. This is God's Century. It must be kept pure. We have God given authority -- the Spirit of power.' As the audience shouted 'famba!' – [lit. 'go for it'!] – he went on, 'what is the secret of the man of God [Archbishop Ezekiel Guti]? prayer and a sinless life. God said to the man of God "fear not and sin not" … If you have a spirit of power and a spirit of love … no girl can come and mess around with you. You will have a boundary… This is the century of God. Other churches are closing down. They have no youth …'

> Then in a final flurry he finished with the words: 'Jesus Christ is all in all. If you are ill – Jesus Christ. If you are in need of money – Jesus Christ. If you need a job – Jesus Christ.'[6]

In the above mini-sermon (and also the previous address on Psalm 46) God was the omnipotent security guard watching over an entire city. He gave his people a 'spirit of power' and created a protective boundary around them. Such a boundary not only provided security from physical threats such as robbery and kidnap but also helped the believer remain pure, able to resist the temptations of the flesh. Moreover, His

8.1 *Evangelist*
Bill John
Chigwenembe

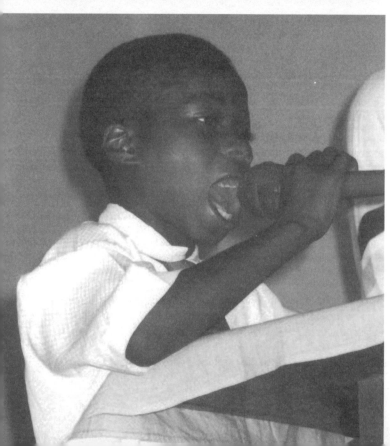

8.2 *Small boy*
preaching

8.3 Woman
praising

8.4 Girl
praising

name, like His blood, protected and empowered. It was not merely a noun but a verb. The word JESUS had incantatory power. It was prayed and spoken over and again like a mantra, willing God into action. The name itself was an answer to problems, if spoken with faith. As with the association with blood, names and naming have a particularly strong resonance in many parts of Africa. Parents choose names with a great deal of care. Often children are named after ancestors to receive their blessing and oversight. At other times they are named to signify events occurring around the time of birth, or to express a virtue or aspiration. Clan names have religious and symbolic connotations (Bourdillon, 1987: 24-6).

The preponderance of images of refuge, security and protection in contemporary Pentecostal preaching in Zimbabwe does suggest that there is an element of escapism or flight from the world in this form of Christian religion. But this is only one theme in the rich collection of sermons I heard. As the citations suggest, there were more upbeat components in the Pentecostal lexicon: status and authority, victory and prosperity. Flight into the sanctuary of the Pentecostal community is often just the first stage of a conversion story. As the believers are remade they move on to view themselves and society from a different perspective.

A Chosen People, a Royal Priesthood: Status and Authority

The most popular sermon text, especially among women, was 1 Peter 2: 9: 'But you are a chosen people, a royal priesthood, a holy nation, a people belonging to God.' Expanding on the passage, the female pastor at Highfields Revival Centre told her audience to have confidence in themselves and to let go of their fears:

> You are heirs to Kingdom of God, Children of God. You are a precious person because you are an heir to the Kingdom of God. As Christians you have an identity card as citizens of the Kingdom of God. You are not an ordinary person. You are not despised, because your identity is not a physical identity, like metal IDs we can lose. It is a spiritual identity ... We don't know the power that is in us as Children of God.. ... The Bible says "By his scars we are healed". As soon as I pronounce that, I am healed. A big truck has to stop because of the authority of a policeman given to him by the government. Our power is greater than that of a policeman or the government because our authority is from on high ... it is not from the government it is from on high... Sometimes you don't come to church because you feel that you have no value or importance but let me say you are valuable and precious before God. [7]

Notions of kinship and descent resonate with a Zimbabwean audience. They are still the means by which wealth and authority are often transferred between families and persons, though usually between men. Kinship is not only the language of 'traditional' politics, it is also an important means of securing jobs, promotions and contracts in the workplace where resources are few and nepotism is rife. Many Zimbabweans would have witnessed the coronation, or installation of a rural chief or headman, rituals which have become more elaborate and more significant in post-colonial Africa than in the recent or distant past. New leadership rituals can be observed as the President and his entourage are ferried around the city in convoys of dark Mercedes accompanied by police and army vehicles, and fêted at lavish state functions in the international hotels. Yet wealth, political authority and status are something that most ZAOGA members experience only at a distance. Some are unemployed or under-employed, others have poorly paid jobs. As the state withdraws from welfare provision it is often experienced through its mechanisms of control. Although the ID card has lost many of its associations with colonial pass-laws, it is still popularly known by the colonial name, *stupa*. It is often checked at roadblocks, used in voter registration and elections, is necessary in most transactions with the state, and is often needed to get work. Like many Zimbabwean citizens, ZAOGA members can feel marginal to the economic and social activities that take place around them. Women and youth are most affected, the consequences directly translated onto their bodies.

While it is accepted that a husband may wander into adulterous liaisons, female infidelity is not viewed with the same fond indulgence. Still required to fulfil her sexual duties to an aberrant husband, a wife is vulnerable to sexually transmitted diseases, especially AIDS. Domestic violence against women is widespread. It accounts for over 60 per cent of all murder cases that pass through the courts. This is in addition to the thousands of women who suffer regular beatings, with figures as high as 32 to 42 per cent in rural areas and small towns. Rape is prevalent both within and outside the home. But in response to these male crimes and incest the courts have been extremely lenient, considering theft of property more heinous. With unemployment high, some women feel obliged to accept 'carpet interviews' in order to secure work. In 1985 it was reported that sexual harassment at work was experienced by 11 to 25 per cent of women. More generally, single women are still stigmatised as prostitutes and those 'caught' wearing mini-skirts have been accused of inviting rape, or worse still assaulted. In spite of their low status and the ever-present threat of male violence, the most vulnerable of female professions – prostitution – has increased as single women desperate for any sort of income have taken to the streets for survival (Getecha and Chipika, 1995: 111, 121; Wood, 1998: 16-18).

Youth are vulnerable to similar ravages. Corporal punishment of children in the late 1990s was so commonplace that it is considered 'normal', occurring in schools (illegally), the courts, and the home. This has been matched by an increase in sexual abuse. Homelessness and insecure and overcrowded accommodation have induced not only more physical abuse but also emotional and sexual violence. A marked increase in rape cases involving minors has been reported in the local press. Orphans living with relatives are particularly vulnerable to sexual abuse, and even more so street children who are often forced to grant sexual favours in return for a warm place to sleep. Higher drop-out rates from schools have created a generation of bored and unfulfilled youth with the associated problems of early sexual relationships, teenage pregnancy, promiscuity, prostitution and forced marriage (Mupedzisiwa, 1997).

Numerous Zimbabweans enter ZAOGA assemblies with low self-esteem, feeling wretched, despised and abused. But within the safe confines of the Pentecostal community they experience a revelation. They learn that they are not a 'nobody but a somebody'. Even though they may not have 'big things' they are nevertheless 'special'. They are no longer just citizens of a state that has broken its promises and increasingly resorts to surveillance and control; they have new *royal* identity as members of the Kingdom of God. And this new identity is not ascribed by means of a flimsy ID card that can be lost. Pentecostals are chosen people, called by name. More than that, they are now holy, set apart, and clean. To ordinary Zimbabweans, the significance of being 'called' cannot be understated. Unlike members of other mass movements, Pentecostals are not part of the great unwashed. They are not just proletarians, workers or cadres. Neither are they 'thugs', a statistic or a potential social problem. They are given a name, told that they are 'unique', and assured that their projects count. At the very heart of their conversion comes the realisation that they still have agency in their lives. The sociologist of religion, David Martin, puts it well: 'For people to be addressed in evangelical language as persons is to be spoken to in terms that truly speak to their condition, confirming beyond the shadow of doubt their dignity, worth and significance.' The message of redemption, or 'freedom from slavery', and the promise of healing resonate powerfully amongst people caught up in every kind of abuse, violation and indebtedness (Martin, 1996: 45-6).

As a royal people, Pentecostals have a new authority by which to live. They are protected and empowered by the blood and name of Jesus Christ. As citizens of the Kingdom of God they participate in a new system of kinship which is not prone to the biases of age and patriarchy. And they have a heavenly ID card that gives them more influence than agents of the state possess. When addressing a ZAOGA student group at the University of Zimbabwe, the pastor at City 1 Assembly took as his texts Genesis 41: 42 and Luke 15: 22. The first is the story of Joseph being placed in charge of Egypt by Pharaoh; the second is the account of the reinstatement of the Prodigal Son by his father. In both stories the subject receives a ring to signify his new-found authority and he is then dressed in fine linen robes. Having retold the stories with great gusto the pastor went on to say, 'God has given us authority. I am above the ordinaries [ordinary people] because of the ring, the ring of power of someone else's name. God has given you authority. He says go and change.'[8]

More than Conquerors: Mission in a Fallen World

With a new identity and authority Pentecostals are encouraged back into the world to lead victorious lives. In Bible studies and sermons, the unredeemed state of being a victim was continually contrasted with the redeemed status of victor. At a Monday evening prayer meeting and Bible study at City 1 Assembly, a young man told those gathered: 'We were victims of inheritance. But now we are no longer victims but conquerors. Greater is he that is in me than he that is in the world [1 John 4: 4]. In Christ we are more than conquerors' [Romans 8: 37]. With a new-found status they can now begin to dream dreams. In September 1995, I accompanied Steve Simango, the Archbishop's son-in-law and itinerant speaker, to Zengesa, a high-density suburb in Seke, a large urban community outside Harare. There, Simango preached to approximately 600 young people on the subject 'Reaching your Destiny':

'We are still in the morning of our lives. I know God has put me on this planet earth for a purpose.' As a female pastor got up to wave her arms in support, shouting 'alleluia', he took his microphone and walked amongst the audience, most of whom looked impressed. He preached against a 'slave mentality', and an 'inferiority complex': 'If you are good at Science don't just settle to be a science teacher in Dzengesa six [a residential area] don't just be a house girl. Daddy has plans for you. ... The Devil is responsible for the genocide in Rwanda, the killings in South Africa, killings in Bosnia. The Devil is responsible for AIDS but Jesus says "I have come that you have life in its fullness" [John 6: 6]. ... Adolescents chill down. You are not the first to grow up. For young people the greatest problem is the flesh. Don't give your body to the Devil. Bad friends. Your friends are thieves, liars and homos [homosexuals] you thought it was only a problem of the West it is also a problem here. ... Prosperity is the plan of God for you. There is no time to feel inferior. My people are not dying because of the Devil but lack of knowledge. You and God are an unbeatable team. If you are a girl and you have potential to go to university and the Chair [of the Youth Ministry] asks you to marry him. Say no! ... you must not just set your sights on marriage to a husband with a car, and a pram with twins in it... See yourself in big time business. ... Today we are going to pull down the limiting factors.'[9]

The preacher was challenging attitudes that disempower a generation of youth across central and southern Africa. There is a shocking sense of self-loathing, inferiority and despair, which, as we have seen in previous chapters, is described as a 'Third World Mentality' by ZAOGA members. It is an attitude of mind which assumes that blacks are morally and intellectually inferior to whites, and are incapable of prospering or running the institutions of the modern state. It is a mentality similar to that which Fanon identified in the era of decolonisation, but which pervades the recent post-colonial era in which the hopes of independence have failed (Fanon, 1965, [1961], 1986 [1967]; Simpson, 1998; Weiss, 2004: 1-20). By invoking the divine promise of 'life in its fullness', the preacher dared his audience, particularly young women, to view their destinies differently.

At other times ZAOGA members were exhorted to see themselves as part of a larger enterprise, as part of a religious movement that counts. In October 1995 there was a Big Sunday celebration for assemblies in the northern suburbs held at the University of Zimbabwe. Overseer Christopher Chadoka, the third most powerful member of the church after Guti and his wife, addressed a gathering of about 350 people. He began by recounting how he had just purchased the former Dutch Reformed Church in Waterfalls on behalf of the movement, and was now also in search of a building in the city centre. Taking Numbers 13: 27-33 as his text, he told the story of Israelite spies returning from Canaan to report a land of milk and honey inhabited by the giant descendants of the Nephilim. He continued:

> Most of you will see giants but don't forget the vision. A long time back it was said in the vision that we were going to get rich. We could not believe it. Some girls cannot believe that they will get married. They see it as a giant. Others can't see how they will get a job. These problems in the home are just grasshoppers. I want to remind you today the organisation we are in is the vision of God. Anything is possible if it is the vision of God. We are going to face lots of giants. We are going to face a lot of problems. We have to return to the vision. ... How many churches can buy 17 trucks in one day and two lorries? If you look at our pastors you won't see them with patches on their backs. They move in cars... which other churches have youth choirs? ... Other churches only have old people in the choir and ... in our church we have youth in choir and the old sitting. ... This is the royal family in the Kingdom of God. [10]

A mixture of Old Testament promise and modernising zeal, Chadoka's address proved to be extremely popular. Many other sermons were rhetorically brilliant and their promises of security and empowerment, status and authority, victory and prosperity were very comforting to their audiences. But were they no more than that? Were the promises ever realised?

Being of Good Character

From the outset Pentecostals are taught to expect and seek change, and to expect an 'experience of the sacred'(Muratorio, 1981: 527). In services they are repeatedly told 'you will never be the same again' or 'you will go home transformed'. There is a constant emphasis on permanent internal revolution. And much of the agency for this personal transformation rests with the individual. The process begins with repentance, necessary for both cleansing and empowerment. The pastor at the rural Nyamasara Assembly informed his audience that it was impossible to 'go to church a prostitute and come back home as a prostitute', or go to church a *n'ganga* [traditional healer] and come back home a *n'ganga*. He told them, 'you need to repent so that God will restore power in you'.[11]

But repentance is only the first stage. There is a continual emphasis on holiness, or good character. Born-agains are exalted to live moral and disciplined lives. The demands made upon them are total and the push for sincerity is relentless. Speakers often chide their audiences into action, rebuking them for coming late, being stingy in giving, forgetting their Bibles and lacking enthusiasm in prayer or singing. In Highfields Revival Centre a female deacon announced, 'I have seen people sitting on benches at the back not the front. They don't know whom they worship.'[12] There is also a constant spotlight on the believer's motives, which must remain pure.

And Born-agains must be vigilant against the Devil and his agents. These evil forces are continually seeking ways of entering the Christian. The believer's body is a temple, a dwelling place for the Holy Spirit. But for God to dwell there it must be kept clean. A visiting preacher at City 1 Assembly told his young audience:

> In scripture the Devil is a snake, a scorpion [Luke 10: 19], you must beware of such demonic forces. As you walk the streets you are thinking about sleeping with another woman. You should say 'Out Satan'. If you open the door, demons can come in. The easiest way of transferring demons into people is sex, just as STD is transferred. The Devil puts people into churches who sleep with people to put devils in them ... We have counselled people who are homosexuals and lesbians ... in our boarding schools, and some are getting into Satanism. ... Some go to n'gangas when they are back in the reserves, others go to false white garment prophets. Paul in Athens burnt books. These evil fetishes can act as a bridge for evil things coming in and out. ... Movies and TV are good things but can be turned into idols. The Devil makes good things bad. ... Some of you have the spirit of gossip, others the 'spirit of rejection'.[13]

Using emotive and powerful imagery, the preacher addressed the then widespread public debate about homosexuality and popular concern about family breakdown in the language of demonology. 'Spirit' was used in two senses: as a very real supernatural entity, which can possess a Christian, and as an idiom for excessive forces that control or create addictions in the believer's life. Although there are a number of weapons against these forces in the Pentecostal armoury, some of which will be discussed below, a good deal of emphasis is placed on self-control. The individual must do his or her utmost to remain pure because he or she is part of a collective in which personal failings can have corporate repercussions. A visiting speaker to City 1 Assembly told the gathering:

> You repent, you leave beer, you leave women, you become a Christian, but you remain with one thing – hating your brother. 1 John 3: 10 tells us it is a disgraceful thing to hate your brother. We must not be like Cain, hating our brother through jealousy. As a prayer band, we don't want to go before God with someone who is unclean. We would talk, testify, after we would sing but we would not even sing properly. I will not allow anyone to gossip about a brother in the church. ... Don't be like white guys in the northern suburbs. They would just meet at golf. They live in houses with a big wall and a small dog. 'Mrs so and so' next door is in hospital but they would not know.[14]

While Pentecostals build walls against the outside world, they tear them down between themselves to allow the free flow of the Holy Spirit and the construction of a holy community.

The Praying Community: Pentecostal Practice

Pentecostals are offered a pattern in Scripture to help redirect their energies and aspirations. Much has been written on the way in which narratives not only represent but also constitute social actors. The Bible in particular provides a rich repertoire of inspiring, empowering stories and images through which believers can redefine themselves. As we have seen, preachers spend a good many hours retelling biblical stories in the contemporary context. But Pentecostals are also expected to study it during their personal devotions and in cell groups. It is a food which must be eaten (Revelation 10: 10) and a weapon to fight the Devil (Ephesians 6).Certain Scriptures, such as those referring to Christ's blood, his name and his resurrection, have a sacred power in themselves. When spoken they can banish evil spirits, and ensure the success of a meeting or sermon. Thus Pentecostals immerse themselves in Scripture. They look forward to reading the Bible, and memorise verses and passages to arm themselves against the Devil and his agents. By so doing their social life becomes 're-storied' in a manner that engenders positive change and meaning.

But more important still is the power of prayer. Pentecostals are 'people who pray at all times'. They pray when they get up and when they go to bed, when they travel, at work in fellowship groups, when they sit down to eat a meal, when they enter each other's homes, when they open a business, but most of all when they are sick, possessed, or face great hardship. In prayer, their struggle for betterment is acted out both through and on the body. There are also particular moments when they come together to pray: prayer meetings, prayer conventions, bible studies and ordinary church services. For those unfamiliar with the Pentecostal practice of prayer, first encounters can be quite shocking. A few do sit or kneel to pray quietly like those in the historic mission churches. More generally the whole body is thrown into the practice, often with great vigour. Many Pentecostals perambulate while praying, some encircle the room, others walk back and forth along an aisle, within an alcove or beside a wall. Some lie prostrate on the floor or under tables and chairs. Others pray facing a wall. Some jump up and down, others appear to be running on the spot in slow motion. A number seem to borrow movements from the martial arts or professional sports, weaving them into their prayers. Fists are clenched, pounded into palms or used to punch the air. Arms are waved or rotated from side to side. Eyes are screwed tightly shut or remain wide open. All of the time there is a great cacophony of sounds as Pentecostals pray aloud together in a mixture of English, ChiShona, and tongues. Their prayers are interspersed with wails, howls, bursts of laughter and the repetition of sacred phrases.

At times it appears as if these meetings are no more than collections of individuals expressing private emotions in public. But these moments of individual expression are co-ordinated to convey a shared sense of prayer. The corporate dimension was most apparent at the annual Prayer Convention, held each November. At one site – Braeside, a suburb near to the airport – groups of women holding hands formed themselves into circles. Moving inwards and outwards like a folk dance, they repeated

the words '*ngarkudswe Jesus* [let Jesus be praised]' in a near-hypnotic state. The following evening a large crowd gathered in a big tent beside the building. They linked arms
and called down the Holy Spirit. Seconds later they were seized by uncontrollable
fits of laughter. Bursting out of the sides of the tents they crawled on their hands and
knees like spiritual drunkards, overcome with elation.

To the outsider such meetings can appear no more than spiritual anarchy, a collective breakdown of emotions. But it is usually a controlled breakdown. During moments
of intensity, pastors and lay leaders were always vigilant. Some church members were
led away to be exorcised because they had exhibited a strange demonic behaviour, 'not
in harmony' with the meeting. The life of prayer is ordered, and good Pentecostals
are familiar with its conventions. This was most apparent in church services which
initially appeared spontaneous but worked to a set pattern. Prior to the formal proceedings there was always a pre-meeting period of prayer, lasting for twenty to thirty
minutes. During this time, believers prayed for the binding of the Devil and that they
may themselves be clean, so that the Holy Spirit would flow and God's works would
be accomplished. Within the service the level of intensity shifted constantly but was
always heightened for the final crescendo. Halfway through the time of praise and
worship, prayers and tongues were offered to God interspersed with choruses. There
were also victory shouts. Stealing and Christianising a refrain from ZANU/PF rallies, the leader would shout '*Pamberi ne* [forward with] ...? ' to which the audience
would reply 'JESUS', waving their arms in solidarity. He then shouted '*Pasi ne* [down
with] ...?' – to which the audience responded '*Satani* [Satan]' gesturing downwards
with their thumbs and then motioning to stamp on him with their feet. A dignified
gesture from an elder or the commencement of a hymn acted to calm the pace of the
service. The appearance of the preacher at the lectern signalled it was time for the
sermon. The psychic pitch again rose as the preacher inspired, cajoled, and exhorted
his audience toward personal and collective transformation. At a well-chosen moment
the lectern was moved to the side and the people rushed forward for prayer. At times
almost everyone would present themselves for the laying on of hands. Some came
in search of a blessing, others sought forgiveness or healing, and still others wanted
deliverance from the evil sprits that bound them. In practice, deliverance and healing
were not isolated events in the believer's life, but a process. Regular church members
would present themselves for prayer week in and week out.

Some Pentecostals, particularly pastors well versed in Scripture, were able to enun-
ciate a theology that underpinned ecstatic behaviour. Thus the exuberant use of the
body was variously ascribed to:

> Love the Lord your God with all your heart, and all your strength [Mark 12: 30]
> Praise the Lord, O my soul; all my innermost being [Psalm 103: 1]
> All manner of prayer [Ephesians 6: 18]

The loud intensity of prayer was explained by:

> Shout for joy to the Lord [Ps 98: 4]
> He offered up prayers and petitions with loud cries and tears [Hebrews 5: 7]
> They lifted their voices together [Acts 4: 24]

Biblical precedent could be found for even the more exotic practices. Thus the Scripture 'the joy of the Lord is my strength' (Nehemiah 8: 10) justified the manifestation

of laughing spirits. And the furious rocking of the body in prayer was explained in terms of the Scripture 'from days of John the Baptist until now the kingdom of heaven has been forcefully advancing' (Matthew 11: 12).

Most Pentecostals, however, offered common sense or psychological explanations for their behaviour. Prayer was a means of release. Problems were literally laughed or cried away. Being 'bathed in the Spirit' healed emotional wounds. Arms were lifted in reverence, supplication and surrender to a transcendental God. Prayer was warfare with the Devil. The body was contorted to will God into action. Likewise the body of the demon-possessed person shook as the evil spirit struggled to retain its host and the exorcists attempted to wrestle it free. Hence Pentecostals were most animated during moments of deliverance: deacons and elders rushed about in loud prayer, seeking a quickening of the Spirit. As those most gifted in exorcism and healing worked on the queues of supplicants, others stood behind them praying in tongues, powering the deliverance like an engine. Amplifying the glossolalia with a microphone enhanced the electrifying effect. Prior to every service at Highfields Revival Centre, a group of young zealots enter a shack beside the church for half an hour of vigorous prayer. The shack was aptly named the 'power house'. Thus, as in other contexts in southern Africa, preachers and leaders work together with the assembly to build waves of 'communal enthusiasm' as a social manifestation of the power of the Holy Spirit. 'The greater the euphoria, the greater the power.' The 'tide of spiritual fervour' is eventually released, directed to the alleviation of individual suffering by means of divine healing and deliverance (Kiernan, 1994: 76).

In a general sense prayer generated a sense of individual and collective effervescence which produced a feeling of great potency among otherwise powerless people. Tongues and other miraculous manifestations brought about a 'recovery of spirit and voice by those previously voiceless and dispirited' (Martin, 1990: 172). The radical changes in behaviour and modes of communication that accompanied praying provided yet another example of rupture, another means of distinguishing and maintaining discontinuity. Tongue-speaking and 'in-filling' by the Holy Spirit were intended to 'seal off' adherents from the vast range of demonic forces that surrounded them in their daily lives (Van Dijk, 1998). Finally, prayer impelled believers back into the world with a renewed sense of confidence inspired by the belief that their petitions to God could bend nature to their interests (Wacker, 2001: 25).[15]

Beyond the ecstatic there were other practices within the culture of the assembly which acted on the believer's life. Visitors to ZAOGA churches were met at the door and accompanied to their place by a smartly dressed usher. Often their bags were carried for them. During the service they were asked to stand up, and were applauded and greeted in the name of Jesus Christ. All were made to feel welcome. The master of ceremonies greeted pastors, preachers, elders and deacons by name, and then greeted each social category, boys, girls, mothers and fathers. Subsequent speakers often repeated these greetings. Everyone was made to feel special. Boys were told they were handsome and girls were told they were beautiful. All were informed that they were 'loved'. Each member of the audience could be asked to greet their neighbour and God with a 'smile offering'. But the process of individuation went far deeper. Within the assembly and beyond, there was a multiplication of roles and offices. Each believer was given something useful to do, and during the service anyone could exercise his or her gifts in singing, prayer, deliverance, preaching. Assemblies were caring and therapeutic communities. Pentecostals believe they can connect with anyone. People were taken for what and who they were, and testified about past lives with an unnerving frankness. Those who laid themselves bare were then ministered to by the laying on of hands. At times believers were called to embrace their neighbours in a Born-again bear hug. With eyes tightly shut, each petitioned loudly for the other's needs. Pentecostalism is a quintessential religion of the body.

The World Beyond Church: Redeeming the Body, Space and Time

The body is not merely the site of struggles with the demonic; it is transformed in the process. As well as being redeemed, healed and delivered of evil spirits, believers are also re-clothed like Joseph and the Prodigal Son: external transformation mirrors internal change. ZAOGA is well known for its hordes of smartly dressed young pastors. It was an unwritten rule that they use their first 'love offerings' to buy a new suit. Often there were collections for the up-keep of the pastor, given that his formal salary was so low. But the smart attire of ordinary assembly members was also striking. Everyone made an effort, from the most humble domestic servant to the most successful businessman. The latter may have augmented his fine suit with a large expensive watch that dangled obtrusively from his wrist. His wife might have had the latest expensive hairdo, but even the poorest church member would be turned out in a clean, well-ironed shirt or blouse. Those sitting at the front – pastors, deacons and elders – made the greatest effort to look smart to set an example to others. Thus, most young men procured a suit by some means, often from the large informal market in second-hand clothing located in downtown Harare. For the most marginal church members, their bodies were one domain over which they had some agency.

Outside of the church the believer was caught up in a believing community. He or she joined a cell group in their locality, participated in the movement's associational life, and was assigned a pastor or elder who cared for them. The world beyond the assembly was also sacralised. Wherever its location, the Pentecostal home became a sanctuary. Filled with Born-again kitsch, the believer was reminded of Christ and scriptural injunctions wherever he or she turned. There were numerous pictures of Christ often looking like a Swedish hippie with blue eyes and fair hair. There were Bible verses, cut out of polystyrene, embroidered onto mini-banners or engraved into cheap copper plate, hung on every wall. There were photographs of key religious events and framed Bible school diplomas and Talents certificates. Books were few and far between; they were usually devotional texts, commentaries, and manuals of spiritual warfare or godly prosperity. The air was filled with Christian music from the radio and audiotapes. Alternatively, ZAOGA members might have listened to the latest big sermon from Ezekiel Guti or the recent teachings from international Born-again superstars, Benny Hinn or John Avanzini. More prosperous Pentecostals could watch these on television and video. Even the motorcar was reclaimed for Christ with bumper-sticker Scriptures and pumping gospel music or taped sermons. The home was also a place of prayer, public and private. Much to the annoyance of neighbours, the smallest township cottage could be filled to the brim with young people, praying and praising God. Often standing, sometimes facing the wall with arms outstretched, they cried out unreservedly. Finally, the home also became a site for business. The refrigerator in the high-density suburb would be packed with Cokes for sale to thirsty neighbours, and a small stall might be placed in front of the home to sell firewood and vegetables to passers-by. And the lounge in the large suburban home may have had a knitting machine or two for the small-scale production of jumpers and cardigans.

The normal week was littered with religious meetings. On Monday there was the evening prayer meeting. On Tuesday cell group leaders were instructed on what to teach in the coming week. Wednesday evening was the first Bible study night. Thursday was the day of women's meetings. On Friday evenings there was the second weekly Bible study and an all-night prayer meeting. On Saturday there was an afternoon choir practice, followed by an evening youth service. There was also the opportunity for evangelism in the morning, when zealous young men and women empowered by a night of prayer became warriors against Satan. Sunday was filled with two or three church services, which seemed to merge into a day-long event. All these meetings were supplemented by the various associations and ministries within ZAOGA that catered for youth, graduates, women, married couples and businessmen. To add variety, there was a Pentecostal liturgical year with regular annual events such as the Anniversary, the Prayer Convention, the Deeper Life Conference, Youth Conventions, and the Pastors' Conference. Thus the believer's social life was re-modelled on the life of the church. There was little time to indulge in polluting, worldly activities.

Redeeming Families

As well as transforming individuals, Pentecostalism restructures families. Because meaningful political change is often hard to bring about in contemporary Africa, improving the chances of social reproduction becomes a priority. Emphasis on character, especially that of the young male, is crucial. The Pentecostal gospel of fidelity, hard work, teetotalism and a peaceful temper re-socialises the young man, drawing him away from a world of violence and promiscuity into a family-orientated life. Money once spent on beer and gambling is reinvested in the home, particularly in education. Failure is not tolerated. Wife-beaters, drunkards, smokers, fornicators and adulterers are subject to church discipline. At times they are hauled up before the assembly in public disgrace. Aberrant elders and deacons are demoted; failed pastors are suspended or sacked.

A key practice contributing to new Pentecostal economic culture is the rejection of what they define as tradition: a reified set of beliefs and practices strongly associated with non-Christian rural culture, focusing on ancestor veneration, possession, ecological cults and witchcraft. In a similar vein to the rejection of old rural sports and pastimes by English Methodists during the Industrial Revolution, Pentecostals are not supposed to participate in family and communal rituals, or provide resources for them (Thompson, 1968: 444-9). Possession rituals, rain-making and first-fruits ceremonies, funeral rites, sessions of divination and beer parties are seen as the profligate invocation of demonic spirits. Acts of traditional commensality are avoided. The church becomes the believer's extended family and ties with kin diminish as energies are refocused on the nuclear family. This new emphasis on the nuclear family is particularly important for second-generation urban Pentecostals, raised in the city. The negation of tradition by Pentecostals is significant in a number of ways. First, women and young men have attacked shrines and holy places and demonised possession rituals that legitimate male gerontocratic elites. Secondly, making a complete break with the past contributes to the creation of free subjects able to embrace modernity. But for our purposes it frees the believer from the exaction of kin and community, facilitating personal accumulation. New converts also become smart in appearance, trustworthy, hard-working and literate, hence employable. Numerous Pentecostals recounted testimonies in which they began their careers as 'garden-boys' or 'house-girls', and eventually became white-collar workers and consumers. Being Born-again can create a 'redemptive uplift'.

New Pentecostals also benefit from the material support of the church community. The believer is immediately supported by a system of informal fraternal networks: small-scale welfare systems found within and between local assemblies and fellowship groups. ZAOGA assemblies act as informal burial societies, financing the travel of the bereaved, the transportation of the body and the cost of the wake. Strong emphasis on the nuclear family and Christian marriage leads to wedding collections. Pentecostals also care for the sick, orphans and widows, and often provide housing in an urban environment where it is scarce and expensive. Furthermore, Born-agains like to employ their own. Richer Pentecostals will often engage poorer church members in their homes, garages, shops, sewing and knitting businesses. Those offering employment, or searching for it, will make their needs known to the assembly. While these processes of economic and social transformation are present in other Zimbabwean Pentecostal churches such as the Apostolic Faith Mission or the Assemblies of God, in ZAOGA they form two pivotal interrelated teachings which are central to the movement's identity.

Talents and the Spirit of Poverty in the 1990s

ZAOGA's doctrine of Talents fosters 'penny capitalism'(Martin, 1990: 206): the vending of cheap foodstuffs and clothes, initially within the religious community but later externally, to finance the expansion of that community. In Chapter 3 we learnt that Talents was pioneered by Nicholas Bhengu, leader of the Assemblies of God South Africa during his 'Back To God' Campaign in Highfield in 1959. It was then perfected by one of ZAOGA's co-founders, Pricilla Ngoma, who taught that women should 'prosper the church', and indirectly themselves, by 'using their hands'. Many women still cook peanuts, chips, fat-cooks (a dough-like substance – *kooksisters* in Afrikaans) and cakes, sell sweets, and sew cushion covers in keeping with the initial conception of the teaching. But others, aided by chip-fryers, popcorn-makers, sewing and knitting machines and paid labour, have launched themselves as successful 'indigenous business women'. Still others make use of the relaxation of customs and currency restrictions to buy and resell at a profit. ZAOGA members are well-known at borders, which they cross regularly to buy bales of clothes, blankets and electrical goods. In some respects ZAOGA members are behaving no differently from many other Zimbabwean women who have turned to self-reliance in the face of the desertion or absence of the male wage-earner, or in response to the rising cost of living. Indeed, Ezekiel Guti's initial enthusiastic promotion of Talents doubtless derived from his mother, Dorcas, whose industriousness and creativity held her family together.

202

A six-month period of Talents will happen about every three years. Guti will first decree which new resources the church needs in the coming years, such as vehicles, computers or new buildings. Talents workers then pledge how much they will earn and begin to work towards it. There are services of encouragement and church members recognised for their financial acumen are called upon to offer advice during assembly meetings. An economic culture is talked into existence as the successful 'testify' about budgeting and market niches. Starter-grants are offered and earnings are recorded on computer. Although some men and children also volunteer for Talents, it is a predominantly female activity. Feminine images are drawn upon to motivate and inspire. Women sing: 'We are working to sweep away poverty' – *tiri kushanda tichakanda zvese* – and often liken the added financial strain of Talents to the experience of carrying and giving birth to a child. Even the process of giving is feminised. Money is collected in *zambias* (chiShona: *mbereko*) – the decorated piece of cloth often wrapped around a woman's waist or used to carry a child on her back. Alternatively, the money is placed in large enamel bowls. Such bowls are normally held by women whilst elders wash their hands, or are used for washing up. But these feminine associations do more than enhance the appeal of Talents; they moralise money. Through Pentecostal agency, money is invested with moral qualities of trust and intimacy by contact with swaddling cloth. Furthermore, association with the washing-up bowls cleanses the notes and the coins. It is clear that money cannot be simply 'credited with an intrinsic power to revolutionise society and culture'. To a large extent its value is derived from 'the cultural matrix into which it is incorporated'. Thus, rather than viewing money as some 'dark satanic force tearing away at the very fabric of society', Zimbabwean Pentecostals seek to transform it for the sake of the Kingdom (Parry and Bloch, 1989: 6).

At the end of Talents, the money is collected with much celebration at provincial-level services. Workers testify how God helped them to make money and each person's earnings are publicised. In what resembles a graduation ceremony, those who have done well are rewarded with certificates. ZAOGA members joke about 'graduating from the school of Talents'. Although the earnings varied from province to province, the amounts of money produced were quite astounding. In 1995 women in Harare West Province, which included the city centre and prosperous northern suburbs, produced a modal average of about Z$5,000 (£365 – the equivalent of a white-collar monthly salary). A few made more than Z$150,000 (£10,950). ZAOGA took enough money to buy 18 brand-new trucks for the provincial overseers and two lorries.

Once the period of Talents is over women are encouraged to continue their production and make money for themselves. Justifying the doctrine to a middle-class and student audience (see below), Ezekiel Guti's wife Eunor told the gathering how it had enhanced her own business interests: 'So have I been brainwashing you? My order from the boutique won't go when Talents finishes.'[16]

The second doctrine, the Spirit of Poverty, became prominent in the mid-1980s but its roots go far deeper. The notion that believers remained poor because of their spiritual condition was first expressed in the movement's sermons preached in the late 1960s and throughout the 1970s. The formal doctrine then evolved by appropriating and indigenising various American prosperity gospel teachings. In particular, ZAOGA's leadership drew from the teaching of the black Bahamas-based preacher, Myles Munroe. Munroe, a graduate of Oral Roberts University, propagated a message that drew heavily from his interaction with the American Civil Rights movement. His own particular brand of the prosperity gospel stressed that God had given dominion of the world to humankind who were responsible for realising their own 'dreams'.[17] He placed a strong emphasis on black pride and self-actualisation. ZAOGA members immediately seized upon his teachings when he first encountered the movement at its 1985 International Deeper Life Conference.[18]

In 1995 the Spirit of Poverty was forcefully expounded during Talents; it was also preached widely by the movement's evangelists on crusades throughout the year and reproduced by pastors, elders and deacons at ordinary church meetings. Fundamentally, the doctrine entails a wide-ranging assault on 'tradition'. While most Pentecostal churches demonise ancestor veneration and spirit possession, ZAOGA's attack is far more systematic and wide-ranging. The teaching can be summarised as follows. Africans stay poor because of a Spirit of Poverty. Even though they are born again, only their soul has in fact been redeemed. The pernicious influence of ancestral spirits remains in the blood. These ancestors were social and economic failures during their own lifetimes. They led lives of violence, indolence, drunkenness, polygamy, ancestor veneration and witchcraft: lives of waste and poverty, rather than accumulation. Their legacy transmitted through their bloodline accounted for the precarious existence of Zimbabweans in the age of neo-liberal economics. Spirits of poverty accounted for the experience of never being able to accumulate: the new shirt burnt by the iron; the car that always breaks down; the money vanishing from a person's pockets with little sense of where it goes. In sum, misfortune is passed from generation to generation via demonic ancestral spirits.

In a sense, the proponents of ZAOGA's Spirit of Poverty doctrine are preaching what older Pentecostal missionaries taught about African culture and religion. In part, the movement's teaching is an inheritance from its Apostolic Faith Mission forebears. However, ZAOGA's evangelists and preachers demonise tradition with more effect because their characterisations stem from first-hand experience. In neo-liberal Zimbabwe in the 1990s the teachings have a different meaning. The working of Talents resonates with ideas of self-reliance, indigenous business and black empowerment propounded by the ruling party and state-controlled media. At the same time, the Spirit of Poverty successfully explains and exploits popular insecurities. In rural areas, it explains to the male householder why his daughters remain unmarried, or are sent home by dissatisfied husbands demanding the return of bride-price. It explains why a family is prone to domestic violence or a plague of avenging spirits – ngozi. The household is simply perpetuating a downward trajectory begun by their progenitors. The aspiring middle classes are thwarted in a different manner by bad ancestral blood. They may be well-off but their children will be dull and need expensive extra schooling; they may fall ill and incur big health bills. Spirit of Poverty doctrine also merges with another ZAOGA teaching, Third World Mentality, to explain Zimbabwe's plight in global terms. In his famous 'Lift Up the Standard' sermon, delivered at the National Sports Stadium in 1988, Guti told those gathered:

> Any nation or country, which worships idols or animals will have problems. Go to any nation where they worship idols or cows, these countries have problems and are poor. I say let's start with God. A nation that puts its trust in witchcraft, must know that witchcraft leads to laziness, hatred and killing one another ... This is the problem with the third world (Guti, 1989: 24).

In a similar manner to the young puritan preachers whom van Dijk studied in Blantyre, those who teach Spirit of Poverty in Zimbabwe use strongly anti-rural sentiments (1992: 168-9). It is almost as if 'rural' equates with 'evil'. The communal lands

204

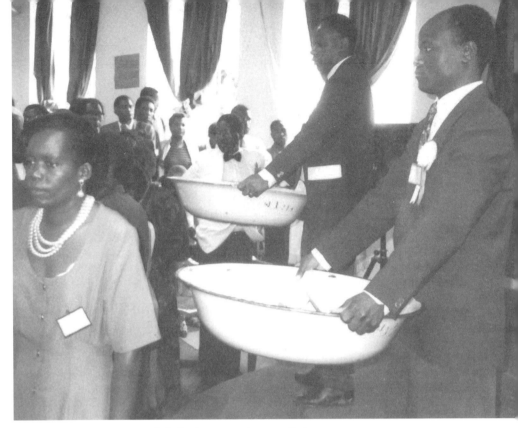

8.5 Lining up to give an offering

8.6 Woman seeking deliverance from the Spirit of Poverty

are the places where demonic ancestral spirits originate, polluted substances are man-
ufactured, witchcraft is rife and non-believing kin pressure or entice Born-agains back
into traditional practices. Like the pioneers of the Industrial Revolution, Pentecostal
preachers and evangelists in ZAOGA constantly seek to fashion an image of rural
idiocy (Thompson, 1968: 445). In ZAOGA there is a strong association between being
Pentecostal, urban and modern. The movement's expansion into rural areas throughout the 1980s and 1990s was viewed as mission work from an urban base.

The doctrine's proponents, evangelists and pastors are skilled in the principles of
stereotyping and masters of acute social observation:

> Your uncle Samanyika, oh, I hate to be called Samanyika. He will call you to go with him to the
> bar. What's the name of the bar here? He will walk like this, this [comic walk swinging his hips
> which prompts cheering and laughing] stopping every woman he meets on the way. That's the
> same demon in you. He is married to eight wives, but still not satisfied ...

> Right now you have a house in the suburbs, but we see you here [Sakubva] often, why? Coz your
> girl friend lives here. In her little room, there is no rocking chair, only bricks. She doesn't have
> a cooker, but only a primer stove. But you spend the whole night there, sitting on the bricks and
> smoke coming into your eyes from the primer stove. You are not doing anything about it. But in
> your own house, you know you have a rocking chair where you can sit.[19]

> You are a Father, you work to earn money. It goes nowhere. You are hopeless... Spirits spoil
> marriages, they make your wife look like a donkey so that you don't feel for her ... Spirits of
> ancestors cause ignorance. When you are asked what is one plus one you say six.[20]

The proponents assert with equal force that other solutions to poverty and misfortune
offered by traditionalists, other denominations and development workers no longer
work: 'your body is covered with a *n'anga's* cuts. You are losing blood every day but
nothing is happening.' The traditional healer's séance and the possession dance are
part of the evangelists' comic repertoire. But just as ineffective is the independent
church prophet with his holy water.[21] Even the more recent solutions proffered by the
agencies prove useless:

> People are trying to give help to third world persons. They find third world persons do not
> prosper. Money is being poured in a bucket. It's being poured in a bucket that has holes. Nothing
> is being achieved. Billions and billions of dollars have been poured out. Hallelujah! But nothing
> is happening in Africa. Africa is remaining under the Spirit of Poverty.[22]

Nevertheless there is deliverance. Christians are taught that they receive freedom
through giving. Blessings come through giving. ZAOGA Pentecostals not only work
Talents; in keeping with mainstream Pentecostalism, they pay tithes. During meetings
they are encouraged to give spontaneous love- and freewill-offerings. Love-offerings
are a reward, or perhaps more accurately a tax, levied from an assembly during the
visit of an overseer or itinerating pastor. They are a supplement to his salary. Freewill-offerings can be for the orphanages, weddings, funerals, hall-hire, evangelistic
campaigns, choir-gowns, musical equipment and public address systems the stuff of
church life. Finally there are special gifts – tribute – for Archbishop Guti, for birthday
and for Christmas.

But deliverance is also a process; a drama acted on the body. At the climax of
crusades or Talents meetings, Christians are given the chance to come forward for

deliverance from their ancestral spirits. At the height of the 1995-96 Talents campaign, Eunor Guti spoke to a gathering of students and middle-class ZAOGA members in a lecture theatre of the University of Zimbabwe.[23] At the end of her sermon Mrs Guti invited her audience to receive deliverance. There was a mad rush forward and attendants had to hurriedly pack away the table/altar, chairs and lectern to make space for 90 per cent of the congregation. For 15 minutes her team delivered a kneeling crowd, four or five rows deep, whilst she continued to recite various phrases into the microphone: 'deliverance, deliverance, deliverance, deliverance in the name of Jesus... blood of Jesus, blood of Jesus, blood of Jesus...'. These incantations, which were interspersed with tongues, had a mesmerising effect. The exorcists worked at a great pace. Some simply touched the forehead of the client, others grasped the temple firmly, rotating the head while gripping the back of the neck. Certain phrases were invoked to hasten deliverance: 'Out vile spirit ... release, release, release ... in the name of Jesus, in the name of Jesus.' Some of those delivered returned quietly to their seats, others fought with the exorcist, their ancestral spirits unwilling to leave their bodies. Others still were 'slain in the spirit'. So overwhelmed were they by the power of the experience that they crawled under chairs or lay on the floor. Some women wept. Parents also presented their children for deliverance, to completely remove the ancestral scourge from their family.

ZAOGA as a Religious Movement

Doubtless many ZAOGA members rushed for deliverance to 'get ahead', drawn by the images of material success, sophistication and modernity actively promoted by the leadership. But it is clear from the hundreds of letters Guti received from ordinary church members that the majority did not so much seek prosperity as security: 'to stay well at home' – *kugara zvakanaka kumusha*.[24] They looked to the church, and to Guti in particular, for protection from ancestral curse and for fertility, healing, employment, good marriages and success in public examinations. These concerns did shift in line with broader socio-economic change. Correspondence concerned with sickness and poverty increased from about 20 per cent to 30 per cent over the period 1992-6. That concerning ancestral curse also grew as 'spirit of poverty' teaching took hold. Doubtless more letters concerning these matters would have been sent if they had not been addressed within the local Pentecostal community. In Chapter 6 we saw that some wrote to Guti as a last resort.

To some extent material and existential desires were satisfied, especially modest ones associated with stable family lives. But the letters to Guti tell us other important things about the movement. Filed separately as 'locals', the letters were personal and spontaneous, very different from normal administrative correspondence on matters of church governance. Another 20 per cent of the correspondence accompanied gifts, usually of money. Some of these were clearly about the politics of patronage, intended to oil the wheels of church government. Some correspondence involved an exchange of gifts. A local church wrote to thank Guti for the gift of Z$6,000 (approx. £470 in December 1994) for roofing (doubtless money from CFNI, Dallas), and sent their own gift in return. Another from Chiredzi accompanied a Christmas present of Z$5,000 (£393) for the Archbishop in return for his gift to the Province of Z$10,000 (£786).

Others appeared to send gifts to obtain promotion, such as the pastor who had collected money within his province for 'Dr Guti's groceries'. Gifts were also sent as 'thank-offerings' in response to blessings. A young man from Harare sent money on passing his exams. A woman from Chitungwiza sent a portion of her first salary in thanks for the Archbishop's guidance. A couple sent money because their daughter had got married in 'a good way' (i.e. a white wedding in church). Finally, gifts came in hope of future blessing. The School of Dress Making in Harare sent Z$5,600 (£440) with the words 'this is a gift as a family. We believe that God shall bless us and the work of the dressmaking in all the provinces.' A couple from Msvingo wrote: 'The Lord spoke to us to give you this amount [Z$20.00].Remember us.'

In some respects the offering of gifts and sacrifices to a holy man to ensure personal security was congruent with traditional belief and practice across much of Africa. But the spontaneity of some of the giving pointed to something beyond. The letters communicated a sense of excitement at being part of a movement, of living out a vision of Biblical Christianity. Indeed the biggest portion of the letters – 40 per cent – was concerned with the progress of the Church. In the missives, the spiritual and physical were intertwined to tell a story of moral and material advance. Some letters were business-like, requesting evangelists, pastors and tracts to enhance local church growth. Others reported progress in tithing, in giving to mission, in the construction of churches, pastors' houses with chicken runs in the back yard, in the purchase of vehicles and musical instruments. Another category brought 'Good News' about successful meetings and conventions, the growth of churches, fellowships and ministries. Many recounted 'visions' or 'miracles' of repentance, healing, and deliverance. A couple from Luveve reported miracles in their church after the Deeper Life meeting. The Archbishop's lessons on church planting and follow-up teams had 'worked well' but they asked for his prayers. Another correspondent wrote to share the story of the miraculous healing of his daughter from a ruptured vein in her head. She had been healed just before surgery. One letter brought news of the police force 'coming to the Lord'. Another described advances made in Mkoba Township: cars had been purchased, membership had grown, and the Girls Fellowship was successful. The correspondent finished by sharing news of the Gospel in Cuba where the Church was growing.

Like the prayers overheard in communal worship, the letters offer a rare glimpse into the interior life of ordinary believers. Some wrote in search of power or 'anointing' to preach or lead. Others recounted inner struggle with weakness or failure requesting prayer for strength, such as the woman from Gokwe who wanted to become a pastor and preach but was too lazy to read Scripture, or the young man who longed to pray but found he had no words. One man wrote to Guti: 'Daddy I am your child who is always crying about the mind ... I am requesting that I may not have lust and I want to continue to love God. I want to remove the spirit of stinginess and jealousy.' Some correspondents agonised about their salvation. A widow expressed regret that she had grown cold towards God: 'my spiritual life leaves a lot to be desired. I no longer attend church regularly and have just grown cold towards things of God. Please Father, I know you are a true prophet of God. May your God help me. I want to see Jesus' face when I die but I think that if he is able to come today I will be able to face him.' Someone else requested prayer simply because his 'his soul was grieved'.

Some correspondents wrote to share an aspiration. Material progress blended into a larger story of redemption and transformation; many dreamed of employment, or promotion at work, studying abroad, or of opening a business. Others had a more straightforward vision for God's work. A young man wrote: 'My request to you is not in material things ... but is to be a pastor with the character of God.' A number of letters pointed to a similar pious devotion, a deep longing to act on belief. A new pastor wrote of his 'desire to bring souls unto the Lord'. Another correspondent felt a 'burden for the work of God in Matabeleland'. One writer simply requested Guti's blessing to preach in Mozambique to bring chiefs to repentance and stem the killing of people through 'evil spirits'. Within Pentecostal movements such as ZAOGA, pragmatic and primitive impulses merged seamlessly in a pervasive sense of God's providence: the desire to marshal one's gifts and resources in a way that will maximise their chances of getting ahead here on earth, blended with an equally profound desire to 'know the divine mind and will' (Wacker, 2001: 11-12).

Conclusion

Contemporary Pentecostalism is a highly successful popular religion: a set of ideas and practices that address adherents' existential concerns for wholeness, purity, meaning and empowerment. But like mission and independent Christianity that took popular form in townships and rural locations across the African continent in the first decades of the twentieth century, contemporary Pentecostalism responds to a specific socio-economic context (Hastings, 1994). Whereas those earlier forms of popular Christianity helped African peasants and labour migrants come to terms with the demands of capitalist imperialism, contemporary Pentecostalism enables African adherents to come to terms with neo-liberalism. It offers 'hope and lived solutions' to combat intensifying poverty, marginalisation and insecurity, problems that arise from structural conditions that are beyond the power of individuals to alter and which their political leaders are unable or unwilling to change. Pentecostalism does not challenge neo-liberalism head on but offers adherents the chance of changing their responses to the 'limiting conditions' its macro-structures create (B. Martin, 1998: 126-8). Most obviously the ascetic codes adopted by converts on joining a Pentecostal community contribute to an all-round betterment. The result of regular employment, restored family relations, active church membership, and of giving up alcohol, drugs and prostitutes, is a regular income and a better managed household economy. But more importantly there are areas of congruence between neo-liberalism and Pentecostalism. The neo-liberal economy requires 'micro-entrepreneurial initiative, an individualised more feminised psyche, a high level of self-motivation, and the flexibility with which to face insecure employment and self-employment, mobility, and the twenty-four-hour working day'. Moreover, in the neo-liberal era 'the need to operate as an individual at the level of the psyche as well as in terms of social and economic ways, becomes ever more imperative'. Pentecostalism is well placed to bring about this cultural transition because its fundamental conception of the human person is as 'a unique, individual soul, named and claimed by God. Its business is the business of self-hood' (B. Martin, 1998: 129). A positive attitude, overcoming fear, a sense of personal destiny, self-worth and self-reliance are key traits in the Pentecostal character that enable adherents to operate as individuals in a volatile labour market. And in such conditions the domesticated Pentecostal male has an advantage over his unreconstructed brethren.

Like neo–liberalism, Pentecostalism also favours competence over status, stressing the importance of 'gifting' and 'being fruitful'. The Pentecostal religious meritocracy has an obvious attraction to women and youth in Zimbabwean society where age and masculinity dominate. But Pentecostalism rejects neo–liberalism's cultural project in which the state, market and media increasingly relate to communities as collections of individual subjects, with little concern for the collective dimensions of social and political life. While a privileged few are able to transpose those aspects of clientelism that best serve their interests into new bureaucratic structures, most are left vulnerable by the erasure of old trusted networks of mutual dependency. In Pentecostalism the urban and rural poor find support as individuals within an intimate voluntary community of believers. At times, old idioms of ethnicity and kinship are deployed and combined with other habits of collective solidarity, but the individual retains autonomy in a body he or she has chosen to join. Within the community of believers, practices of mutual support, the promotion of education, training, and participation in the work of the church endow members with a sense of individual responsibility and the experience of leadership. 'Individualisation and the voluntaristic collective creation of new social capital thus occur in tandem'(B. Martin, 1989: 130). The strict ascetic codes reinforced by the authority of the pastorate and legitimised by their sacred character provide a firm foundation upon which autonomy and self–control can be constructed. Of crucial importance is Pentecostalism's capacity to redeem, restore and re–pattern the family as the primary defence against the destructive effects of neo–liberalism. For the chosen few believers who do find real economic prosperity, Pentecostal doctrine provides a moral map to help them navigate the lures and pitfalls of the contemporary world.

But dreams, desires and visions remain important: modernity is always an aspiration rather than a condition. Hope is vitally important for Africa's youth, who swell Pentecostalism's ranks but who remain enticed by the 'presence of commodities and electronically available images only recently available' which go to 'an ever-narrowing range of people' (Weiss, 2004: 8). Modernity's unrealised nature makes Pentecostals forward-thinking, and vigilant for nefarious forces – spiritual, social and material – that prevent them from ever quite reaching their goals. A female pastor at City 2 Assembly in David Livingstone Avenue told her audience: 'We are priests for our families, breaking the traditions of our forefathers, saving our families from calamities: daughters not marrying, sickness and poverty.'

Notes

[1] *Electronic Mail and Guardian*, 20 January 1998. The cost of the basic staple, mealie meal, rose by 81 per cent between November 1997 and January 1998.
[2] Dates of meetings: Charter, 30-31 October 1995; Sekubva, 31 October – 1 November 1995; Braeside, 15-16 March 1996; Chisipite, 30-31 January 1996.
[3] Int.DM64, Paul Saungweme.
[4] City 1 Assembly, Baines Avenue, Harare, 21 January 1996.
[5] City 1 Assembly, Baines Avenue, Harare, 9 May 1996.
[6] Highfields Revival Centre, Highfields, Harare, 29 October 1995.
[7] Highfields Revival Centre, Highfields, Harare, 28th January 1996.
[8] University of Zimbabwe, Mt Pleasant, Harare, 20 October 1995.
[9] Zengesa Assembly, Seke, Harare, 30 September 1995.
[10] University of Zimbabwe, Mt Pleasant, Harare, 5 November 1995.
[11] City 1 Assembly, Baines Avenue, Harare, 19 November 1995.

12 Highfields Revival Centre, Highfield, 2 December 1995.
13 City 1 Assembly, Baines Avenue, Harare, 16 September 1996.
14 City 1 Assembly, Baines Avenue, Harare, 19 November 1995.
15 Seven Lectures on Demonology, file, Sermons, ZAW.
16 Eunor Guti, Sermon, Mt Pleasant Big Sunday, 8 October 1995.
17 Int.DM108, Reverend Ronnie Meek; Sermon, Myles Munroe, International Leadership Conference, Harare Sheraton, 1993, file, Sermons, ZAW.
18 Other black proponents of the prosperity gospel were Bertril Baird and James Bell from Trinidad. IntDM108, Ronnie Meek; Int.DM105, Gayle Erwin.
19 Sermon, Evangelist Bill John Chigwenembe, Mutare for Jesus Campaign, Sakubva Stadium, 31 October 1995. Chigwenembe confessed to despising rural culture. Int.DM9, Bill John Chigwenembe.
20 Sermon, Paul Saungweme, ZAOGA Crusade, Charter 30 October 1995.
21 Evangelist Bill John Chigwenembe, Mutare for Jesus Campaign, Sakubva Stadium, 31 October 1995.
22 Sermon, Eunor Guti, Mount Pleasant Big Sunday, University of Zimbabwe, 8 October 1995.
23 Ibid..
24 File, Locals 1992-6, ZAW. Given that the letters were often about personal and private matters I did not record names and addresses, merely the gender of the correspondent and the region they came from. The remaining 10 per cent concerned a range of miscellaneous issues such as requests to study at AMFCC and preaching invitations to Ezekiel and Eunor Guti. The volume of the correspondence was quite considerable: approximately 250 letters in 1992; 200 in 1993; and 480 in 1994.

9

Conclusion

Introduction: Historicising Pentecostalism

This study of the origins and evolution of ZAOGA has been one of intersecting histories. It has situated the story of Zimbabwean Pentecostalism within the setting of colonial and post-colonial Zimbabwe, but also within larger regional patterns of labour migrancy and missionary endeavour. Beyond that, it has located Pentecostal developments within the ongoing encounter with the USA.

The opening chapters of the book began in the United States and South Africa. They showed how Pentecostalism, as a collection of vital and powerful idioms about illness and healing, evil and purity, made striking connections with peoples sharing common historical experiences of marginalisation from established religion and from the effects of twentieth-century industrial capitalism. Pentecostalism took root so quickly in southern Africa and in other classic mission fields because it moved along well-established networks of non-conformity and radical evangelicalism in printed tracts and by word of mouth. It had a remarkable capacity to localise itself, taking on distinct meanings in different local contexts. Its initial scorn for formal theological education, its reliance on lay initiative, and its acceptance of belief in the supernatural made it particularly responsive to local and national agendas. The maverick missionaries, street preachers, roving evangelists, self-styled prophets and pastors in tiny chapels who propelled the movement forward (and continue to do so) were usually of the people. They had little or no specialised training, spoke the same language as their flocks, shared their perspectives and were dependent on them for their maintenance. Hence, they were open to local agendas and often drawn into popular struggles. Given that the most important qualification for the office of Pentecostal pastor was baptism in the Holy Spirit – a qualification usually acquired with extraordinary speed by converts – it is not surprising that Pentecostalism has been so open to such local and personal creativity.

In its opening phases Pentecostalism is often quintessential popular religion: the faith of 'people who have little contact with institutional churches, little religious training and who get their religious information through informal channels' (B. Wilson, 1999: 100). It is highly syncretistic. Ideas and practices from traditional religion are borrowed, and then recoded within a Christian system of ideas where they

212

take on a new form and significance. Popular Pentecostalism often lacks intellectual cohesion, but it helps practitioners come to terms with existential passions empowering them through faith to deal with concerns for health, wealth and protection against evil. However, as missionaries, ambitious pastors and evangelists seek to mould disparate groups into denominations, so Pentecostalism manifests developmental tensions. These are contradictions inherent in Pentecostalism and which are continually being worked out. The first tension is that between the populist-voluntarist origins of movements and an increasingly authoritarian leadership. The second is the tension between sectarian sources and the drive for respectability, recognition and an embrace of the world. The third lies in the balance between its capacity to expand among the masses, by remaining of the masses, and its ability to improve their lot. The strong desire to evangelise and expand a movement's social base, and yet at the same time encourage social mobility, can create class tensions. Finally, there are tensions of gender and generation. Pentecostalism has a particular appeal to women and youth and other socially marginal categories. In founding moments it often manifests a strong egalitarianism whereby the gifts of the Holy Spirit and revelation through the Holy Spirit are universal, and differences of race, gender and class are diminished. Moreover, it has the potential to challenge and undermine patriarchal ancestor religion through idioms of deliverance and demonisation.

Because of its inherent openness to outside stimulus, Pentecostalism is also animated by transformational as well as developmental tensions. Zimbabwean Pentecostalism has shifted in response to local stimuli and the wider social and economic change that has come with transitions from the colonial to post-colonial, and from the age of state intervention to the age of neo-liberal economics. These internal and external motors of change collided and conflated to create very specific forms of Pentecostalism in southern Africa and beyond. They also partly explain the contradictory picture of Pentecostalism which has emerged in scholarly literature: local versus global; American versus African; populist and egalitarian versus authoritarian and hierarchical. Conclusions about Pentecostalism also vary because of differences in scholarly methodology. Research that focuses on church elites, their relations with church councils, missionary organisations and NGOs, and their activities at conferences and conventions will by its nature produce a very one-sided picture. Such research describes a context in which the external, the American and the electronic are most manifest (Gifford, 1998). In-depth fieldwork in a township or rural location produces a very different picture. Ordinary rank-and-file church members have very different agendas from elites. They are often too busy earning a living to attend weekday conventions, and would probably not be able afford the fees to enter high-profile events in plush hotels and conference centres. In order to apprehend the immensely varied nature of Pentecostal religious movements, research must be both historical and ethnographic, and multi-sited. Only this approach will capture shifts within Pentecostalism across time and space.

From the outset, Pentecostal Christianity took very different pathways once it landed on southern African soil and escaped missionary control. In Southern Rhodesia, the absence of white Anglo-Saxon, middle-class missionary supervision and a virtually autonomous black section led the state to view the Apostolic Faith Mission as subversive 'pseudo religion' akin to the prophetic movements of Masowe and Maranke. Members of all three churches engaged in witchcraft eradication, night dances on mountain-tops, wore white robes, experienced ecstatic trances and practised Hebrew-style purity taboos. Here the crisis of mission Christianity and popular fears of witchcraft profoundly shaped the AFM during the 1930s, the decade in which it experienced its most dramatic rural growth. In South Africa, the black AFM maintained close relations with a similar form of Christian independency: Zionism. It spawned numerous Zionist offshoots, but was not viewed as subversive by the state because of the appearance of white supervision. Meanwhile, white AFM Pentecostalism gradually insinuated itself into the dominant Afrikaner religio-political culture, its socially mobile members drawing on their Dutch Reform Church heritage to gain respectability.

Standing in the Southern Rhodesian trajectory, but coming later in the 1960s, ZAOGA-style Pentecostalism differed again. In its early stages of growth, the movement was also propelled by the evangelising zeal of young men and women driven by the urgency of Christ's imminent return. But these religious agents lived in a world of even more complex and far-reaching networks of labour migrancy. They had been drawn into the Rhodesian capital to serve its increasing need for labour in the postwar industrial boom. Many eventually returned home to villages and townships in other cities to found local assemblies, constructing simple mud or brick buildings as places of worship. These labour migrants were driven by the desire to maintain their Pentecostal society within a society. From the early 1970s onwards, but particularly after independence, the movement expanded and modernised by making connections with global Born-again Christianity, drawing resources from the American Bible Belt, appropriating western Pentecostal signs and practices. In the 1980s the dangers of schism and global homogenisation grew. Control was maintained through authoritarian government, and the circulation of a printed sacred history and locally produced audio-visual media intended to reinforce identity. Although exploiting, even flaunting, its connections with American Christianity, ZAOGA nevertheless resisted these external influences by centrally controlling American missionary activity, mobilising its own resources and making a vigorous critique of Western Christianity couched in the language of indigenous authenticity. From the mid-1980s the movement's direction and government has been an elite affair controlled by religious executives who are 'frequent flyers and faxers' (Hannerz, 1996: 29). However, most proselytism remains the province of labour migrants and humble pastors and their flocks. Real religious growth, as elsewhere, has come about through low-key, face-to-face encounters, and not by appeals to the mass media or large evangelistic crusades, as is often suggested.

Over four decades ZAOGA/FIFMI has evolved from a religious movement with strong links to Christian independency into what Richard Werbner describes as a 'territorial' organisation with a hierarchy of ordered centres resembling that of historic mission churches (Werbner, 1989: 315-17). Or as Adrian Hastings put it, 'a small *communauté de base* with some intense shared religious insights and fellowship' has become 'a "church" – an ongoing network of congregations held together by an "objective" order of name, ministry, [and] stabilised particular tradition' (Hastings, 1979: 268). As ZAOGA evolved, so the strong adventism that drove the movement in the early stages of growth shifted from a motive force to a point of doctrine, and the leadership has grown ever more concerned with maintenance and memorialisation. Nevertheless, the familiar sociological story of the transition of sect to church has not been as neat or as complete as the theory. As long as Guti lives, charisma remains a force to be reckoned with. The leader's idiosyncrasies and personal revelations often thwart attempts at bureaucratisation.

This account of southern African Pentecostalism's interaction with America revises scholarly understanding of Christian independency in two ways. First, for too long its study has been limited by the tendency of some scholars to ignore religious traditions other than those of the 'historic' European churches. This ignorance of other missionary impulses has meant that African Christian movements, which emerged out of the encounter with both black and white America, have been characterised as merely 'African'. Secondly, it is clear that ZAOGA has changed from being one kind of Pentecostal Church – urban underclass with strong roots in a rural prophetic Christianity – to other kinds: international, institutional and at times prosperity-based. Analysts have often sought to divide up these categories of Pentecostalism as though they represent distinct rather than related and successive strands. This study's broad historical and international perspective makes these former analyses of independency and Pentecostalism even more difficult to sustain. Likewise, the label 'neo-Pentecostal' makes little sense for large transnational movements such as ZAOGA. With churches spread across the region, each at a different stage in their development, the movement as a whole embodies a number of historical stages.

This study has also shown how the drive to evangelise has been central to the making of ZAOGA and the broader Pentecostal movement, and therefore helps revise earlier explanations of Pentecostalism's appeal. The majority of ZAOGA converts 'like the majority of converts in Latin America, Africa and elsewhere have been rural migrants to cities, people at the lower end of the social class scale, or rural stay-at-homes displaced from the centre of their own worlds by social change' (Robbins, 2004a: 123-4). Many of the first classics of Pentecostal history and ethnography deployed arguments of disorganisation and deprivation to make sense of these patterns of adherence. Those cut adrift in a rapidly changing environment found sojourn in new intense and intimate communities of faith, protected from the runaway world by firm moral boundaries. And those who felt deprived found solace in ecstatic release, millennial promise, and a new egalitarian earthly community where all were valued. While there is some truth in these explanations, disorganisation and deprivation do not explain the contemporary appeal of Pentecostalism to young, upwardly mobile, middle-class congregations in the West, or in African and Asian cities. And when these theories are used they are often applied in a tautological manner, 'making the fact of conversion the proof of prior experiences of deprivation and anomie'. Such models also exclude the vast range of explanations – moral, material and metaphysical – that Pentecostals themselves use to account for their conversion. More to the point, they ignore the defining place of evangelism within broader Pentecostal culture. Driven by the urgency of Christ's imminent return, Pentecostals go out in faith convinced that they are evangelists and missionaries, equipped through the gifts of the Spirit (Robbins, 2004a: 124; Wacker, 2001: 199-202).

Religious Transnationalism and Globalisation: American or African Religion?

At first glance, Pentecostalism's adversarial stance toward ancestor veneration, possession cults and other traditional practices can make it appear out of step with 'traditional African thinking' (Gifford, 1998: 177). But when viewed as the latest variant of three or more centuries of cyclical societal cleansing, characterised by the destruction of polluted objects and the demonising of a range of religious entities, it appears far less alien and threatening (De Creamer, Fox & Vansina,1976; Maxwell, 1999). Moreover, as Birgit Meyer has shown, 'the negative incorporation of spiritual entities in African religious traditions into the image of the Christian Devil' amounts to another form of local appropriation. 'In this way, the "old" and forbidden, from which Christians were required to distance themselves, remained available, albeit in a new form' (Meyer, 2004: 455; 1999). One does not have to look very far to find other forms of appropriation within Pentecostalism based on a more positive appreciation of African traditions. An obvious example is Gospel music. Singing in the vernacular backed by traditional instruments, Zimbabwean musicians reflect on a range of issues that concern ordinary citizens. Their songs address 'the reality of suffering, disease, moral decay, oppressive spiritual forces [and] death', but also exhibit a 'commitment to African progress' (Chatindo, 2002: 56, 67).

It should be apparent from this historical account of a Pentecostal religious movement that questions concerning authenticity are somewhat facile. The diverse sets of idioms and ideas that became Pentecostalism emerged from a number of locations throughout the world: from the mission fields and local churches of Africa and India as well as from America and Western Europe. It is fitting that a religion that has global ambitions is in essence a composite deriving from religious communities across the world. Yet Pentecostalism's propensity towards adaptation and appropriation meant that ideas and practices from one source rapidly took on new meanings in the hands of local agents in another context. Pentecostalism is at once global and local. There are commonalities in forms of organisation and leadership, in styles of oratory and proselytisation, but Pentecostalism is as diverse as the range of contexts its ideas and practices encounter. Within ZAOGA/FIFMI the faith and practice of the Mozambican leader, Mateus Simau, differ considerably from the slick electronic religion of his Zimbabwean overlords. While he survived the travails of Frelimo and Renamo sustained by the hope and endurance found in the Psalms, some Zimbabwean leaders sought material advance to the point of covetousness. The latter's aspirations were very different from their counterparts in rural areas and urban townships who were merely intent on survival. In Malawi, where politics were always less racialised than in Zimbabwe, a different set of local meanings has emerged. Malawian Pentecostals declare independence in a purely religious sense that claims membership of the global community of believers and expresses radical separation from the inequalities created by worldly black pastors and greedy white missionaries. Zimbabwean, Mozambican and Malawian brands of Pentecostalism are different from some of those found in Kenya, which remain close to North American missionary sources and appear 'utterly foreign' and 'terrifyingly transcendental'. They are distinct again from West African Pentecostalism, which defines itself against a very different pantheon of spirits (Englund, 2003; Lonsdale, 2002:189; Kalu, 1998: 244-5; Meyer, 1999). The existence of different Pentecostal communities; Zimbabwean, Nigerian, Jamaican, Brazilian and Anglo-Saxon, often in tension with each other in American and European cities, is the most powerful illustration of how culturally bound Pentecostalism can become.

Movements of religious Diaspora and religious elites are also a weighty reminder that Pentecostal cultural flows go in many directions, and not only from north to south. Nevertheless, the vast movement of Born-again resources and personnel from the

USA to Africa in the 1980s does raise important questions about a 'second missionisa-tion', and cultural and political autonomy (Gifford, 1991; Lonsdale, 2002). American resources do have a great appeal to African Born-agains. American Born-agains can be well intentioned and their generous offers of financial and technological aid represent easy pickings for impecunious Africans. But it is important to distinguish between the power of American Christians to attract foreign connections and any influence those connections might have (Freston, 2001: 289). Although ZAOGA's leaders rail against dependency and white missionary arrogance, Ezekiel Guti has consistently and clan-destinely used American money to finance his own patronage system and consolidate his position within the movement. Movements like ZAOGA obey a double impera-tive: they tighten boundaries to maintain control over their members while at the same time extending connections into the wider world of economics, politics and the media to ensure their own reproduction and expansion.

Perceptions are vital. Points of entry or connection with religious movements like ZAOGA are crucial in shaping conclusions. Pentecostal leaders are a prime example of the sheer range of forces that give African Pentecostalism its contemporary vigour. The likes of Archbishop Guti are 'Janus-faced', exhibiting different persona for dif-ferent constituencies. From the international perspective, the Archbishop participates in a network of high-flying religious executives who travel the convention circuits exchanging the latest Holy Spirit-inspired 'teachings' and physical manifestations of spiritual 'gifts'. For the most part he looks like his American counterparts, dressed in an Armani suit, sporting a Rolex watch and travelling in a classic German car. From the local perspective he looks very different.

From a Zimbabwean standpoint, Guti's achievements and appeal result from the amalgam of roles he performs – old and new, secular and religious – which find force in both continuity and change. Even though he leads a transnational community which transcends old ties of kinship and newer bonds of ethnicity and nation, he is nevertheless admired as a man of prayer for protection and healing, two of the essential functions of a traditional religious leader. Even though some of the gifts he receives – sofas, vacuum cleaners and packet milk drinks – are different from those given to diviners and mediums, they have a similar function, namely to encourage him to petition God on behalf of the supplicant. But while Guti's roles are congruent with African cosmological beliefs, they are expressed in the Christian, particularly Pentecostal, idiom of the Holy Spirit and understood within the context of Bibli-cal Christianity. There are other continuities and changes too. To some extent Guti's insistence on the virtues of industry and sobriety, domesticity and self-discipline places him in a trajectory of white and black American missionary tradition, which, in part, sought to create a disciplined subject for the needs of capitalist imperialism. His attack on witchcraft, ancestor veneration and possession cults as wasteful, idolatrous and regressive would win him accolades from many missionaries past and present. But his critique of the missionary tradition for its racism and creation of dependency tempers his criticism of African culture. And while endorsing capitalism's capacity to create autonomous, socially mobile citizens, he is critical of its global inequalities and the liberal secular humanist culture that often accompanies it. Guti is more of a 'culture broker' than a bald advocate of Westernisation. He encourages his followers to adopt *strands* of Western modernity, but simultaneously affirms the worth of Afri-can culture, specifically its Christian heritage, its ancient civilisations and its more recently imagined patriarchal family values. His success lies in his ability to draw upon commonly understood notions about the past and familiar aspects of contemporary culture to rationalise desired changes (Hegland, 1987: 4).

Yet in the realm of cultural change Guti can once again be located in a prior African tradition of prophetic utterance and innovation. Within this trajectory of religious change, prophets, first traditional and then Christian, can be credited with challenging old structures and ideas, and envisioning alternatives that were impossible for elders to conceive because of their different relation to capitalist production (Van Binsbergen, 1981: 172–9). Guti arrayed himself against elders – traditional, Christian and nationalist. Many of his social teachings amount to petit bourgeois respectability, but he is far more than an emergent class leader. On the range of issues the Archbishop addresses – moral, material and political – he is the descendant of the community leaders of the 1950s.

As ZAOGA has grown, so Guti's functions have multiplied: apostle, prophet, culture-broker and community leader. But the Archbishop is more than the sum of all these parts. The roles fuse to create a new figure on Africa's contemporary social landscape, the Pentecostal big man. Among their ranks are the likes of Otabil and Duncan-Williams from Ghana, Nevers Mumba from Zambia and Simeon Kayiwa from Uganda. Like the more secular *chefs*, these men possess great material and social resources , and are able to use their connections and influence to 'get things done'. As corruption and inefficiency mire African states, the Pentecostal big man grows more important. Most of them are disparaging about working for the state, and advocate the liberating potential of having one's own business (Gifford, 1998). Although citizens are informed about the failings of these new leaders through journalistic exposés, Pentecostal big men often have more popular legitimacy than compromised politicians, particularly in the eyes of their loyal followers.

The confidence of Pentecostal big men is often most manifest in the management of their movements' international branches. While ZAOGA resists external missionary dominance, it produces its own authoritarianism as a means to bind a large and unwieldy constituency. ZAOGA exports a highly localised set of doctrines and practices, in particular a leadership cult and a specific sacred history. There is tension in the movement between its centre and its peripheries. The leadership cult, authoritarian government and the sacred history have most influence at the centre, around Zimbabwe's capital, Harare, and the eastern Shona areas. In Mozambique, South Africa and England there is opposition to this distinctive part of ZAOGA's ideology. In these peripheries it is seen as Zimbabwean cultural dominance. But across the globe ZAOGA adherents actively proclaim their evangelical message. They resist secular humanism and liberal Christianity, finding common cause with conservatives on matters of gender and sexuality.

Pentecostalism and Politics

The shifts and tensions within Pentecostal movements are well illustrated through the example of ZAOGA's changing relation to politics. The dominant political culture of nationalism coloured the power-struggles between ZAOGA's founders and South African Pentecostals. But like their forebear Nicholas Bhengu, who left the South African Communist Party to take up a preaching ministry, the faction that eventually became ZAOGA initially eschewed formal politics. Instead they focused on leading respectable and vindicated lives. Economic change took priority over political change as ZAOGA's leaders preached a gospel of sobriety and industry built on family life. Such was the efficacy of this strategy that by Independence the movement had mushroomed on a transnational scale. But not for the first time ZAOGA was threatened by its own success. As a territory-wide religious movement with great potential for youth and multi-ethnic mobilisation, it was a threat to the new Zimbabwean state, jealous of its own legitimacy. Thus the movement was subject to a good deal of surveillance, not least because of its seeming connection with Ndabiningi Sithole. Its chance did not come until a shift in ZANU/PF's political fortunes. By the late 1980s the ruling party's legitimacy was beginning to wane. Dogged by corruption scandals, poor human rights records and economic downturn, the support of mainline churches was no longer automatic, and ZAOGA offered it much needed support. But ZAOGA's drive for political recognition was motivated by more than political expediency. It had a good deal of ideological sympathy with the ruling party's agenda of cultural nationalism, particularly notions of self-reliance and black autonomy. Moreover, there was some convergence on 'moral' questions, particularly sexual mores and family life.

If ZAOGA's greatest political moment came in 1995, when Mugabe launched his presidential campaign at one of their rallies, the relationship began to unravel soon afterwards. As ZANU/PF's legitimacy grew ever more tenuous, it began to encourage a destructive wave of farm invasions in the face of growing opposition from the MDC, and ZAOGA's loyalties shifted once again. Given that its membership in the townships were terrorised by a coalition of war veterans, police and army who saw them as potential MDC supporters, ZAOGA could not but heed their voice. But the leadership also had strong ideological reasons for distancing itself from ZANU/PF. Economic stability was crucial for one of ZAOGA's key tenets, social mobility. The collapse of the economy undermined its gospel of prosperity. Mugabe had lost his chance.

If the movement's relations with formal politics have been diverse and contradictory, so have its prospects as a potentially progressive element in civil society. While arguments about Pentecostalism's democratising force are generally 'speculative', the stuff of the *longue durée*, at the level of the local gathering there is at least a sign of an alternative pluralist and egalitarian political culture (Robbins, 2004a: 135; Martin, 1990: 267-8, 286-8). Local level financial accountability is assured, as tithes and offerings are recorded with mathematical accuracy. In pre-service Bible studies Scripture is debated with tolerance and mutual respect. Elections for the posts of deacons and elders are scrupulously conducted. Women and youth participate fully in assembly leadership, given opportunity through the multiplication of roles within the hierarchy. They are subsequently encouraged to seek greater responsibility in their careers and public life. Another source of egalitarianism lies in the movement's associational life. These organisations, which are lay-run and removed from the hierarchy, operate with a degree of autonomy. Particularly influential are the student and post-graduate associations. Their educated elite memberships are well-read and travelled. They have other models of church government to compare with ZAOGA, as well as a financial independence. And just as the egalitarian culture found in its assemblies is in symbiosis with the radical local politics, so student and post-graduate leaders are influenced by Western-derived rights discourses. At the very least the culture of the assembly creates active independent-minded citizens, a necessity in many overbearing African states.

In contrast, ZAOGA's leaders who are on the frontline in mediating relations with wider society are often the first to lose touch with their egalitarian origins and become corrupted by worldly ambitions. In the 1980s this tendency within the leadership to lose touch with its roots first manifested itself in a series of highly publicised schisms. Since then it has become increasingly drawn into the dominant political culture of 'chefism', nepotism and tribalism. Yet, Guti's political machinations have so far had little effect on ZAOGA's membership. Because Pentecostalism has voluntarist origins and has traditionally sought separation from the world, it is not possible to associate ZAOGA members *en masse* with any specific political or economic programme. Moreover, once the apolitical tradition has been rejected, Pentecostal leaders 'cannot close the gates totally to alternative forms of politicisation' (Freston, 2001: 306). As we have seen, ZAOGA's younger pastors and urban population have made their own different political choices. By the 1990s the populist voluntarism, which launched the movement in its early stages, was in contradiction with the chefist command from the centre. Finally, there are limits on centralising authority. ZAOGA has spawned a host of schismatic movements, seeking to escape the dominant faction's centralising control, dividing the Pentecostal field further.

Pentecostal ideology limits its engagement with formal politics. First and foremost, Pentecostalism seeks personal and cultural reformation rather than social transformation. Driven by the urgency of Christ's imminent return and his commandment to make disciples, Pentecostals almost always make politics subservient to proselytism. The state is not Pentecostalism's primary concern. Its fire is directed primarily at other elements within civil society, though not to the exclusion of the state's present regime. It is critical of institutions fostering secular or liberal values, and of media agencies which encourage immorality and promiscuity. Pentecostals also criticise the historic mission churches for being 'cold', 'worldly', 'unsaved', and 'demon possessed'. These are its major rivals and it is mainly in this context that the state assumes importance. ZAOGA's leadership is accomplished in what Paul Freston describes as 'time serving', 'the art of keeping oneself close to power, regardless of ideology or principle, in order to receive benefits' (Freston, 1994: 563). The end is 'ecclesiastical corporatism', the enlisting of state resources for church aggrandisement (Freston, 2001: 285). Favours with customs control, visas for foreign travel, planning permission for new buildings, and media contracts give them an important advantage over their competitors.

ZAOGA's leaders aggressively seek to dominate the religious field. It blocks the entry of other evangelical bodies into schools and colleges and competes for sites of worship in rural and urban locations. Its supposed interdenominational organisations act as fronts for recruitment from other churches. ZAOGA has also come into conflict with overseas donors for refusing to share aid with smaller ministries and churches. In sum, it appears little interested in a plurality of opinion, either within the church or outside it, or in the processes of negotiation typical of a 'civil' society. Despite the 'noisiness' (Freston, 1996: 164) of ZAOGA's arrival on the political scene, its importance must not be exaggerated. The Catholic Church's political activity is less visible because it has direct access to government ministers, many of whom are Catholics. And, with decades of experience, Catholic Bishops are deft in the art of *realpolitik*. While government ministers recognise the political significance of ZAOGA's large constituency, they still acknowledge that the Catholic, Anglican and Methodist churches have more political clout arising from their vast mission infrastructures of health and education.[1]

Finally, Pentecostal spirituality does not necessarily de-politicise issues. A theology of 'deliverance from demons' does not automatically mystify those social and economic processes that scar adherents' lives (Gifford, 1998: 332). Rather it provides a language for discussing the forces that act on their lives in ways that believers can understand and confront. The idioms of spirits and demons are in their own way no more mysterious or abstract than the language of structure and process deployed by social scientists.[2] Moreover, it does not take too much imagination to grasp the politically destabilising potential of some spiritual injunctions. Refrains such as 'fear God not man' or the assertion of first loyalty to a Holy Nation where status and citizenship are redefined can, as David Martin suggests, 'divest systems of authority of their justification and turn law into a matter of inward judgement and sincerity, rather than external observance'. Likewise, the egalitarianism of the Holy Spirit, and its attendant inclusive distribution of 'gifts' independent of age, gender and class, 'subverts every principle of social honour, inherent status, and necessary mediation' (2001: 12). As Karen Fields illustrated two decades ago, culture and politics do not readily separate into discreet analytical categories for the convenience of social scientists (1985).

Pentecostalism and Cultural Reformation

Pentecostalism does have a political import but it is not primarily concerned with formal political change. Although much of the contemporary research on Pentecostalism considers the activities of prosperous young believers who attend Born-again conventions in plush hotels and worship in carpeted, air-conditioned churches, most Pentecostals are in fact poor. They are mostly remote from the political and educated classes, and at a good distance from the spoils of the state. In such circumstances 'they alter what is in their capacity to alter, beginning with themselves' (Martin, 2001:12). People are often drawn to Pentecostalism through a search for healing. But Pentecostalism also attracts and retains its following through its ability to 'call' people as individuals. Preachers concentrate on probing the basic questions of what it means to be a person. In particular, they address key existential concerns for wholeness, purity, meaning and empowerment. The person is recreated and maintained in a state of purity. Those who have abused, or taken moral shortcuts to survive or achieve worldly riches, are washed clean by Christ's blood, able to embrace a future where past sins are not revisited. And those who have been victims of poverty and exploitation are freed from shame, embarrassment and fear. Such liberation is achieved not only through the remaking of personal narratives, but through the actual bodily experience of the Pentecostal service. The experience of the Holy Sprit can be so profound that it wrenches lives out of downward spirals of abuse and self-loathing. These are, of course, only changes in states of being, but they are not to be taken lightly. Informants spoke repeatedly of the self-respect and feeling of empowerment they had gained from a 'clean conscience' and sense of 'moral victory'.

The binding of wounds is only the first stage of the Born-again story. Once reborn, the convert is a person of consequence, value and authority: a 'member of a chosen people, a royal priesthood, a holy nation' [1 Peter 2]. They are dressed in God's 'finest robes' and given His 'ring of authority' [Luke 15]. Inside the assembly, believers' horizons widen. They see people not too different from themselves leading, speaking, singing and organising. By example, new converts come to discover gifts and talents they never knew they had. There are enough examples of leadership adorned with the trappings of success to inspire the faithful on to better things. Pentecostalism begins by remaking individuals, but it rapidly progresses to the remaking of the family. While the leaders and members of ZAOGA have exhibited a quixotic response to formal politics, particularly cultural nationalism, over the decades their commitment to max-imising the chances of social reproduction has been unwavering. Given the choice, they have consistently opted for making families rather than making revolutions. They have been guided by the doctrine of 'the spirit of poverty', which causes them to reflect on mentalities that lead to decay and inspire a break from traditions that are perceived to hold them back.

Zimbabwean Pentecostalism has evolved in relation to politics, shaped by shifts from anti-colonial nationalism to one-partyism and the current attempts by the ruling party to cling to power. And movements such as ZAOGA have developed a critique of the dominant political culture, violence, authoritarianism and clientelism, even if the leadership sometimes replicates some of these traits. However, the shifting economic context has been no less important. The movement was born in the age of late colonial capitalism amid the social disruption of post-war industrialisation and urbanisation. It later mushroomed in the era of neo-liberal economics, an era of declining state pro-vision, inflation and growing unemployment. Given the *immorality* of the dominant political culture and the inability of the state to bring about political change that is both meaningful and lasting, ZAOGA members have sought an alternative route to development through self-improvement. Its rhetoric has shifted from righteousness and respectability to deliverance from the spirit of poverty, but the focus on the well-being of the family has remained the same. Such an emphasis on economic uplift rather than political advance is nothing new. Black Americans, Christian and Islam-ic, have often deployed this strategy in the context of frustrated political ambitions (Campbell, 1995; Tinaz, 1996).

There are real limits to Pentecostal transformation of self and family. The gap between leaders and followers tends to widen, causing ever more schism and internal migration within the wider Born-again movement. Moreover, changing the sub-structure of individual personalities does not end all social and political ills. Contrary to Guti's teaching, wars are caused by more than a 'failure to listen' (1993a). And the forces of global capitalism combined with the corruption and political violence of some African states, all demonic in the broadest sense of the word, can leave even the most determined believer on the margins of poverty. Third World Christians are often more sinned against than sinning. But, given that health and a stable family life are often the only resources available to the poor, Pentecostalism at least helps them to protect and marshal these valuable commodities to the best of their abilities. At their heart, move-ments like ZAOGA prod their members towards security rather than prosperity. The Pentecostal ethos is one that stresses coping, and the avoidance of extreme poverty and ill-health, rather than success.[3] Security and prosperity are opposite poles on the same continuum, but the distinction is important because most Zimbabweans, like most Africans, are poor and far removed from the 'name it and claim it' theology exempli-fied by the likes of Kenneth Hagin and Kenneth and Gloria Copeland. At their most basic level the ascetic codes that accompany Pentecostal practice pull believers out of poverty, or at least prevent them from slipping over the edge.

Pentecostalism: A Religious Movement at the Turn of the Twenty-First Century

Given the choice, Pentecostals spend their time within their religious communities. The primary concern of the assembly is the resolution of private rather than public problems. 'It is far more in terms of prayer that they understand themselves, hold their members and discover a future laced with hope' (Hastings, 1979: 265). In these communities Pentecostals build testimonies that clothe 'individual lives with timeless significance', locating the believer's personal narrative within a larger 'magnificent drama in which cosmic good vanquished cosmic evil' (Wacker, 2001: 69). The novelty of being called by name draws many out of the historic mission churches. Although popular Christianity, whatever its tradition, can offer adherents personal security, the historic movements are further down the road of bureacratisation and routinisation. In such circumstances the 'crowd' church can prevail, whereby large congregations meet just once a week, and allow only a superficial practice of faith.[4] Such problems are only just beginning to affect Pentecostals and at present believers respond by moving to newer, more intimate Pentecostal gatherings.

Pentecostal movements such as ZAOGA are not escapist. They are not a defensive and non-constructive reaction to social disruption. They do not fit into the schema often used to explain social movements in which their activity is explained in terms of anomie, alienation and crisis. Instead, as Mary Hegland argues, they are better understood as movements which are both 'the cause and effect of change', as adaptive mechanisms through which 'change is shaped and directed'.[5] Religious movements can thus be creative, innovative and active responses to change and to the perceived needs of society, groups and individuals. Pentecostals seek not only to respond to change but also to bring about change through their own activity – to form a society better able to provide for human needs as well as address their own interests. Adherents are not refugees retreating from frightening new circumstances, but are courageous, confident and able people who actively seek to influence their lives and social environment according to their own ideals and aims, their conduct motivated by hope, optimism and determination rather than by despair and defeat (Hegland, 1987: 3). Although often poor and marginal, contemporary Pentecostals are not humble people. In much of Africa and beyond they are on the offensive. Their leaders purchase real estate in city centres and elite members build high-tech churches with air-conditioning, closed-circuit TV and plush decor. Politicians treat them with respect, assiduously attend Born-again conventions and appropriate the language of renewal, mindful of the size of the growing Born-again community. Other elements in the religious field have innovated in response to the Pentecostal upsurge. Anglicans, Catholics and Methodists have adopted Charismatic renewal, 'jazzed' up their worship, and adopted evangelical church growth strategies to maintain numbers, particularly amongst the young.

As a religious movement, African Pentecostalism draws force by standing within two great traditions of religious renewal and innovation. The first is an internal one, best documented in Central Africa but also present in West and southern Africa. In essence, the tradition is one of personal security movements, whose adherents have acted collectively in pursuit of harmony or 'good life': fertility of women; a successful

223

hunt; abundant harvests; material wealth and prosperity; salvation; protection against evil, sorcery or witchcraft (De Creamer, Fox and Vansina, 1976: 467-8; Maxwell, 1999). This internal dynamic has collided and conflated with an external Protestant one, from which Africans have derived the spiritual and ideological resources of Biblical Christianity. These two cycles have come together to form the back-cloth to the great prophetic movements of twentieth-century Africa: Zionist and Aladura Christianity, the movements of Garrick Sokari Braide and William Wadé Harris. Contemporary Pentecostalism stands at the end of this trajectory. Given their desire to associate themselves with modernity and to cast themselves as 'international', African Pentecostals play down links with movements of Christian independency. Their notion of the good life has evolved to include exam success, correct emigration papers, successful business and the latest commodities alongside the more fundamental material and existential concerns. The practice and idiom of witchcraft eradication have been Christianised further than within the prophetic movements. But continuities in terms of membership and practice show that contemporary African Pentecostalism lies firmly in independency's shadow. It is a similar trajectory to the development of Jamaican Christianity. Here Pentecostalism legitimated Zion Revivalism, which had floated free from a text-based Christianity (Austin-Broos, 2001: 157). In Africa, missionary-derived Pentecostalism legitimated the practices of Zionist, Apostolic and Aladura churches. The founders of ZAOGA encountered in Pentecostalism a Biblical justification for healing and exorcism, which they had already experienced in Christian independency. Such insights should cause us to reflect on how scholars study the widespread African conversion to Christianity. To frame the question in terms of how missionaries imposed Christianity ascribes too much historical agency to them (Comaroff and Comaroff, 1991, 1997). It also obscures how Africans actively sought out the spiritual and intellectual resources of Biblical Christianity.

It is important, however, to return to the problematic posed in the Introduction concerning Pentecostalism's take-off in much of sub-Saharan Africa during the last two decades of the twentieth century – decades which mark the neo-liberal era. It is obvious that Pentecostalism is popular religion *par excellence*, a powerful collection of idioms readily available to the laity. But Pentecostalism is simultaneously existential and historically specific.

Throughout the last century Pentecostals consistently pitted themselves against 'large institutions and personal aggregations that seemed to stand in their way' (Wacker, 2001: 194-6). With them, ZAOGA members fought against traditions, mentalities and conglomerates, physical and spiritual, that blocked their entrance into modernity. But from the 1980s onwards ZAOGA was particularly well equipped to respond to modernity's latest neo-liberal incarnation. Contemporary Pentecostalism's capacity for individuation, through enabling believers to rewrite their own personal narrative and break with the past, symbolised through violent exorcism, proved immensely important. Although essentially a religious movement which offers the path to salvation through healing and personal transformation, Pentecostalism creates a modern individual subject well suited to the demands of the post-industrial economic culture found in parts of the Southern hemisphere. In the late colonial era Pentecostal religion helped create the disciplined wage labourer capable of meeting the needs of farm and factory production; today it engenders the flexibility, trust and self-motivation required by the lightly supervised sectors of the service economy (B. Martin, 1995). Pentecostalism's fit with neo-liberal modernity is further enhanced by its love affair with the electronic media and its emphasis on accumulation, even conspicuous consumption.

However, individuation can be overemphasised (Englund and Leach, 2000: 233-6). Because the promises of modernity never fully materialise, and neo-liberal economics create unprecedented levels of insecurity and volatility, Pentecostalism rejects neo-liberalism's cultural agenda of atomisation that strips away old networks of social support. Instead, Pentecostal assemblies provide new forms of communality and a new moral order derived from sacred text and transcendent experience. Within their local churches adherents can find stability and security as they collectively strive toward something better. Believers willingly embrace the conservative ascetic code, rigorously enforced by an authoritarian pastorate, because it offers the rewards of self-disciplined freedom and new sources of social capital (B.Martin, 1998: 137). The religious community becomes a place where members are captured by a vision and offered a compelling alternative pattern for society. The intimacy of this new 'surrogate family' (Meyer, 2004: 461) reveals how, in spite of the shortcomings of leaders and failed hopes of material advance, Pentecostals like those in ZAOGA still 'love' their church.

Pentecostals, however ordinary, also find hope through being 'part of a worldwide movement of *winners*' (B. Martin, 1998: 123). Re-enacting the powerful drama of the Acts of the Apostles in a contemporary setting, believers imagine new identities that transcend the nation-state. They envisage a pan-African identity where blacks are delivered from deference to whites, are proud of their heritage, and claim the Christian mantle from the secularised and apostate Western church. Alternatively they see themselves as part of a global Born-again identity, an international community of the 'saved'. As a confident young female Zambian pastor told those gathered for morning devotions at ZAOGA Headquarters in Waterfalls, Harare: 'It was the Devil who gave Africans a Third World mentality. But God did not create a Third World Person, only First World People.'[6] These transnational and global identities grow more important as Zimbabweans, like many of their African neighbours, lose faith in the 'national ideal' and the ability of their state to better their lives. The emancipatory potential of Zimbabwean nationalism has not been realised. And the secular gospel of 'development' is met with growing cynicism about its utility and Western biases. The Born-again alternatives at least appear to work. Their transnational identities are embodied in 'mission plants' in adjacent countries and amongst the Diaspora in Europe. Moreover, they are enacted in international conventions and circuits, and imagined in the electronic and printed media. But most of all, Pentecostals provide 'stable or fulfilling structures of sociality' in their extensive networks of small religious communities meeting in homes, classrooms, cinemas, sports centres and church buildings which span vast regions (Austin-Broos, 2001: 159). Heaven may be the final destination, but in the meantime, membership of a transnational religious community represents an acceptable halfway house. To be Born-again in ZAOGA is to be part of something big, part of something that counts.

Notes

1 Int.DM113, William Gumbochena.
2 This does not mean that Pentecostals do not understand the language of social science. It is clear that Guti and others have a clear grasp of the implications of structural adjustment (Guti, 1994a).

225

[3] Robbins, 2004a: 137.
[4] See *The African Synod Prepares*, 1991: 28. Also *Zimbabwe Project News Bulletin*, October 1982, in which Bishop Hatendi accused the majority of black Anglicans of using the church as a social or cultural club.
[5] Hegland, 1987: 3, citing Gerlach and Hine (1979: xiv).
[6] Fieldwork notes, 3 October 1995.

Sources & References

Archival Sources

Apostolic Faith Mission, Lyndhurst, South Africa (AFM)
File, William Branham, ND
File, Buck's Farm, ND
File, General Native Correspondence
File, S. Harris, 1914-82
File, F.D. Johnstone, 1913-50
File, Kruger, 1923-72
File, O.P. Teichart, 1944-67
File, W.L. Wilson, 1939-78
File, W.K. Wilson, 1932-nd.
File, Young Persons Union Committee Minutes, 1953

Annual General Native Workers Conference Minutes, 1947-53
Executive Council Minutes, February 1909-April 1925, 1932, 1943, 1944
Missionary Committee Minute Book, February 1920-February 1936
Sending Committee Minutes, August 1915-January 1920, 1946-49

The Comforter (and Messenger of Hope) [Also known as *Die Trooster*]
Southern Rhodesia Pentecostal Light Bearer

**Assemblies of God Zimbabwe Archives (formerly Springfield, USA),
    Borrowdale, Harare, (AOGZ)**
Larry Malcolm 1981. 'Development of the Assemblies of God in Zimbabwe', mimeograph.
John Elliot 1990. 'History of General Council and Other A/G Groups. Based on Discussion with
    Samuel Ndove and Conversations with Mischeck Chimsoro', mimeograph.
'Zimbabwe Past and Present', nd
'Work of the Assemblies of God in Rhodesia', nd
File, Bible College
File, Correspondence relating to Ascot Church 1968-78
File, District Council Financial Reports
File, Church Reports
File, Correspondence with Government
File, Formative Period
File, General Council Finances
File, General Council Minutes
File, Personnel 1968-71

Journals
Advance (Assemblies of God, Springfield USA) 1986
Mountain Movers (Assemblies of God, Springfield USA) 1986
Pentecostal Evangel (Assemblies of God, Springfield USA) 1959, 1968, 1970-71, 1984-86

(Papers in the Possession of) Desmond Cartwright, Cardiff, Wales
B.J. Britz, 'Facts about Pentecost in Southern Rhodesia', ca. 1952
H.W. Greenaway, Report on Visit to South Africa, ca. May 1958
Notes of a meeting held in Fairview Assembly Hall, South Africa, 24 May 1958

Christ for the Nations, Dallas, USA
Journals
Christ for the Nations, Dallas
Revival Report (CFNI Dallas)

Donald Gee Centre for Charismatic Research, Mattersey, Doncaster, England

Journals
Confidence February
Intercessory Missionary
Pentecost: A Review of World-wide Pentecostal Missionary and Revival News
Pentecostal Testimony
Pentecostal Witness
Pentecostal Wonders
Redemption Tidings
Revival News: Being the Organ of the Revival League of Jamaica
Showers of Blessing
The Apostolic Faith (Los Angeles)
The Apostolic Faith (Portland)
The Apostolic Herald
The Apostolic Light
The Apostolic Messenger
The Children's Paper
The Latter Rain
The Upper Room

Tracts
Anonymous, *Healed Through Praise*, ca. 1915
T.B. Barratt, (nd) *The Twentieth Century Revival. Some Facts and General Information*
– (nd) *The Gift of Tongues: What Is It? Being a Reply to Dr A.C. Dixon* and *Pentecost not Hypnotism*
A. Boddy, *Pentecost at Sunderland: Testimony of a Lancashire Builder*, ca. 1907
H. Musgrave Reade, (nd) *Christ or Socialism*
C. Polhill, *A China Missionary's Witness*, ca.1908

(Papers in the Possession of) Jeremiah Kainga, Harare, Zimbabwe
Correspondence 1964-67

(Papers in Possession of) David Maxwell, Keele, England
Mrs M. Chesve, Diary Extracts, transcribed January 1996
Constitution of Pentecost Assemblies of God, March 1967 (original with David Choto)
Jean Henderson, Diary, 1993-94, Annotated Notes, Pastors' Conference, November 1996.
John James , Letters and Correspondence, ca. 1990-92
Wilson Mabasa, 'How FIFM Started', ca. 1994, & Notes on the Origins of FIFM in South Africa ca. 1994
Mbare Region, Letter, 1996
Liniah Rusere, (nd) written testimony
Wycliffe Bible Translators, Mwani Strategy Document, ca. 1994

National Archives of Zimbabwe, Harare, Zimbabwe (NAZ)
N3/5/3-4 Churches and Missions, 1919-32
S138/17/1 CNC's Correspondence and other papers, 1924-25
S138/17/2 CNC's Correspondence and other papers, 1925-28
S138/22 CNC's Correspondence and other papers, 1931-33
S138/140 CNC's Correspondence, Zionist Activities, 1924-34

S138/148 CNC's Correspondence, Apostolic Faith Church, 1923–32
S138/176 CNC's Correspondence, Pentecostal Mission of Southern Rhodesia, 1924–28
S235/511 vol.1 Annual Report, Wedza, 1933
S661 [] 1932–33
S1032 [] Hartley 1932–33
S1219 Departmental Circulars, 1913–34
S1542/M8 Missions and Churches, 1934–38
S1542/M8B vol. 1, Apostolic Faith Mission
S1542/M8B vol. 2, Apostolic Faith Mission1934–39
S1542/P10 Pseudo Religions, 1934–36
S2805/3423 Highfield Village Settlement, 1955–57
S2805/3918/20/1 Native Townships, 1948–50
S2805/3918/20/2 Native Townships, 1950–54
S2805/3918/20/3 Native Townships, 1954–57
S2805/4329/5 Native Housing Conference Minutes, 1953
S2810/2340 Apostolic Faith Mission of South Africa, 1935–54
S2810/2358/1 Apostolic Faith, Hartley, 1931–45
S2810/2358/2 Missions and Churches, Hartley, 1940–56
S2810/2366 Missions and Churches, Salisbury, 1940–56
S2810/2630 Assemblies of God, 1949–53
S2810/4082 Latter Rain Assemblies of South Africa, 1939–51
S2810/4424 Full Gospel Church, 1935–56
S2810/4469 African Apostolic Faith Mission of Southern Rhodesia, 1943–55
S2811/9 University of Rhodesia and Nyasaland Socio–economic Survey, 1955–66
S2824/3 The Korsten Basket Makers, 1957–63
S2827/2/2/8 vol 4. Annual Report, Bindura, 1961
S3330/T1/35/22/2 Highfield State of Emergency, 1964–65
Annual Reports of the Director of Native Administration, 1951–57
Annual Reports of the Director of Native Administration, 1958–61

Gen P - Sen 'From the Bush to the Pulpit: Autobiography of M.J. Sengwayo, Rhodesia, affiliated to
the Apostolic Faith Mission, Portland, Oregon, USA' (mimeograph).

AOH/4 Interview, Amon Nengomasha 17 February & 3 March 1977
AOH/4 Interview, Jeremiah Jack Dzuke 17 February & 3 March 1977

Pentecostal Assemblies of Zimbabwe (formerly Canada), Harare, Zimbabwe (PAOZ)
File, Bhengu 1960–69
File, General Correspondence 1962–67

Wesleyan Methodist Archives, Harare (WMA)
Minutes of Salisbury District Synod Meeting, January 11-17, 1922
Minutes of Salisbury District Leaders Meeting, November 29, 1935
Minutes of Leaders Meeting, June 11, 1936

Zimbabwe Assemblies of God Africa, Archives, Waterfalls, Harare, Zimbabwe (ZAW)
File, AOGA correspondence 1964–80
File, British South Africa Police 1963–79
File Christ for the Nations Institute (CNFI) Dallas
File, Constitutions & Ministries
File, Deeper Life 1974–96
Executive Minutes 1977-84, 1988–90
File, Ezekiel Guti Evangelistic Association (EGEA) (ca. 1981-94)
File, Finance 1976–94
File, General Reports ca.1980-96

File, Gracious Women 1988-96
File, Histories (ca. 1967-93)
File, Internal Correspondence to Dr Guti
File, International Third World Leaders Association (ITWLA) 1993-96
File, Locals, 1992-96
File, Mashonaland East 1987-88
File, Missions: Botswana, England (London), Kenya, Malawi, Mozambique, Nigeria, South Africa and Namibia, Swaziland, Tanzania, Zaire, Zambia 1969-96
File, Newsletters, 1981-96
File, Non-Denominational USA 1983-95
File, Non-Denominational Correspondence, Nigeria & Overseas 1975
File, Overseas
File, Relations with Government (Rhodesian and Zimbabwean)
File, Press Cuttings
File, Sermons
File, Sponsors 1981-96
File, Statistics

ZAOGA Publications

Tracts and Booklets
Africa Multination for Christ College
Africa Multination for Christ College Correspondence Division
Africa Multination for Christ College Evening Classes
Christ for Zimbabwe Technical College 1983 Brochure
Ezekiel Guti Saints Relief Fund
Forward in Faith Children's Home
Forward in Faith Child Evangelism Ministry (1)
Forward in Faith Child Evangelism Ministry (2)
Forward in Faith College and High School Ministry
Girls Fellowship
Gracious Women's Fellowship International
Gracious Women's Fellowship International Self Evaluation Booklet
Gracious Women's Fellowship International Song Book
Gracious Single Women's Fellowship
Holy Matrimony and the Dead
Information about the Ministries
Husbands Agape Fellowship International
Marriage Enrichment Expo' 95
Pray for Africa. Forward in Faith Ministries
Presenting Africa Multination for Christ Institute
Presenting Christ for Zimbabwe Institute
Single Women
Tithes
What is Gracious Women?

Periodicals
Africa Arise (ZAOGA)
This is That (ZAOGA) 1991-1995
The Macedonian Call (Forward in Faith International) 1972

Booklets by Ezekiel Guti
nd-a. *Where is Heaven?* Waterfalls, ZAOGA Forward in Faith Publications.

nd-b. *Laws of Leadership*. Waterfalls, ZAOGA Forward in Faith Publications

nd-c. *Relay of Three Leaders*. Waterfalls, ZAOGA Forward in Faith Publications.

nd-d. *Do you Know your God?* Waterfalls, ZAOGA Forward in Faith Publications.

nd-e. *Ezekiel in the Holy Land*. Waterfalls, ZAOGA Forward in Faith Publications.

nd-f. [with Eunor Guti] *Pathway to Praise and Worship*. Waterfalls, ZAOGA Forward in Faith Publications.

nd-g. *Preparation for Church Growth*. Waterfalls, ZAOGA Forward in Faith Publications.

nd-h. *Teaching Prayer and Intercession for Leaders*. Waterfalls, ZAOGA Forward in Faith Publications.

nd-i. *Changes Come through Pressure*. Waterfalls, ZAOGA Forward in Faith Publications.

1989. *The Sacred Book of ZAOGA Forward in Faith to the Leaders and the Saints, pt.1*, Waterfalls, ZAOGA.

1991. *Effective Preaching that Draws People to God*. Harare, EGEA Publications.

1992a. *New Believer's Guide for Christian Success*. Harare, EGEA Publications.

1992b. *The Longest Recorded Prayer of Jesus*. Harare, EGEA Publications.

1992c. *Zimbabwe Assemblies of God, Africa. Guidance, Rules and Policy of the Local Assemblies*. ZAOGA.

1992d. *Human Beings Cannot Change Without Pressure*. Harare, EGEA Publications.

1993a. *Hearing and Listening is a Problem Even in the Home*. Harare, EGEA Publications.

1993b. *Saved, Baptised & Filled with the Holy Spirit*. Harare, EGEA Publications.

1993c. *Principles of the Doctrine of Christ*. Harare, EGEA Publications.

1994a. *The Church and Political Responsibility*, Harare, EGEA Publications.

1994b. *Does Your Marriage Look Like This?* Harare, EGEA Publications.

1994c. *So I am an Elder. What am I Expected of?* [sic.] Harare, EGEA Publications.

1994d. *Restoring the Purpose of True Cost of Leadership*. Harare, EGEA Publications.

1995a. *The Sacred Book of ZAOGA Forward in Faith to the Leaders and the Saints, pt. 2*, Waterfalls, ZAOGA.

1995b. *SH-hh Shut Your Mouth: Marriage and Young Couples Character*, Harare, EGEA Publications.

1995c. *What makes Church to Grow.* [sic] Harare, EGEA Publications.

1995d. *The Vision that Gives You Direction and Produces Faith*. Harare, EGEA Publications.

1995e. *Guidance and Example of Praying Church* [sic] Harare, EGEA Publications.

1999. *History of ZAOGA Forward in Faith. The Book of Remembrance. How it Began and Where it is Going*. Harare, EGEA Publications.

Other ZAOGA Booklets

Mudere, Chipo. 1993. *A Place for the Woman*. Harare, EGEA Publications.

Mukonoweshuro, Sharai. 1993. *He Has All the Power*. Harare, EGEA Publications.

Takavarasha, Robert M. (nd), *The Remained Unspoken of the African Apostle*.

Zimbabwean/southern African Newspapers

Electronic Mail and Guardian
Kawadzana (Produced by the Highfield Township Administration) 1964–70
The African Weekly 1957–60
The Rhodesian Herald 1960, 1973, 1975
The Daily News 1957–60 & 2001–02
The Herald 1986, 1996, 2001
Sunday News

Zimbabwean Monthlies

Christian Concorde 1999
Gospel in Transit 1999
Horizon
Moto 1986, 1988, 1995, 1996
Parade 1987, 1994–96

Southern African Political and Economic Monthly
Zimbabwe Project News Bulletin, 1982

Oral Sources

All interviews conducted by David Maxwell except where otherwise noted.

Zimbabwe Assemblies of God Africa/Forward in Faith Mission International (ZAOGA/FIMI), Past and Present
1. Joaô Almeida (m) Pemba, Mozambique, 29 June 1996
2. Phil Austin (m) AMFCC, Glen Norah, Zimbabwe, 26 October 1995
3. – Edinburgh, 29 April 2003
4. Christopher Chadoka (m) Overseer, ZAOGA,Waterfalls, Zimbabwe,16 November 1995
5. Veronica Chaipa (f) Kazozo Village, Katerere, Zimbabwe, 19 April 1996
6. Godfrey Chakanyuka (m) Gleview, Zimbabwe, 26 January 1996
7. Martin Chesve (m) & Mrs Chesve (f) Belvedere, Zimbabwe, 7 December 1995
8. Israel Chibisa (m) Raungwe, Katerere, Zimbabwe, 1993 int. by Tom Riyo (TR)
9. Bill John Chigwenembe (m) Evangelist, ZAOGA, AMFC, Glen Norah, Zimbabwe, 8 November 1995
10. Adiel Chikobvu (m) University of Zimbabwe, Zimbabwe, 23 October 1995
11. Dias Chikodo (m) Chiwariria village, Katerere, Zimbabwe, 22 March 1996
12. Tendai Chikumbindi (f) Ruangwe, Katerere, Zimbabwe, 21 April 1996
13. Vidah Chitatse (f) Ruangwe, Katerere, Zimbabwe, 3 February 1996 int. by Samson Mudzudza (SM)
14. City Assembly Youth (Bradley (m) Jacqueline (f) Mavis (f) Mhike (m) Phildah (f) Rangarirai (m) Avenues, Harare, Zimbabwe, 17 December 1995
15. Debson Chizivano (m) Highfield, Zimbabwe, 13 June 1996
16. Joseph Choto (m) Bulawayo, Zimbabwe, June 1996.
17. Mr Chuma (m) Pastor, Nyamanda, Zimbabwe, 11 August 1996
18. Martin (m) and Mary (f) Cooper, Borrowdale, Zimbabwe, 15 November 1995
19. Mrs Dinari, Highfield, Zimbabwe, 15 February 1996 int. by Elisha Manzou (EM)
20. Norman Dzinduwa (m) Overseer, ZAOGA, Mutare, Zimbabwe, 1 November 1995
21. Anna Goche, Highfield, Zimbabwe, 15 February 1996 int. by Elisha Manzou (EM)
22. Ezekiel Guti (m) Archbishop, Waterfalls, Zimbabwe, 11 October1995
23. – Glen Lorne, Zimbabwe, 5 February 1996
24. Jean Henderson (f) Borehamwood, England, 3 January 1997
25. Jenny (f) and John James (m) Edgware, England, 2 January 1997
26. Gwen (f) and Davison (m) Kanokanga, Greendale, Zimbabwe, 25 April 1996
27. Mr Kapandura (m) Overseer, Bindura, Zimbabwe, May 1995.
28. Johanes Kasese (m) Msasa, Zimbabwe, 10 August 1999
29. Lazarus Kataya (m) Kuwadzana, Zimbabwe, 18 January 1996
30. Paul Kimaruh (m) Pastor, ZAOGA, Kenya, AMFCC, Glen Norah, Zimbabwe, 8 February 1996
31. Daniel Kovera (m) Soshanguve, South Africa, 20 May 1996
32. Edna Lajabu (f) Highfield, Zimbabwe, 13 March 1996
33. Norah Lajabu (f) Evangelist, ZAOGA, AMFCC, Glen Norah, Zimbabwe, 24 January 1996
34. Joseph Lebea (m) Soshanguve, South Africa, 21 May 1996
35. Wilson Mabasa (m) Overseer, FIFMI South Africa, Mamelodi, South Africa, 20 May 1996
36. Tichaona Mabasari (m) Mhokore, Katerere, Zimbabwe, 1996 int. by Simba Chikodo (SM)
37. Mr Madziya, Highfield, Zimbabwe, 16 April 1996 int. by Elisha Manzou (EM)
38. Doreen Makoma (f) Mhokore, Katerere, Zimbabwe, 1996 int. by Simba Chikodo (SM)
39. Innocent Makwarimba, (m) Glen Norah, Zimbabwe, 10 July 1996
40. John Mangisa (m) Pastor, AMFCC, Glen Norah, Harare, Zimbabwe, 13 February 1996

41. Bartholomew (m) and Appiah (f) Manjoro, Leaders of Faith World Ministries, Belvedere, Harare, Zimbabwe, 27 April 1996
42. Jason Marowa (m) Chaplain-General, Police Headquarters, Harare, Zimbabwe, 12 December 1995
43. – Borrowdale, Zimbabwe, 11 July 2001
44. Lydia Masimbe (f) and Ida Chikono (f) Dublin House, Harare, Zimbabwe, 15 February 1996
45. Jorge Joaquim Matus (m) Pastor, Pemba, Mozambique 28 June 1996
46. Lazarus Mavhura (m), Mufakose, Zimbabwe, 25 August 1999
47. Jack Mhondiwa (m) Overseer, ZAOGA, Waterfalls, Zimbabwe, 16 April 1996
48. Simon Monde (m) Pastor, Leader of Zaire Assemblies, AMFCC, Glen Norah, Zimbabwe, 7 February 1996
49. Anna Mturi (f) with Perpetua Mkodzansi (f) and Stella Dembedze (f) Mhondoro, Zimbabwe, 10 December 1995
50. Luxford Muchenje (m) Harare Polytechnique, Zimbabwe, 14 June 1996
51. Servias Mugava (m) Central Fire Station, Harare, Zimbabwe, November 1995
52. Paul Mutumi (m) Ruangwe, Katerere, Zimbabwe, 21 April 1996
53. Pricilla Ngoma (f) AMFCC, Glen Norah, Zimbabwe, 10 November 1995
54. – Waterfalls, Zimbabwe, 4 June 1996
55. Caleb Ngorima (m) AMFCC, Zimbabwe, 9 November 1995
56. Sophia Nyandoro (f) and Stella Masiku (f) Ruangwe, Katerere, Zimbabwe, 19 April 1996
57. Grace Nyati (f) Avondale, Harare, Zimbabwe, 24 July 1996
58. Mary Rembo (f) Bindura, Zimbabwe, 10 January 1995
59. Liniah Rusere (f) Waterfalls, Zimbabwe, 13 December 1995
60. Mrs Sagandira (f) Mhokore, Katerere, Zimbabwe, 1996 int. by Simba Chikodo (SM)
61. Joshua (m) and Mabel (f) Samasuwo, Edgware, London, 8 August 1994
62. Abel Sande (m) Leader of Ambassadors of Christ (co-founder of ZAOGA), and Waterfalls, Zimbabwe, 30 April 1996
63. – Waterfalls, Harare, 30 August 1999
64. Paul Saungweme (m) Evangelist, ZAOGA, Glen Norah, Zimbabwe, 11 October 1995
65. Steve Simango (m) Pastor, Waterfalls, Zimbabwe, 6 December 1995
66. Mateus Simao (m) Leader of ADDA, Mozambique, 12 December 1995
67. Fernado Sumunitato (m) Pastor, Pemba, Mozambique, 28 June 1996
68. Nyarai Teta (f) Ruangwe, Katerere, Zimbabwe, 29 February 1996 int. by Samson Mudzudza (SM)
69. Mrs Willis, Avenues, Zimbabwe, July 1996 int. by Elisha Manzou (EM)

Apostolic Faith Mission (AFM)
70. I.S. Burger (m) President of the AFM, Lyndhurst, South Africa, 20 May 1996
71. Florence Goneke (f) and Peter Marovha (m) Waterfalls, Zimbabwe, 22 December 1995
72. Cleopas Gwanzura (m) Prospect, Zimbabwe, 1 July 1997
73. Samson Gwanzura (m) and Kuitenyi Msike (m) Zimbabwe, ca. 1994 int. by Titus Murefu (TM)
74. Samson (m) and Laiza Gwanzura (f) Chiweshe, Zimbabwe, 8 August 1996
75. Maweni Lazurus M'kombe (m), Mount Pleasant, Zimbabwe, 11 July 2001
76. Kuitenyi Msike (m) Msana, Zimbabwe, 15 August 1996
77. Constanatine Murefu (m) Principal, Living Waters Bible College, Harare, Zimbabwe, 30 August 1996
78. Titus Murefu (m) Overseer,Waterfalls, Zimbabwe, 31 July 1996
79. Jeries Mvenge (m) Pastor, Mutare, Zimbabwe, 19 July 1996

Other Church Leaders and Members in southern Africa
80. John Bond (m) Vice-Chairman, Assemblies of God South Africa, Johannesburg, South Africa, 15 May 1996
81. Bacai Casimba (m) Pemba, Mozambique, 29 June 1996
82. Wilson Chibisa (m) Pastor, Elim Mission, Katerere, Zimbabwe, 19 July 1996
83. Misheck Chimsoro (m) Superintendent of the Assemblies of God, Zimbabwe, (formerly

Springfield, USA) Vainona, Zimbabwe, 25 March 1996

84. Antonio F. Da Sousa (m) Pastor, Evangelical Assemblies of God, Pemba, Mozambique, 27 June 1996
85. Phineas Dube (m) Minister, Central Baptist Church, Harare, Zimbabwe, 1 March 1996
86. – Avondale, 11 July 2001
87. Wilson Dube (m) General Secretary, Pentecostal Assemblies of Zimbabwe (formerly Canada), Harare, Zimbabwe, 1995.
88. Enoch Dzihwema (m) Regina Coeli Mission, Nyanga, Zimbabwe, 11 August 1996
89. Nigel Johnson SJ (m) University of Zimbabwe, Zimbabwe, 31 July 1996
90. Jeremiah Kainga (m) Msasa, Zimbabwe, 6 August 1996
91. Noel Kasu (m) Nyamudeza village, Katerere, Zimbabwe, 20 April 1996
92. Murombedzi Kuchera (m) General Secretary of the Zimbabwe Council of Churches, Harare, Zimbabwe, 17 April 1996
93. Benjamin Leach (m) Resthaven, Harare, Zimbabwe, 31 May 1996
94. Ngwisa Mkandla (m) Senior Pastor, Faith Ministries, Harare, Zimbabwe, 7 May 1996
95. Pedro Muianga (m) Pastor, Assemblies of God, Evangélica, Pemba, Mozambique, 26 June 1996
96. Amaro Valeiro Mwitu (m) Catholic Priest, Pemba, Mozambique, 30 June 1996
97. Tobias Nyatsambo (m) National Director, Scripture Union, Harare, Zimbabwe, 8 July 1996
98. Ephriam Satuku (m) Vice-Chair, Elim Mission, Raungwe, Katerere, Zimbabwe, 18 July 1996
99. Isias Tete (m) Pastor in the Zion Church, Pemba, Mozambique, 29 June 1996
100. Stella Tsengo (f) Pastor, Mughodi Church, Katerere, Zimbabwe, 1996 int. by Simba Chikodo (SM)
101. Frederico (m) and Amina (f) Vincente, Nanlia, Cabo Delgado, Mozambique, 1 July 1996

Born-again Leaders and Workers based in the USA
102. Randy Bozarth (m) Vice-President, Christ for the Nations Institute, Dallas, 22 April 1997
103. John Carver (m) Christ for the Nations, Dallas, 22 April 1997
104. Bruce Coble (m) AOG Pastor, Smyrna, Tennessee, 25 April 1997
105. Gayle Erwin (m) Pastor Cathedral City, California, 29 April 1997
106. Sally Horton (f) Coordinator, Literature Project, Christ for the Nations Institute, Dallas, 24 April 1997
107. John McLennon (m) Marlborough, Harare, Zimbabwe, 20 June 1996
108. Ronnie Meek (m) AOG Pastor, Smyrna, Tennessee, 26 April 1997
109. Edward Michaelson (m) and Charles Bullock (m) Friends Christian University, USA, 11 December 1995
110. Howard Reents (f) Academic Dean, Christ for the Nations Institute, Dallas, 24 April 1997.
111. Bernice Watson (f) Coordinator, Native Church Program, Christ for the Nations Institute, Dallas, 24 April 1997

Zimbabwean Politicians and Academics
112. Dumiso Dabengwa (m) Minister for Home Affairs, Ministry for Home Affairs, Harare, Zimbabwe, 1996
113. William Gumbochena (m) Deputy Minister for Education and Culture, Ministry of Education and Culture, Harare, Zimbabwe, 31 July 1996
114. John Makumbe (m) Cranborne, Zimbabwe, 18 January 1996
115. Olivia Muchena (f) Deputy Minister for Lands, Ministry of Agriculture and Land, Zimbabwe, 30 August 1999

References

Alexander, J., J. McGregor & T.O. Ranger. 2000. *Violence and Memory: One Hundred Years in the 'Dark Forests' of Matabeleland.* Oxford, James Currey.
Ambler, Charles. 2001. 'Popular Films and Colonial Audiences: The Movies in Northern Rhodesia'.

American Historical Review. 106, 1.

Anderson, Allan. 1992. *Bazalwane. African Pentecostals in South Africa*. Pretoria, UNISA.

– 2004. *An Introduction to Pentecostalism*. Cambridge, Cambridge University Press.

Anderson, Benedict. 1991. *Imagined Communities: Reflections on the Origin and Spread of Nationalism*. London, Verso (revised edition).

Anderson, R. M. 1979. *Vision of the Disinherited. The Making of American Pentecostalism*. New York, Oxford University Press.

Appadurai, Arjun. 1990. 'Disjuncture and Difference in the Global Cultural Economy'. *Public Culture*. 2.

Atterbury, P. 2001. 'Steam and Speed: Industry, Transport and Communications' in J. Mackenzie (ed.), *The Victorian Vision. Inventing New Britain*. London, V&A Publications.

Austen, Ralph. 1987. *African Economic History. Internal Development and External Dependency*. London, James Currey.

Austin-Broos, Diane. 1997. *Jamaica Genesis: Religion and the Politics of Moral Order*. Chicago, IL, Chicago University Press.

– 2001. 'Jamaican Pentecostalism: Transnational Relations and the Nation-State', in André Corten and Ruth Marshall-Fratani (eds.), *Between Babel and Pentecost. Transnational Pentecostalism in Africa and Latin America*. London, Hurst and Co.

Balcomb, Anthony. 2004. 'From Apartheid to the New Dispensation: Evangelicals and the Democratisation of South Africa'. *Journal of Religion in Africa*. 34. 1-2.

Barnes, Teresa. 1999. *'We Women Worked so Hard': Gender, Urbanization, and Social Reproduction in Colonial Harare, Zimbabwe, 1930-56*. Oxford, James Currey.

Barraclough, G. 1967. *An Introduction to Contemporary History*. Harmondsworth, Penguin.

Bartleman, F. 1980. [1925]. *Azusa Street*. South Plainfield, NJ, Bridge Publishing.

Baur, John. 1994. *2000 Years of Christianity in Africa. An African History*. Nairobi, Paulines Press.

Bayart, J.-F. 1993. *The State in Africa: The Politics of the Belly*. London, Longman.

Bayly, C. 2004. *The Birth of the Modern World 1780-1914*. Oxford, Blackwell.

Bays, D. 1995. 'Indigenous Protestant Churches in China 1900-1937: A Pentecostal Case Study', in S. Kaplan (ed.), *Indigenous Responses to Western Christianity*. New York, New York University Press.

Beach, David. 1994. *The Shona and their Neighbours*. Oxford, Blackwell.

Bhabha, Homi. 1994. *The Location of Culture*. London, Routledge.

Bhebe, N. & T. Ranger (eds). 1995. *Zimbabwe's Guerrilla War*, Vol. II, *Society*. Harare, Baobab.

Birmingham, David, & Phyllis Martin (eds). 1998. *History of Central Africa. The Contemporary Years since 1960*. London, Longman.

Blumhofer, E. L. 1993. *Restoring the Faith. The Assemblies of God, Pentecostalism and American Culture*. Urbana, University of Illinois.

Bourdillon, Michael. 1987. *Shona Peoples: Ethnography of the Contemporary Shona, with Special Reference to Religion*. Gweru, Mambo Press.

Bruce, Steve. 1996. *Religion in the Modern World. From Cathedrals to Cults*. Oxford, Oxford University Press.

Burger, I.S. 1995. 'A Historical Perspective on the Apostolic Faith Mission of South Africa', ms.

Burke, Timothy. 1996. *Lifebuoy Men, Lux Women. Commodification, Consumption, Cleanliness in Modern Zimbabwe*. Durham, NC, and London, Duke University Press.

Burpeau, Kemp. 2002. 'A Historical Study of John Graham Lake and South African/United States Pentecostalism'. PhD Thesis, Rhodes University.

Burton, W. 1934. *When God Makes a Pastor*. London, Victory Press.

Callaway, H. 1993. 'Purity and Exotica in Legitimating Empire: Cultural Constructions of Gender, Sexuality and Race', in T.O. Ranger & Olufemi Vaughan (eds), *Legitimacy and the State in Twentieth Century Africa*. London, Macmillan.

Campbell, James. 1995. *Songs of Zion. The African Methodist Episcopal Church in the United States and South Africa*. Oxford, Oxford University Press.

– 2002. 'African American Missionaries and the Colonial State: AME South Africa', in H. Bernt Hansen & M. Twaddle (eds), *Christian Missionaries and the State in the Third World*. Oxford, James Currey.

Cartwright, Desmond. 1991. 'Pentecostal Origins from a Global Perspective', ms., Brighton.

Cerillo, A. Jr & G. Wacker. 2001. 'Bibliography and Historiography' in S. Burgess (ed.), *International Dictionary of Pentecostal and Charismatic Movements*. Grand Rapids, MI, Zondervan.

Chabal, Patrick & J. Daloz. 1999. *Africa Works. Disorder as a Political Instrument*. Oxford, James Currey.

Chakanza, J.C. 1983. *An Annotated List of Independent Churches in Malawi 1900-1981*. University of Malawi, Department of Religious Studies.

Chatindo, E. 2002. *Singing Culture. A Study of Gospel Music in Zimbabwe*. Uppsala, The Nordic Africa Institute.

Cleary, E. L., & J. Sepulveda. 1997. 'Chilean Pentecostalism: Coming of Age', in E.L. Cleary & H.W. Stewart-Gambino (eds), *Power, Politics and Pentecostals in Latin America*. Boulder, CO, Westview Press.

Comaroff, Jean. 1985. *Body of Power, Spirit of Resistance: The Culture and History of a South African People*. Chicago, IL, University of Chicago.

Comaroff, J. & J. 1991. *Of Revelation and Revolution. Christianity, Colonialism and Consciousness in South Africa*. Vol.1. Chicago, IL, University of Chicago Press.

– (eds). 1993. *Modernity and Its Malcontents. Ritual and Power in Post-colonial Africa*. Chicago, IL, University of Chicago.

– 1997. *Of Revelation and Revolution. The Dialectics of Modernity on a South African Frontier*. vol.2. Chicago, IL, University of Chicago Press.

Cooper, Frederick. 1994. 'Conflict and Connection: Rethinking Colonial African History'. *American Historical Review*. 99.

– 2001. 'What is the Concept of Globalisation Good For? An African Historian's Perspective'. *African Affairs*. 100, 399.

– 2002. *Africa Since 1940. The Past of the Present*, Cambridge, Cambridge University Press.

Coquery-Vidrovitch, Catherine. 1991. 'The Process of Urbanization in Africa (From the Origins to the Beginning of Independence)'. *African Studies Review*. 34, 1.

Craemer, W de, R. Fox & J. Vansina. 1976. 'Religious Movements in Central Africa: A Theoretical Study'. *Comparative Studies in Society and History*. 18, 4.

Daneel, Martinus. 1971. *Old and New in Southern Shona Independent Churches*. Vol. I, *Background and Rise of the Major Movements*. The Hague, Mouton, Afrika-Studiecentrum.

– 1974. *Old and New in Southern Shona Independent Churches*. Vol.2, *Church Growth - Causative Factors and Recruitment Techniques*. The Hague, Mouton, Afrika-Studiecentrum.

– 1988. *Old and New in Southern Shona Independent Churches*. Vol.3, *Leadership and Fission Dynamics*. Gweru, Mambo Press.

– 1987. *Quest for Belonging*. Gweru, Mambo Press.

– 1989. *Fambidzano, Ecumenical Movement of Shona Independent Churches*. Gweru, Mambo Press.

Davie, Grace. 2002. *Europe: The Exceptional Case. Parameters of Faith in the Modern World*. London, Darton, Longman and Todd.

Dayton, Donald. 1987. *Theological Roots of Pentecostalism*. Grand Rapids, MI, Francis Asbury Press.

Dillon-Malone, C. 1978. *The Korsten Basketmakers. A Study of the Masowe Apostles, An Indigenous African Religious Movement*. Manchester, Manchester University Press.

Dodge, Ann. 1987. 'A Historical and Analytical Overview of North American Protestant Missions in Zimbabwe: 1890-1987'. Masters in Sacred Theology Dissertation, Yale University.

Dubb, Allie. 1976. *Community of the Saved: An African Revivalist Church in the East Cape*. Johannesburg, Witwatersrand University Press.

Dube, L.M. 1984. 'The Spirit of Purity: A Study of the African Independent Church of Overseer (Madida), South of Gwanda, Matabeleland South, South West of Zimbabwe'. MA Dissertation, Department of Religious Studies, University of Zimbabwe.

Ekeh, Peter. 1975. 'Colonialism and the Two Publics in Africa: A Theoretical Statement'. *Comparative Studies in Society and History*. 3.

Ellis, Stephen. 1995. 'Liberia 1989-1994: A Study of Ethnic and Spiritual Violence'. *African Affairs*. 94, 375.

– 2002. 'Writing Histories of Contemporary Africa'. *Journal of African History*. 43.

Ellis, Stephen & G. ter Haar. 1998. 'Religion and Politics in Sub-Saharan Africa'. *Journal of Modern African Studies*. 36, 2.

Englund, Harri, & James Leach. 2000. 'Ethnography and Meta-Narratives of Modernity'. *Current Anthropology*. 41, 2.

– 2003, 'Christian Independency and Global Membership: Pentecostal Extraversions in Malawi'. *Journal of Religion in Africa*. 33.1.

Erwin, Gayle, D. (nd) *African Prophet: The Story of Ezekiel Guti. As Told to Gayle Erwin* ms..

– (nd) *The African Apostle: The Life of Ezekiel Guti*. Waterfalls, ZAOGA.

– ca. 1997. *That Reminds Me of a Story*. ms.

– ca. 1997. 'Tourist or Teacher? or Incarnational Foreign Missionary, or How to Overcome "White Think" in Cross Cultural Missionaries'. ms.

Etherington, Norman. 1996. 'Recent Trends in the Historiography of Christianity in Southern Africa'. *Journal of Southern African Studies*. 22, 2.

Featherstone, Mike, Scott Lash & Roland Robertson (eds). 1995. *Global Modernities*. London, Sage.

Ferguson, Adam. 1768. *An Essay on the History of Civil Society*, London, Millar and Cadell.

Fields, K. 1985. *Revival and Rebellion in Colonial Africa*. Princeton, NJ, Princeton University Press.

Freston, P. 1994. 'Popular Protestants in Brazilian Politics: A Novel Turn in Sect-State Relations'. *Social Compass*. 41, 4.

– 1995. 'Pentecostalism in Brazil: A Brief History'. *Religion*. 25.

– 1996. 'The Protestant Eruption into Modern Brazilian Politics'. *Journal of Contemporary Religion*. 11, 2.

– 2001. *Evangelicals and Politics in Asia, Africa and Latin America*. Cambridge, Cambridge University Press.

– (forthcoming) 'Globalisation, Religion and Evangelical Christianity: A Sociological Meditation from the Third World', ms.

Gee, Donald. 1967. *Wind and Flame*. London, AoG Publishing House.

Gerlach, L. &V. Hine. 1979. *People, Power, Change: Movements of Social Transformation*. Indianapolis, IN, Bobbs-Merrill.

Getecha, Ciru & Jesimen Chipika. 1995. *Zimbabwe Women's Voices*. Harare, Zimbabwe Women's Resource Centre and Network.

Giddens, Anthony. 1990. *The Consequences of Modernity*. Stanford, CA, Stanford University Press.

Gifford, Paul, 1987. '"Africa Shall be Saved": An Appraisal of Reinhard Bonnke's Pan-African Crusade'. *Journal of Religion in Africa*. 17, 1.

– 1989. *Religion and Oppression*. Harare, Ecumenical Documentation and Information Centre (EDICESA).

– 1991. *The New Crusaders. Christianity and the New Right in Southern Africa*. London, Pluto.

– 1994. 'Some Recent Developments in African Christianity'. *African Affairs*. 93, 373.

– 1995. (ed.) *The Christian Churches and the Democratisation of Africa*. Leiden, E.J. Brill.

– 1998. *African Christianity: Its Public Role*. London, Hurst & Co.

– 2004. *Ghana's New Christianity. Pentecostalism in a Globalising African Economy*. London, Hurst & Co.

Gill, L. 1990. '"Like a Veil to Cover Them": Women and Pentecostal Movements in La Paz'. *American Ethnologist*. 17, 4.

Goodhew, David. 2000. 'Working Class Respectability: The Example of the Western Areas of Johannesburg, 1930-55'. *Journal of African History*. 41.

Gray, Richard. 1990. *Black Christians and White Missionaries*. New Haven, CT, Yale University Press.

Haliburton, G. 1976. 'Edward Lion of Lesotho'. *Mohlomi, Journal of Southern African Historical Studies*. 1.

Hallencreutz, C. 1988. 'Ecumenical Challenges in Independent Zimbabwe: ZCC 1980-1985', in C. Hallencreutz & A. Moyo (eds), *Church and State in Zimbabwe*. Gweru, Mambo Press.

– 1998. *Religion and Politics in Harare, 1890-1980*. Uppsala, Swedish Institute of Missionary Research.

237

Hammar, Amanda & Brian Raftopoulos. 2004. 'Zimbabwe's Unfinished Business: Rethinking Land, State and Nation' in A. Hammar, B. Raftopoulos and Stig Jensen (eds), *Zimbabwe's Unfinished Business: Rethinking, Land, State and Nation in the Context of Crisis*. Harare, Weaver Press.

Hannerz, Ulf. 1996. *Transnational Connections: Culture, People, Places*. London, Routledge.

Hastings, A. 1976. *African Christianity: An Essay in Interpretation*. London, Geoffrey Chapman.

– 1979. *A History of African Christianity 1950-1975*. Cambridge, Cambridge University Press.

– 1989. *African Catholicism*. London, SCM Press.

– 1994. *The Church in Africa 1450-1950*. Oxford, Clarendon Press.

Hegland, Mary Elaine.1987. 'Introduction', in Richard T. Antoun and Mary Elaine Hegland (eds), *Religious Resurgence. Contemporary Cases in Islam, Christianity, and Judaism*. Syracuse, NY, Syracuse University Press.

Herbst, J. 1991. *State Politics in Zimbabwe*. Harare, University of Zimbabwe Publications.

Hofmeyr, Isabel. 2002. 'Dreams, Documents and "Fetishes": African Christian Interpretations of Pilgrims Progress'. *Journal of Religion in Africa*. 32, 4.

Hollenweger, Walter. 1972. *The Pentecostals*. London, SCM Press.

Iliffe, John. 1979. *A Modern History of Tanganyika*. Cambridge, Cambridge University Press.

Isichei, Elizabeth. 1995. *A History of Christianity in Africa. From Antiquity to the Present*. London, SPCK.

Jeater, Diana. 1993. *Marriage, Perversion and Power. The Construction of Moral Discourse in Southern Rhodesia 1894-1930*. Oxford, Clarendon Press.

Jenkins, Philip. 2002. *The Next Christendom: The Coming of Global Christianity*. New York, Oxford University Press.

Journal of Religion in Africa. 2004. 'Civic and Uncivic Religion'. 34, 4.

Jules-Rosette, Bennetta. 1975. *African Apostles. Ritual and Conversion in the Church of John Maranke*. Ithaca, NY, and London, Cornell University Press.

Kalu, Ogbu. U. 1998a. 'The Practice of Victorious Life: Pentecostal Political Theology and Practice in Nigeria, 1970-1996'. *Mission*. 5, 2.

– 1998b. 'The Third Response: Pentecostalism and the Reconstruction of Christian Experience in Africa, 1970-1995'. *Journal of African Christian Thought*. 1, 2.

Kamau, Francis. 1991. 'Leadership Development for the Assemblies of God Church in Kenya'. MA Thesis, Fuller Theological Seminary.

Kay, P. 1996. 'Cecil Polhill, The Pentecostal Missionary Union, and the Fourfold Gospel with Healing and Speaking in Tongues: Signs of a New Movement in Missions'. North Atlantic Missiology Project, Position Paper no.20.

Khoser, Khalid (ed.). 2003. *New African Diasporas*. London, Routledge.

Kiernan, J. 1994. 'Variations on a Christian Theme. The Healing Synthesis of Zulu Zionism', in C. Stewart and R. Shaw (eds), *Syncretism/Anti-Syncretism*. London, Routledge.

Kileff, C. 1975. 'Black Suburbanites: An African Elite in Salisbury, Rhodesia', in C. Kileff and W.C. Pendleton (eds), *Urban Man in Southern Africa*. Gwelo, Mambo Press.

Lan, David. 1985. *Guns and Rain. Guerrillas and Spirit Mediums in Zimbabwe's War of Liberation*. London, James Currey.

Langerman, Jan. 1983. 'Apostolic Faith Mission of South Africa: A Revitalisation of the Theological Concepts of Church Ministry'. D.Min., Fuller Theological Seminary.

Lehmann, D. 1996. *Struggle for the Spirit. Religious Transformation and Popular Culture in Brazil and Latin America*. Cambridge, Polity Press.

– 1998. 'Fundamentalism and Globalism'. *Third World Quarterly*. 19, 4.

Lindsay, F. 1976. *My Diary Secrets*. Dallas, TX, Christ for the Nations, Inc.

– 1984. *Freda. The Widow who took up the Mantle*, Dallas, TX, Christ for the Nations, Inc.

Lindsay, Gordon. 1986. *John Alexander Dowie: A Life Story of Trials, Tragedies and Triumphs*. Dallas, TX, Christ for the Nations, Inc.

– 1994. *J.G. Lake – Apostle to Africa*. Dallas, TX, Christ for the Nations, Inc.

– (ed.) 1994. *The Astounding Diary of Dr John G. Lake*. Dallas, TX, Christ for the Nations Inc.

– (ed.) 1995. *The John G. Lake Sermons on Dominion over Demons, Disease and Death*. Dallas, TX, Christ for the Nations, Inc.

Lonsdale, John. 2002. 'Kikuyu Christianities: A History of Intimate Diversity' in David Maxwell (ed.) with Ingrid Lawrie, *Christianity and the African Imagination. Essays in Honour o, Hastings.* Leiden, E. J. Brill.

Lugard, F. 1922. *The Dual Mandate in British Tropical Africa.* London, W. Blackwood and Sons.

Lungu, Stephen. 1994. *Freedom Fighter.* Crowborough, Monarch.

MacGaffey, Janet, and Rémy Bazenguissa-Ganga. 2000. *Congo-Paris: Transnational Traders on the Margins of the Law.* Oxford, James Currey.

Marshall, Ruth. 1993. "'Power in the Name of Jesus": Social Transformation and Pentecostalism in Western Nigeria "Revisited"', in Terence Ranger and Olufemi Vaughan (eds), *Legitimacy and the State in 20th Century Africa.* Oxford, St Antony's Macmillan Series.

— 1995. '"God is Not a Democrat": Pentecostalism and Democratisation in Nigeria', in Paul Gifford (ed.), *The Christian Churches and the Democratisation of Africa.* Leiden, E. J. Brill.

— 1998.'Mediating the Global and the Local in Nigerian Pentecostalism'. *Journal of Religion in Africa.* 28, 3.

Martin, Bernice. 1995. 'New Mutations of the Protestant Ethic'. *Religion.* 25.

— 1998. 'From Pre- to Post-Modernity in Latin America: The Case of Pentecostalism', in P. Heelas (ed.), *Religion, Modernity and Post-Modernity.* Oxford, Blackwell.

— 2001. 'The Pentecostal Gender Paradox', in Richard K. Fenn (ed.), *The Blackwell Companion to the Sociology of Religion.* Oxford, Blackwell.

Martin, David. 1990. *Tongues of Fire. The Explosion of Protestantism in Latin America.* Oxford, Blackwell.

— 1996. *Forbidden Revolutions. Pentecostalism in Latin America and Catholicism in Eastern Europe.* London, SPCK.

— 2001. *Pentecostalism: The World is Their Parish.* Oxford, Blackwell.

Marty, Martin, E. and R. Scott Appleby (eds). 1991. *Fundamentalisms Observed.* Chicago, IL, University of Chicago Press.

— 1993a. *Fundamentalisms and Society.* Chicago, IL, University of Chicago Press.

— 1993b. *Fundamentalisms and the State.* Chicago, IL, University of Chicago Press.

— 1994. *Accounting for Fundamentalisms.* Chicago, IL, University of Chicago Press.

— 1995. *Fundamentalisms Comprehended.* Chicago, IL, University of Chicago Press.

Mate, R. 2002. 'Wombs as God's Laboratories: Pentecostal Discourses of Femininity in Zimbabwe'. *Africa.* 72, 4.

Maxwell, David. 1995. 'The Church and Democratisation in Africa: The Case of Zimbabwe', in P. Gifford (ed.), *The Christian Churches and the Democratisation of Africa.* Leiden, E. J. Brill.

— 1999. *Christians and Chiefs in Zimbabwe: A Social History of the Hwesa People c.1870s-1990s.* Edinburgh, International African Library.

— 2000. '"Catch the Cockerel Before Dawn": Pentecostalism and Politics in Post-Colonial Zimbabwe'. *Africa.* 70, 2.

— 2001. '"Sacred History, Social History": Traditions and Texts in the Making of a Southern African Transnational Religious Movement'. *Comparative Studies in Society and History.* 43, 3.

— 2005. 'Decolonisation', in Norman Etherington (ed.), *Missions and Empire, The Oxford History of the British Empire Companion Series.* Oxford, Oxford University Press.

— (2006). 'Post-colonial Christianity in Africa', in Hugh McLeod (ed.), *The Cambridge History of Christianity.* Vol.9, *World Christianity.* Cambridge, Cambridge University Press.

Mayer, Philip. 1961. *Townsmen or Tribesmen. Conservatism and the Process of Urbanisation in a South African City.* Cape Town, Oxford University Press.

— 1963. 'Some Forms of Religious Organisation among Africans in a South African City', in K. Little (ed.), *Urbanisation and African Social Change.* Edinburgh, Centre for African Studies.

Mbembe, A. 1992. 'Provisional Notes on the Postcolony'. *Africa.* 62, 1.

McClintock, Ann. 1994. *Imperial Leather. Race, Gender and Sexuality in the Colonial Contest.* London and New York, Routledge.

McGee,G. 1988. 'The Azusa Street Revival and Twentieth Century Missions'. *International Bulletin of Missionary Research.* 12, 2.

— (nd), 'From East to West: The Early Pentecostal Movement in India and its Influence in the West', ms.

Meyer, Birgit. 1995. '"Delivered from the Powers of Darkness". Confessions about Satanic Riches

in Christian Ghana'. *Africa.* 65, 2.
- 1996. 'Commodities and the Power of Prayer. Pentecostalist Attitudes Towards Consumption in Contemporary Ghana'. Paper for the conference 'Globalisation and the Construction of Communal Identities', Amsterdam.
- 1998. '"Make a Complete Break with the Past": Memory and Post-colonial Modernity in Ghanaian Pentecostalist Discourse'. *Journal of Religion in Africa.* 28, 3.
- 1999. *Translating the Devil. Religion and Modernity Among the Ewe of Ghana.* Edinburgh, International African Library.
- 2000. 'Comment on Ethnography and Meta-Narratives of Modernity'. *Current Anthropology.* 41, 2.
- 2004. 'Christianity in Africa: From African Independent Churches to Pentecostal-Charismatic Churches'. *Annual Review of Anthropology.* 33.
Miller, Daniel. 1995. 'Introduction: Anthropology, Modernity and Consumption', in Daniel Miller (ed.), *Worlds Apart: Modernity Through the Prism of the Local.* London, Routledge.
Monga, C. 1996. *The Anthropology of Anger. Civil Society and Democracy in Africa.* Boulder, CO, Lynn Rienner.
Mupedziswa, R. 1997. *Empowerment or Repression. ESAP and Children in Zimbabwe.* Gweru, Mambo Press and Silveira House.
Muratorio, B. 1981. 'Protestantism, Ethnicity and Class in Chimborazo', in N. Whitten (ed.), *Cultural Transformations and Ethnicity in Modern Ecuador.* Urbana, IL, University of Illinois Press.
Murphree, Marshall. 1969. *Christianity and the Shona.* London, Athlone Press.
Murray, Colin. 1999. 'The Father, the Son and the Holy Spirit: Resistance and Abuse in the Life of Solomon Lion (1908-1987)'. *Journal of Religion in Africa.* 29, 3.
Ncube, W. 1989. 'The Post Unity Period: Developments, Benefits and Problems', in C. Banana (ed.), *Turmoil and Tenacity. Zimbabwe 1890-1990.* Harare, College Press.
Neinkirchen, C. 1994. 'Conflicting Visions of the Past. The Prophetic Use of History in the Early American Pentecostal-Charismatic Movements', in K. Poewe (ed.), *Charismatic Christianity as a Global Culture.* Columbia SC, University of South Carolina Press.
Nottage, Robert, 2000. 'Becoming Respectable': Social Stratification in Salisbury, 1948 to 1965'. BA Honours Dissertation, History Department, Keele University.
Ojo. Matthews. 1988a. 'Deeper Christian Life Ministry: A Case Study of Charismatic Movements in Western Nigeria'. *Journal of Religion in Africa.* 28, 2.
- 1988b. 'The Contextual Significance of the Charismatic Movements in Independent Nigeria'. *Africa.* 2, 58.
- 2001. 'African Charismatics', in Stephen D. Glazier (ed.), *Encyclopaedia of African and African-American Religions.* New York, Routledge.
Parry, Jonathan and Maurice Bloch. 1989. 'Introduction', in J. Parry and M. Bloch (eds), *Money and the Morality of Exchange.* Cambridge, Cambridge University Press.
Peel, J.D.Y. 1968. *Aladura: A Religious Movement Among the Yoruba.* Oxford, Oxford University Press.
- 1994. 'Historicity and Pluralism in Some Recent Studies of Yoruba Religion'. *Africa,* 64, 1.
- 1995. 'For Who Hath Despised the Day of Small Things? Missionary Narratives and Historical Anthropology'. *Comparative Studies in Society and History.* 37, 3.
- 2000. *Religious Encounter and the Making of the Yoruba.* Bloomington, IN, Indiana University Press.
- 2002. 'Christianity and the Logic of Nationalist Assertion in Wole Soyinka's *Isara*', in David Maxwell (ed.) with Ingrid Lawrie, *Christianity and the African Imagination. Essays in Honour of Adrian Hastings.* Leiden, E. J. Brill.
Phimister, I. 1988. *The Economic and Social History of Zimbabwe 1890-1948: Capital Accumulation and Class Struggle.* London, Longman.
Phimister, I., and Brian Raftopoulos. 1997. *'Keep on Knocking'. A History of the Labour Movement in Zimbabwe 1900-97.* Harare, Baobab Books.
- 2000. '"*Kana sora ratswa ngaritswe*". African Nationalists and Black Workers: The 1948 General Strike in Colonial Zimbabwe'. *Journal of Historical Sociology.* 13, 3.
Prakash, Gyan. 1990. 'Writing Post-Orientalist Histories of the Third World: Perspectives from

Indian Historiography'. *Comparative Studies in Society and History*. 32,1.

Raftopoulos, Brian. 1999. 'Problematising Nationalism in Zimbabwe: A Historiographical Review'. *Zambezia* XXVI (ii).

Raftopoulos, Brian. 2001. 'The Labour Movement and the Emergence of Opposition Politics in Zimbabwe', in B. Raftopoulos and Lloyd Sachikonye (eds), *Striking Back: The Labour Movement and the Post-Colonial State in Zimbabwe 1980–2000*. Harare, Weaver Press.

Ranger, T.O. 1970. *The African Voice in Southern Rhodesia 1898-1930*. London, Heinemann.

– 1982a. 'Mchape: A Study in Diffusion and Interpretation', ms.

– 1982b. 'Medical Science and Pentecost: The Dilemma of Anglicanism in Africa', in W.J. Sheils (ed.), *The Church and Healing*. Oxford, Blackwell.

– 1985a. 'Concluding Summary', in K. Holst-Peterson (ed.), *Religion, Development and African Identity*. Uppsala, Scandinavian Institute of African Studies.

– 1985b. *Peasant Consciousness and Guerrilla War in Zimbabwe*. London, James Currey.

– 1986. 'Religious Movements and Politics in Sub-Saharan Africa'. *African Studies Review*. 29, 2.

– 1987. 'Taking Hold of the Land: Holy Places and Pilgrimages in Twentieth Century Zimbabwe'. *Past and Present*. 117.

– 1994. 'JSAS and the Study of Religion', Journal of Southern African Studies 25th Anniversary Conference, 'Paradigms Lost, Paradigms Regained', York University, ms.

– 1995. *Are We Not Also Men? The Samkange Family and African Politics in Zimbabwe, 1920 - 64*. London, James Currey.

– 1999. *Voices from the Rocks: Nature, Culture and History in the Matopos Hills of Zimbabwe*, Oxford, James Currey.

– 2002. '"Taking on the Missionary's Task": African Spirituality and the Mission Churches of Manicaland in the 1930s', in David Maxwell (ed.) with Ingrid Lawrie, *Christianity and the African Imagination. Essays in Honour of Adrian Hastings*. Leiden, E. J. Brill.

– 2003. 'Introduction', in T. Ranger (ed.), *The Historical Dimensions of Democracy and Human Rights in Zimbabwe*. Harare, University of Zimbabwe Publications.

– (ed.) forthcoming. *Evangelical Christianity and Democracy in Africa*. Oxford, Oxford University Press.

Robbins, Joel. 2004a. 'The Globalization of Pentecostal and Charismatic Christianity'. *Annual Review of Anthropology*. 33.

– 2004b. *Becoming Sinners. Christianity and Moral Torment in a Papua New Guinea Society*. Berkeley, CA, University of California Press.

Robert, Dana. 2000. 'Shifting Southward: Global Christianity since 1945'. *International Bulletin of Missionary Research*. 24, 2.

– 2003. *Occupy until I Come. A.T. Pierson and the Evangelisation of the World*. Grand Rapids, MI, Eerdmans.

Robertson, Roland. 1995. 'Glocalization: Time-Space and Homogeneity-Heterogeneity', in Mike Featherstone, Scott Lash and Roland Robertson (eds), *Global Modernities*. London, Sage.

Ryan, J. 2001. 'Images and Impressions: Printing, Reproduction and Photography', in J. Mackenzie (ed.), *The Victorian Vision. Inventing New Britain*. London, V&A Publications.

Sachikonye, Lloyd (ed.). 1995. *Democracy, Civil Society and the State. Social Movements in Southern Africa*. Harare, SAPES Trust.

Scarnecchia, Timothy. 1993. 'The Politics of Gender and Class in the Creation of African Communities, Salisbury, Rhodesia, 1937-1957'. PhD Thesis, University of Michigan.

– 1996. 'Poor Women and Nationalist Politics: Alliances and Fissures in the Formation of a Nationalist Political Movement in Salisbury, Rhodesia, 1950-56'. *Journal of African History*. 37.

– 1997. 'Mai Chaza's *Guta re Jehova* (City of God): Gender, Healing and Urban Identity in an African Independent Church'. *Journal of Southern African Studies*. 23, 1.

Schoffeleers. Matthew. 1985. *Pentecostalism and Neo-Traditionalism: The Religious Polarization of a Rural District in Southern Malawi*. Amsterdam, Amsterdam Free University Press.

Schwartz, N. 1994. 'Christianity and the Construction of Global History. The Example of Legio Maria', in K. Poewe (ed.), *Charismatic Christianity as a Global Culture*. Columbia, SC, University of South Carolina Press.

Shaw, R., & C. Stewart. 1994. 'Introduction' in R. Shaw and C. Stewart (eds), *Syncretism/Anti-*

Syncretism: The Politics of Religious Synthesis. Routledge, London.

Simpson, Anthony. 1998. '"Memory and Becoming Chosen Other": Fundamentalist Elite Making in a Zambian Catholic Mission School', in Richard Werbner (ed.), *Memory and the Postcolony: African Anthropology and the Critique of Power*. London, Zed Books.

Sivan, E., and M. Friedman (eds). 1991. *Religious Radicalism and Politics in the Middle East*. Albany, NY, State University of New York Press.

Stopforth, P. 1972. *Two Aspects of Social Change in Highfield African Township*. Occasional Paper No. 7. Department of Sociology, , University of Rhodesia.

Stuart, O.W. 1989. 'Good Boys, Footballers and Strikers: African Social Change in Bulawayo, 1933-1953'. PhD Thesis, School of Oriental and African Studies, London.

Sundkler, Bengt. 1948 (2nd edn., 1961). *Bantu Prophets in South Africa*. London, Lutterworth Press.

– 1976. *Zulu Zion and Some Swazi Zionists*. Oxford, Oxford University Press.

– & Christopher Steed. 2000. *A History of the Church in Africa*. Cambridge, Cambridge University Press.

Synan, H.V. 1971. *The Holiness-Pentecostal Movement in the United States*. Grand Rapids, MI, Eerdmans.

Taylor, M.J. 1994. 'Publish and Be Blessed. A Case Study in Early Pentecostal Publishing History, 1906-1926'. PhD Thesis, Department of Theology, University of Birmingham.

The African Synod Prepares. 1991. Harare, Pastoral Centre.

Thompson, Edward. 1968. *The Making of the English Working Class*. London, Penguin.

Tinaz, Nuri. 1996. 'The Nation of Islam: Historical Evolution and Transformation of the Movement'. *Journal of Muslim Affairs*. 16, 2.

Ukah, Asonzeh F.K. 2003. 'Advertising God: Nigerian Christian Video-Films and the Power of Consumer Culture'. *Journal of Religion in Africa*. 33, 2.

Van Binsbergen, W. 1981. *Religious Change in Zambia. Exploratory Studies*. London, Kegan Paul International.

Van Dijk, Rijk. 1992. 'Young Puritan Preachers in post-Independence Malawi'. *Africa*. 62, 2.

– 1997. 'From Camp to Encompassment: Discourses of Trans-subjectivity in Ghanaian Pentecostal Diaspora'. *Journal of Religion in Africa*. 27, 1.

– 1998. 'Pentecostalism, Cultural Memory and the State: Contested Representations of Time in Pentecostal Malawi', in Richard Werbner (ed.) *Memory and the Postcolony: African Anthropology and the Critique of Power*. London, Zed Books.

Van Onselen, Charles. 1976. *Chibaro. African Mine Labour in Southern Rhodesia*. London, Pluto Press.

– 1982. *Studies in the Social and Economic History of the Witwatersrand 1886-1914*. Vol. 1, *New Babylon*. Johannesburg, Ravan.

Wacker, Grant. 1995. 'Searching for Eden with a Satellite Dish: Primitivism, Pragmatism and the Pentecostal Character', in R.T. Hughes (ed.), *The Primitive Church in the Modern World*. Urbana and Chicago, IL, University of Illinois Press.

– 1996. 'Travail of a Broken Family: Evangelical Responses to Pentecostalism in America, 1906-1916'. *Journal of Ecclesiastical History*. 47, 3.

– 2001. *Heaven Below: Early Pentecostals and American Culture*, Cambridge, MA, Harvard University Press.

Walls, A. 1976. 'Towards Understanding Africa's Place in Christian History', in J.S. Pobee (ed.), *Religion in a Pluralistic Society*. Leidon, E.J. Brill.

Watt, P. 1992. *From Africa's Soil. The Story of the Assemblies of God in Southern Africa*. Cape Town, Struik Christian Books.

Weber, Max. [1930] 1990. *The Protestant Ethic and the Spirit of Capitalism*. London, Allen & Unwin.

Weiss, B. 2004. 'Introduction', in B. Weiss (ed.), *Producing African Futures. Ritual and Reproduction in a Neo-Liberal Age*. Leiden, E. J. Brill.

Werbner, P. 1990. *The Migration Process: Capital, Gifts and Offerings among British Pakistanis*. Oxford, Berg.

– 1996. 'The Making of Muslim Dissent: Hybridized Discourses, Lay Preachers, and Radical

Rhetoric among British Pakistanis'. *American Ethnologist.* 23, 1.

Werbner, R. P. 1989. *Ritual Passage, Sacred Journey. The Process and Organisation of Religious Movement.* Manchester, Manchester University Press.

— 1991. *Tears of the Dead. The Social Biography of an African Family.* Edinburgh, Edinburgh University Press.

— 1995. 'Human Rights and Moral Knowledge: Arguments of Accountability in Zimbabwe', in M. Strathern (ed.), *Shifting Contexts. Transformations in Anthropological Knowledge.* London, Routledge.

— 1996. 'Introduction: Multiple Identities, Plural Arenas', in R.P. Werbner and T.O. Ranger (eds.), *Postcolonial Identities in Africa.* London, Zed Books.

— 1998. 'Memory, State Memorialism and the Postcolony', in R.P. Werbner (ed.), *Memory and the Postcolony: African Anthropology and the Critique of Power.* London, Zed Books.

West, Harry. (forthcoming). *Kupilikula: Governance and the Invisible Realm in Mueda Mozambique.* Chicago, IL, University of Chicago Press.

West, Martin. 1975. *Bishops and Prophets in a Black City. African Independent Churches in Soweto, Johannesburg.* Cape Town, David Philip.

West, Michael. 1990. 'African Middle Class Formation in Colonial Salisbury, 1890-1965'. PhD Thesis, Harvard University.

— 1997. 'Liquor and Libido: Joint Drinking and the Politics of Sexual Control in Colonial Zimbabwe'. *Journal of Social History.* 30, 3.

— 2002. *The Rise of an African Middle Class: Colonial Zimbabwe, 1898-1965.* Bloomington, IN, Indiana University Press.

Wilson. B. 1999. *Christianity.* London, Routledge.

Wilson, Bryan. R. 1961. *Sects and Society: the Sociology of Three Religious Groups in Britain.* London, Heinemann.

Wood, J. 1998. 'Women in Zimbabwe since Independence'. BA Honours Dissertation, Keele University.

243

Index

God, Africa(n) (AOGA), 1-15,
57, 109-226; finances (Resources),
109, 110, 112, 113, 118, 127, 142,
148, 149, 151-4, 164, 167, 171-2,
176, 177, 178, 180, 187, 202-7,
217; international character, 114,
121, 124, 131, 133-4, 140, 145,
147, 148, 150, 158, 159 167, 174,
175, 178, 179, 192, 200, 215, 217,
218, 224, 225; preaching, 110, 111,

113, 115, 120, 121, 129, 133, 134,
138, 139, 143, 145, 146, 149, 154,
155, 156, 157, 158, 166, 169, 170,
175, 185, 187-97, 202-11, 218;
services, 114, 127, 129, 146, 184-
200, 202-11; ZAOGA Ministries
and Fellowships, 131, 132, 133, 142,
145, 147, 151, 152, 158, 159, 161,
172, 176